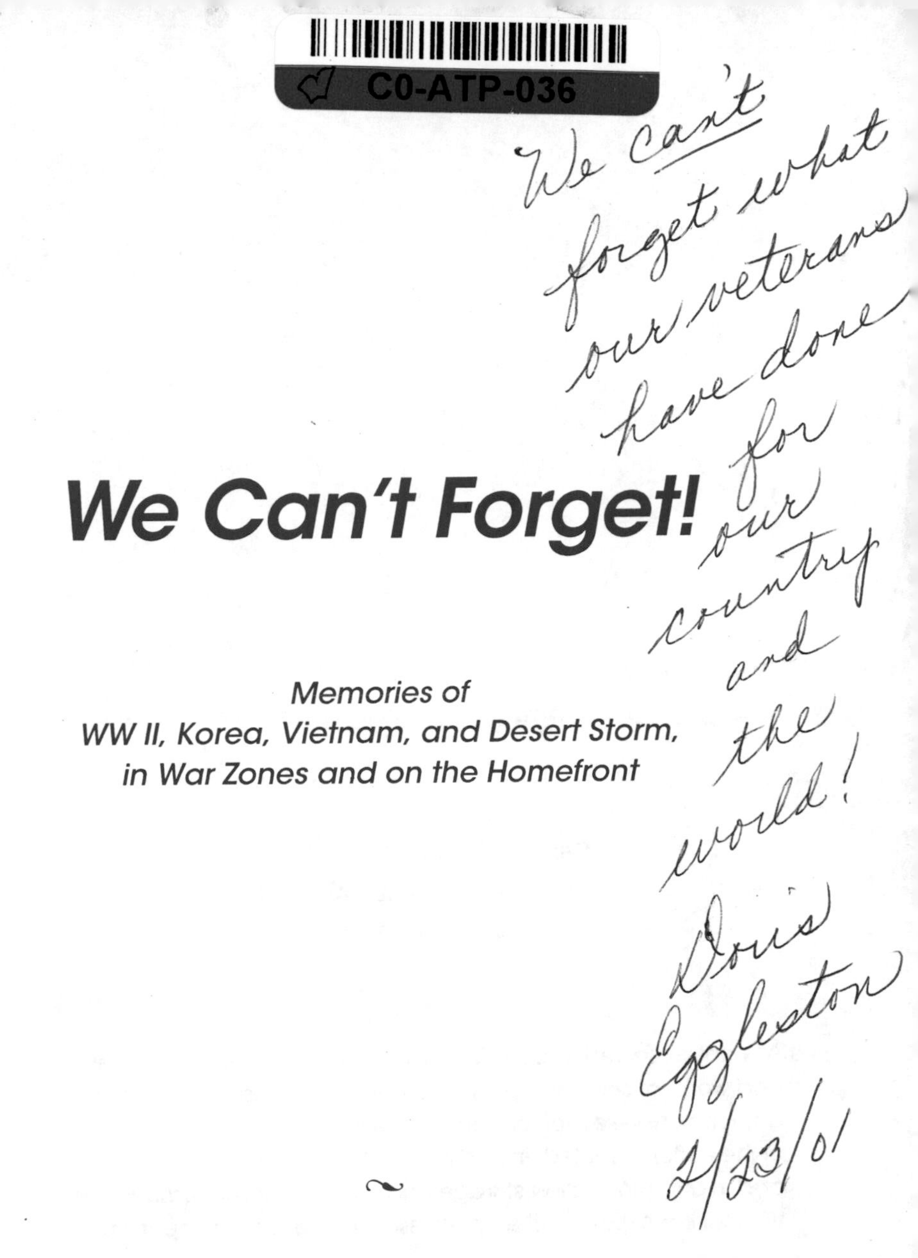

We Can't Forget!

Memories of
WW II, Korea, Vietnam, and Desert Storm,
in War Zones and on the Homefront

Doris Eggleston

CHICAGO SPECTRUM PRESS
1571 Sherman Ave., Annex C
Evanston, Illinois 60201

Printed in the U.S.A.

10 9 8 7 6 5 4 3 2

Books can be ordered directly from Doris Eggleston:
204 Charles Ave., Sidney, OH 45368

ISBN: 1-886094-20-9

This book is dedicated to all those who have risked their lives for their country and to those who gave the necessary support to make it all possible.

Thanks to all the veterans who have taken time to write out their memories and send them to me; and to Ralph L. Greene, Texarkana, Arkansas, World War II veteran, for supplying me with so much background material and so many pictures.

Thanks to the librarians at Amos Memorial Library in Sidney, Ohio, who have been so helpful with my research; to Betty McCasland for reading the manuscript and giving suggestions, and just always being there to talk to; to my husband who has been my reader, my *gofer*, and who has given assistance in so many ways; to our daughters and their families who have given moral support.

Troy, Ohio. Doris Eggleston.

TABLE OF CONTENTS

KOREA

VIETNAM

DESERT STORM

INTRODUCTION

We Can't Forget! is a compilation of personal military stories from WW II, Korea, Vietnam, and Desert Storm. Veterans of the army, navy, marines, and air force, officers as well as enlisted men and women, from eleven states, as well as one from Germany and one from Russia, with stories in their own words, draw us into their situations, arousing feelings of compassion, disbelief, anger...

The stories are divided into four sections, with each section introduced by a brief synopsis of that war, giving more attention to behind-the-scenes information rather than battles, peering at the individuals involved.

In the synopses I have used many quotations from military books, which lend authenticity. I am not an expert on war, but this book is not intended to be a military treatise. It is for lay people like myself. If I found these quotations to be interesting and enlightening, hopefully other lay people will, also.

Following the synopsis is a description of the homefront at the time of each war, showing that war involves everyone, not just those in the military. There is a personal story of a civilian librarian for the air force in Japan; a civilian office worker in Washington, D.C.; and an anonymous mother of a son sent to Vietnam. Boots & Coots, a fire-fighting company from Houston, Texas, reports on extinguishing oil fires in Kuwait. To give an idea of how the rest of the world coped, there are stories of the homefront in England, Holland, and Germany during WW II.

The purpose of this book is not only to honor all veterans but to remind people of what our country has gone through in the last 50 years. People need to be aware of these horrible times! While the younger people probably know about Desert Storm, they may never have read or heard much about WW II, Korea, and Vietnam. Others may have forgotten.

We Can't Forget! is not a detailed description of the war. It is a condensed, easy-to-read version, an orientation. Similarities and differences can be noted in the experiences covering the fifty-year period. Reading about the four wars in chronological order may put them more in perspective. People who would not read a military book could become absorbed in—*We Can't Forget!*

WORLD WAR II

SYNOPSIS

Hitler rose to power and in little more than a single decade controlled the biggest part of Europe. Considered to be an extremely evil man, it has been said that Hitler cannot be judged by the standards of ordinary men.

We in a democracy find it difficult to comprehend how, under Hitler, in a police state, the citizen had no voice but was at the mercy of the police. Fear replaced law.

In 1931 a marriage code was adopted which required any man in Hitler's Elite Guard (the SS) to prove that his bride had pure Aryan blood for at least two centuries. These brides were required to attend special SS schools to ready themselves to be Aryan mothers.

Hitler thought of Jews as sub-humans. They did not fit in with his idea of a master race, that being those with pure Aryan blood. Thus was established the centers for racial extermination. By 1943 Auschwitz-Birkenau was quite advanced in performing mass murder.

Alaska Veterans Memorial, Mile 147.2 George Parks Highway. Five sculpted upright slabs, statue and flagpole: Army, Marine Corps, Navy, Air Force, National Guard.
Doris Eggleston

Millions were taken to labor camps where they were worked to death or to concentration camps and put to death. Over 10,000,000 lost their lives after 1941 in these camps. At Dachau and other concentration camps, the SS men were expected to practice brutality with the prisoners in their charge.

Severe Nazi medical experiments started at Dachau using living human subjects, POWs or captured civilians, including many interned Jews, without their permission.

On September 3, 1939, both Britain and France declared war on Germany after Hitler invaded Poland two days earlier, starting his long succession of aggressions. Hitler did not really want a full-scale war with the British. Considering them as fellow Aryans, he hoped they would eventually recognize his supremacy and join him in ruling the lesser races of the world.

The first several months after the declaration of war were known as The Phoney War in England because there were no important land battles, even though Allied convoys were being raided. The time was used to prepare for war. The British were issued gas masks, and air raid precautions with blackouts were instituted. Stained glass windows of churches, art treasures, and other valuable and irreplaceable items were removed to safer places. Hospital patients, children, and government departments were evacuated. The Women's Land Army was formed, with young women learning to milk cows, plough the fields, and take over the work of the farmers.

When Belgium surrendered to Germany, more than 336,000 British, French, and Belgian troops retreated to Dunkirk on the northern French coast. (June, 1940) They were rescued by British military and civilian ships, as well as fishing boats, motorboats, and vessels of all kinds. Many were killed or drowned trying to get to the boats; 40,000 men were left to be captured by the Germans. Both the British and French people had difficulty accepting the idea of war until the daring escape at Dunkirk. There the *spirit of Dunkirk* was born and became the rallying force.

During this time Hitler was conducting a great propaganda war in his country, creating the mood he wanted. His philosophy was that propaganda need not tell the whole truth; it should only include that which favored his side.

After a nine-day German offensive in their country, France signed an armistice with Germany, June, 1940. Hitler specified that France was to survive as a sovereign power and she and her fleet would not go over to Britain.

Also in June, 1940, shortly before France fell, Mussolini (Italy) declared war against France and England. The hearts of the Italian people were not with this announcement. For the last hundred years they had been *with* France and *against* the Germans. Hitler sent forces, under the direction of General Romel, the Desert Fox, to aid the Italians in their move against British holdings in Africa. Egypt was particularly important to Britain (and to America) because of its proximity to the oilfields in Iraq and Persia (and the Suez Canal), which supplied its military forces. And the British bases in the Middle East needed supplies that came by convoy through the Mediterranean. Mussolini also realized that the Ploesti oilfields in Rumania, which produced 90 percent of the Luftwaffe's gasoline, had to be protected and kept from the Allies. (In 1944 the Allied bombers did pound at these oilfields.)

Later Mussolini was ousted by his countrymen but rescued by German Commandos. However, in April, 1945, Mussolini was captured and executed by the Italians.

Within 48 hours after Dunkirk, 30 German bombers (Luftwaffe), and Messerschmitt 109Es, attacked Britain. In later nightly raids several hundred, and even a thousand, planes were used in what the British called the *Blitz*.

Even though the British air defense system was the most technically advanced in the world and radar could pick up enemy formations before they crossed the French coast and give warning, still, within three months, in London alone, 12,696 civilians were killed by bombs. In one month more than 10,000 bombs were dropped on the city. But this proved costly to the Germans, also, with their having lost 2,375 planes and crews in daylight raids alone.

Not until 1944 did Germany start sending the buzz bombs, the first ground-to-ground guided missiles, to England. These bombs carried one ton of explosives and made a loud-enough noise that the people knew when they were coming, but still, they killed thousands of persons by the end of the war.

Following the bombing of London, the British bombed the German capital, which enraged Hitler—he and Goring thought this could never happen. Hitler soon turned his attention to Russia.

After the fall of France, the U.S. started mechanizing its army, expanding its aircraft industry, and sending planes, as well as arms and destroyers, to Britain. Some of the rifles we sent had been used in the first World War. Ammunition was so scarce that firing an extra round was a serious matter.

Peacetime conscription was begun in the U.S. in September, 1940.

In 1939, the U.S. had about 174,000 men in the army and went to six million by 1945; 126,400 in the navy to 3,400,000; 26,000 in the army Air Corps to 2,400,000; 19,700 in the Marine Corps to 484,000; 10,000 in the Coast Guard to 170,000. It went from 2,500 planes to 80,000; 760 warships to 2,500.

German submarines (U Boats) constantly menaced Allied shipping. The German pocket battleships were smaller but faster than Allied battleships. U-boats were formed into *wolf-packs* of eight or nine and sometimes as many as twenty or more, to attack ships.

By July 1940, 400,000 tons of Allied shipping, which was the lifeline for the British, had been sunk. By November, 1941, their losses were up to 350,000 tons per month to German submarines and Luftwaffe (air force). It was the middle of 1941 before the rebuilding of the Royal Navy had progressed to the point where they could provide escorts clear across the Atlantic.

England's planes did not have equipment as of today. Until 1941 the navigators had to get their positions from using the stars and radio signals sent up from various ground locations.

Lend-lease was instituted in March, 1941. President Franklin D. Roosevelt had said: *If Britain were to be defeated... all of us, in all the Americas, would be living at the point of a gun, a gun loaded with explosive bullets, economic as well as military. We must produce arms and ships with every energy and resource we can command...* Congress agreed to use $7,000,000,000 for the production of aircraft, tanks, cannon, raw materials, factory equipment, and food to help those nations that were considered vital to America's security. This equipment and supplies would be lent-leased. During the next four years the U.S. sent more than $50,000,000,000 worth of war materials to the Allies.

Hitler tried to woo Yugoslavia over to him. But Yugoslavia greatly favored the Allies and it tried to evade the issue with

Hitler. After three months, Hitler's patience ran out. He considered Yugoslavia's actions as an insult and determined to destroy them through continuous day and night air attacks.

On June 9, 1942, Hitler said he wanted to make an example of a town, so he chose Lidice and issued orders that all men be shot and the women taken to concentration camps. Those children thought suitable should be given to families of SS men; the rest, re-educated in other ways. Then the village should be burned.

After taking over Yugoslavia, the Germans conquered Greece and then Crete, thereby controlling all the Balkan countries.

The U.S. had been watching Hitler's advances across Europe and debating whether it should join the fight against him. Congress and the American people were isolationists. Most were for the Allied cause but didn't want to send troops. Roosevelt was trying to walk the tight line.

At the same time Roosevelt (1939) was worrying about Europe and trying to maintain neutrality, as polls indicated the people wanted, a congressman demanded that Japan, because of its aggression in China and the Far East, be taken off the *most-favored nation* basis for trade.

On September 27, 1940, Japan signed a Pact with the Axis powers.

On July 26, 1941, the U.S. froze Japan's funds in America and put a ban on oil exports to Japan, which practically eliminated trade between the two countries. Britain and Holland did the same, altogether cutting out 90% of Japan's oil imports.

On November 26 a ten-point peace plan was given to the Japanese, which they did not accept. From then on the President and Congress felt it was just a waiting game until war started with Japan. Although the U.S. was not aware of it, in Japan the go-ahead signal had been given on November 25 for the December 7 attack on Pearl Harbor.

The Japanese attacked Pearl Harbor on a peaceful Sunday morning, a few minutes before 0800 hours, December 7, 1941. They launched around 360 torpedo planes, bombers, and fighters, hitting nineteen American warships, with eighteen being sunk or severely damaged; they destroyed about 170 planes and killed approximately 3,700 people, all in one hour and forty-five minutes.

In "Pearl Harbor, the Attack," an article included in *History of the Second World War*, it was mentioned that a couple of trainee radar operators tracked the approach of planes from 137 miles, but were told to disregard the contact because the planes were probably Fortresses expected to arrive that morning from the mainland.

In *Goodbye, Darkness*, Manchester said that U.S. Intelligence had decoded messages from Japan to its embassy saying the attack on Pearl Harbor would take place on December 7. The commanding officer did nothing.

Rear Admiral Layton in *And I Was There* stated that much of the intelligence that had been received in Washington had not been passed on to the commander at Pearl Harbor. Had it been immediately passed on, they would have realized that a Japanese attack was actually planned.

The devastating blow at Pearl Harbor united the American people and brought the U.S. into the war. On December 8, 1941, Roosevelt asked Congress for a declaration of war against Japan, stating that December 7 was *a date which will live in infamy.* Churchill also declared war on Japan. Churchill told the American Congress "that in the Pacific war the British will fight 'side by side with you while there is breath in our bodies and blood flows in our veins.'"[1]

On December II Germany and Italy declared war on the U.S. Now it was Britain, USSR, and the U.S. (Allies) against Germany, Italy, and Japan (the Axis).

While the U.S. was recovering from the shock of the attack and preparing for war, Japan continued its offensive throughout the western half of the Pacific, as far south as Australia. They also took Attu and Kiska in the Aleutians in the summer of 1942. U.S. forces recovered them in the summer of 1943.

"... the Nipponese blitz had swept up a million square miles, almost a seventh of the globe, an area three times as large as the United States and Europe combined."[2]

General MacArthur, commander of the U.S. forces in the Far East, withdrew his forces from Luzon to Bataan. He expected the arrival of planes and warships to aid in the bitter fight, but when no help came, Bataan and then Corregidor surrendered. MacArthur promised the Filipino people, *I shall return*. Many of his 60,000 men, captured by the Japanese, were taken for the

"...ten-day, seventy-five-mile notorious Death March to POW cages in northern Luzon."[3] When the prisoners couldn't keep up, they were shot. They received no water, many dying from thirst; many were beaten, tortured, and beheaded.

During the opening months of the war, the Japanese achieved almost complete success in the air. The Allies did not have the number of planes needed nor did the planes have the speed and maneuverability necessary to cope with the Zero fighter. Morale in the United States was very low, and a daring plan was conceived to strike back at Japan.

In April, 1942, Lt. Col. James H. Doolittle led a raid on Japan. Because there were no land bases close enough to fly to Japan, the U.S. Air Force decided to try something never before done, flying land-based bombers from an aircraft carrier. After the attack, the bombers would fly to various points in China. Besides lifting the morale of the Allies, the successful raid was a pschological shock for Japan.

The Allies felt it essential that China (under leadership of Chiang Kai-shek) be able to continue fighting the Japanese. With Japan blocking all Chinese seaports, the only way to get supplies was through Burma, the back door, the Burma Road being 720 miles long. By this route, the Chinese armies could be supplied and any American air bases in China maintained.

An American Air Volunteer Group, called the Flying Tigers, under Col. Claire L. Chennault, came to Chinese aid in 1942. Later his group became the 14th Air Force. Also, Lt. Gen. Joseph W. Stilwell was leading an American military mission to advise and help the Chinese army. He trained them to use American equipment, which they hoped would come over the Burma Road or the Hump (Himalaya Mountains).

In the jungles where America's men had to fight, "... New Guineas's animal life would give the bravest man pause. Hideous crabs scuttle underfoot. Reptiles are coiled around tree limbs. And somewhere in this green hell lurk scorpions, bats, baboons, spiny anteaters, ratlike bandicoots, cassowaries, wild boars, and crocodiles... a soggy miasma of disease-bearing insects, snakes, precipitous slopes, mire, swamps, heat, humidity, landslides of falling rock, and rushing rivers to cross, rivers whose creatures include bloodsucking leeches with circles of tiny teeth, like lampreys..."[4]

Men also had to contend with fevers and jungle diseases. But, as the American G.I.s are prone to do, they tried to lighten the situation by joking about it.

Midway (June, 1942) was the turning point in the South Pacific war. The Japanese wrongfully assumed that their Midway attack would be over long before any enemy aircraft carriers could arrive in the area, but Adm. Nimitz foresaw the enemy moves and wiped out half of its carrier strength. This, plus air strength, was never regained by Japan.

About the same time as this Midway victory, America's increase in production was well underway. By the end of June, 1942, every week there were more and better Allied planes. Australia was the base for planes to attack the Japanese positions in the South Pacific. From then on, the Allies were on the offensive; Japan on the defensive.

Now, with the Allies being on the offensive, all the islands previously taken by the Japanese had to be recaptured. Guadalcanal was the first attempt. Then on to the Solomon Islands, the Admiralties, the Gilberts, the Marshalls, the Carolines, the Marianas, and the Philippines (with the promised return of MacArthur three years later).

On the transports, waiting to disembark at Guadalcanal, "... enlisted men had been quiet, though awake, writing letters, sharpening bayonets, blackening the sights of rifles and carbines, checking machine-gun belts to make certain they wouldn't jam in the Brownings, rummaging in packs to be sure they had C-rations. They carried canteens, Kabar knives, and first aid kits hooked to web belts; packs of cigarettes, Zippo lighters, shaving gear, skivvies, mess kits, shelter halves, ponchos, two extra bandoliers of ammunition for each man, clean socks, and, hanging from straps and web belts like ripe fruit waiting to be plucked, hand grenades... There wasn't much room to mill... There was no place to sit... vitality surged through you like a powerful drug, even though the idea of death held no attraction for you. Your mood was... a melange of apprehension, cowardice, curiosity, and envy..."[5]

"A Marine in an amphibious assault was a beast of burden. He shouldered, on the average, 84.3 pounds, which made him the most heavily laden foot soldier in the history of warfare. Some men carried much more: 20-pound BARs (Browning Automatic Rifles), 45-pound 81-millimeter mortar base plates, 47-pound mortar bipods, 36-pound light machine guns, 41-pound heavy machine guns, and heavy machine-gun tripods, over 53 pounds. A man thus encumbered was expected to swing down the ropes like Tarzan. It was a dangerous business..."[6]

It had been agreed by Roosevelt and Churchill that the European war should be finished first and then they would concentrate on the Pacific Theater. As a result, most military goods were being sent there, while food and supplies, fuel, and even men, were short in the Pacific. Men lost weight, some as much as twenty-five pounds during an assault and were suffering from fatigue. Night blindness was a problem due to a shortage of vitamin A. However, when the Japs fled and left a supply of food, even though it was not what they were accustomed to eating, the Marines made good use of it. They were also grateful for the equipment left behind.

At Tarawa the men had a problem with their new camouflage suits. The suits were not porous, they didn't breathe. As a result, the men were miserable and lost pounds.

"You could always tell whether men were moving up or coming off the line. Usually those coming off... had a different look—dull, sightless eyes showing the strain, misery, shock, sleeplessness, and, in veteran fighters, the supreme indifference of young men who have lost their youth and will never recover it."[7]

Digging a foxhole was always first on the list when stopping for the day—it came before rations or rest, no matter how tired or hungry they were. Usually there was a buddy in the foxhole and each took turns—one watching and one sleeping. Tree branches kept the guys off the wet ground in case it rained, but lying on the branches was not so comfortable.

"Such was our trade and our Stone Age life: knowing our weapons and how to use them, knowing the enemy's weapons and trying to avoid them, bitching about those behind our lines who didn't have to fight, dreaming of home, fantasizing about girls, controlling our terror, bathing when we could, if only in a water-filled shell hole, and blessing the corpsmen with their morphine syringes, plasma, and guts in risking death to bring back the wounded... To each of us the most important place in the world was his foxhole."[8]

Iwo Jima was bombed and shelled for seven months before the invasion. It would place the Allies within 750 miles of Tokyo. On February 19, 1945, 60,000 Marines landed and met savage opposition. After 26 days of heavy fighting, it fell to Allies.

"Those men on the line were my family, my home. They were closer to me than I can say, closer than any friends had been or ever would be. They had never let me down, and I couldn't do it to them... Men, I now knew, do not fight for flag or country, for the Marine Corps or glory or any other abstraction. They fight for one another. Any man in combat who lacks comrades who will die for him, or for whom he is willing to die, is not a man at all. He is truly damned."[9]

On to Okinawa. Long-distance bombing from China had been practiced on Japan, but after the Allies' capture of Iwo Jima, night bombing raids on Japan increased, using up to a thousand planes a night. By the summer of 1945, more than 40 percent of Tokyo, as well as 65 other cities, was in ruins.

On August 6, 1945, a B-29, the *Enola Gay* dropped the first atomic bomb used in warfare on Hiroshima. The second one was dropped three days later on Nagasaki. About 70,000 people were killed at Hiroshima and 40,000 at Nagasaki.

During this period when the Allies were getting closer to Japan, kamikaze pilots were a menace to American shipping, as they dived into their targets, willing to sacrifice their lives.

At one time America thought it might help to have Russia in the Pacific War, but as time went on, they changed their minds. One of the reasons for using the atomic bomb was to get the Japanese to surrender quickly before the Soviet Union, under the leadership of Joseph Stalin, declared war. And it did declare war on Japan two days after the first atomic bomb was dropped.

On the Atlantic side, in June, 1941, Germany invaded the USSR. They sealed off Leningrad, thinking it would fall shortly. Instead, everyone rose to the cause, and the city endured for 900 days until the Soviets finally broke through the German blockade. At least 632,000 people had died of starvation.

Hitler thought that bombing the Soviet's industries would bring the USSR to its knees. But instead, the industries were hastily moved and revitalized and produced more and better tanks, guns, and aircraft.

Some of the most vicious combat was in the battle for Stalingrad. German forces were practically annihilated. They were finding that they were not invincible after all.

Because of the rains, mud, terrible cold, snow and frost, and the counter-offensive of the Soviets, Hitler abandoned the Moscow offensive within 19 miles of Moscow and started a retreat.

Churchill said they had to bomb Germany day and night, more and more. They would, in the spring of 1942, using saturation bombing, send a thousand bombers over one major German city in a single night.

The crew members of the Memphis Belle became "the first U.S. bomber crew to survive 25 combat missions over Nazi-occupied Europe. The mortality rate among American bomber crews was so high (about 80 percent) that military commanders feared mutiny among U.S. air crews and put a cap of 25 on the number of missions they were required to fly."[10]

In 1942 the Americans and the British, in their first experience of joint planning and operations, invaded Morocco and Algeria, to cut the enemy's supply lines and establish a base from which they could launch attacks. General Eisenhower was given overall command.

After see-sawing back and forth across Africa with bitter fighting and stubborn resistance, the end came in May 1943. Fighting continued on to Sicily and Italy.

Early in 1943 plans started for the Allied invasion of the Normandy Coast (France). By the spring of 1944 England, in preparation for D-Day, was bustling with activity—shipbuilding, production of equipment, training of helpers of all imaginable natures, activities covering all facets of war. Men in secret were checking on the geological composition of beaches along the enemy coast to know that equipment would not get bogged down; they were checking for mines, for tidal conditions, and for anything that might present D-Day problems.

Much of England was forbidden territory to civilians and millions of extra troops. There was a huge invasion of people, besides all the airfields, camps, and vehicle parks.

With all the military traffic, civilian movement was practically impossible. Most civilians had no means of traveling other than by bicycle or foot.

By June, 1944, there were over 1,500,000 members of the U.S. armed forces in Britain. Besides the supplies and equipment that they brought with them, they received 750,000 tons a month. All of these went through ports assigned to them. Getting all the men, equipment, and supplies to the right places at the right times, and in the right order, required the utmost in organization and planning.

On April 26 everything was ready. Security was tight. There was no way such a massive buildup could be concealed. But hopefully, details of the time and place of the operation could be kept a mystery. The Allies were aided in their secrecy by the fact that German air power had diminished and reconnaissance flights over England had been discontinued.

D-Day would require the initial transporting of 185,000 men and 20,000 vehicles, followed by steady replacements. Besides 4,200 landing ships and craft carrying in these troops and vehicles, warships, merchant ships, and other vessels would number more than 2,000. Over a thousand planes and gliders would drop approximately 20,000 paratroopers behind the beaches. An additional 10,000 aircraft would add to the naval fire power.

One hundred forty-six Mulberry units (artificial harbors) would be taken across the Channel by 3,000 tugs, small craft, and barges.

Germany controlled 3,000 miles of coastline but had no way of guarding that much. It was becoming very difficult to move men and equipment from one place to another. The Allies had, for sixty days prior to D-Day (April and May) been bombing rail lines, bridges, airfields, and cutting communication in France and Belgium. Transportation was reduced to bicycle or horse and cart. So for them it was a matter of deciding when and where Allied forces would invade. German Intelligence felt sure the attack would be some time in May through August, 1944, at high tide and the place to be either the Pas de Calais or Normandy, and that Cherbourg would be the natural port.

But the decision was Hitler's. He was the one in charge. He made all the decisions and then told his officers. There was no single military man in charge and this, according to a general who worked in his headquarters, proved to be disastrous in the end.

The Allied navy and air force had to have daylight for bombardment and to see they were landing troops in the right places. For navigation purposes, moonlight was preferred. Because of underwater beach obstacles, landing three to four hours before high tide was necessary. Out of each month there were only three days that met all of these specific requirements.

The development of the *Mulberries* (artificial harbors) was directed by Churchill, who insisted that they had to float up and down with the tide. The outer breakwater, 200 ft. long, had to be towed across the Channel, making it possible for ships or barges to land in the sheltered water area. Later an average of 6,500 vehicles and nearly 40,000 tons of stores landed in these sheltered waters weekly.

An underwater pipeline was built from England to the French coast so that eventually fuel was drawn directly from England.

The logistics of an operation of this magnitude were monumental and everything could be upset by some chance happening, a change in the weather, for instance.

There were many months of disagreement, tension, and painstaking detailed planning before D-Day in this coordinated effort with Britain, America, Canada, Belgium, Holland, Poland, Norway, Czeckoslovakia, Australia, New Zealand, plus the French resisters.

D-Day, June 6, 1944, had been planned for June 4, but weather was too bad then and on the 5th, General Eisenhower decided the risk must be taken on June 6. The infantry waded ashore under a cloudy, overcast sky, with Allied ships firing 200 tons of shells a minute at the German coastal batteries. There was no air opposition because the Allied planes had overpowered the German air force before the day of the invasion. By the eighth day the Normandy beaches had been won, but with heavy losses.

The Allied drive in Italy swung to the West, clearing the Germans from France, and liberating Paris in August, 1944, while the Russian armies rolled toward Berlin from the east, ridding the Nazis from the Baltic States. Many, however, felt there was not much difference between the brutality of the German and Russian armies.

The Allies were closing in on the Germans from all directions. They had entered Rome hours before the Normandy landing.

Russian troops reached Berlin in April and the Germans there surrendered on May 2, followed by the surrender of all of Germany on May 7. The unconditional surrender was signed by a high official on May 7, 1945. Eisenhower's chief of staff signed for the Allies. After 5 years, 8 months, and 7 days, the European phase of WW II had ended. Hitler, along with his wife, Eva Braun, committed suicide on April 30, 1945. (She had been his longtime mistress, but they were married the day before the suicide.) V-E (Victory in Europe) Day was declared to be May 8, 1945.

In June Berlin was divided, according to former agreement of the Allied leaders, into four zones: American, British, French, and Soviet.

On September 2, 1945, aboard the battleship Missouri, Japan officially surrendered. MacArthur signed for the Allied Powers and Adm. Nimitz for the U.S. President Truman declared September 2 as V-J (Victory over Japan) Day.

Although figures vary, more than 10 million Allied servicemen and nearly 6 million military men from the Axis countries died in the war. WW II cost more than $1,150,000,000,000. More than 50 countries took part in the war. It has been estimated that civilian and military dead total 55 million.

The Allies destroyed more than 56,000 German aircraft, and dumped about 2,700,000 tons of bombs in Europe. American pilots flew over 750,000 bomber and nearly a million fighter sorties. The British flew nearly 700,000 bomber and 1,700,000 fighter sorties.

An American woman who broadcast propaganda for the Axis, known as Axis Sally, was convicted of treason and went to prison. Tokyo Rose had made propaganda broadcasts for Japan and was also charged with treason.

Tank, Courtesy George J. Young

Photos courtesy Ralph L. Greene

WORLD WAR II

HOMEFRONT

Probably everyone that was living at the time remembers what he or she was doing on December 7, 1941, when the announcement came on radio, *Pearl Harbor has been attacked.* The world was stunned. President Roosevelt said it was *a date that would live in infamy.* His speech declaring war on Japan aroused feelings of shock, fear, patriotism, revenge. Young men, and older men, too, rushed to enlist. Many couldn't wait to get into the action; others enlisted in order to get into the branch of service they preferred. If they were single and between the ages of eighteen and thirty-five, or married and between eighteen and twenty-six, and hadn't enlisted first, they were drafted. A picture of Uncle Sam pointing his finger and saying *Uncle Sam Wants You,* was posted in buses, trains, in public buildings; in other words, you couldn't miss it.

Exemptions were made for those men working in occupations necessary to the war effort, those in college, those married with children (although many of those were taken later, also), those not passing the physical (4F), and those who were conscientious objectors. Regarding 4F, William Manchester said in *The Glory and the Dream* that nearly half the men called up in 1941, having grown up during the depression years, were refused because of malnutrition.

Women's units included the WACs (Army), WAVEs (Navy), WAFs (Ferrying Command), SPARs (Coast Guard). There was also a unit for the Marines. Many parents were quite hesitant about their daughters joining these groups, going into what was predominantly male forces.

Trains and buses were commandeered for movement of troops. Other citizens were asked not to travel unless it was absolutely essential.

Most every family had someone in service, if not a family member, friends. We heard on the radio and read in the newspapers about Lt. James H. Doolittle leading a bombing raid on Tokyo. We learned about the kamikaze, or suicide planes of the Japanese. We gloried in the turning of the tables with the battle of Midway, after so many losses in the Pacific. Maps and world globes were found in virtually every home. Names we had never

Jeeps. Courtesy Ralph L. Greene

heard of, such as the Coral Sea, Guadalcanal, Tarawa, Kwajalein, Eniwetok, Saipan, Tinian, Leyte, Okinawa, became household words. Any one of us from that period could identify the picture of the American flag being raised on Mt. Suribachi, Iwo Jima.

The Flying Tigers became famous for their work in the China and Burma area. Our hearts were with General Douglas MacArthur when he said, *I shall return,* as he left the Philippines. And all of us harbored a special hate for Tokyo Rose and Axis Sally for trying to break the morale of our men by broadcasting that they were forgotten at home, that their wives and sweethearts were going out with other men, that they weren't being told the truth about the war, on and on. And, the unfortunate thing was that some men *were* forgotten by girlfriends, or even wives, as soon as they were out of sight. The Dear John letters, ones telling guys that their girls had found someone else, became all too common. The song "Don't Sit Under the Apple Tree with Anyone Else but Me" was the dream of the serviceman.

The description of the atomic bomb attacks on Hiroshima and Nagasaki astounded us. Theoretically they saved the lives of from a half million to a million of our GIs in combat. We were glad to think of their saving the lives of our boys and that those bombings might soon bring the war to an end, but at the same time, most people were frightened by the thought of the atrocious thing we had done and what it would lead to in the future.

Ernie Pyle became famous for his war coverage in the newspapers as well as in his book, *Brave Men.* He was buried in Hawaii after being killed by Japanese machine gun fire. People have long since made a point of going to his graveside in Hawaii.

On radio Lowell Thomas, H.V. Kaltenborn, and Edward R. Murrow kept us informed. We flocked to the movies to see the latest newsreels. Occasionally parents would get lucky and see their sons in the newsreel or the March of Time. Or if anyone saw someone he or she knew in the newsreel, it was common practice to call the parents or wife. The projectionist, in our small towns, anyway, would then run the film several times for the loved ones after the feature was over. Desert Storm was so different in that we could actually see on TV what was happening at the moment.

We suffered for the troops as they went through Africa and Italy and France. No matter how rough the American troops were having it, the reporters said the GIs were always ready and willing to share their candy bars, or whatever else they might have, with children along the way.

Then the landing on the Normandy Coast with General Dwight D. Eisenhower in charge gave us hope that the end might be in sight in Europe.

Personal animosity toward Japanese Americans on the West Coast ran rampant. With the fear of treachery, those Japanese American citizens were hustled off by our government to internment camps or relocation centers. They had to leave homes and jobs to become virtually prisoners. Although people of German and Italian heritage were not interned as a group, they were under surveillance and prone to rough language and treatment by average citizens.

We were often told that our great American sense of humor was what got us through, GIs and folks back home. Bill Mauldin helped the servicemen's morale through his cartoons of Joe and Willie, two haggard, unshaven soldiers (dogfaces) in the GI paper, "The Stars and Stripes," and with his book, *Up Front.* Sad Sack also appeared spoofing army life. Joe Palooka kept up with the others by joining the army. Other cartoons in the funny papers joined the war effort, too. *Let the Good Times Roll* stated that "although youngsters read most of the ten-cent 'funny books,' men in uniform were a close second; a thirty-five thousand copy special edition of Superman was dispatched monthly to our overseas forces."[11]

Two of the principal slang expressions at the time were: "Hubba, Hubba" and "Kilroy was here." One can still be surprised occasionally in various places around the world to find that Kilroy, after all these years, can be seen carved on a tree or imprinted on rock.

The USO, which celebrated its fiftieth anniversary in 1990, tried to be an all-encompassing unit to entertain and help servicemen. They provided donuts and coffee in bus and train stations, where our boys were amassed. Near bases or shipping-out points the USO had entertainment centers with food, dancing, and girls (under strict regulations). Girls from each town, and especially in college towns, volunteered to work in these centers, as well as visiting the guys in hospitals. Campuses were practically devoid of men unless there was an ROTC base there. Men who did not pass the draft physical and were classed as 4F, plus conscientious objectors, and some exempted students, were scattered over campuses, but generally speaking, college students were mostly girls.

With all that was being done to help and entertain the servicemen, they were still lonely. Many of them looked for feminine company and found it with prostitutes hanging around the military bases. Some of the girls at home looked for male company wherever they could find it. Moral behavior hit a low.

Churches opened their doors to these men away from home. Families invited them to dinner. Lists of names and addresses were circulated so that girls and other people could write to the servicemen, ones they hadn't even met, assure their getting mail. It was not uncommon for girls to be writing to ten, fifteen, twenty, or more servicemen. People were encouraged to write, write, write, to keep up morale. The government facilitated the movement of this mail by initiating V-Mail, similar to today's forty-five cent aerograms. Only then V-Mail was three cents (or six cents for airmail), the same price as regular first-class mail. It had the advantage of being light weight, with writing on the inside, address on the outside (after folding). The two daily deliveries of mail, morning and afternoon, in towns and cities, were the highlights of the days. This two-delivery-a-day service slipped away in post-war years.

Until recent years there were no zip codes. For a short period cities had area numbers, so the address was typed as Columbus 9, Ohio.

Mail was censored. Sometimes big sections of a letter from a serviceman were cut out. Newspapers and radio also operated under strict codes. The public, in general, was constantly reminded about not giving away information that might be of value to the enemy. A very familiar poster said, *A slip of the lips sinks ships.* Some guys and families developed code words so they could pass on messages as to where they were because an outright statement would have been cut out by the censors.

With all the thousands of servicemen, sometimes there was a coincidental meeting at some far corner of the world of two friends or guys from the same home town. Or in one case, two friends of my husband were on ships that passed. Since the radio couldn't be used, the signalman was nice enough to use the signal lights to convey the greetings from one buddy to the other.

As mentioned earlier, patriotism was running high. Mothers felt they should do anything possible for servicemen around them in hopes that other mothers would do the same for their sons.

Many of the mothers never had the opportunity to see their sons again. They, or the wives, waited at home, hoping the dreaded telegram from the government, starting with, "We regret to inform you..." would not come. Gold stars displayed on a white silk background hung in the windows of homes where the son did not return. The Gold Star Mothers were well known for helping the sons of other mothers. The same kind of pennants hung in windows of other people with sons or daughters in service, but those stars were blue. The nationwide organization of Gold Star Mothers was started in 1928 and is based in Washington, D.C. Their purpose is to assist veterans and their dependents remember those who died in battle.

Quick marriages were commonplace. The boy wanted to know his high school sweetheart would be waiting for him on his return. Or many weekend romances with the girl he met at the USO or church might end in a wedding.

Government boards or agencies were set up to handle almost any kind of problem that might arise during wartime. There were so many they used almost every letter of the alphabet. There were ones for housing, labor, price control, rationing—you name it, we had it. Examples: Office of Price Administration, Office of War Information, Office of Civilian Supply, National Relocation Authority. Ones who worked in Washington at the time said it was a busy, busy place. According to William Manchester, "By the war's end the OPA... had 73 thousand full-time employees, 200 thousand volunteers."[12]

While I did not accept a position in Washington, I passed the Civil Service test as a stenographer, salary to be seventeen hundred fifty-two dollars a year, and received the following information about Washington:

"The Washington War Housing Center has on its lists approximately 4000 available rooms in the metropolitan area of Washington... All rooms are inspected, and unless they meet required standards of health, safety and comfort, they are not listed as available... Single rooms average around $25 per month; double rooms average $20 per month per person... Where there are two or more persons in a room, prices for room and board average $40 to $55 a month for each person... Streetcar and bus fares within the district of Columbia are 10 cents... Taxi rates are charged by zones. There are four zones with the following rates for one person: 30, 50, 70, and 90 cents.

"There are a large number of centers in Washington where girls who are employed by the government may participate in recreational facilities, provided for servicemen and war workers... A number of government establishments, such as the War and Navy Departments, the War Production Board, have employee counselors who are doing much to acquaint any government workers in Washington with existing recreational facilities... The people are interesting. Celebrities, members of the armed forces, as well as just plain people visit or live in Washington... On weekends soldiers, sailors and marines from nearby camps visit Washington. On Saturday nights Washington's amusement places are well attended by young people. Because there are so many young government workers in Washington, the great majority of them from out-of-town—it's easy to make friends."[13]

Rationing on the homefront of gasoline, tires, shoes, and foods such as meat, sugar, coffee, helped to make these things available to the troops. A gasoline sticker was posted on each car windshield indicating the owner's driving status: A, pleasure only; B, drives to work; C, drives at work; D, emergency vehicle. The A sticker entitled the driver to three gallons a week. This gasoline rationing seemed to cause more complaints than anything else and dealing on the black market became common.

Even though there was not much driving, eventually tires wore out and had to be retreaded. This, too, took special permission; need had to be shown. Mechanics were kept busy repairing cars; cars could not be replaced. New ones were not available. All metal was being used for tanks and war material or equipment. Carpooling was used extensively, although it was called ride sharing.

Not a dropful of coffee or a spoonful of sugar was wasted. In fact, desserts were rare, as were large pieces of meat, such as chops or steaks. Stews, soups, and casseroles were the order of the day. One ration book was issued for sugar and coffee; another for canned foods; another for meat. The one for meat contained red and blue stamps equal to ten points. Meat in the store case was marked not only with price but the number of points needed per pound. Red and blue tokens, worth one point each, were used to make change. Immediately after Pearl Harbor, each man, woman, and child was limited to one half pound of sugar a week, but that ration was increased later.

Recycling was popular during this war period: old hose, nylon or silk, newspapers, rubber, and any kind of metal, including toothpaste tubes and old pots and pans, were saved and turned in. Fenced-in areas on courthouse lawns were common collection centers. Even bacon grease and other fats were collected to be used in making ammunitions.

Families were encouraged to have Victory Gardens to supply some of their own food and leave more for the servicemen. Window boxes, as well as flowerbeds and corners of yards, were devoted to this purpose. People who had never gardened before willingly took on this new challenge. Supposedly, there were eighteen million gardens in the U.S. at that time.

Since shoes were also rationed to three pairs a year, we didn't run to the store and buy a new pair when the sole wore out; that sole was replaced. Shoe repair shops had booming business. However, that had been true since the depression era. People had no money for new shoes then, so many times cardboard was used as an inner lining. Mother or Dad traced around the foot with a pencil, cut out the cardboard, and inserted it in the shoe. If the outer sole came loose, some kids held it on with a rubber band or piece of string. It was not unusual to see kids at school with those rubber bands, or cord, around their shoes. If they had a few extra cents, they could buy outer soles and glue them on. A shoestring was not thrown away just because it broke; sometimes a string would have four or five knots tied in it.

Holes in socks were darned; runners in hose were sewed up. People learned to be very conservative; but again, having just come out of the depression years, it was not that different.

As a substitute for the unavailable stockings, some girls wore leg makeup. It was a liquid, similar to today's face makeup, but was gratefully dispensed with when hose again became obtainable. The leg makeup was messy to apply and got on the bottom of dresses and other clothes. And if it rained, disaster! Since most hose at that time had seams in the back, some girls even drew lines up the back of their legs with eye markers.

All consumer goods were scarce because raw materials that were needed for war production were used to that end. Workers were concentrated in war production. Unemployment was forgotten. Factories were competing to meet quotas set by the government. Workers felt an obligation to produce as much as possible. If quotas were met, government officials would come to the factory, laud the workers and present a large Army-Navy E Award (for Excellence), the banner thereafter being displayed in a prominent place. Each worker was made to feel proud. This was an incentive to produce even more the following months. Patriotism was at a peak. The *American Chronicle* mentioned one problem: manufacture of alarm clocks had ceased and, as a result, thousands were late to work.

The following statistics, taken from *The Glory and the Dream,* give credence to the dedication of the American workers. During the period of the war we produced "296,429 warplanes; 102,351 tanks; 2,455,964 trucks; 87,620 warships; 5,425 cargo ships; plus all the arms and ammunition."[14] Kaiser was producing one ship a day.

This was the birth of Rosie the Riveter. With so many men going to the armed forces, there was a dearth in the factories. Women whose place had heretofore been in the homes, now were needed in the working place. They donned the slacks or coveralls, started carrying lunchboxes, and learned to operate drill presses, all kinds of equipment and machinery; thus started the saga of women in the workplace. My mother was one of the first to answer the call in an airplane factory. I doubt if she was ever happier. Being a very independent person, she loved the challenge of proving she could operate every piece of machinery as well as any man. Pay in these factories was also good, so families began to come out of the slump of the depression. Still in 1940 "... half of the nation's children were in families with an annual income of less than fifteen hundred dollars a year."[15] The term *latchkey kids* was coined when mothers started working in the defense plants and children came home from school to an empty house.

To finance the war, war or defense or victory bonds were sold, similar to today's U.S. Savings bonds. The other names were used for patriotic purposes. Citizens were encouraged at their workplaces to buy these bonds. To facilitate payment, money could be deducted from paychecks for a continuous contribution. Even children at school were encouraged to buy stamps which could be pasted into a booklet until the designated amount of the bond had been collected. Signs were in public buildings, on billboards, and frequent announcements were on the radio appealing to citizens to buy these bonds.

Newspapers and magazines also carried advertisements for these bonds. Superman was even used on posters to sell bonds. Songs were composed. Sales competitions were arranged. Kate Smith seemed to be everywhere keeping people in a patriotic mood by singing "God Bless America." Movie stars made personal appearance tours over the country urging citizens to support our boys by buying bonds.

The stars passed out many autographed pictures for guys to put on their locker doors. Some of the favorite pinup girls were Betty Grable, Rita Hayworth, Jane Russell, and Cyd Charisse. Since these guys were separated from girls, they boosted their morale by plastering walls and doors of lockers with sexy pictures. So arose the term, *pinup girls.*

Speaking of stars touring, Glen Miller, the popular band leader, had gone into the air corps and was being used to entertain troops. All Americans were saddened when his plane crashed en route to an appearance for the troops.

Other big-name bands were: Tommy Dorsey, Jimmy Dorsey, Benny Goodman, Stan Kenton, Guy Lombardo, Artie Shaw, Kay Keysor, Harry James, Claude Thornhill, Duke Ellington, Count Basie, Louis Armstrong—on and on.

Popular singers were: Frank Sinatra, Perry Como, Bing Crosby, Johnny Ray, Tony Bennett, Nat King Cole, Jo Stafford, Doris Day, Rosemary Clooney, Margaret Whiting, Patti Page, Lena Horne, The Andrews Sisters, the Mills Brothers, the Ink Spots...

Most of the songs related to the war: A Boy in Khaki, A Girl in Lace; Little Bo Peep has Lost her Jeep; This is the Army, Mr. Jones; I Left my Heart at the Stage Door Canteen; When the Lights go on Again all Over the World; I'll Never Smile Again; Harbor Lights; Boogie Woogie Bugle Boy; I'll be Seeing You; Sentimental Journey; I'll Walk Alone; You'd be so Nice to Come Home to; and the all-time favorite, White Christmas—all recorded on the big 78 records.

Air-raid drills were organized by Civil Defense groups in towns and cities all over the United States. Each street had an air-raid warden. People became plane spotters, learning to identify planes and taking their turns watching for hostile ones. Many places, especially along the coasts, had blackouts. Schools participated in air-raid drills, with children getting under desks and putting their hands over their heads. Many women across the U.S. volunteered every spare minute to roll bandages for the Red Cross. Blood Banks had no problem getting volunteers to donate blood.

Victory did come, and President Truman proclaimed May 8, 1945, as V-E Day (Victory in Europe). Likewise, he proclaimed September 2, 1945, as V-J Day (Victory in Japan). The world was saddened that President Roosevelt had died in April, 1945, not getting to see the end of the long struggle.

On V-E and V-J Days people all over the United States, in big cities and small towns, went wild; they were ecstatic. Streets were filled with people throwing confetti or whatever, dancing, grabbing and kissing one another, crying with happiness. With the zeal and intensity of emotion, windows were broken. Some liquor stores had to close. No New Year's Eve could compare. But at the other end of the spectrum, many churches were filled to overflowing.

While Hitler was blitzing England almost every night trying to force a surrender, England was using radar, a secret development, to track the Luftwaffe. Also through the war came new or improved flame throwers, rocket launchers, jet engines, amphibious assault boats, long-range navigational aids, devices for detecting submarines, radar bombsights. Wider use of penicillin, DDT, and blood plasma was initiated.

After the war, to help work out the present and future problems among countries, the United Nations was chartered. And then, of course, Russia divided Germany with the Berlin Wall. When Russia blocked all transportation routes into West Berlin, Western Allies organized the airlift, landing a plane every forty-five seconds for almost a year until the blockade was lifted.

In 1976 the effects of the Wall were imprinted on my mind when I taveled to Berlin and mirrors on dollies were run under our bus, dogs sniffed everything, ill-disposed guards scrutinized our faces and our passport pictures. Guns were pointed in our direction from various angles. An American high school girl that accompanied us, one that ordinarily seemed as though she didn't take life very seriously, upon our return to the western area, fell down and kissed the ground. East German people stood on their balconies of apartment houses immediately beyond the Wall, sadly watching us enjoying our freedom on the western side.

Quite a problem arose after the war (1945) when GIs brought war brides home from Europe or Japan. Feelings were so strong here that many families could not accept a daughter-in-law of that heritage. Many townspeople caused unpleasant incidents. The brides, being far away from their own people and land, many times not being able to speak much English, did not receive the welcome and help they needed.

The Baby Boom started when the war ended and the GIs returned home. Houses were at a premium. Construction soared, starting the rush to the suburbs, creating the new concept of suburbia. With suburbia came the lines of houses all alike and the jokes about men not being able to find their own house, especially if they had a few drinks under their belt. Suburbia caused men to commute between home and work. Station wgons became the distinguishing mark of the suburban housewife, giving room to haul her own kids, plus friends' and neighbors' kids to ball practice, Scouts, etc. Neighbors in these housing areas found it fun to have backyard picnics together, starting the barbecue tradition. And the topic of conversation with the men was the new power lawn mowers.

The next twenty years or so were changed by the increased population of babies, then young children, then teenagers, then college students. Marketing was geared to these different age groups, as they progressed. Business was booming. They were the consumers. Older people, who had to tighten their belts during the depression and the war, did not feel quite as secure about money. They were more likely to hold on to what they had and not spend quite so freely as the younger folks.

A much more mobile society developed. Men who had never thought of going to college before the war could now go with the government paying the bill, thanks to the GI Bill. Campuses were flooded with older men. Whereas during the war there were practically no men on campus unless there was an ROTC unit there, now they were taking over, but it was a completely different age group. A great many of them were already married, so a new campus concept developed, housing for married students. Quonset huts (rounded metal buildings used during the war), trailers, and prefabricated units appeared to alleviate the housing problem.

After graduation, jobs were offered in other areas of the country. GIs had met and married girls from other areas of the United States and the world. Their perspective of their hometown and the country had changed. Transportation was improving rapidly, making it easier to move from place to place.

With all this mobility, the need for babysitters arose. Young parents were no longer living close to their parents so Grandma and Grandpa couldn't help to take care of the children. So what better way could there be than to have the older girl down the street come to keep their children? The idea caught on fast. Parents loved having their new freedom and teenagers loved having the opportunity to make that money. Suburbia became a viable social outlet, a way of making friends in strange surroundings.

Also, along with the Baby Boom came Dr. Spock and his idea of permissiveness; that is, be flexible; don't stick to schedules; do what you think the baby needs or wants. His book on raising children became new parents' law.

During the separation in wartime years, some husbands and wives had grown apart. Women had to take care of themselves; they had to make their own decisions. They were no longer the dependent housewives. The men had seen the war; they had seen their buddies, as well as strangers, hurt or killed. Their nerves were shattered. Many were disabled. The two people who had loved one another before the war now were different people; they coudn't understand one another or communicate.

Many men could not find work. It was taking time for manufacturers to switch back from wartime to peacetime production. And then the question of seniority arose—who should have the jobs, the ones who had been working during the war or the returned veterans? Many women who had been working while the men were away did not want to give up their jobs and their independence. They were not satisfied with staying at home and raising a family. Some opted for not having children at all. These feelings emerged from wartime work and escalated gradually into the Equal Rights Amendment.

Morals changed. Having premarital sex and living together before marriage became the thing to do. Divorce rates shot up. Children with divorced parents became the rule rather than the exception.

During the war, black men served honorably in the armed forces. Black women were allowed to work in places where they were not permitted before, even though they were given the lowliest jobs. This acted as an impetus for the Civil Rights Movement, with Dr. Martin Luther King as leader.

General Motors, Ford, and Chrysler were the big auto makers. There was also Studebaker for a while, AMC, and Kaiser-Frazer with the Henry J. They didn't need to worry about competition from Japan. There were no Hondas, Toyotas, Nissans. In fact, before World War II, Japan made trinkets and rather poor-quality items. Japan's industrial prowess arose after the war when the United States was helping Japan to rebuild in order to become self-sufficient.

JAMES BRENTLINGER

SIDNEY, OHIO

MP, 397th Battalion, T/4 Sgt., Army, 1945-47, WW II
Basic Training: Camp Robinson, Little Rock, AR
Duty in Germany

Basic Training was a very growing experience for most all of us. The average age then was 18-19. Our squad commander was only 21 and a 2d Lieutenant. We kidded him about not being old enough to shave yet, and by doing so, he insisted we all shave every day, even though every other day would have been enough. (At that time I only had to shave about every three days.)

It was a time of leaving your boyhood behind and attempting to enter manhood. That was the most difficult for a lot of the young men, but for myself and a great number of others, the responsibility was accepted, and it made us all better citizens for the future.

On the weekly menu at the mess hall in Basic Training was usually what they called Lamb Stew. But, surrounding the camp area was a huge goat farm, and we all knew where the lamb stew came from; you could smell it cooking long before you got to the mess hall. That was the time to hit the PX for canteen sandwiches and pass up the mess hall. Only the hardy with no nose and no taste could handle that once-a-week meal!

After Basic Training was over (16 weeks) our platoon was shipped out to New York, then by Victory Ship (SS Coal Jr.) to Bremerhaven, Germany, to join the occupational forces there. I was assigned to a military police battalion, the 397th.

For a short time I was doing MP duty at the Palace of Justice in Nuremburg, guarding all the entrances. That was the time of the trials of the German officers for the acts against prisoners during the war, such names as Goering, Hess, etc.

Then I was reassigned to riding supply trains to all points of Europe. I was stationed in Furth, Germany, and my partner and I worked as a team, taking the supply train to its destination and seeing that all the contents reached there intact.

The biggest risk was carrying gasoline in open gondola cars in stacks and rows of filled five-gallon cans. When the train would slow down for a water stop or small town, the Germans or French would try to board the train and pilfer the cars or throw the gas cans off to their waiting cohorts on the ground. Our job was to see that they did not do this! I found a system that seemed to work—rather than shooting at them all the time (and sometimes that was necessary), we would carry extra supplies of food and necessities and give to the people we passed that really needed them.

My experience in the service was most gratifying and took me to ten or twelve European countries, from Germany into France, Austria, Switzerland, Italy, and all over.

I could go on and on, but I won't. But, if I had it to do over again, I would like to do it all over again!

CHARLES BRISTLINE

Gunner, 727th Squadron, 451st Bomb Group, WW II
Duty in European Theater

Princess Catherine was a member of the Romanian Royal Family. She never got along with the Germans or Communist regime and she let them know that. She took care of our low level raid boys for a whole year. Then when we got there she did what she could for us. She came through with the Royal Family and investigated the camp. King Michael was only 14 at the time and she brought the King through along with the Royal Family. I was a T/Sgt. with a group of 25 other enlisted men when they came through. She came over to our group and said, "Is there something you want?" One of the other boys in the back said, "Yes, we want to know when we are getting out!" She looked around and looked back at us, and said, "Wait till the 27th of August." The night of the 27th they opened the gates and we walked out.

The Princess lost everything. She lost all of her holdings in Romania. She was no longer accepted under the new regime because she had fought Communism. She came to America and fought for three years to stay here. A few of our prison boys helped as much as we could. She was allowed to stay in this country...

Thirty some years ago I got a call one day while I was out. They said it was Princess Catherine. I said, "Did she say she would call back!" YES! So I was home an hour or so and she called back.

There was a man from Harrisburg who had been a prisoner with us. I live in Hummelston, which is nine miles away. Anyway, he was working for the newspaper. So we got the Princess and took her out to dinner and visited with her.

I went to the POW Reunion... at Colorado Springs. This was 30 years after our dinner date. We walked into the hospitality room. I introduced my wife to the Princess and said hello to her. I said, "I guess you don't remember me." She said, "What do you mean? I remember the newspaper man from Harrisburg and you're the man from Hullsberg." After 30 years she remembered me. She has a fantastic mind and a fantastic memory. Of course she calls all of us ex-prisoners, "HER BOYS."

Editor's Note: ...She is responsible for saving hundreds of American fliers from German hands, not only from the 451st but from the entire 15th Air Force.

Reprinted with permission from Michael D. Hill, Editor, *The Fight'n 451st Bomb Group (H).*

Warren Cadwallader using Piball (weather balloon)

WARREN CADWALLADER

FT. WAYNE, INDIANA

Weather Observer, Corporal, Army Air Corps, 1945-47
Basic Training: Sheppard Field, Texas
Duty in Philippines and Japan

1945 was an upbeat year for me, as it was for many people in America. I remember celebrating the end of the war, knowing the killing was over, and my three brothers in the service would soon be coming home, alive and well.

Brother Raymond would assume the job of helping our parents on the family farm, and this left me free to enlist in the Army Air Corps.

As a member of the occupation troops, we arrived at Manila, Philippines. Two weeks later we were transferred to Japan, and I served most of the remaining time at the Itazuke army air base at Fukuoka on Kyushu Island.

What do I remember about these times? I remember the rusted ships resting on the bottom of Manila Harbor, looking like statues in the water.

I remember walking through the city of Nagasaki one year after the atom bombing and seeing the complete destruction of a city. The eyes of the survivors reflected much sorrow.

I remember large Japanese crowds gathering on the sidewalk just to see General MacArthur arriving and leaving his office. I believe at that time they had a greater respect for MacArthur than they did for their emperor. They were quick to adjust to peace and rebuild for the future (look where Japan is today).

I remember the great friends I met from all areas of the USA. In a way, I believe we were diplomats of our country and were a small part of the WW II story.

The most unforgettable event was the final day at the weather station before I was due to return to the USA. The Japanese personnel presented me with several small gifts. I felt like I had made some friends. I wonder where and how these people are today.

A CHAIRBORNE CLERK

AIR FORCE SERGEANT, WW II

"...Chairborne, that's me. They carried me to Australia and sat me at a typewriter. Every second week I got a day off and went for long walks. But most of the time I sat. Sat and typed... Me, I was at a headquarters all the time. I'm lucky. Two and a half years over there and no one ever shot at me. And I never shot at anybody else. Hell, I wasn't really in the war."

In the AAF there are 337,000 men assigned specifically to administrative work, and a great many more who actually do it... They are the men who've fought their war with Typewriters, Desk, Standard, wondering if what they're doing affects the war at all. Lots of them have been bombed and strafed. Some have been killed. But even when they experience enemy action they have to sit there and take it. They rarely get a chance to fight back.

The papers slide over their desks in posts smack on the equator where they have to put talcum powder on their hands and arms to keep from rubbing all the ink off the papers; in underground shelters north of Nome they work through the arctic twilight with feet on top of kerosene stoves and fingers blue from cold. They realize that the inconvenience they endure is nothing compared to the violent hardships of combat troops—they keep telling themselves that, but all the time there's the boredom and monotony of the carefully trite official correspondence—and a guilty feeling that they're not contributing to the war.

Well, without them we could give up now. Without the steady clack clack of thousands of typewriters there'd be no spare parts and no replacement airplanes; no rotation policy, no troop movements, no pay, no courts martial, no uniforms, no gasoline; there'd be no duty rosters and no overnight passes, no PXs and no .50 caliber ammunition—or guns. There'd be no promotion on either side of the ocean, no food, no war—no victory...

They're guys who stood next to you at induction center and felt the same emotions you did—were just as ready as you to take whatever came, combat or kitchen police. They're good soldiers who do what they're told knowing they're lucky in lots of ways, but who, for the most part, devoutly wish they weren't.

Quoted from the article, "405—Clerk, Typist," by Major Luther Davis, April, 1945, *Air Force,* p. 26.

WILLARD R. COLGATE

HAINES CITY, FLORIDA

1st Loader on right Twin Forty, Seaman 1st Class, Navy,
1944-45, WW II
Basic Training: Great Lakes, Illinois
Duty at ATB Camp Bradford, North Fork, VA; USS LST 655 Pacific

Entered service August, 1944, when I was 24, from Columbus, Ohio, and was sent to Great Lakes, IL for 11 1/2 weeks of boot camp. Our company received the rooster flag the last six weeks of boot camp for rating the highest in drills and barracks inspections. In marching, we didn't carry real rifles—they had steel barrels and looked like rifles but didn't shoot. Our company marched in Navy Day Parade in Chicago, a long distance.

After boot camp and Amphibious Training at Camp Bradford, VA, I went to North Fork, VA, aboard LST 655 (Landing Ship Tank) to Hoboken, NJ. We were in dry dock for thirty-one days while they refitted the ship. It had made a trip to France and now was back for a replacement crew.

The LST had 112 men plus officers. It was equipped with a twin 40-mm. gun (better than 14 inches probably. Used mostly for shooting aircraft) on the bow; six 20-mm. guns around the ship; and a single 40-mm. gun in the stern. They never shot a plane; shot at drones (practice ones, mechanically controlled). The ship had a deck for hauling tanks. When coming close to shore, it drops anchor close to sand and lowers a ramp for the tanks, men, whatever, to unload. Some islands had the motorized ducks and the navy guys would send them out to the ships to get supplies.

At the New York side, after loading an LCT and crew, we started for the Pacific as part of a large convoy. An LCT is smaller—12 men, no guns. It hauls men to shore and lets them out and is used to get supplies from the big ship.

Arriving at San Juan, Puerto Rico, after 10 or 11 days, we donned our dress whites and marched to the naval base where we spent one day while supplies were loaded; then on to Panama City for two days. I was able to buy three pairs of silk stockings for my wife; they were hard to get at home. I mailed them, as well as some other things, while there. She got everything but the stockings. Apparently someone in the post office liked or needed the stockings, too. The song, Rum and Coca Cola, was popular at that time and we heard it everywhere.

After taking five or six hours, I think, to go through the Panama Canal, we went on to San Diego, to Honolulu, Hawaii, and then to Eniwetok in the Marshall Islands. Stopped there long enough to attend services at the base church—didn't get to see the native people or the island. Went on to Guam and let a chief off; on to Saipan—pulled right up to the beach, unloaded the tanks and trucks, pulled away from the beach and launched the LCT.

The next morning was Sunday, and we were anchored out in the bay. During an air raid, another ship pulled in where we had been and a suicide plane dived into the bow and killed three guys. Also, the night we pulled in we had five air raids; everyone had to man their guns, but we didn't have to use them, fortunately.

During the five nights there we had four or five air raids per night. Everyone was scared the first time, but after we'd been through it three nights, we got used to it. The LST had a fog generator and we would lay a smoke screen at night, before the planes arrived; not in daytime.

When we returned to Saipan it was already secured and things were pretty well cleaned up. We were busy unloading and loading the ship so didn't see much of the island. There were a lot of Seabees there. Were there three days, picked up some army men and carried them to Okinawa. One night we had an air raid and the fog generator caught fire. The flames were coming up around the gun tower on the stern. I was loader on the right twin 40. They gave us orders to abandon the gun tub. When I jumped out, my foot hit something and I hurt my back. By that time, the air raid was over.

We needed sugar on the ship, so three of us went in a jeep to get some. The building was full, clear to the roof, of sugar. Some of it was as hard as rock. We threw sacks around till we found some that was soft.

From Okinawa we returned to Saipan, where they were preparing for the invasion of Japan; they had dropped the two atomic bombs on Japan. Soon the word was received that Japan wanted to surrender. We returned to Okinawa to drop off soldiers and were there when two Japanese officers arrived at a little island next to Okinawa. They got on an American plane and proceeded (from a very small airstrip) to Manila to sign surrender papers on the Missouri. This little island was where Ernie Pyle, the newsman, was killed; there's a little cross marking the spot.

While in the Philippines, my buddy and I went ashore and he got pretty well *lit.* We went into a little place to get coffee before going back to ship, and there was an old lady sitting there in a rocking chair. My buddy went over, lifted the woman up out of the chair, picked up the rocker and started back to the ship with it. We got back to the Higgins boat, he put the rocking chair aboard, got it unloaded, and carried it down to his place.

Next morning I heard these very determined footsteps, and there was the skipper. The lady wanted her rocking chair back. The skipper said, "You're going to take that rocking chair back and apologize to her! If there's any damage, you are going to pay for it!" So he took it back and the lady said there was no damage—she was just glad to get her chair back. They never punished him in any way, but he'd never been in trouble before.

We headed for Fuson, Korea, and while on the way, spotted two mines. They gave us orders to go out around them and stand by. After two hours we proceeded on.

Another ship in our convoy picked up two Japanese in a small boat, transferred them to another LST, and tied their boat on behind ours. Before we arrived at Fuson, their boat fell apart and sank. We got there late, was almost dark when we arrived. During the night orders were received for everyone who was eligible to return to Okinawa and then return home.

On the way home there was a storm. They tried to go out around it, but then had to return to base twice. One ship lost its bow doors—just broke off. The ship got back to base okay because behind the doors the ramp had rubber seals to keep it from leaking. Some of the ships that were anchored at the base sank. We lost one of our emergency rafts. One LST started breaking up and they hurried welders out to it and managed to save it. When an LST is empty, it rolls like a washtub.

We were three days late getting into Treasure Island, California. About 13 knots (approximately 15 miles per hours) was as fast as we usually went. We all had to remain there until all gear was shipped home.

Top: Willard R. Colgate. Bottom: LST (Landing Ship, Tank)
Courtesy Willard R. Colgate

After a liberty in San Francisco, I boarded a troop train for Great Lakes, IL. The trip took six days and nights, arriving one day before Thanksgiving. We spent Thanksgiving Day in Great Lakes; got mustered out and discharged the following day.

Our crew was great—couldn't have had a better one. We got a recommendation for a job well done.

The worst part was being away from my wife and three kids. One fellow aboard had six children. Going over we didn't get mail for 33 days and then it started catching up, so that made things better. Mail service was pretty good.

The last two months before I left Curtis-Wright, making airplane propeller parts, I was training women to take the men's jobs. There was only one man on my line when I left, and he was at least 60; all the rest were women.

We came in under the Golden Gate Bridge. Two ships with entertainers came out to meet us, with bands playing.

WILLIAM H. DEAM

SIDNEY, OHIO

B-26 Marauder Pilot, Ist Lt., Army Air Corps, 1942-45, WW II
Basic Training: Ft. Belvoir, VA; Maxwell Field, AL
Duty in European Theatre of Operations

There were three stages of flight training—primary was with single open cockpit with civilian instructors. Most of the would-be pilots that washed out did it here in this first phase. Some got airsick, some didn't have coordination, some had attitude problems. If you didn't solo within 8 hours, you probably would become a gunner.

The second phase had military instructors and we started flying nights. I had my biggest problem there—was hard for me to land at night.

Received my wings and commission of Second Lieutenant in January, 1943, and went on to B-26 school in Shreveport, LA.

We flew a B-26 Marauder over to England by the southern route, first stop being Puerto Rico. Then on to Brazil for 2 stops, then to Ascension Islands, about halfway between Brazil and Africa. Each of us had an air transport navigator, pilot, co-pilot, engineer. There was a number of planes, but we didn't fly in formation. An extra bomb bay gas tank had been put in each plane. That ATC could shoot the stars and know where we were all the time.

Went from the Islands to Monrovia, Africa, to the Sahara Desert, and to Marrakech, Morocco; from there to Bath in Southwestern England. We took leave of our planes there and went to Belfast, Ireland, for two weeks of combat training. I particularly remember their telling us that if we found ourselves grounded in Germany, not to give ourselves up to civilians. They have had a rough time and many of them do not treat Americans kindly. Avoid them at all costs. Try to find the military.

In England there were probably a minimum of two hundred airbases. We never had trouble getting gas for the planes or ammunition.

We started flying over Germany a couple of months before D-Day. By that time most of the German fighters had been pulled back into home country to protect Germany against the RAF at night and the B-17s and B-24s in the daytime. So we seldom ran into any fighters.

A tour of duty on a B-26 was 65 missions. If you flew a lead mission, they gave you an extra half credit. I flew on them four times, getting two extra credits, so was rotated back to the States after 63 missions. Most of my missions were in support of Gen. Patton's Third Army. I was co-pilot until I flew over 50 missions.

With us, we lost more planes through pilot error, mechanical failure, and weather conditions than to enemy action. We lost four crews before we left England because of collision—they just ran into one another getting into formation.

Most of our flights were about 400 miles, 800 miles round trip.

When we moved across the Channel from England to Normandy, we lived in tents in an apple orchard, which was also occupied by a British POW camp for German prisoners. This was known as Airstrip #13 which was the 13th airstrip built by the U.S. Army Engineers in Normandy, and it consisted of steel matting for runways.

We took part in the Battle of the Bulge—that and D-Day stand out in my mind more than other missions. In the Battle of the Bulge we were on 24-hour alert; they didn't know from which direction the Germans would break through, if they broke through, and we were not that far removed from that area. It was winter, thick fog, cloud cover, short days. There were 12 to 14 days straight when we couldn't fly; we were sitting on the ground just waiting. The Germans caught the Allies off guard. That's why they made such a drastic bulge in the lines—no air support available. The Germans threw hundreds of tanks and airplanes into that effort, a tremendous amount of fire power. Our guys didn't have air support. When the weather cleared and we got into the air, fighters and bombers, then that turned the tables.

I was in the 394th Bomb Group, 587th Squadron. We were called the Bridge Busters—bombed more bridges than anything else, highway and railroad, but also airfields and ammunition dumps.

Early groups tried low-level bombing and it was a disaster. They changed tactics. There were 54 planes in a maximum effort. To keep the Germans from zeroing in with their flak at one level, the lead box (each box being 18 planes) would be at 12,000 ft.; high box at 13,000 ft.; low box at 11,000 ft. Losses went down. About the maximum a B-26 could get up with a bomb load and full gas load was 15,000 ft.

A crew consisted of six people—pilot, co-pilot, bombardier, and three gunners. The lead crew carried seven—added a navigator. Otherwise, the bombardier was also trained in navigation. We had a form of radar called a G-Box—very early stages of radar. The navigator could use it to help determine location.

On our 59th mission, December 2, 1944, we were going to Saarlautern, Germany, and were supposed to have fighter escort. The fighter escort didn't arrive on time so we had to circle until it arrived. That was the beginning of things going wrong. A cold front was to be moving in off the English Channel. We were supposed to get back in plenty of time, but it moved quicker than they thought, and we had gotten off to a late start. When we started back, we ran into bad weather. Tried to get underneath cloud cover, down about 500 ft. The hills were 1,000 ft., so we knew we were in trouble. By that time we had broken up and everyone was on his own. We tried to make radio contact; no base was open that we could reach. We decided to try to go above the cloud cover. It was pouring down rain and the higher we got, the colder it got, and we iced up. Gas gauges were down to practically nothing. No way could we stay with that plane. The navigator couldn't see ground so he couldn't figure out where we were, but we knew we were in Allied territory (this was after D-Day). We dropped the nose wheel, landing gear, and the three of us in front dropped out through the nose wheel; the three in back went out the back window; never saw each other until some time later.

I lost my flying boots when my parachute opened, but had a pair of oxfords on under them. Everyone got down without a problem. When I broke out of the clouds, no more than 500 ft. above ground, all I could see was trees. Then I noticed a mud lane. My chute got caught in a tree, but I was on the ground. This was the first time I had parachuted; they had told us what to do but gave us no training. I walked down the mud lane and found a man leading a draft horse. This was France, on the French-Belgian border. I tried to tell the man I was American but we couldn't understand each other. He motioned for me to follow him; took me to a house in a small village, about a mile. Three of the crew were already there. This fellow was head of the Free French in that area and had communication with military police. After three or four hours a command car picked us up and took us back to the base. No one got hurt, so we were lucky.

On my last mission, the 63rd, we were going to bomb a bridge fifteen or twenty miles east of Cologne. We got low on gas; engine acted up. We dropped out of formation and no longer had fighter escort. The German air force was practically non-existent by that time. We were to call the fighter patrol if we had trouble. It was just a matter of minutes after we called until they were there. We didn't have enough gas left to get back to camp. We saw an emergency landing strip (one direction only) outside Luxembourg, a steel matted strip. We couldn't make any contact with this emergency strip. There was snow on the ground. We made a poor choice, but we landed down wind instead of into the wind, and that increased our speed. We went scooting in, probably with a ground speed of 150 or 160 miles per hour when we hit that steel mat. At the far end of the 5,000 or 6,000 ft. runway there was nothing but trees and an American anti-aircraft battery dug in. There was no way we were going to stop. So we jerked the wheels up, no gas left so we weren't worried about fire, and skidded. Tore the plane up some, but we stayed on the runway, got stopped, and got out. The B-26 was done for.

No sooner had we gotten out than a kid in a P-47 came in and did the same thing. He didn't hit our plane; got stopped in time. So there were two planes setting there with the wheels up.

Somebody picked us up, took us to downtown Luxembourg, and put us up in a hotel. This hotel was being used for the headquarters of a U.S. Infantry Division. We told the major we would like to go up to the front lines, 30 or 40 miles away. Later when the front was quiet, he got a Jeep and took us up. A couple of German tanks that they had destroyed were setting there, still smoking. The Germans killed the day before were still stacked up in the street. One guy wanted to trade a German Luger for my flight boots. It was winter, cold and snowy, and I wanted to keep my boots. Ours were all fleece lined, but his were just like work shoes. My hat was off to those guys on the front lines—was wintertime and their living conditions were absolutely horrible. It didn't take us long to get out of there. We were thankful to be in the Air Corps.

FREDERICK J. EGBERT

ANNA, OHIO

Captain's Guard, PFC, Marines, 1944-46, WW II
Basic Training: Parris Island, SC
Duty on aircraft carrier, USS Lake Champlain; and
light cruiser, Oregon City

I left for the military service on December 15, 1944, and having never been on a train, bus, or plane, this was something totally exciting for me. Upon arriving in Columbus, Ohio, to be inducted, I was asked what branch of the service I wanted. I said, "Navy." At the Navy Department the Navy officer told the Marine sergeant, "Here are six men for your quota." That was how I got into the Marines.

I took my boot training at Parris Island, SC, and infantry training in Camp LeJune, NC. From there I went to San Diego, California, to sea school. This was to be a three-month schooling, but I received only two weeks of training and one week of mess duty. Then we were shipped by train back to Norfolk, Virginia, to go overseas on an aircraft carrier, the Lake Champlain.

This was a large ship with a flight deck that was 946 ft. long. To this farm boy, that was big! In fact, the first night I was on it, I got lost and had to ask for directions. This was a new ship, so we took it on its first trip to Cuba. It was on the ship that my eardrum burst from a five-inch shell concussion.

I will say we had good cooks on board ship; they baked their own bread, and to me, it was very close to Mother's.

Possibly the toughest part of my cruise, and the thing I'll never forget, is having to bury a person at sea.

However, there were several enjoyable things and one happened while I was in San Diego. A troop from Hollywood came to entertain us and I was selected to go backstage after the show to help them load their bus. That way I got to meet them in person.

Another enjoyable thing was when Germany surrendered. I was on liberty in Norfolk, Virginia, and my, what a celebration that was! I never was hugged and kissed so much by so many strangers. But I enjoyed it!

Frederick J. Egbert

After Japan surrendered, I was transferred to a light cruiser ship named the Oregon City. Since it was a new ship, we took it for its first cruise to Cuba, also.

While I was on the Lake Champlain aircraft carrier, I went to Naples, Italy, and South Hampton, England. In fact, on one trip to Europe, we set a record for being the fastest ship to cross the Atlantic. I still have the certificate given out by the ship's captain to everyone, stating that we were part of the world record.

ALFRED E. EGGLESTON

SIDNEY, OHIO

Weather Observer, Corporal, Air Corps, WW II
Basic Training: Keesler Field, Biloxi, MS
Duty in Philippines; Japan

Our troop ship, the Marine Jumper, was loaded with men from all branches of the service. The favorite pastimes seemed to be card games and dice. One of the articles in the daily paper, The Jumper Journal, published on ship, was "Kilroy is Aboard," by Sylvester Neal:

"Despite all attempts by port officials, military police, and Army personnel, Kilroy has managed to slip aboard the Marine Jumper unobserved. Grim testimony of this were the words scrawled on a cabin wall, 'Kilroy is here, 17 July, 1946.' Handwriting experts have assured us that it was without a doubt the handwriting of Kilroy.

"This ambiguous E.M. who has held every rank and grade from a five star General to a lowly yardbird trainee is believed to have disguised himself as a duffle bag. The announcement of his presence aboard has been hotly denied by numerous other ships, submarines, airplanes, dirigibles, and hundreds of army camps and naval stations who have all claimed his presence.

"Various observers have given this description of Kilroy: Anywhere from four feet eleven inches to six feet eight inches, weighing somewhere between 100 and 400 pounds, has fucha colored eyes, greenish yellow teeth and has red hair with a blonde streak down the middle. If anyone is seen answering the above description he should be stripped of all identification and unceremoniously thrown overboard."

The Marine Jumper was headed for Manila, in the Philippines. The loud speaker informed us when we were passing Corregidor; our ship took on a strange reverence as we passed by, everyone knowing of the heroism there during its final days. That was also true in Manila Bay as our ship maneuvered around the sunken superstructures.

During the short time in the Philippines, I guarded Japanese POWs. We weren't afraid of the prisoners running away—they were very meek—but of protecting them from the local Filipinos who were wanting revenge after the atrocities during the Japanese occupation.

In Tokyo the Japanese stopped on the street and bowed as General MacArthur's motorcade passed by. The devastation of blocks and blocks of the city, due to the bombings by the American Air Corps, was quite depressing.

My final assignment was at Itazuke Air Base in Kyushu Province (southern-most island). The clothing worn by local people was nearing the rag stage. Small children had their heads shaved. Many of them had sores on their heads which were treated with a white salve. Some simply had large scabs.

Our barracks was like a factory building. The former occupants of this walled-in area was a Japanese cavalry unit. Some of the horses were still housed here and were available for our recreational use.

As I rode out into the countryside and was approaching a cluster of farm houses or a small village, many of the parents and children were scampering to get inside their homes to hide. I guess they had been told about the bad Americans. By the time I reached the houses, the area was deserted. On some occasions later, I noticed small heads peeping out of doorways or at the openings in the walls that surrounded their house. If I stopped and looked back, no movement could be detected. Knowing that these innocent children of war had no experience with candy bars, I began taking some of my rationed candy bars and left them beside the courtyards.

The children of school age usually wore black jackets and backpacks. Hearing some oral recitation one day, I went to a small village school and looked through the sliding door. All students and the teacher were sitting on a mat in a circle. The room was bare, and each student had his books and papers stacked beside him. When they discovered they were being observed, they seemed uneasy, so I retreated. Little did I know at the time I would retire from the school business.

Our weather station used Japanese radio operators to collect weather data from other weather stations. I noticed one operator had a pair of unusually shaped ears and he seemed to sniffle all the time. Later I learned he had been a lieutenant assigned to recover people from the Nagasaki rubble, being subjected to very intense radiation. As they were digging into the rubble, there were pockets of extreme heat trapped in some underground caverns. When those pockets were uncovered, they burned the lieutenant's ears.

At Itazuke Air Base in Japan, being a weather observer meant a lot of *eyeballing* was done every 30 minutes and an hourly radio report was sent out to other air bases in Japan. These reports contained the amount of cloud cover, type of clouds, direction they were moving and their estimated height. Sometimes as planes were inbound (mostly Mustang P-51s), they could give us the clouds' height as they broke though the cloud cover. Every six hours we would send up a piball, a balloon filled with a measured amount of helium, that was tracked by an instrument (theodolite) on the ground, giving us the wind direction at a certain altitude. On clear days a white balloon was used; on overcast days, a red one.

This theodolite was something like a telescope. We knew the balloon ascended at 30 ft. a minute. Using the calibration of the theodolite, we could determine the angle and precise

Alfred E. Eggleston: Using piball to gather weather information.

direction of the balloon. With this information we could determine wind direction and velocity.

I wore a telephone headset with a mike. A beeper on the theodolite sounded every minute. I'd check the calibrations and report them to the other observer and he'd record the information on a graph which would indicate the speed and direction of the wind.

The piball was approximately 30 inches in diameter and was a good quality rubber, but would explode at approximately 8-10,000 feet. By this time the balloon was only a speck in the sky. At night a white paper lantern was attached with a burning candle inside (sometimes the lantern caught fire) so we could follow the balloon.

Weather maps were made each 24 hours. Information from all surrounding weather stations was collected by radio code and then decoded and placed on the large map. Each weather station was numbered and all weather information was transferred to this large map, covering Japan, parts of Russia, China, Philippines, and several islands. With this information, the forecast could be determined. There were no weather satellites or radar to help in forecasting.

Planes leaving for other destinations always stopped by our station to check the type of weather they could anticipate on their journey.

Alfred E. Eggleston making gas for piball.

KARL EICHHORN

726TH Squadron, 451st Bomb Group, WW II
Duty in European Theater

It might be useful at this point to describe the mechanics of loading bombs and to identify the types of bombs we used. We had a curious organizational structure with respect to handling of bombs and ammunitions. Each Bomb Squadron had assigned to it three or four Ordnance men. These soldiers were actually in the Army Ordnance Corps, assigned to the Air Force. On their uniforms they wore the Ordnance Corps insignia, rather than the Air Force insignia. (Likewise, we also had two men assigned to each Squadron from the Army Chemical Corps to serve as gas-protection specialists.) Ordnance was responsible for the transportation of bombs and ammunitions from ports like Naples and Bari, where it arrived via cargo vessels, to bomb dumps located near each bomber base. When orders were received for certain bombs to be loaded, the Ordnance people, who operated the bomb dumps, would load the appropriate bombs on special bomb trailers and haul them to the airfield where they unloaded the required number beside each aircraft. At that point we Armorers took over and loaded the bombs into the planes. After loading, the Ordnance people would return to mount the steel fins on the larger demolition bombs and to install the fuzes in each bomb. The fins had to be installed after loading to prevent damage from handling. Ordnance was also responsible for installing the arming wires on the fuzes, but we often helped with that job.

Most of the larger general purpose demolition bombs had a fuze installed in both the nose and tail, where there were threaded recesses to receive them. Smaller incendiary and fragmentation bombs usually carried only one fuze. The small 25 lb. anti-personnel fragmentation bombs, which were mounted in clusters of six were shipped in wood boxes, with the fuzes already installed. We hated to load fragmentation bombs because they were so awkward and hard to handle, but we loved the cases they came in as we used the wood to construct floors for our tents.

The fuze (yes, it is properly spelled with a "z"!) contained a very sensitive explosive train which actually detonated the T.N.T. in the bomb. Each fuze was normally in a *safe* condition. It had a small propeller at the end which was locked into position with a removable safety pin, much like a cotter pin. In flight, on the way to the target, the Bombardier had to remove this pin from each bomb fuze and bring them back so that the armorer could verify that all arming pins had been removed. After the bomb was dropped, air flow would rotate the propellers rapidly and after a set number of revolutions the fuze would be armed and ready to explode the bomb on contact. Some fuzes could be adjusted for a predetermined time delay so that, for example, a bomb would not explode when it hit a factory roof, but a brief time later, after it was inside the building. Sometimes we used fuzes with a long time delay, of perhaps several hours. These we called *booby-trap* fuzes as they caused a buried bomb to explode under the earth long after it landed. In addition, these fuzes had another nasty feature. Two ball-bearings rode with tapered tracks on opposite sides of the fuze. As it was screwed into the bomb these balls recessed into the deep part of the track, causing no interference. But when anyone tried to disarm the bomb by removing the fuze, the balls would jam against the thread, penetrate the thin wall of the fuze and instantly detonate the bomb. Even we could not

Karl Eichhorn, with permission from Karl F. Eichorn, Jr., and, Bob Karstensen, Sr., Publisher of *Ad-Lib, 451st Bomb Group (H)*

remove these things. When a plane had to abort a mission and return with unused bombs, they were usually dropped *safe* into the Adriatic Sea. It was just too dangerous to try to unload them on the ground for reuse, with those fuzes installed.

Since, after the Bombardier had removed the arming pins in flight, air flow through the bomb Bay might cause the fuze propellers to rotate and arm the bombs inside the plane, a second safety device, called an arming wire, was used. This was a long brass wire with a ring in the center. The two ends of the wire were inserted through the two fuze propellers to prevent their rotation and the center ring was attached to a special spring-loaded snap on the bomb shackle. When the bomb was released, by way of the bombsight, this retainer snap would be locked closed thus securing the arming wire, which pulled free of the fuzes as the bomb dropped and remained attached to the shackle within the aircraft. Normally, when bombs were *salvoed* mechanically, the retainer snap was NOT locked and the arming wire ring would pull out of the shackle and fall with the bomb, thus preventing the fuzes from arming during free fall. In practice, because there were many missions, especially later in '44 when it was desired to drop armed bombs in salvo, we often hooked the ring of the arming wire over one of the shackle arms so that there was no way any bomb could fall in a safe condition.

During our first several weeks of combat missions we loaded bombs in the standard approved manner. Two hand-operated winches, which had a long steel cable with a hook on the end wound around the drum, were mounted on the inside of the bomb rack to be loaded. The bomb, say a 500 pounder, was rolled under the bomb bay by hand and positioned under the rack. A heavy-duty double web sling, with attach points at each end, was positioned under the bomb. Next, the winch cables, rigged through pulleys and hooks, were connected to the bomb sling. Then two men, one on each winch, would slowly crank the bomb to the proper place on the rack; starting at the top, while a third man guided the bomb up and finally connected the shackle into the large snaps on the rack. When the first rack was loaded the winches had to be removed and re-positioned on the next rack. A B-24 could carry a total of twelve 500 lb. bombs and it would take three men at least 75 to 90 minutes to load one plane. Crews often had to load four planes in a night, so the work went on until the wee hours of the morning.

Later on we came up with a much easier loading method, which I will describe later. It was contrary to all standing tech orders, but it was so much simpler that one man, if necessary, could load a plane all by himself, in less time than three men using the approved loading method.

Smaller bombs, such as the 100 lb. incendiaries; the demo bombs; and the fragmentation bomb clusters (frags) were hand loaded by two men without winches. These smaller bombs were loaded five to a rack; a total of twenty per plane. Later on, by using some special cables we devised, we were able to double our loads of incendiary and fragmentation bombs. The 250 and 300 lb. demolition bombs were loaded at the same positions as the 500 pounders (i.e. twelve per plane). While we winched the upper one up, we often tried to speed the work by manually lifting the two lower 250 lb. bombs into position. In retrospect, this was a stupid thing to do, as someone could have been badly injured if one of those bombs had dropped. As it was, three of us developed hernias. The 1,000 lb. bombs were loaded two to a bay; a total of eight per plane, and for 2,000 lb. bombs we had to install special auxiliary racks in each bomb bay, each of which held only one bomb, for a maximum load of four bombs.

All of the above were maximum loads. For long missions deep into Germany, our planes often carried smaller loads; such as ten 500 pounders; six 1,000 pounders, and three 2,000 pounders. By far the bomb we most freqently used was the 500 lb. General Purpose (G.P.) demolition bomb...

When the AF Headquarters called the Bomb Groups to give orders for the next day's bomb load, they used code words for each type bomb. I can recall only that the frag clusters were Lightnings; 500 pounders were Liberators; and the 2,000 pounders were Thunderbolts.

Overall during our service in the 15th Army Air Force, the 451st Bomb Group flew 245 combat missions, the first on 30 January 1944, and the last on 26 April 1945.

...It was common knowledge that there was a large Italian German bomb and ammunition dump on a small hill near our field. On Sunday, 19 March, a group of us from the Armament Section decided to go and see what was there while the planes were on their mission. We took a weapons carrier and drove up a dirt road to the dump. The first thing we saw was a very large aerial bomb of at least 1,000 to 1,500 kilos. From its general design we decided it was Italian, rather than German. We looked it over very carefully to verify that the fuzes had been removed, then when we were quite sure it was safe, several guys sat on the thing and the rest stood behind while I took their picture.

There was almost every sort of ordnance in that dump that one could imagine. We could see several sizes of bombs, a huge pile of artillery shells, and scattered all about were a variety of anti-tank and anti-personnel mines. One of our fellows started to walk into the dump but the rest of us told him to get the hell out, which he did.

Just two days later I was sickened to learn that two of the gunners on my plane, *Big Mogul,* Sergeants David Hall and Robert Whitney, had gone to the same dump and both been killed by an anti-personnel mine. No one else was present and no one knew what had happened, though there was speculation that one of them may have fired his pistol into the mess. If so, it was an incredibly stupid thing to do, as the whole dump might have gone up. The mine that killed them was a German *Bouncing Betty* anti-personnel mine, sometimes called a *Butterfly* mine. When triggered they jump up and explode shrapnel at waist height. One man was dead and the other dying when they were discovered. Both were buried at the U.S. Military Cemetery in Bari. They were friends and I was sick about it. I wondered if I had mentioned the big bomb to them and if so, whether that had led them to visit the dump. I still wonder when I think of it. After their deaths the Air Force declared the area off limits, but it was too late for them. There must have been hundreds of abandoned bomb and munitions dumps scattered all over Europe after the war. Whatever became of them? How many children may have died playing in such places?

Reprinted with permission from Karl F. Eichhorn, Jr., and Bob Karstensen, Sr., Publisher of *Ad-Lib, 451st Bomb Group (H).*

DOROTHY (Lathrop) FALKE

SIDNEY, OHIO

Office Work, PhM1c, US Navy WAVEs, 1943-45, WW II.
Basic Training: Cedar Falls, Iowa.
Duty at Washington, D.C. and Midshipmen's School, Chicago.

I had a brother on the USS Boise, which was surrounded by Japanese, and we wondered if they would make it back to the States. I was working at the VA Hospital in Dayton, Ohio, as a stenographer, so decided to quit and do my part by joining the WAVEs.

By train we went to the U.S. Naval Training Center for WAVEs on the campus of Iowa State Teachers College. We got our sheets and other things and were assigned four to a room (bunk beds).

Physicals and shots came next, which caused some crying among the girls at night.

We did a lot of marching, and I loved it, even in the rain, but there was no other physical training. Marching really gave us an appetite and we had good food. We had duties but didn't have to wash walls and scrub decks like the guys. We were to keep our rooms neat, but no inspections.

We learned about the different military services. There were 700 girls and 60 were chosen to go to the Bureau of Medicine and Surgery, Washington, D.C., after graduation. But there we just typed, and it really got boring.

While stationed in Washington, however, several of us girls went to the USO Building. One time a guy was getting the machine ready to play dance music. There was a piano in the room, so I played and we all sang until he got the machine fixed. You could also make records in there, and one time I was going to make one to send home. (Making a record at that time was a big deal!) I turned on the machine, started to talk, and got so tickled at talking to a machine that I couldn't finish.

One Sunday evening we went out to eat and had a hot beef sandwich, baked beans, and milk for thirty-five cents. And we got a breakfast of orange juice, doughnut, and coffee for twenty cents.

After about three months, three of us asked for transfers. We had the rating of Y3C, but we wanted to do hospital work, and to do that we had to be PhM3C, so we were transferred to Bainbridge,

Maryland, and took a four-week course. I had the same subjects as my sister who was in nurse's training, but I certainly was not a nurse. One time I was to give a guy a shot, and when I started to push it in his skin, the needle bent and that did it for me. My boss said it wasn't necessary that I give a shot, thank goodness.

While in Bainbridge, we went to an amphitheater and saw Joan Blondell in person. We got to sit with the officers. There were 3,000 people there but 30,000 had wanted to go.

Several of us girls went to New York one weekend and met a lady who owned a mansion. She let us stay there for fifty cents. We saw Glen Miller in person and took a tour of New York.

After graduation I was sent to the U.S. Naval Midshipmen's School at Northwestern University, Chicago, and was secretary to the Medical Officer. By that time I had a rating of PhM1c and later was up for Chief. I and three other girls had an apartment in the Plaza Hotel, which we had to pay for.

One winter weekend I went to my home in Illinois. Because of ice on the day I was to return, I was a day late. My friends were worried and said, "The Captain is really mad, and you are really going to get it!" When he called me in, I told him the truth and he said it was okay. Later on I received a Commendation from that same Captain.

Incidentally, we wore silk hose; nylons were not in yet. And when I was a PhM2c, my check was for $128 a month. It would have been a bit less when I first went in and a bit more when I was discharged.

I really enjoyed being in the WAVES and my brother made it home in good shape.

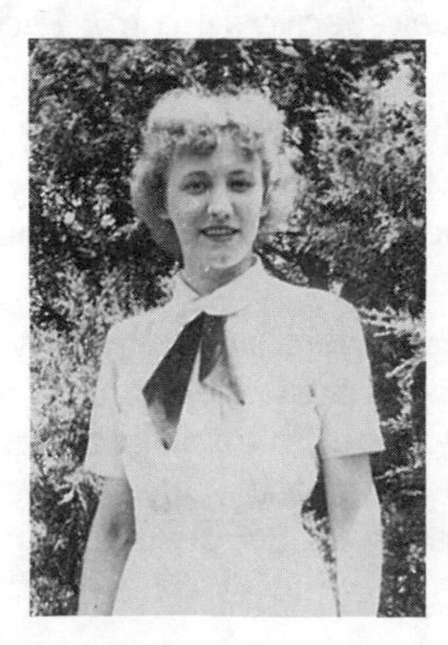

Dorothy (Lathrop) Falke

JOE FARROW

LARGO, FLORIDA

M/Sgt., Bombardier, 8th Air Force, 748th Bomb Group
Duty in Europe

Our crew of the U.S. Army Air Force was made up in Gulfport, Mississippi, and it didn't take long for us to become close friends. We went to Savannah, Georgia, and a brand new B-17 was waiting for us. After instrument orientation and checking out the aircraft (about 3 days), we left for England, going along the coast to New England. I was very fortunate to fly over the house that I was born in, just south of Boston.

We went on to Goosebay, Labrador, then to Greenland, Scotland, and to Peterboro, England. Our 748th Bomb Squadron, called the Fireball Express, did a little training together, became quite close, and knew we could depend upon one another in combat. But it wasn't very long before we found that those close feelings can be very painful.

It was on our third mission that we lost quite a few aircraft and some close buddies. They were flying almost directly beside us when hit by enemy aircraft. We saw their plane on fire, hoping and praying they would get out on time. We saw some of the fellows bail out, but their chutes were on fire. We had felt that if we got in trouble and the aircraft went down, we had a means of getting to safety by bailing out. But this didn't work with our close friends.

After ten missions we were sent back for some R & R (rest and relaxation) and a week's leave, and the English people showed us great hospitality.

It was the policy that if you had finished 24 missions, you would be sent back to the States or where you would be useful in training new crew members. We were for that, but it wasn't meant to be.

On July 22, 1944, we were shot down. We were on a mission heading for the northern part of Germany, a big industrial area. On the bomb run we couldn't continue because of a lack of communication, foul-up in plans, or whatever. There was another group flying underneath us. So, consequently, we had to head to our secondary target, which was a railroad junction outside the city. We thought it would be a lot easier target as far as flak was concerned, but we ran into all kinds of problems. Our bomb doors were open and we were flying at an altitude of around 35,000 feet. We received a hit close to the bottom of the aircraft, off to the side, and part of the flak came up through the open bomb bay doors and shot away the elevator and rudder control cables. Consequently, the aircraft went into a steep dive. Being way up in the nose, everything started falling down on top of me, and I panicked somewhat. I pulled off my flak suit, oxygen mask, radio equipment, etc. and tried to get up out of there, but there was too much stuff falling down. But we had a fantastic pilot who managed to pull the aircraft out of its dive by using the full flaps on the wings. Even though he brought the plane out of the dive, we were losing altitude rapidly, and he couldn't turn the plane around because of loss of rudder control.

When we were down to about 21 or 22,000 feet, we were being hit with 20 mm shells, which they can throw up in the air pretty rapidly. So the pilot ordered us to bail out.

I went out through the escape hatch, not looking forward to the idea. I was very nervous and, before I left, noticed that I had already pulled the D ring or rip cord, which fastens on to the parachute. You pull that and it releases the chute on your back. Since I had already pulled this ring, I thought the chute was never going to open.

It was so peaceful and quiet as I was descending that it seemed there wasn't even a war going on. This was out in the country. When I reached the ground, the German guards were waiting for me. There were a lot of aircraft coming down that day, a lot of activity in the area. I got out of my chute and the wind blew it up against the fence. Some farm girls immediately grabbed it, wanting to keep it because of the material. On the harness were my shoes; all I had on were these little flying slippers, which were not of much use on the ground. The leader of this group signalled to the girls to bring my harness back, which they did.

When the guard approached me, he thought at first I was a German flyer because there was a German plane going down as well as ours. Then he thought I was British. I understood some German, but I couldn't speak it very well. As soon as I explained I was an American, he came over, pulled down the zipper of my flying jacket and reached inside under my left arm where I had the shoulder holster containing a 45. While they were pointing their rifles and shotguns at me with my hands up, he knew exactly where to go and what to look for. There was no hesitation. It seemed he had done this before.

He took my 45 and I was very apprehensive about what was going to happen next. We were told that if we ever did go down over enemy territory that we should try by all means to stay away from civilians and, if capture was inevitable, to turn ourselves in to the German soldiers. Civilians were capturing airmen and bringing them down to the village area and hanging them. They figured we were coming over and deliberately bombing their homes, churches, etc. indiscriminately, not just going for military targets, which was not true. Sometimes it would look that way because when you do this kind of bombing, this saturation bombing, you cover a tremendous big area with a lot of aircraft, and some of the bombs would not go right on target. So it was understandable why some of the people were upset.

I was fortunate that the leader of this group took me back to the anti-aircraft battery which shot down our aircraft. It was getting on into the day and they kept me there a while, trying to get information. All I gave them was what was on my dog tags, but they wanted more than that.

When it started getting dark, I was put on the back of a truck, all alone, and was still very nervous. I heard a lot of commotion and there were a lot of soldiers with another prisoner. They put him in the truck with me, and it was our pilot. I was smoking at that time and he had his cigarettes with him, which they did not confiscate. So he reached down into his flying outfit and pulled out a sterling cigarette case. We both could tell that one of the guards was going to try to get the case. One guard approached him, said he wanted the case, but the pilot said he wasn't going to give it to them. The guy started poking the pilot with his rifle, but he still didn't surrender the case. At that moment a German officer came around and reprimanded this guy unbelievably. We realized then that they would leave us alone and wouldn't bother us any more.

Before long they had the rest of the crew and brought us all together except for our radio operator. He had the misfortune of landing on a roof of a nearby home and broke his ankle. They took him to a hospital, put a set of pins in the ankle, and was well treated.

When we left this anti-aircraft battery, they took us to a place that reminded me of a western country jail. We were kept there in one big room, with a dirt floor, for about four or five days, and weren't treated too badly.

On about the fifth day they took us to the big interrogation center outside Frankfort, which had a tremendous big railroad station. This interrogation center was used primarily for airmen. I believe this was one of the hardest ordeals I had gone through. We had to fill out cards with serial number, if we were married, where we were from, so that they could let the Red Cross know if anything happened to us. They took our pictures. Then we were separated and each one was put into an individual cell, which was possibly six ft. long and four ft. wide, maybe a little more, just big enough for a cot to fit in. There were no windows, just one door. You didn't see anybody or get a chance to talk to anyone. There were no toilet facilities. If you had to use their facilities, there was a string inside the door and it dropped a little flag on the outside of the door. The guard would make sure no one else was in the toilet area. They wanted to make sure that you didn't talk to anyone.

We received one meal a day, which was in the late evening and was something like potato soup with not much in it. We could have all the water we needed.

After seven days of this, we started to lose a little bit of weight and wondered what would be next. A lot of things went through my mind: Where are my pals? What happened to them? I got very anxious wanting to see somebody, to talk to somebody. I think it was all part of the psychological plan to get us to talk.

At the end of the seventh day I was brought out of my cell and taken upstairs to a beautiful office, which had the aroma of the food that had been eaten there. In the room where I was waiting, there was every conceivable kind of aircraft pictures, German, American, British, French. And a lot of detailed structural plans. Everything was very well kept; the furniture was beautiful. All was in very good taste.

A young man came in, spoke perfect English, opened up a huge big folder and started going through it. Wanted to know if I would like a cigarette. Hadn't had a cigarette for some time and not much food. I leaned across his desk and reached for the cigarette, which was American. He lighted it for me. Not having smoked for a while, I got very light-headed and fell back into the chair, but I enjoyed it. He sat there making small talk about how were they treating me, was I getting enough food, was I feeling all right. When I told him how I felt, just getting one bowl of soup a day, he said he would have to rectify that. As he kept up the small talk, every so often he would put in an interrogation bit. What was the name of the target where we were going? So I would give him my name, rank, and serial number. He would go back to the small talk again and then insert the question about what our target was. This kept on for a good hour, and he didn't get too much information from me. He said, "I probably know more about your outfit than you do yourself." He opened another big loose-leaf book and started relating to me some facts that were amazing. He told me when we left Savannah, Georgia, the route that we had taken, when we left for Labrador, for Greenland. He had the days down exactly when and where. I had completely forgotten the exact days, but to them it must have been of importance.

He knew some of the officers that were in our group, some in our squadron. People planted in there must have given them plenty of information. They probably picked up information, too, from men that were captured and interrogated.

Interrogation was over, our crew was all together, and they took us to a small detention camp, where we stayed approximately ten days. They took all our clothes and we went through a delousing program. They issued us new American uniforms, no insignia. It was here that I had my first encounter with the real experience of being a POW. I realized that this was what it was going to be like being behind barbed wire and with German soldiers surrounding us with guns. It took a little while to get used to this fact. It affects your psychological well-being. Some of the men could accept this rather readily; others couldn't. You had to realize and understand that this was the beginning. You were going to be here a while. You don't think you will be liberated for some time. No sign of any victories at that time.

We could walk around in this small camp area, like a quarter-mile track. They had a small warning fence on the outside of this track, and we couldn't go near, or over, that fence. We could walk around the track as much as we wanted. There was a single wire about two ft. off the ground. Beyond that, at a distance of possibly 25 or 30 ft., was another high barbed wire fence, 10 or

12 ft. in the air. There was a space of about six ft. and then another high fence.

One day when we were walking around on the track we saw a young fellow, by himself, that seemed very depressed. He went over this small warning fence and started heading toward the tall barbed wire fence. The guards blew their whistles to try to deter him. We were hollering at him, too, but he never looked back once. He started climbing the fence; then dropped down from the fence and got into the small space between the two fences and, as he started to go up the second one, the Germans started shooting. They hit him once. He stopped, hesitated, and then kept climbing. He got up to the top of that second fence, dropped to the ground. Shooting at him then was pretty strong. They hit him again. He went down, got up and then started a slow trot. He disappeared over a small rise and we couldn't see him. The guards went out with their dogs. We were all ordered into our barracks and told to stay inside but heard the rapid firing, and it was all over. Half an hour later they called us all out again, lined us up, and without any explanation, brought the soldier in on a stretcher, dead, of course. They paraded him up and down in front of us so we were sure what would happen to us if we tried to escape. We were dismissed and sent back to the barracks.

There wasn't too much food there, but it wasn't bad. After about ten days we were assembled, put on a train and brought down to the Frankfort railroad station, put on a troop train which, supposedly, they were using for carrying Red Cross materials and POWs. We learned afterward that they were using these trains for carrying their own troops, supplies, and whatever.

While on this train, before we even pulled out of the station, an air raid took place and we were taken down into the shelters below the Frankfort station. There was a lot of bombing all around us and a lot of damage was done to the tracks. That meant a delay in our leaving the Frankfort area.

After the repairs, we went back to the train and it proceeded, as it was getting dark. Then the train came to an abrupt stop; this time we were being attacked by the British night fighters. They hit the train, not paying much attention to Red Cross markings because they knew that it wasn't necessarily so. They were strafing the train and we were not allowed to get off. The German soldiers were on each side of the embankment of the tracks to make sure none of us escaped. The strafing came right down through the middle of the train, through the roof, and some bullets took the collar right off the engineer's flying jacket; he wasn't hurt one bit. God showed his message and kept us safe.

I will backtrack a little to when we were in the country jail. The city of Muenster was severely damaged and it was very difficult to get any vehicles through the city area. Consequently, the soldiers made us walk to where trucks were to take us to the interrogation center. It was then that I realized how much damage these bombs could cause. When you are in an aircraft, flying 35 to 40,000 ft. above, and you press a button, bombs fall away on the target and you're gone and you never see the damage that these bombs can do. Walking through the city that we had bombed and seeing nothing but rubble, I started to cry because I realized I could have been responsible for a lot of this. The statement War is Hell is true.

Back to my journey from Frankfort to the southern part of Germany—we ended up in Nuremberg, where the war crime trials were held later. The Olympics were held in 1938 or 1936 there when Jesse Owens showed Hitler he didn't have the mighty race he thought he had. We were situated in a huge camp outside the city, but I never did get to see the stadium. There were British and Americans there; Russian soldiers were kept separate; something like 30,000 POWs. We were there quite a while and treatment wasn't too bad, but the food was terrible. We weren't getting much at all. They were trying to distribute Red Cross parcels, which we were supposed to have had regularly once a week, but we didn't get them that often. When we did get some, they had punched holes in the cans of perishables so that there was no way you could store up any food articles or any items you might possibly use for escape. Much of the stuff had to be used right away. Cigarettes were taken out of the boxes, and the chocolate candy bars were gone. There was some concentrated and dehydrated food, which was better than what we were getting from the camp.

Sleeping accommodations were not great. We slept on the floor and had two blankets for two men for a while. We put one blanket partially around on the floor and up around us and then the other one over us. If we had any type of food, it had to be under the blankets. We'd pull the blanket up over our heads because the rats would come out and crawl up over the blanket. It wasn't a very pleasant feeling.

We lost track of time. Some of us went on small work details. As time went on, we knew things were getting kind of tough for the Germans because food kept getting tighter and tighter and security tightened up, too. It was amazing how rumors could get around inside a POW camp, but we were informed we were in the way of fighting. Russians from the East and Americans from the West, or maybe in reverse, I forgot my directions now. They had to move us out of there, but they couldn't move everyone at one time. They didn't have enough vehicles available, so many of us would have to leave, hit the road and march to the next destination.

At one time there were close to 10,000 soldiers on the road heading for a destination out of the line of fighting. We were in the countryside, in the southern part, which reminded me so much of the New England area. We were fortunate that it wasn't too cold.

The second night two of our fighter planes, P-47s, came over. The Germans neglected to inform the Americans and the British Intelligence that they were moving us out from Nuremberg to a new destination and that these POWs would be out on the road. The pilots came over, saw 10,000 men marching on these roads, and figured we were enemy soldiers. They strafed the column. There were some hit, some killed, but most of us managed to get off the road and out of the way. The guards wouldn't let us go too far, just to the side of the road.

The next day the commander of the POWs, a Colonel from West Point, a fighter pilot, told the German commanding officers that we were not going to move any farther until they would allow some of the soldiers to go ahead and put out in the open fields with toilet paper "POW," and they agreed to that. After we did this and identified ourselves, every day these fighter pilots would come over, check our position, and do the barrel roll over us. We knew then that we were going to be okay. They would be looking out for us.

There was no food available for us on this march. Whatever food we had we scrounged in the countryside, grasshoppers, frogs, etc. Maybe eight or ten fellows would group together and designate one person to cook whatever they could find. I was designated cook in our group. We managed to make little types of frying pans, and they would let us build little fires at night. We would share, depending upon one another.

During this forced march, I first encountered personally some brutality from German guards. One fellow with whom I became very close was sickly, had a bad case of dysentery and was becoming very weak. I helped him with a strong shoulder and, quite a few times, didn't think he would make it. One time he stopped to rest and the guy in charge would not let me give him any assistance. When I tried to lift him off the ground, the guy started poking him, trying to make him get up. He gave him a rifle butt on the side of the head. He didn't move. I don't know what happened after that, but I'm afraid he didn't make it.

We continued on the march. A lot of the fellows were having trouble with lice and diseases that go along with not being able to keep yourself clean. We were allowed to go over to a small stream and sit on the side. We took all our clothes off. Someone managed to get a razor blade, and we shaved all the hair off that we could where we were being bothered with lice and had become infected. We washed our clothes the best we could and then put them back on while still wet.

We continued on, now about the fifth day, still scrounging to find food. Some guys grabbed a few chickens, and I saw a barrel in a barn that I thought had wheat in it. There was an older German guard following me around; he could speak a little broken English and I could speak just a very little German. Some of the guys found some eggs. Someone had saved some powdered milk, so I said we were going to have some pancakes. This guard that I talked to a little was circling around our fire with a big smile on his face. When I started putting it all together, he kept saying, "Nix, nein gut." Well, nothing happened, it was just a big glob. It turned out that what I thought was wheat was chicken mash. The guys said this was going to be my last day of cooking, but we ate it, and I'm here to tell about it, so it couldn't have been too bad.

Some of the security guards, the younger men, started to disappear. We were being guarded mostly by the older men. We were warned that the Hungarian SS troopers were in this area and that we better not try to make any escape. They had the reputation of being very mean, as some of the men found out. Some thought they knew more than the men directing us on this march, and they tried to escape. They didn't get very far. We discovered a day later that they were caught in a nearby woods and were executed. So we all stayed together pretty close.

About the ninth day we reached a small village area. There was Stalag 7A; Nuremberg was 13D. Now a POW camp, this 7A was formerly some type of permanent prison. There were quite a few British personnel there already that had been wounded. The buildings were all concrete, and accommodations were much better than any of our previous ones. We had some decent meals, and medical attention was given to fellows that were in pretty bad shape.

While there we learned that our troops were getting very close to us. The Russians were pushing on one side and Gen. Patton was pushing from the other. We had been there almost two weeks when told to make some trenches inside the compound area that we could lie down in.

It wasn't too long after that, on a Sunday morning, that we heard a small aircraft, looked like a Piper Cub, and we knew it was an artillery spotter. German guards started firing because the plane wasn't very high off the ground, 200 ft. or so. He was flying for Gen. Patton's outfit, so he'd know just where this POW camp was located. As it happened on that Sunday, this aircraft spotter came in and then we could hear a lot of fighting closeby. We knew things were getting close.

The next day through the gate came a tank. Prior to this, we noticed a lot of the guards had taken off; they didn't hang around after the aircraft spotter came. They were the older guards. When the tank came through, there was no resistance whatsoever. The second tank came through and there was the General himself. He really was a soldier's soldier. He was so proud in this tank. He had his two guns on. In my estimation, he was one of the greatest inspirational leaders in WW II. He certainly didn't go for the political stuff. He wanted to be out there all the time with his men, right in the thick of the battle.

We didn't get to celebrate with General Patton because he just kept on going. But after his tank, there were jeeps with medical people, priests, and a lot of alcoholic beverages for the soldiers who could enjoy it. So there was quite a big celebration, but a lot of us were still pretty sick and weak from dysentery, malnutrition, etc. The way the General had taken the whole town, his tanks were on both sides of this camp and both sides of the town. In the center of the tanks on either side, as far as the eye could see down the road, were trucks, trucks, trucks. They were taking the prisoners out from the camp to an emergency landing field that they had captured. The British wounded went first because they had been there the longest. Then the Americans. They went non-stop to an airfield that they had captured. C-47s would come in and take as many soldiers as they could in each one.

From this captured airfield we went to Rheims, France, and from there to a quarantine camp called Camp Lucky Strike. We were welcomed there with open arms and received the best medical treatment and the best food available. After about two weeks there, we went home. They wanted to make sure we could make the trip home safely and that there were no communicable diseases. Most of our problems were from dysentery, stomach troubles, and under-nourishment. A lot of us had psychological and mental problems, which a lot still have today.

EARL FOGT

SIDNEY, OHIO

Hdq. Platoon/Supply Sgt., T4/Sgt., 321st Infantry, 81st Div., 1943-46,WW II
Basic Training: Camp Adair, Oregon
Duty in Pacific Area

Our unit, the 321st Combat Team, had started over the side of the troop ship to the amphibian landing craft below, in preparation to land on the island of Angaur. As my turn came to climb down the net, the clasp on my high school graduation watch let go and started to fall toward the water. By some quirk, it snagged on to the net near the landing craft. I called down to alert someone to recover my watch before it came loose and dropped into the water. When I arrived at the bottom of the net, my watch was returned to me.

We descended the landing net into the landing craft and pulled away to await the completion of the loading process. As we started for shore, there were naturally many types of questions that came to mind: What kind of reception would we get from the Japs? Exactly how many Japs were on the island? What type of fire power would we encounter, etc?

As we neared the beach, I happened to look back to see there was no navy man steering our landing craft. He wasn't there. I could see only a helmet sticking up and then noticed that ropes were tied to the steering mechanism and our driver was operating from a *low profile*. He was not going to expose himself unless he had to. I guess you call that *Yankee ingenuity*. It didn't make me feel any better having no gun fire from the Japs. I guess we all felt uneasy and were wondering what the enemy was planning. They hit us a short time later.

After our landing on Angaur, we moved inland to our first day's objective. Our particular section of the front line was situated in a rocky area. As we prepared for the night, we found the ground too filled with rocks to dig our foxholes. We rummaged around and found some corrugated roofing which we used and stacked rocks against it for protection. During the night we heard scratching noises coming from the corrugated roofing. Being jumpy since landing, we were greatly relieved to discover a land crab as the noise maker. What a relief!

The Japs didn't hit us on the landing day. They evidently watched us as we moved in and dug in. That night they hit us; next morning we pulled back to regroup due to our losses.

I had been designated to be the runner from the front line to the command post. After the Japs had tried several attacks to push us back, due to our losses I was told to remain on the front line. After stringing wire and C-ration cans in front of our foxhole, three of us settled in our foxhole home. Before long, the cans rattled. Haskel J. Morris of North Carolina jumped up and shot. He dropped the Jap with one shot. From that time on, Haskel was known as One-Shot Haskel.

Foxhole life was not the most convenient life: not enough room to stretch out for sleeping; bodily functions had to take place, so the helmet often had to be used and then the contents pitched out. Helmets were also used to warm the water that heated our C-rations.

As replacements were coming in, one was killed by a Jap sniper just after his arrival. A small pocket of Japanese had been overlooked as we were mopping up the stragglers. We eliminated the pocket, but not soon enough to save that new replacement.

After the Japanese surrendered, Amori, Japan, was our assignment for occupation. We prepared for Thanksgiving, 1945. The cooks were up early to get things started; however, a fire started and the alarm went out. Our flimsy barracks went up in flames at an exceptionally fast rate. Troops bailed out, some even jumping from the second floor. Luckily, no one was hurt, but my job as supply sergeant started with trying to scrounge up replacements for the clothing and equipment lost in the fire.

Earl Fogt

J. EDWIN FRIDLEY

ANNA, OHIO

Scout, Cpl., Infantry, 1942-45, WW II
Basic Training: Ft. Lewis, Washington
Duty in European Theater

STANLEY LAMBERT

EWING, NEBRASKA

Rifleman, Scout, Cpl., Infantry, 1943-45, WW II
Basic Training: Ft. Leonard Wood, MD.
Duty in European Theater

(Together Ed and Stan remembered their days as POWs in Germany)

Remember how we dug potatoes out of those potato patches? The Germans came out waving pistols trying to chase us POWs out of the potato patches. We went through those like moles.

We were staying in that barn. A horse had been strafed and was lying beside the road. We tried to cut it up and cook it over fire—ate it almost raw. There were about a thousand of us.

The best soup we had while we were POWs was the time that P-51 shot that horse. They hauled him up and put him in the soup.

Did they catch you with a rutabaga? They slapped you up good, didn't they?

That rutabaga fell out of a coat and the guy motioned to me to pick it up and take it back to camp. I didn't get beat up, though. Some of those guards let us get by with taking food when we were around the vegetable piles. The only time I got beat up was down there in the cook shack. I was carrying some stuff down for the Germans. They had a pile of potatoes there and I tried to get one into my pocket. The guy hit me on the face several times; he didn't really beat me up.

That red-headed guard gave me fits. I had pictures on me. They would take them and stamp them and then you could keep them. I had hidden mine in a seam on the bottom of my shirttail. Family pictures. The redhead hadn't found them. When he did, he took them and made a lot of noise, really created a scene. They had to have something to make their day. Some of those guys were sadistic. We had three or four that should have been in a psycho ward.

I was working for that engineering outfit. They had a dozen shovels in a wagon. We were taking that stuff down that steep hill to the Elbe River to get on the ferry to take it across. There were three or four guys on the tongue and six or eight guys on each side of the wagon, hanging on to the wheels to keep it from running away going down that hill. We got it down there. Took all that across the river—this bunch of skinny POWs.

We had a wheelbarrow, three of us and that German civilian that was in that engineering outfit. We brought back a load of coal. We took turns pushing that wheelbarrow. Going down wasn't bad, but coming back up! We were lucky if we pushed it the length of this room. Another guy would have to take over. The German guard felt pretty sorry for us. He said that us guys just didn't get enough to eat to push a wheelbarrow. We finally made it back to camp. The civilians used the coal in their houses. With some of these work details, Germans would come out of their houses with food to give to us, but as soon as they saw German guards, they'd go back into the house.

We had two guys that took off and we covered up for them for two or three days. That guard, Pop, must have been sixty years old. Most decent guard we had. They shipped him out cause he lost some of the men out of his barracks. We caused him to go to a Russian prison; he probably never lived through it.

That one work camp wasn't more than twenty or twenty-five miles from Czeckoslovakia. Dresden was upstream, about twenty-five miles. After it got bombed, we got a lot of the trash flowing in the river by our camp. That strong wind blew a lot of refuse down, too. That was the time when one of the guards, *Snake Eyes,* turned nasty because his wife and family had been killed in Dresden. We sent some guys to help clean up Dresden. I don't think they ever got out. I heard a couple got shot for looting. They were starving to death. They probably grabbed anything they could to eat.

Old Mort usually was slow in getting out in the morning. One morning Snake Eyes shot off a blank right in Mort's seat. Some time later then, when we were working down there by the river, Mort caught that rabbit and was about to skin it when he thought of Snake Eyes and dropped that rabbit in a hurry. He still got it in the back with Snake Eyes' rifle, though.

I heard the Russians talked to certain guys and asked if there were any guards they didn't like and then the Russians took them out, gave them their guns, and made them shoot those guards. That's the story I heard. Life was cheap to them. They drank all the Schnapps they could find. They were getting even for Stalingrad. The Germans had raped, looted, and burned everything across Russia. There was no honor among thieves. We listened to those guns those last six weeks we were in prison camp.

On the way to that one work camp, there were ninety-five of us in a little boxcar. These were like the ones from WW I, the *forty by eights* that would carry eight horses. We were in there for best of three days. The last day they opened up the car and let us get some ice and we brought it back for water. They gave us some bread, but everybody was so dehydrated that they couldn't eat. They bombed that railroad yard that day and it killed three or four of our guards. They were pretty scared. It hit one of the cars up to the front end of the train. The cars rocked.

There were always fifteen or twenty guys standing up because there wasn't room for everyone to sit down. When we sat down we pulled our knees up and the next guy sat down and leaned right up against your stomach. You used your helmet to eat out of, to go to the bathroom in, and everything.

This was on our way to prison camp. When we got captured, we walked for five or six days. After we were captured, they asked my rank and serial number and then they didn't ask anything else.

We knew one another before we were captured. When we got to this last camp where we stayed three months, we were in the same hut, fleabag. Had that fifteen-watt bulb hanging from the ceiling. We got up on this stool, stripped naked, and pulled off all the body lice we could find. We turned our underwear inside out and picked them off and then turned them right side out and picked them off. Then we put the underwear back on and hoped we could get to sleep before another batch hatched out. Fleas and bedbugs from those old straw ticks!

I went out to the outhouse. Nature called pretty frequently because we had diarrhea. There were partitions between the holes. I wondered why because GIs are not all that modest. We needed wood and somebody smuggled this bucksaw into camp. We pulled pins out of the door and had that door and that partition over to our hut and turned into firewood pretty fast.

They steamed our clothes, deloused them. In that one place, they used cyanide to delouse them. The Germans had all the windows open. In our hut the guys were too lazy or too tired to close the windows. But in another barracks the gas got so strong it killed four or five.

In that last camp they would walk us every two or three weeks to get a shower—five or six miles.

Friday night party was cleaning the barracks and equipment. Everything had to be shipshape for Saturday morning inspection. If the officer came through and didn't find anything, he was disappointed. He would stand up on something to see where he couldn't reach, to see if he could find some dust.

We caught one guy in the barracks stealing and we took a pocket knife out and cut all his hair off. He was stealing food. You could steal all you wanted to off the Germans, but you couldn't steal off a brother Yankee or you'd get beat up. They caught this guy redhanded. We had Red Cross parcels and he got into them. He was hauling them up to the barracks for distribution. We had been missing a little stuff and there were any number of guys held under suspicion. Those Red Cross parcels had chocolate bars, and powdered milk, dried fruit, and some tea or coffee, and cigarettes. Some of these we'd trade with the Germans to get extra bread.

One guy wanted cigarettes so badly he'd trade his bowl of soup for one. He didn't last long, cause we didn't have that much to eat. We'd get a chunk of bread about an inch thick, sometimes a bit of margerine or marmalade, some slimey cheese, and once a bit of blood sausage. Then the soup in the evening. A number of guys died from malnutrition.

That's demoralizing to suspect guys in the barracks. Well, we took care of him. I think somebody took him over and threw him in the latrine. That was the dumbest thing they could have done because he had to come back and live with us and we had no water to wash with or nothing. I think it was the more unforgiving types that did that.

You know why the notch is in the dogtags, don't you? When they're dead, you put that notch between their teeth and hit him on the jaw to drive it up in. If you're dead, you don't feel it. Then they can always identify the body. The chain might come off from your neck.

When we were finally in Camp Lucky Strike in France, waiting to come home, I was trying to get my fill of milk. I saw some cows tethered in the field by the camp and twice a day they were taken in for milking. I started across the field with two empty wine bottles. A little girl met me at the door saying, "Ching gum, ching gum." Then her mother came to the door, and with the French words one of my tentmates had taught me, I stumbled, "Voo-layvoo vondo laet?" To which she asked, "Milk?" Anyway, I got my milk then and several more times, always taking "ching gum" or candy for the little girl.

Pay in 1943: \$50 a month for privates; \$114 for 1st sergeants; \$1800 a year for 2d Lieutenants.

Stanley Lambert

DONALD MAX GARMAN

WEST LIBERTY, OHIO

Combat Infantry, PFC, Army, 1943-45, WW II
Basic Trainjng: Camp Croft, SC
Duty in European Theater

Shortly after graduating, I was in the army. This was almost two years after WW II started and they were making possible plans of invasion of France. They were needing lots of foot soldiers because of expected losses.

I took my basic training with a lot of fellows from home at Camp Croft, a temporary training center for infantry. After thirteen weeks here, we were supposed to be ready for combat. These fellows were from the age of 18 to about 34, all thrown together, and believe me, when a fellow is 34 and you are 18, that seems old!

We were shipped out of New York in June, 1944, and after a short stay in England, at a place called Hinten, St. George, which was like a little tent city, we crossed the English Channel to France. This was a few days after D-Day, so the beach was still a mess. We walked the distance from the beach to the front lines. This was something that was hard to comprehend because it was all happening so fast. In fact, I was in and out of combat so fast that a lot of things seem vague.

I was sent in as one of the replacements for fellows that had already gotten hurt. I was with all new personnel, but met Ben Hinkle, about 34 or 35, from my hometown. He was in the same platoon with me, so I was looking forward to having someone like him to lean on since he was a seasoned veteran. Within a few days after I got to know him, Ben was killed by a sniper. That sure loosened me up and made me realize what could happen.

On August 25, six days before my nineteenth birthday, I was laying on a hospital bed in England, having been evacuated by an airplane back across the Channel. I was hit by small mortar fire at close range, but being only about fifty millimeters, there was no concussion, so I did not lose consciousness until the medics started giving me morphine and blood plasma.

Donald Max Garman

About Christmastime in 1944, I was sent back to the States on a hospital ship. I arrived in New York City and was taken by train to a hospital in California. I was discharged from the hospital and military service in September, 1945.

As to being in the hospital in England, I was to be 19 years old in about five or six days. The thing I remember well was how good the Red Cross was to me, not just my birthday, but the full length of my stay. You get to know the fellows real well that are in a big ward. Some were recovering and being sent back to the front lines in France, while to my surprise, some were being court-marshalled for shooting themselves in the hand or foot.

Most of my injuries were to my head and hands. With casts on both hands and arms, it was rough going to the restroom. One of the ward boys said he would rather help me with my call to duty than to be dodging bullets.

It really wasn't as bad coming back home from the war as I had been imagining while laying around the hospital for over a year. I worked at a factory that built hearses and ambulances before I left for the military, so that job was still waiting when I got back. I suppose I did have a little bit of insecurity at first, but when you think of some of those guys in the hospital that were much worse, it helps to forget.

NAOMI (Hopper) GASAWAY

SIDNEY, OHIO

Secretary, Quartermaster Dept., Staff Sgt., Marine Corps, 1943-45, WW II
Basic Training: Huntington College, New York City
Duty at Quantico, VA

When Pearl Harbor was attacked on December 7, 1941, I was attending a football game in Washington, D.C. The attack was announced over the PA system; the fans became extremely silent as shock set in; the game was finished with little enthusiasm.

The Marine Corps did not start recruiting women until 1943, and I was among the first group to enlist. Our basic training was for six weeks at Huntington College in New York. We were not issued uniforms for several weeks. Eventually we were issued green wool uniforms for winter and green and white striped seersuckers for summer. The seersucker skirt was gored—to be different, some of us creased the seams of the skirt, which was frowned upon.

Ration books were issued for meats, butter, sugar, oils, coffee, canned goods, shoes, *silk* hosiery, gasoline, and cigarettes.

At Huntington College we studied the history of the Marine Corps, learned to stand inspection, and how to march. We did not have rigorous physical training, mainly calisthenics. From Huntington College I was sent to Quartermaster School in Camp LeJeune, North Carolina.

We were not well liked by the fellows. First of all, most fellows did not want women in the Corps. Secondly, we had to use men's barracks and mess hall. We did have to clean the barracks, but did not have KP duty. We had guard duty, but no guns.

Eventually we did date the fellows. We were not close to a city, so it was a big deal to go to a small town nearby to get a meal.

I was one of the lucky girls and felt proud to be chosen for pictures for recruitment posters, which were placed in front of post offices and other public buildings. I was pleased when the recruitment poster made the New York Times and other newspapers.

When I finished Quartermaster School, I asked to be sent to the west coast, but was sent to Quantico, Virginia. My job was secretarial duties in the Quartermaster's office. I reached the rank of Staff Sergeant, and my pay was $98 per month. I was a cheerleader for the Quantico football team, which was fun.

Lady Marines were not permitted to go overseas. However, in 1945, they did start to send us to Hawaii. I signed up to go, but the war ended—Hallelujah! We were given leave that night, so I went home to Washington, D.C. I will never forget the sheer pandemonium at Union Station!

We were issued mustering out papers and pay—first time I had ever seen a one-hundred dollar bill. After being mustered out, my military service helped me get a job at the Navy Dept.

It was a great experience and I am proud to have served in the U.S. Marine Corps.

Naomi Gasaway

KERMIT H. GEORGE

BLUFFTON, INDIANA

Platoon Leader, Adjutant, 1st Lt., Army, 302nd Combat Engineers, 77th Div. and the 127th Airborne Engineers (Paratroopers), 11th Airborne Div. 1943-46, WW II
Basic Training: Ft. McClellan, AL
Duty in Pacific Theater—Guam, Okinawa, Philippines, and Japan

During infantry basic training at Ft. McClellan, Alabama, the captain of our training company was a very devout Christian and at each meal in the mess hall directed that everyone remain standing until he asked a blessing or said grace. Several of us thought this was fine and respected him for it. However, the company First Sergeant, a Regular Army man of many years' service, thought this was a lot of foolishness, or at least inappropriate. One day the captain was absent from a meal for some reason. Everyone stood at the tables, waiting and looking around awkwardly, until finally the First Sergeant blurted, "All right, God damn it, somebody pray!" I don't even remember what happened after that. Most of us were raw trainees, too scared or at least hesitant to speak up, but we must have somehow eaten.

Several months later I was taking some specialized training at Auburn University, Alabama. Pete had the uncanny ability to know the time of day (or night) within a very few minutes without benefit of any watch, clock, or any other device. Everyone would ask, "Hey, Pete, what time is it?" And Pete would reply almost instantly, always correct within a minute or two. His fame grew as others learned of his ability, but it eventually became his undoing. Some of the fellows out *on the town* at some tavern or the PX would make substantial bets with fellows from another company that they could go wake up Pete and he'd know just what time it was. The first few times Pete would give the correct time and his friends won their bets. But as this went on, Pete became tired of being wakened in the middle of the night, and finally started deliberately giving the time wrong by about half an hour. The bets stopped and Pete was able to get a sound night's sleep again.

Years later while serving as an officer in the combat engineers in the Pacific, we had invaded the Japanese-held island of Okinawa near Japan. Our navy formed a double circle of ships around the island (we called it the picket line) to protect us, as the Japanese would send attack bombing planes over at night to bomb our positions. Almost all these planes would be shot down by fire from the navy ships before reaching the island, but occasionally a plane would get through the picket line and we would hear it far overhead. Our large searchlights would swing their beams back and forth across the sky until one picked him up and the other searchlights would also converge on the plane. Instantly dozens of anti-aircraft guns would open up and the dark sky would be bright with streaks of tracer bullets. The Japanese pilot would twist and turn to try to get his plane out of the searchlights but at least one was able to stick with him and soon the plane would be hit and would come spiraling down in flames against the black sky. In spite of the fact that he was trying to drop a bomb on us, I felt sorry for the Japanese pilot, one poor fellow up there against all those odds.

A few months later, as we were preparing for the invasion of Japan, the atomic bombs were dropped. Although this was horrible for the people of Hiroshima and Nagasaki, the resultant surrender by Japan prevented far more casualties on both sides had we been forced to invade Japan.

WHAYLAND H. GREENE

BELCHER, LA

Rifleman; Platoon Runner; Squad Leader, S/Sgt., Army, 126th Infantry, 32nd Div., 1943-46, WW II
Basic Training: Camp Fannin, Texas
Duty in Pacific Theater

Sometime after our physical, a Corporal came by and said in a real nice, polite voice, "Would you men please follow me." Then he had us raise our right hands and repeat what he was saying. After that he walked into the other room and in a loud, rough voice said, "You miserable, sick looking bunch of kids come in here on the double." Being in the Army about 30 seconds, we did not know what on the double meant. After being shoved through the door, we soon learned and never forgot all the time we were in the service. I could not believe that was the same man that had been so nice and polite just minutes before. I think it had something to do with us raising our right hands.

After a three-day pass, the sergeant reviewed different ways to kill the enemy. He said, "Be sure to remember to hit him real hard with your bayonet and holler loud at the same time. Then when you start to pull it out, be sure to kick him hard in the stomach. You see, it hangs between the rib bones and is hard to pull out sometimes." He went through each weapon even down to the knife. At the end, he asked if there were any questions. I raised my hand. "What is it this time, Greene?" I said, "Sgt., I have this killing down pretty pat. What I want to know is, when do we get to the class where you learn how to keep from getting killed? That's what I am most interested in." He said, "I am glad you asked that. I could look at some of you and tell you did not understand, especially you." So he went all through it again how to kill. At the end he said, "It's all in the same class. You kill to keep from getting killed."

On Leyte it rained every day or every night and sometimes day and night. We had been wet about twenty-six days. We went to another area and were sent out on patrol just to see what we were about to run up against. We did run into some

Japs and the lieutenant told us to turn around and come back because we were just on a reconnaissance patrol.

On the way back, Smitty was running just behind me and a machine gun was firing at us. He was hit in the head and it killed him. My feet were hurting so bad that I couldn't run fast when they were shooting at me. I had jungle rot on them real bad. When we got back, the medic looked at them and said I should have been in the hospital several days ago, so he sent me back with the litter train as a guard. I got to the hospital and my boots were almost rotted off. The doctor had to cut my socks off; they had grown to the skin on my feet and blood came off with the rotten socks.

We were in a tent hospital and sleeping on cots. It felt like a nice hotel after being in mud for so long. They took real good care of me and when it was about time to be released, the doctor came by and asked if I was from the company that they were getting so many wounded from. When I told him I was, he said, "I'm going to let you stay here until tomorrow." I said, "Thank you, Sir."

When I went back to the front, I met James Bryant and he said the day after I left that five out of the six men of the squad I was in, had been hit.

We continued what they called a mopping up exercise and soon the battle of Leyte was over. In those 47 days of battle on Leyte, 6700 Japs and 401 32nd Division men died.

It was time to go to Luzon Island. The beach had already been secured. When we were ready to unload from the boat, they put us in life boats that were hanging on the side of the ship. They were about to lower us to the water when we had an air attack. Thankfully, our planes were able to take care of the Jap planes before they got to us.

Well, it was time for Lt. Coolie, with our platoon, to try to take that hill. We were all real nervous and I asked the lieutenant if he was ready to go get 'em. He said, "Greene, I'm not any more ready to go get 'em than you are." So I said, "If that's the case, let's *don't* go get 'em." He said, "I wish it could be like that."

I was platoon runner at this time and carried a little 536 radio for the lieutenant so we could keep in contact with the company commander. As we started up the hill we were drawing fire from a machine gun, rifles and hand grenades, but we continued slowly moving up the hill. Our men that were up the hill just a little farther pinned down the machine gun and killed several of the Japs and even occupied some of the Jap holes. Four or more were almost to the top of the hill when the Japs started shelling us with a large mortar from another hill. One shell hit real close to us and killed Lt. Coolie. A piece of shrapnel had gone through Valentine's helmet. He was bleeding a lot but did not seem to be hit real bad.

A piece hit Bryant in the wrist. Weaver got hit. The breath was knocked out of me and the 536 radio had been destroyed. I had just gotten in contact with the company commander and handed the radio to Lt. Coolie. The lieutenant was now dead. In just a few seconds, after I got my breath back, the sergeant asked how bad it was. At first I told him that I thought real bad, but found out it was just a little piece of shrapnel in my leg and the rest of it was just concussion. The sergeant said for us to pull back before we all got killed. By the time Valentine and Bryant and others started back down the hill, we were all ready to get the heck out of there.

We all started back at once and when we did, the machine gun raised up and helped us get down the hill a little faster. We got almost back with the wounded and something hit a man named Camarino in the head and killed him. He used to kid me about being the only man in C Company that could still get in the show for a dime.

When things settled down again, I thought, What a price to pay for a small hill in these islands! I think in two days we had eight men killed and twelve wounded on that hill.

I looked around and all I could see were more hills and small mountains. It looked to me that there were enough for the Japs and us, too, but we always seemed to want the same hill. We would take one from them by day and they would try to take it back from us that night or a few nights later. I asked the sergeant why that little hill was so important to us. He said that it was because the Japs had it and that Gen. Douglas MacArthur had told our division commander, Gen. Gill, to keep every hill we had and take every one that the Japs had.

One night on Leyte four of us were guarding a trail. We dug two holes, but were taking turns sitting against a large tree. The early part of the night they had told us to be real careful because an American patrol might be coming in the early part of the night. Smitty was sitting guard and it must have been about three or four o'clock in the morning when we heard Smitty say, "Halt! Halt! Who goes there?"—then he fired twice before he got all of that out of his mouth. A few minutes after I heard the two shots I asked him what he saw. He said two Japs had walked right up on him and he got one and thinks he got the other one.

It was my turn to guard the trail. It started to get daylight, and it scared me when I looked down and saw that dead Jap near my feet. I didn't have any idea that the Jap had gotten that close to Smitty before he shot him. The Jap fell over in the edge of the hole that Smitty and another man had been sleeping in. Smitty was later killed by a machine gun.

Once on Luzon Island when we were dug in on a hill, the Japs started dropping artillery shells near us. They dropped one in front of us, one to the rear of us, and one to each side. We had been told that was the way the artillery zeroed their guns in on the position that they were about to shell. Some times they would do it real soon and some times they would wait until night. But we knew it was coming and it was just a matter of time. You might know we dug our holes a little deeper.

Not expecting it to come when it did, a man from Georgia got out of his hole to go to another one nearby to get a chew of tobacco from a friend. The Japs started shelling and one of the first shells hit near Carter and killed him. He didn't even get to enjoy that chew of tobacco.

It was time to start that push again. The sergeant that was to take charge had about 104-degree fever, so they had to get Sgt. Hale to take his place. Sgt. Hale was a real good combat soldier. I remember that he had jungle rot on his hands with white gauze wrapped around them. I remember his wiping mud on the gauze so it could not be seen so easily. They had gone only a few feet and ran into lots of Japs. There was lots of shooting from both sides. A man from Texas was hit in the top of his head, right through his helmet. It knocked him down, but did not kill him. Several more men were wounded. It was decided that there were too many Japs for such a few men, so they were ordered back. Sgt. Hale let his men get back to their holes and turned and started back himself. Just a few steps after he turned and started back, a Jap shot him in his back. He was dead instantly. He was real close to my hole and I saw him fall. It really bothered me because we had gotten to be good friends. Another sergeant checked to be sure he was dead and told me to get my head down since I could not do anything for him. They would not let us move him at that time because they said someone else would get killed trying to do it. A few hours later they had me pull him up the hill to our holes; he had already begun to get stiff. After the war was over, Valentine and his wife and my wife and I went to see his family in Gates, Tennessee.

We were making a push down a creek bed and came to a place where the Japs had left a dog tied to a tree. We think the dog was left there to let them know when we were getting close. We did not want to kill the dog, but had to because he would keep giving our position away.

About one-fourth mile from there we made contact with the Japs. We were both doing a lot of shooting. Soon one of our men was hit on the side of his head. The bullet just grazed him, but he was bleeding pretty bad. I was down behind a large rock and told the man to get behind the big rock and I would get a Medic to him. He said, "Get a Medic to me, Hell! I'm going to the Medic!" and he never slowed down until he got to the Medic.

To let you know how messed up your thinking can get in times like that, no one would hesitate to shoot a Jap, but no one wanted to shoot the dog.

You always had to carry on a little foolishness to keep from going crazy. After a little skirmish I looked at the lieutenant and said, "Boy, that really cost the taxpayers a lot of money!" He said, "It sure did!"

It was not too long before we heard about the big bomb. I think the next day we heard about another one and that Japan had surrendered. I don't believe anyone could have been happier than we were unless it was the Japanese soldiers that were in that area.

Now it was our job to get the Japanese to come in and lay down their arms. Our second platoon started up the hill to make contact with them. They took a note in English and some cigarettes and candy bars. The first Japs that they came in contact with did not have the news the war was over and they fired at our men. Our men left the note, cigarettes, and candy bars, marked the area, and came back down the hill.

The next day it was Lt. Kedrick's time to try to make contact and he told me to get my squad ready. I guess I was as nervous at this time as I ever was. While carrying a white flag, we reached the place where the note and cigarettes were left and noticed they were gone. Just a little farther up the hill, we could see heads looking out around some trees. They did not fire. Our lieutenant hollered at them and said the Japanese had surrendered. They hollered back and said the Americans had surrendered. Our lieutenant asked if anyone could speak English; one said, "Very little." He got four of them to meet four of us halfway. In five minutes we were smoking cigarettes, laughing, and trying to talk. They told us to come back tomorrow and they would have a higher ranking officer with them.

When we returned, the officer said that they could not come in until they got direct orders from Gen. Yamashita. He was to them what General Douglas MacArthur was to us.

After two weeks they came in and laid their weapons down. From then on they were not Japs any more; they were Japanese soldiers. The hate was gone just that quick. One of the first things we did was to set up a tent for a hospital for the ones that were too sick and badly hurt to make the trip out of the area.

I still think we have the greatest country in the world and I would fight for it again if it became necessary, but I do think some of our leaders have some of their priorities in the wrong place. May God continue to bless this great country of ours!

Whayland H. Greene

MATHIAS J. HENMAN

SIDNEY, OHIO (DECEASED)

Cook, Corporal, Army Air Force, 1943-46, WW II
Basic training: Keesler Field, Biloxi, MS
Duty in England, France (Normandy), Belgium, Germany

I lived in 7-man tents most of the time, the kind you saw in Mash. In England I lived in tents all the time except when I was in the hospital barracks after I broke my ankle. It was before winter had set in, but was still damp and cold, mostly because of the fog. We did have a small stove, maybe two or three ft. high and about a foot in diameter. We didn't always have fuel to burn, though. One time while trying to start a fire, I poured gasoline on it. It really took off and caught a newspaper afire that a guy was reading—happened to be The Sidney *Daily News*. We got the fire out okay, though—no catastrophe.

Water from a creek was brought to the base in tank trucks and purified and guys carried some to their tents in five-gallon buckets or whatever was available. We took the liner out of our helmets and heated water in them to wash in.

I broke my ankle when I stepped out of a truck backwards. After six weeks in the hospital, all of the stuff I had left in the tent was gone—clothes, my watch, personal items that I kept in a little box. We didn't have radios because they took tubes—no transistors at that time.

When we were stationed near Paris, France, we stayed at a chateau around one of the largest wineries in France, Rothchilds. But it was not operating and there was no wine left around anywhere. The building was completely empty; the Germans had used it as a radio station. There were tunnels from the main building to the outer buildings. While there was no wine in the buildings, some guys managed to get some. If they had money, it seemed the French could find things to sell them.

When I was first sent overseas, I was issued a British jacket because of a lack of proper clothing, as this country was not prepared for war. Guys were issued long winter coats but we couldn't wear them all of the time. The Eisenhower jacket wasn't out at the time, but later we were issued one of those.

I had a carbine rifle issued to me and every tenth man was issued a Thompson machine gun. There was no training with them in basic or when they were issued. You were just expected to know how to use them. In fact, in basic training we only had wood guns because there weren't enough to go around. We used real rifles on the rifle range but that was the only time.

I think the Germans were better trained than we were because they had been at it for a long time. We had to prepare in such a hurry. We trained in P39s in the States. Overseas we didn't have any of them; had P47s.

I went to England on an English luxury liner named The Sterling Castle. This ship was very similar to the Queen Mary liner but had been converted to a troop ship, so we saw none of the luxury. The huge ballroom was full of bunks, three or four high. When we got in line for breakfast, it was almost dinner time when we got through. The weather was real bad and lots of guys were sick. We were traveling in a convoy and, with the weather so bad, there was a constant watch to make sure we didn't ram another ship. I had watch duty and had to crawl up in the gun turret and watch for subs. It was funny—I couldn't even see my hand it was so dark, so how could I see a sub!

The Belgium government gave each man in the 404th Air Force Fighter Group a commendation for helping to liberate Belgium. All the bridges were destroyed across the Rhine River, so our engineers made a bridge out of boats so we could cross into Germany from Belgium. They used what was available—something like LCUs, maybe ten or fifteen of them.

I met Mickey Rooney at a USO show in a hangar in Belgium, and played some poker with him. A lieutenant was giving Mickey hell for being late for a show and Mr. Rooney told the lieutenant he was running the show. Most of the guys treated Mickey just like one of the guys.

After V-E Day (5/8/45) the civilians would ransack our garbage and ask for the leftover food on our plates because they were starving. My mother sent me some unpopped popcorn while I was stationed in Belgium. When we popped it, it scared the civilians because they said they never had seen that kind of food. When fresh food was not available and we were moving from one location to another, we ate K-Rations and C-Rations (Spam and a chocolate bar that was so hard you could have pounded nails with it, plus cigarettes) that came in a box.

I was a cook, and when we got fresh chicken it came with only the feathers removed. I had to clean them inside and out. The intestines, etc. were still in the inside. Usually we deep fried the chicken. The hams were salt cured and tasted real salty when served. The milk we received was all powdered and had to be mixed with water. We had to be careful in preparing powdered eggs and cook them right before they were to be served because if they set too long, they turned green. Sometimes we made donuts. Our supplies were brought to us by truck. Cigarettes were five cents a package; no tax.

We had six or seven gasoline stoves to cook on. Each one was about four ft. long and average stove height. We moved the burners to the top to fry pancakes or something and then moved them to the bottom if we wanted to use the oven. When we had to move to another air base, we, the cooks, had to move our own equipment. We lifted the whole stoves—they didn't come apart. There were six or seven of us that cooked for two hundred fifty people.

The fighter planes stayed close to the troops during battles because of the distance they could fly. We who were at the air base could go up on a hill and watch them bomb a short distance away. The distance the planes could fly was limited because they were loaded with bombs or belly tanks full of gasoline. When we were at our first air base near Bormouth, England, we had an all-dirt runway. After the rains came, they had to put a steel runway down because the planes bogged down in mud when they tried to take off to bomb Germany. That steel-mat runway rattled and banged—sounded like the airplane was falling apart.

When the Germans surrendered, we sat in Germany for approximately two months. Then when V-J Day came (9/2/45) and ended the war, I had enough points (even though I was single) to be shipped back to the states and qualify for my honorable discharge.

ALFRED L. HENRY

VERSAILLES, OHIO

Squad Leader, ST/Sgt., Army, 1942-45, WW II
Basic Training: Camp Atterbury, IN
Duty in European theater

After training for the invasion in a staging area in England, on June 8, 1944, we crossed the English Channel, going ashore to relieve the 101st Airborne. Just off shore we left the small boats we had boarded to cross the channel. The water was waist deep and we had to hold our weapons up out of the water to keep them dry. As we waded ashore on to the beach at Normandy, we had to step over bodies and debris and seek cover from enemy fire. The bodies were scattered on the beach like railroad ties.

We moved in a short distance and had to hold our position at the front until July 4, 1944. We tried to move forward that morning but were stopped by the swamps. We lost a lot of good men that day.

I saw the first man in my squad killed; it hurts to see young men you trained with for twenty months die. We finally broke through and moved forward on July 10 or 11, taking the small town of Saint Eny, but were driven back. We had orders to move some distance beyond town and dig in and hold our position. We hadn't had time to dig deep enough when we were shelled. A shell hit three feet from our slit trench, and I was hit in the knee and hip. At first I thought I was okay, but when I moved, I could feel a burning sensation. I turned to Sam Oliver, one of our scouts, who had dug in with me. When I couldn't get any response from him, I called for a medic. The medic found Sam had been killed from concussion. I walked back to the aid station and was sent to the rear.

The hospital in England couldn't remove all the shrapnel, so I still carry some of it in my hip and knee. After a while in the hospital, I met a man from my Company who told me he had just left my twin brother. My twin brother and I had gone into the service at the same time—I to E Co., 331st Infantry Regiment, 83rd Infantry Division; he to L Co., 329th Infantry Regiment, 83rd Infantry Division. We hadn't seen each other for more than six months. I called the hospital where he was and his doctor said he had been sent back to duty the day before I called. It was then that I decided to volunteer to go back to my unit. That was the only way I could get back with the men I already knew like family.

Shortly after rejoining my Company, I was hit in the other leg. I had the medic dress it so I could remain with the men I knew.

We worked our way across France to Luxembourg where more replacements joined us and we moved on to the Hurtgen Forest. There we took a small town, Gey, at the edge of the forest. We started with a full platoon of thirty-eight men and when we came together afterwards, there were only seven of us left. Some were missing in action and some were wounded. This was around Christmastime and things were not jolly.

We then got more replacements and were back up to full squads. But there was little time for rest. We were called upon to move to the Ardennes Forest where the Germans were moving. We moved at night to our position to attack early in the morning of January 10 or 11, 1945. I had the lead squad and Lt. Clark and I started out first. We hadn't gone far when Lt. Clark was struck by fire from our own Division Recon who thought we were Germans.

I had orders to continue on with the platoon. Not more than a thousand yards or so farther, I saw a tree lying across the path in the forest and I told my scouts to cover me while I had a look. To my surprise, Germans came out of the forest, dropping their weapons and putting their hands over their heads. I don't know how many surrendered, but they were coming out of the forest four, six, and sometimes eight abreast.

However, the lull in the action did not last long. The Germans zeroed in on our position and started shelling us. Their men, along with ours, were being hurt. We were told to dig in and hold our position. But you can't dig to do any good with snow on the ground that is two and three feet deep.

It wasn't long until I was hit again in the same leg as the first time. This time the calf muscle was shot away. I was trying to put a tourniquet above my knee to stop the bleeding when a young scout, who had just come as a replacement, said, "I'll help you, Sarge." Just as he knelt down in front of me to help, a shell hit him in the back and he fell on top of me. I laid him over as easy as I could and called the medic, but he was already dead. If it hadn't been for him, I wouldn't be writing this. I'll never forget his name, PFC John T. DiMaurco. I wish I knew where he was from so I could tell his family he was a good soldier. I never could tell Sam Oliver's mother about how Sam had died. She wrote me years ago, but I couldn't talk about it then.

I was helped out of the forest by another sergeant who had been wounded in the elbow. I held on to his other shoulder and hopped on one leg for about three-fourths of a mile. Then I was taken to an Evac hospital and given first aid. I had started to smoke and was up to two packs a day in just eight weeks. But when the doctor gave me a shot of morphine, I lit up and he slapped the cigarette out of my mouth. I quit for good and haven't smoked since.

I was sent to Le Mans, France, and lay on my back for over a month before my wound was sewn shut. While I was in the hospital, I got a big surprise. My twin brother came to visit me. My wife and I had gotten married while I was at Breckenridge. Before I went overseas, we made up a code that I could use to write her where I was at all times. Since my brother was dating her sister, she was able to tell him where I was. I still find my wedding and seeing my brother as my two most important days. I found out that day that he had been sent to the MPs from the hospital. After I got back on my feet, I, too, was sent to an MP outfit. After fifty years, I don't remember the outfit. I did come home with the 75th Division, on the point system.

I had a thirteen-month old daughter that I had never seen. She was born when I was in Luxembourg. I got a big shock and scare one day when the MPs came to my Company and took me back to the Allied Command. They had found a body with a shirt with my name and number on it. The War Department had sent my wife a telegram saying that I had been killed in action. Two officers had come from Dayton to Wilson Memorial Hospital in Sidney to give her the news when she had just given birth to our daughter. She didn't believe them because she had received a letter from me written two days after the date they had listed for my death.

After they took me back to Allied Command, they asked me hundreds of questions about the United States and my family. (My twin brother and I had ten other siblings.) They asked names, ages, lifestyle, etc. In the end, they made me sign seven copies and sent them through the chains of command.

I learned to know a lot of good officers and men. I wonder how any of us survived to come home.

ROBERT KARSTENSEN

Nose Gunner, 724th Squadron, 451stBomb Group, WW II
Basic Training: Miami Beach, FL
Duty In European Theater

Our first mission on July 12 gave us our first taste of combat. I had no difficulty with enemy fighters (they stayed away—word must have preceded us) but I was confronted with a faulty British (Brown) electrical flying suit. Seems that I had an electrical short in the upper leg. I never realized I was afire; I thought blue smoke and plexi-glass reflections were all a part of what combat was all about.

When it dawned on me that the smoke was emanating from my suit, I was forced to *pull the plug.* This left me in rather a precarious situation; freeze to death in the 50 below temperature, or fricassee myself with the suit on. The situation was relieved when I alternated freezing and frying by plugging the cord back in and beating out the fire on the pant leg till I got warm and toasty, then unplugging and letting the cold take its grip. T'was an interesting first encounter with combat.

Reprinted with permission from Robert Karstensen and Michael D. Hill, Editor, *The Fight'n 451st Bomb Group (H).*

WILLIAM KINGSEED

PIQUA, OHIO

Cook, Navy, WW II
Basic Training, Norfolk, VA
Duty at Pearl Harbor, Pacific Theater

As he and the chief gunner's mate stood drinking coffee outside the galley of the USS Macdonaugh anchored at Pearl Harbor, William Kingseed was puzzled by all the aircraft flying over on an otherwise peaceful morning in Hawaii.

The morning of Dec. 7, 1941, had begun like many others for Kingseed, who served as the ship's cook. "I cooked breakfast that morning," he said, recollecting the number of men eating was less than normal because it was a Sunday. "They didn't all have to get up."

"We just stood there and watched them for awhile," said Kingseed. "I wondered what the Army was doing flying around so much on a Sunday morning."

His question was soon answered when his shipmate took another look and declared, "Those are Jap planes."

Amid the explosions, fire, and smoke that followed after the enemy warplanes dropped their torpedoes and bombs, Kingseed witnessed the destruction that would shock the United States into entering World War II.

"I saw the old (USS) Utah get hit and roll over," Kingseed said. The aged battleship was being used as a target vessel by the Navy. Historians of the Pearl Harbor attack believe Japanese pilots mistook the Utah for an active duty battleship, and so targeted it.

"They were after the battleships. That was their main target," said Kingseed, whose ship the Macdonaugh was a destroyer. It was anchored with a nest of other destroyers and took no direct hits during the attack.

The Macdonaugh and the other ships soon entered the battle, though, directing antiaircraft fire at the waves of enemy planes. "We put up as much fire as we could from then on," said Kingseed, who helped man a gun. The battle continued for about an hour and a half. "It seemed like they just kept coming," he said of the low-flying Japanese aircraft.

"It was a terrible mess. Everything was all on fire. There were explosions everywhere."

Most of the Macdonaugh's officers were on overnight liberty, he noted. Only one was on board the ship at the time of the attack. Despite this, and the crew's lack of combat experience, everyone carried out their duties. "You had the training. I can't recall a whole lot of confusion. I don't think anybody was scared. Not that anybody was that brave. You were trained for that. You probably didn't have time (to be scared)."

After the battle, the Macdonaugh sailed out of the harbor, giving Kingseed a chance to see the devastation wrought on battleship row, where the Arizona, the Oklahoma, and the West Virginia lay in ruins.

The Macdonaugh got out of the harbor at about noon that day. There was fear that the Japanese might folow up their air attack with a landing of troops on the Hawaiian Islands. "Nobody knew what was going on. I think they definitely could have done a landing," Kingseed stated. The Macdonaugh and some other warships which escaped damage patroled around the islands for a couple of days.

He said such an invasion was not in the planning by the Japanese, whose aim was to inflict severe damage on the U.S. Pacific fleet. Luckily for the Americans, their aircraft carriers were at sea when the Japanese attacked, preventing further destruction that might have crippled for a longer period of time the U.S. military's ability to respond.

Kingseed said his ship was not involved in operations to rescue men wounded in the attack, explaining the Macdonaugh was tied to a tender and undergoing repairs at the time of the attack and was taking power from the tender. The ship's own power had been shut down and could not immediately be restored.

The Macdonaugh, with Kingseed aboard, went on to serve throughout the rest of the war, earning 13 battle stars in engagements such as Guadalcanal, the Battle of the Philippine Sea, and "the Marianas Turkey Shoot."

None of these battles, however, had the impact on Kingseed that the surprise attack on Pearl Harbor did. "Anytime after that, you knew what was going on," he said...

Reprinted with permission from *The Sidney* (Ohio) *Daily News* and Mike Seffrin.

William Kingseed

MERLE LARSON

Pilot, 727th Squadron, 451st Bomb Group, WW II
Duty in European Theater

As an overseas hobby, I built a propeller driven auto from junked airplane parts. Before starting the project, I was considering the building of a light airplane around a Fiat motor! It was a fascinating project and kept my mind occupied between missions. The other guys were going "stir crazy," sweating out the next mission. I was worried about solving the next problem of my project.

It had P-40 wheels; B-24 tail skid shock struts; a pre-war Fiat airplane engine, 7 cyl 100 h.p. (something like a Warner). The frame was the top of an Italian tri-motor bomber, like they bombed Ethiopia with. The prop and mag were big problems. I made a prop out of steel tubing and covered the blades with a mattress cover (excellent quality canvas) and doped with airplane dope. It worked well and even survived running through tall weeds. The mag problem was solved with hot ignition (an old motorcycle battery). I built the distributor system. I needed some ungodly ratio of gears between the distributor cam and the rotor (I think it was 4:9). The cam came from a P-38 and the breaker points from a B-24 or vise-versa. I solved the gear problem by divorcing the cam and rotor depts. I drove the cam from the mag drive and drove the distributor rotor from the tachometer drive. The distributor block and rotor were made from plexiglass.

The master brake cylinder was from an ME-109 (with round wingtips). I completed the project and drove it around the base for some time. Finally I tipped it over and almost killed my asst. crew chief. We all were pretty lucky. I gave it to some ground crew personnel when I left Italy. I understand they got another prop for it and got it going again.

We called this thing "ROYAL PROD JR."

Reprinted with permission from Michael D. Hill, editor, *The Fight'n 451st Bomb Group (H).*

MARY McCALLA

SIDNEY, OHIO

Club Director, American Red Cross, 1945-47, WW II
Duty in Italy

DONALD McCALLA

SIDNEY, OHIO

88th Div. MP, PFC, Infantry, 1944-46, WW II
Basic Training: Camp Blanding
Duty in Italy

Don McCalla, Sidney, OH, had come to Italy in November, 1944, and joined the 34th Infantry Division at Montecatini. After the war in Europe ended, he was transferred to the 88th Division for occupation duty. Having been made an MP, he was given a two-week assignment in Venice with seven other MPs. They were on duty part time, keeping GIs, who had come to see Venice, in line.

Mary Beth Hartson, Oberlin, OH, had joined the American Red Cross in May, 1945, and was sent to Montecatini in July, and on to Venice, Italy, in August of that year.

One of the first places the MPs headed for was the American Red Cross Club on San Marco Square. Here three American girls gave a touch of home, with friendship, sightseeing hints, and just a nice place to relax.

American service people ate their meals at a small restaurant nearby where each person had to sign in. This is how Don found out Mary's last name. In the two weeks he was in Venice, they often ate together and Don would sign in for both of them. One evening the whole gang rode the Vaporetto over to the Lido to see a USO show at the big theater there.

There is nothing very unusual in this story so far. But thirty years later, in 1975, Don's wife of thirty-six years died after a long illness. On the very same day of her death, Mary's divorce became final. Don wondered about Mary, where was she, was she married, and so he wrote to her college for information. He learned that she was living in Oberlin and had a *Mrs.* affixed to her name. The letter to her was much harder, but he got it sent, and soon she answered.

Mary did not remember Don at that time, as she had known literally hundreds of soldiers in her two years with ARC and, of course, it was thirty years later! When he came for the first visit, she did remember the gondola ride he had taken her on and also recalled his waiting for her to go to the restaurant. He told her that he had fallen in love with her back in Venice and that he had never forgotten her. He recalled that she had refused to kiss him in the gondola because he was married.

Don and Mary were married on Thanksgiving Day, 1975, and have lived happily in Sidney, Ohio, ever since.

JANICE (Schlagetter) McGRATH

SIDNEY, OHIO

Driver - Dispatcher, T-4, Army Ordnance (WAC), 1943-45, WW II
Basic Training: Ft. Oglethorp, GA
Duty at Aberdeen, Maryland

I was inducted on January 2, 1943, at Columbus, Ohio, and went to Ft. Oglethorp, Georgia, for four weeks of basic training. We were issued clothing, everything from top to bottom, including underwear and hose—service weight so they wouldn't get runners quite so easily. When we did get runners, we turned the hose in and were issued new ones. With our dress uniform we had what we called stovepipe hats, but when the WAAC (Women's Auxiliary Army Corps) was changed to regular army (August, 1942, I think—Women's Army Corps), then we received the overseas-type hat. Girls wore very little makeup, maybe just some lipstick.

We had basic army routine, physical training much like men had, calisthenics, pushups, etc.

Our barracks were regular army and very rough. Had bed check at night. We changed our own sheets and turned them in at the designated area; took turns cleaning the barracks, doing KP, etc.

Our group was sent to Arkansas State Teachers College, Conway, Arkansas, for six weeks of training in army administration procedures. I did not have an office background. We had no choice but were sent as a group. We learned all types of office work. Very nice place. No civilians there, the army had taken it over.

After graduation, some of us were sent to Aberdeen Proving Grounds, Maryland (Ordnance). On arrival at Aberdeen we found it was a regular army post (WW I) and had been manned by civilians from that area (office work). So our whole company had to be reassigned. We were given a list of jobs we could try for. I chose transportation, which I had wanted originally.

Clockwise from bottom left; Janice (Schlagetter) McGrath in summer Fatigue Dress and shorts, in dress, in working clothes,

Our job in Headquarters Motor Pool was to drive all officers that called for transportation. We graduated from 3/4 ton trucks to staff cars. Aberdeen was a place where all weapons and vehicles the army used were tested. Some girls were on vehicles that were tested, tanks, etc; some in Ballistic lab where some parts of the atom bomb were worked on. Therefore, when a foreign dignitary or one of our own known generals came to Washington, he, or they, were brought to Aberdeen where we drove them around on demonstrations. Hap Arnold, Wainwright, Russian delegations, are a few I remember. It was a very interesting post, so much going on, and we were always treated with the greatest respect.

I received a commendation ribbon for my service as Dispatcher, Headquarters Motor Pool, at Aberdeen. I was responsible for assigning thirty or so girls to their driving assignments. There were many visitors. During that time our group had worked on a project for nearly a week, 24 hours a day—something to do with the loading of a transport at our airport.

There are many incidents that happened that made the life interesting. We were always part of what was happening because we had seen it tested there, at least we drivers did. All types of vehicles, guns, hand to eighteen-inch battleship guns, all types of bombings.

We didn't have much free time (worked all different hours) because ours was mostly a civilian post and they only got one day a month off. So it would take us a while to get a three-day pass. Then New York was our goal.

ROBERT C. McMILLEN

SPRINGFIELD, OHIO

Paratrooper, Corporal, Army, 1943-46, WW II
Basic Training: Ft. Benning, GA
Duty in Southwest Pacific

I was inducted into the army in January, 1943, and from there was sent to Ft. Sill, OK, to take basic training in field artillery. But before completion of basic training, they came through and asked if anyone with more braun than brains would like to volunteer for the paratroops. This sounded like a pretty good deal to me and especially when my pay was fifty dollars a month and the paratroopers got one hundred dollars a month. So I wrote a letter to my mother and father and asked what they thought of my joining the paratroops. Before I could get their answer, I had already volunteered and was on a train heading for Ft. Benning, GA.

My memories are mostly from the main combat I was in when jumping on Corregidor and returning it to the armed forces of the U.S., taking it back from the Japanese who had taken it from Wainwright and MacArthur. This jump occurred on Feb. 16 and we had quite a few casualties, but not as many as the Japanese did.

When they picked me up on the island of Mindoro for this jump, I was under a physician's care for the shingles, and, at that time, they said, "We can make arrangements so you don't have to make this jump because it will be very painful for you." Being young and foolish, I said I'd like to go with my buddies, so they packed cotton all over the shingles scabs and gave me some pills for the pain. Off we went into the wild blue yonder to make history.

We jumped between 400 and 600 feet, which is not very high, permitting maybe one oscillation before hitting the ground. We had reserve chutes, but there wouldn't have been any time to use them. My jump landed me near the parade field at Corregidor. My feet had gotten up into my suspension lines; I was coming down and cracked the ground pretty hard and injured my back. I crawled into a mortar hole to spend the night. There was a lot of machine gun fire and a lot of action around me.

During the night I felt some things crawling around and biting me. The next morning I found I had gotten into a bunch of red ants, which wasn't very pleasant. And also I was taking cover from what I thought was Japanese machine gun fire and it was my own men, so I had to get straightened out there in a hurry.

There were a lot of hardships on the soldiers at this time. Our water supply wasn't very adequate and they would have to drop our water by air. We had jungle rations and C-rations for food that are okay when you're hungry. Besides the fierce fighting, there were an awful lot of bodies around, Japanese bodies that were deteriorating and the blowflies were so thick that they'd land on you and you could just pick them off with your fingers. If you wanted to eat something, you'd have to open your mouth and fan your hand at the same time to keep them from flying into your mouth. We were dirty most of the time; there was no way we could keep clean.

We, in time, finally took the island back from the Japanese. Their casualties were extremely heavy. There were just a few hundred prisoners taken out of six thousand that were on that small island. And they were mostly Tiger Imperial Marines, which were the cream of the crop of the Japanese.

I watched Gen. MacArthur come ashore and come up to the parade ground and make a speech to us about taking back this land from which he had been run off. My regimental combat team was given a presidential citation for this action.

Something along the more humorous route, when we were on an island in the Dutch East Indies, an Indian friend of mine by the name of George Whitewater (he was later killed), and I were going through the jungle. Rising up all around us was a bunch of natives that came up with their spears and pointed to George saying, "Hopanese, Hopanese." They thought he was Japanese because he had dark Indian skin, plus he had been taking malaria tablets, which we all had. They gave him sort of a yellow cast. It was hard talking them out of doing something to George because they had been so mistreated by the Japanese that they wanted some revenge right then and there. They did finally permit us to go on our way and on with the job that we were doing.

Being a paratrooper does not necessarily mean that all your combat is done by parachute jumping. We made seven beach landings. It seemed that every time I got on a landing craft for a beach landing, it would come up short of the beach and I'd have to go into the water almost up to my armpits. And maybe the landing craft next to me would go right up so the guys could walk right off on to dry land. It just wasn't my cup of tea.

Also, when we were on the island of Leyte, it was the monsoon season. We slept in jungle hammocks, stringing them up between two trees. We had a cover, a roof, over them with mosquito netting between that and the part you slept on. It so happened that mine leaked, and at night before I crawled in, I'd have to dump the water out. Going through the swamps and things, we'd be covered with leeches, so we'd have to pick them off of each other.

We were sent to Australia for some jungle training, and while there I developed appendicitis and had to have my appendix removed. While recuperating from that, I continued with my jungle warfare training; from there we were put on Dutch boats with a Javanese crew. The boats were old, had wooden decks. So we went up into New Guinea on that type of boat.

We were treated very, very well, just like royalty, when we came home from overseas. It seemed that no one could do enough for a serviceman, and that was greatly appreciated. In other conflicts, Vietnam for example, this didn't happen, but in WW II they just went all out for the GIs.

I did enjoy being in the service; I think it was good for me, physically and mentally. I was drafted out of my senior year in high school, along with four other members of the senior class. We were permitted to graduate that year, but I could not get a leave to come home for graduation. So at graduation, my mother, along with the other four mothers, were presented with our diplomas.

Robert McMillen

MARY McNEIL

SIDNEY, OHIO

Machine filing, 2/Class Seaman, WAVEs (Navy), 1944-46, WW II
Basic Training: Hunter College, New York City
Duty at Bureau of Personnel, Washington, D.C.

When leaving home by over-night train on December 14, 1944 (my first experience on a train), we didn't know our destination, but it was to be Hunter College. We had active physical training, marched from class to class, and stood inspection every Saturday morning with women officers.

After six weeks several of us were sent to Wave Qts. K, a new Wave Barracks located across from Ft. Meyers Army Post and just down the road from Arlington Cemetery. We worked at the Bureau of Personnel, walking back and forth.

We went in to D.C. at night on the bus (sometimes by myself) and never felt afraid. People were very friendly. We met guys and went out with them. We were bused to other camps for dances. The situation was very different from today.

When coming home for Christmas in 1945, the train was so crowded that I had to sit on my suitcase in the aisle. Going back I rode between the cars from Baltimore to Washington.

As for laundry, at the camp they did our bedding and towels every week, but we had to do our personal things.

Mary McNeil

RALPH E. MONROE

TRABUCO CANYON, CALIFORNIA

Pilot, Colonel, USAF, 1941-63, WW II, Korea
Basic Training: California
Duty in European Theater; Korea

...It did not take the pilot long to have his first major crash, but he certainly was not alone. Along with other inexperienced pilots, Monroe was selected to ferry fighter aircraft to Rio De Janeiro, Brazil. Due to a lack of communication and fuel, along with bad weather, the airplanes had to make forced landings on a beach in Venezuela. There were 10 planes and they lost four and two pilots. 'There were aircraft strewn all over the beach,' Monroe remembers.

When it was his turn to land, there was no place left on the beach as planes were scattered all over. He landed so the end of his plane ran into his friend's plane in front. These two planes eventually were melded together, with his plane's back and the other's front.

The pilots were on the beach three days before they were rescued in a small boat.

When World War II began, Monroe was trained in the B-24 Liberator plane, a four-engine bomber with propeller and crew of 10.

'I flew 52 missions over southern Europe,' Monroe said. Stationed in northern Africa and then Italy, his missions included five times going over the heavily-defended Ploesti in Romania. On one of his returns from Ploesti, with an engine damaged, Monroe could not keep up with the rest of the pack and was a target for German fighter planes. Another engine was hit and he had two crew members hurt.

Monroe decided to try to land on an island in the Adriatic Sea on the way home, but the island field was strewn with other planes that had been forced to land. The pilot received word from the island tower: 'I was number 12 in the traffic pattern to crash land.'

Since they had wounded and could not parachute out, the crew took a vote and decided to try to make it back to Italy. In Bari, Italy, Monroe crash landed the plane, which had hydraulic

problems, one engine out and one engine partially gone. Since he could not brake well, the plane ran off the field but no one received additional injuries. There was, however, one surprised guard. This guard had been sneaking a nap under a cot in a tent at the end of the runway. Monroe's plane picked up the tent and contents and left the guard lying there.

During World War II, Monroe was operations officer of the 485th Bomber Group, which included four squadrons and 60 aircraft. 'For a young guy who hardly knew his own name, it was a lot of responsibility for expensive aircraft and people,' Monroe said.

He left for the war as a second lieutenant and came back from action as a major. After completing his 50-plus missions while the war was still going, Monroe was sent to Wright Patterson Air Force Base in Dayton as a test pilot. He went to test pilot school with Yeager.

In 1948 he retired out of the military as a lt. colonel.

Reprinted with permission of *The Sidney* (Ohio) *Daily News* and Christine Henderson

(See Korea section for a continuation of Col. Monroe's experiences.)

RICHARD L. MORRIS

BELLEFONTAINE, OHIO

Medic, T/5 Cpl., Army, 1943-46, WW II
Basic Training: Camp Hathway, Vancouver, WA
Duty in Germany

Our mess hall was on the ground floor next to the street, in a building taken over by the army. When we went to the mess hall and stood in line for chow, the kids would look through the windows and watch us eat. Blinds were put up so the kids could not see in. So some of us would take a child by the hand and take them in the mess hall with us. We shared our dinner with them. Soon we got orders to stop doing this. We all felt bad about it. So then the kids would wait outside and take food from our trays before it hit the garbage can. It was heart-rending.

JOHN O'CONNER

451st Bomb Group, WW II
Duty in European Theater

...With the coming of spring in Castelluccia (our permanent base), the airbase was ready and in need of some sort of revival of creative activity...

It was decided that Special Services would canvas the Group, survey the... files of all personnel, and then come up with a list of potential musicians, singers, or what have you. Those identified would be interviewed and the most eligible would be invited to audition. Hopefully the final culling would produce sufficient talent for at least a ten man show-dance band plus several vocalists.

And what about the piano, drums, guitar and accordion. Where would they come from and how much would they cost? Lt. Coffey had it all figured out. He would get Col. Eaton's OK for O'Conner to fly the "Unholy Three"—Coffey, O'Conner, and the Chaplin's pianist—to Naples Capodacina airbase. From there, Lt. Coffey's buddy, a US Navy Special Services type, would assist the three Air Force troops in locating and purchasing a used Italian piano, a hand crafted guitar, and a trap drum set complete with Turkish cymbals. The Navy would also furnish one of their trucks to haul the instruments back to Capodacina where they would be loaded into the bomb bay of O'Conner's B-24, and flown back to Castelluccia.

Except for one unforeseen hitch, that's exactly what happened. It seemed that when the old piano (and we do mean old—we only paid $50 for it) was being hoisted into the empty bomb bay of the Liberator, the retaining straps holding up the piano were improperly fastened to the bomb shackles.The flight to Castelluccia was without incident. When the 451st BG ordnance personnel attempted to off load the piano onto their GI truck, the shackles inadvertently loosened the retaining ropes, which in turn fell like the 2,000 lb. "block buster" it was, directly onto the parking apron where it,—yes—you guessed it, "exploded" into a thousand pieces! It took the better part of an hour to pick up the parts—keys, strings, pedals, hammers, etc.—clean up the mess, and haul the remaining fractured hulk to the "new" band building—the old Villa cow barn, south of Group headquarters.

Word of the great piano fiasco spread quickly through the Group. It wasn't long before two GIs, who were former piano tuners and rebuilders, offered their remedial services to Lt. Coffey. They assured him that they were quite capable of putting the piano's pieces together and rebuilding the old relic of the 1800s in time for the debut concert of the new 451st BG "Star Dusters." Believe it or not, the volunteer tuner-builders were true to their word. They not only met the SSO concert deadline, but they also spruced up the new "Steinway" so well, it looked better than the original!

In spite of the attractive facade of the new instrument, some uneasiness and apprehension on the part of most of the band members concerning the quality of the piano reconstruction—something like the "fickle finger of fate"—prevailed for several days before the "Star Dusters" debut, and continued up to curtain time on the evening of the outdoor twilight concert show.

The program got off to a rousing start, with days of hype-type build up and expectations riding high, the Group audience, including the brass and invited local guests, were "brimmed to the rim." They came to relax and enjoy themselves and the band was primed to help their audience do just that!

As the band proceeded from one tune to another, strange things began to happen to our Neapolitan antique. During the first chorus of the "San Drew Sisters" rendition of "I'll be Seeing You," the loud-soft brass pedal broke off from the piano and fell to the stage floor with a couple of loud klunks—much to the chagrin of the "Sisters" and the band. Several tunes later, while our 2nd Lt. piano soloist from the 727th BS was playing his featured arrangement of "Moonglow," two of the piano strings—middle A-flat and low C—snapped suddenly as he arpeggioed up and down the keyboard during the final ending. To add insult to injury, while band vocalist, "Sad Sack" Clamser, of Crew #11, was singing the popular "Maresy Doates"—also an audience favorite, our "Steinway Grand" literally exploded in mid-chorus, scattering strings, hammers, and several black and white keys all about the stage! The band kept playing and the "Sack" continued singing as if nothing had happened. The poor Lieutenant had enough, so he hurriedly abandoned his soloist position behind the ivories and quickly departed the stage through the side exit. As the audience laughed and guffawed, several band members shook their heads back and forth as if to say: "We told you so!"

Strangely enough, the broken piano "act" brought down the house (as well as the "Steinway"). No amount of explanation by Lt. Coffey could convince the audience that the piano's demise was not planned for the show but was the real McCoy—an actual accident—and a real disappointment for the band. It took another trip to Naples to purchase old and new replacement parts, and an extra two weeks to repair and doctor up the instrument, and to make it playable for the "Star Dusters" first Officers Club party and dance at Castelluccia. From that point on, the old piano performed like the veteran it was. It was our understanding that the "Neapolitan 88" continued to be a popular fixture at the Villa Castelluccia until the 451st BG departed for the ZI after VE Day.

Reprinted with permission from Michael D. Hill, Editor, *The Fight'n 451st Bomb Group[(H).*

LAWRENCE PIPER

ANNA, OHIO

Rifleman, Corporal, 65th Infantry Div., 3d Army, 1942-46, WW II
Basic Training: Camp Wheeler, Georgia
Duty in France, Germany, Belgium, Austria

I had read about soldiers returning home after the Civil War to the ruins of their home, mostly Confederate soldiers. Only after seeing this type of destruction first-hand can anyone know what it is.

I remember seeing at least a bushel basket of German marks in the bank we entered. The marks were useless, not a thing to buy, and money without any value.

The basic needs were food and heat. People gathered up twigs, a quarter inch in diameter or less, for cooking and heating.

The German army had horse-drawn wagons toward the end of the war because their trucks had all been bombed out and strafed and gasoline was short. They had boys in the army, eleven, twelve, thirteen years old, barely able to carry a gun.

When a horse was killed in some manner or other, the civilians would gather around with knives and pans to hack off pieces of meat and carry it away. There were children waiting at the trash cans at the mess hall, holding a container like half a Karo syrup can. Most of the GIs saved some of their chow for these hungry youngsters. The hunger was always around.

There was an older man (but younger than some called into duty for the Nazis) walking along a railroad track. He was famished. The soldiers on the train I was riding took the hard crackers from their K-rations and threw them to him. With no pride left, the traveler grabbed up the crackers and quickly forced them into his mouth with both hands.

I have gone into houses where the meal was potato soup and black bread and was still on the table, left by people fleeing the war. In many cases the people returned to their house, which was worse when they returned than when they left.

Groups of people released from concentration camps were walking the roads, both directions, with their few possessions in a little four-wheel or two-wheel cart, all happy to be free, saluting all GIs and trucks that passed. I don't know if they ever returned to where they wanted to go, and if they did, if there was anything left. This was not the glory of war, the superman or military god; this was old people, women and children with only one way to go and that was to us.

At one of the 65th division's reunions, a man I was with most of the war asked if I remembered when he and I were scouting at the head of our company and I shot through a clump of trees. Three German soldiers came out with their hands up. My buddy wanted to know how I knew these soldiers were in the trees. I didn't know anyone was in the trees. I just fired my rifle on a whim and was as surprised as he was to see the soldiers.

Another veteran at one of the reunions was telling of crossing the Danube River in an eight-man rubber boat well after dark. He and seven other men were in a boat using paddles and their rifle butts to row. They couldn't get away from the bank no matter how hard they paddled. It was discovered the engineer who loaded them into the boat tied the boat to the bank and no one had released it. This was just many of the foul-ups that happened in battle; many were far more serious.

When we first entered Germany, we saw huge signs on buildings spelling "Maggi." We all believed it had to be some kind of a drink. We finally found a bottle with a picture of a hunter sitting on a log with a dog beside him. The label said, "Maggi." We all figured this was some kind of liquor. We broke it open and all had a shot—it was barbecue sauce.

I know of two men who were killed opening bottles on shelves of a lab in a German industrial complex. No doubt other men lost their lives by not being able to read labels on bottles, cans, or anything else.

Not all casualties were enemy-inflicted. I spent some time in a Paris hospital. The man in the bed next to me had two broken legs. A French taxi driver drove on to the sidewalk and ran over him. The man with the broken legs had a girlfriend who was a nurse in England. She sent him a box filled with bottles of shampoo. She had removed the shampoo and put brandy in the bottles. That night he got looped and tried to walk on his broken legs. The hospital ward was in quite an uproar, but the man's legs were not injured. The Lord watches over drunks.

Speaking of drunks, two buddies of mine had plenty to drink (there was plenty all over Germany and France if you wanted to find it). They were searching houses for items to liberate, in other words, looting. Now these houses had been bombed. When these houses were hit, it seemed they fell apart in the partition. The whole back part of a building would be down in rubble and the front part would be standing. One man was upstairs, opened the door, stepped out and fell clear down in a pile of rubble. The second man followed in behind him, opened the door, stepped out and fell right on top of the first one. Neither man was hurt, except for a headache the next day.

I had a friend when we were both in the army air corps, prior to being sent to the infantry. He was always getting into trouble. Before we crossed the Danube River, someone said A Company was moving up. I slipped back through this woods we were in, and sure enough, here they come, all strung out along the side ditches, and I saw my friend right away. He was carrying a two-burner kerosene stove and had a pair of German pants on. When I got to talk to him, I asked what in the world he was doing with a stove. He said he got tired of eating his rations cold, and when they stopped, he was going to warm them up. I said, "What are you doing with German pants on?" "Well, I got tired of sleeping in my clothes all the time. The other night we got run out before I could get my clothes so I took these pants off a German prisoner of war." I guess you try to revert back to the way you've always been rather than being uncomfortable all the time, but it doesn't always work out.

There were a lot of other experiences I had that were not very happy, and I don't want to talk about them. My buddies and I at reunions think of the things that were funny to us, and informative, rather than the dark side of the war. I just hope that nobody else ever has to go to war any time.

RAYMOND POPPE

BOTKINS, OHIO

Tech. Sgt., 34th Reg., Army Combat Engineers, 1941-454, WWII
Basic Training: Ft. Belvoir, Virginia
Duty in Pacific

While in Basic Training at Ft. Belvoir, which is only a forty-five minute ride by bus from Washington, D.C., we had the privilege of spending much of our spare time touring our nation's capital. One Saturday morning, Senator Bankhead from Alabama was in his office and asked us in for a chat. He asked each of us our home state; then gave us a brief line-up of pending legislation. One of the bills was a pay raise from $21 to $60 per month for buck privates. We talked with him in September, 1941, and in April, 1942, we got the raise, four months after war was declared.

We left Ft. Belvoir on October 2, at 11 o'clock P.M. by train, with no knowledge of destination; woke up the next morning in North Carolina. That day we traveled through Georgia and Alabama, crossing the Mississippi River at Vicksburg, Mississippi, and arriving in Shreveport, Louisiana, by morning. We traveled from there to Houston, Texas, and across the southern part of Texas to Del Rio. We followed the Rio Grande River several miles, then headed north to Alpine and Pecos, Texas.

For the noon meal we stopped on a siding in western Texas. You could not see a tree over six feet tall and no buildings or animals except a few jackrabbits. Army cooks prepared the meals for this trip in a baggage car near the front of the train. We ate from mess kits and washed them in hot water heated on the train.

After our meal we made a large circle, about one-half mile in diameter, and at the sound of the train whistle, everyone started walking toward the center of this circle. The jackrabbits really came out of the sagebrush. They would run in circles, then run between or jump over our heads. It is amazing how high they can jump. The only rabbit we captured received a broken front leg from being hit by a mess kit thrown by one of our men. We were told by the engineer that would not have caught the rabbit if his back leg had been broken. Jackrabbits can leap with one broken back leg but cannot get into the air with a broken front leg.

Later that day another troop train pulled alongside of us at Pecos, Texas. We talked with the guys, and they were from Ft. Belvoir, having left on Sunday, October 3. They crossed the Mississippi in New Orleans, and had traveled the southern part of states we had crossed.

Our travel took us through Carlsbad, Roswell, to Albuquerque, New Mexico; from Flagstaff, Arizona, through Barstow, Bakersfield, and on to San Francisco, California. The last two days the other train had followed us. Upon arrival in San Francisco on October 9, there was another troop train setting along the siding at the piers. This train had left at a different time from Ft. Belvoir and had traveled a different route. They crossed the Mississippi River at Memphis, Tennessee. All three trains left at different times and traveled different routes but arrived at loading piers at San Francisco within the hour.

The next thing we saw was a large contingent of Military Police in full dress, forming two lines from those troop trains to the gang plank of St. Mehiel. It took less than an hour to unload 1100 men from three trains and load on to the St. Mehiel. The St. Mehiel was a German troop ship, captured in WWI, and put into service early in the year 1941. We were not told our destination, but crates in the cargo were labeled Honolulu, Hawaii.

We shipped out of San Francisco on St. Mehiel on October 10. We had not been away from port but a few minutes when a call came for all enlisted army personnel to line up for shots. We received three shots but were not told what they were for. We had our evening meal at sea. Shortly after coming up topside, we started hitting the swales, which rocked the ship. The St. Mehiel had too much width for its length, which made the ship rock more than most ships. We had roll call of all army personnel on ship. Calling the names of 1100 soldiers took a long time. Some of these men were hanging their heads over the sides, relieving themselves of their previously-eaten meal. Personally, I made it pretty good 'til the ship started to smell from those who didn't make it to the side.

We spent most of the following six days eating shoestring potatoes and lemon drops. We came topside in the evenings when it was cool and watched the movies. On October 17 we arrived in Honolulu. There was the usual scene for ships coming into port at Honolulu: Young boys around the ship diving down to retrieve coins that were thrown into the water. Women were sitting on benches with big rolls of leis, which they were selling to new arrivals.

Two lines of MPs formed a path for us to walk from ship to train. These trains were on narrow gauge track with light weight coaches and small engines. In fact, the train and engines were usually used to haul sugar cane from field to the sugar mill. We were taken to Schofield Barracks, which is up the mountain in the center of the island of Oahu. When we came to an incline, the railroad added another engine to pull up-hill.

We arrived at Schofield Barracks in the afternoon, with horrible weather. It had been raining all day, and we stood in the rain while they called off the names for the different companies. By the time we got to our barracks, we were tired and our clothes were soaked. Since our bags were made of cotton and did not shed water, as those used later, the contents were soaked, too.

The barracks in which we were housed were built just prior to our arrival, with no grass or sidewalks. Footing was muddy and slippery. Through all this dismal weather, we became a part of the 34th Engineer Regiment, activated at Schofield Barracks, October 17, 1941.

I was assigned to the motor pool and took a crash course in operating: dump truck, bulldozer, road grader, drag line, and air compressor.

October 26, 1941, we loaded all our gear and drove in convoy to the north shore of Oahu. There we lived in tents with a mission to build a railroad from Haliewa to the northern part of Oahu, the railroad to be used to move guns and supplies to defend the north shores.

At 7 o'clock A.M., December 6, three trucks headed for Ft. Kamehameha. Each of us was given a map of the island with the route lined in red and instructions to make sure we were at the supply depot by 10 o'clock A.M. The motor sergeant also told us that Hickam Field PX was a good place to eat. He told us to pick up supplies first and stop on our way home, as he wanted to make sure we got the supplies. The PX was in the same building as the mess hall for all enlisted personnel on Hickam Field. Each of us ordered a bowl of chili, large hamburger, and milkshake. The bill, 40 cents each.

Our trip back to camp followed the highway from Hickam Field around Pearl Harbor.The harbor was beautiful with five battleships, large and small destroyers, and tankers lined up at different parts of the harbor. We later learned that two of them, the Arizona and the Utah, were sunk the next day. We got back around 1 o'clock and spent the afternoon playing touch football.

That evening the first sergeant told us in camp that we were allowed to go to Kawailoa. This was a small village with a service station, general store, and bar. We didn't see many in the general store, but the bar was filled with soldiers. We had our first taste of sake, an alcoholic drink brewed on the island. We were back in camp by midnight.

The following morning, which was Sunday, one of the men from my tent went to breakfast, asked me to go along, but the sack felt good. When he came back, he told us the air force was on maneuvers, and I should see all the planes. We threw back the tent flaps and stuck out our heads, seeing 50 or 60 planes in formation coming over our area. Not realizing they were Japanese planes, we decided to let them maneuver and we'd go back to sleep.

The first sergeant blew his whistle for everyone to fall in columns of three. Some of us fell in with civilian clothes, as it was Sunday. The sergeant gave us the riot act about wearing civilian clothes when we were at war. The company commander came out and told us the Japanese planes had attacked Schofield Barracks and Wheeler Field.

There was an emergency landing field joining our camp on the north side of the island. Planes were coming to Hawaii from the States and couldn't land at Hickam or Wheeler Field, so they came out to the emergency landing field. One Japanese fighter plane followed one of these American planes. He fired on the landing plane and came over our area firing on us while we were lined up. Luckily for us, no one was hit, but we did not take time for dismissal. The plane circled over the ocean and came back over our area, but we didn't hear any shots fired.

We had not been issued guns in Hawaii as our main objective was to build a railroad. Later, a truck from Schofield brought us M-1 rifles, which we had never seen before; during basic training, we had used Springfields. We had to clean cosmoline off the guns and received instruction on how to take the M-1 apart, clean and load it; also got some safety rules.

When working on the railroad we ate from china and silver. However, starting that day, everyone had to eat from mess kits. That afternoon, we loaded a truck with the china and silverware to take back to Schofield and to pick up bread and other supplies for camp.

The trip was fine until we went through Wheeler Field on the way to our home barracks. The main street through Wheeler Field was blown up and hangars were on fire. Military Police rerouted traffic on narrow streets through officers' quarters. We had long waits at certain points, and it was getting late when we arrived at our home barracks. We drove around to the kitchen to unload dishes and silverware and to load bread. The bread was baked at the bakery in Schofield and delivered to different units in clean mattress covers.

We couldn't get the back door of the kitchen open as a bomb had been dropped on the motor pool parking lot and blacktop had been hurled on top of the kitchen. The front door opened without any trouble. We unloaded the dishes and silverware, cleaned dirt and blacktop off the bread, and loaded it on to the truck. We drove to the supply room and loaded supplies for camp.

As it was getting dark when we headed back to camp, we were instructed to use black-out lights on the truck. Black-out lights are small blue bulbs in the headlights that are focused down and to the side. We couldn't see ahead any distance. The mess sergeant watched the right side of the road so we didn't go into the ditch while I watched the left side for oncoming traffic. Wheeler Field still had some fires burning, which gave us enough light going through the officers' quarters. Highway traffic was practically nil.

We had seen soldiers guarding major bridges on our way in to Schofield earlier that day but were not aware they would be there at night. At the first bridge we heard "Halt!" We stopped, then were given the command to identify ourselves. The mess sergeant informed me that it was my duty as driver to respond. Upon giving my name and rank, we were asked to identify our organization, destination, and purpose for travel. We also had to tell the type of vehicle, describe the cargo, and give the number of people in the vehicle.

As we approached the bridge, we were ordered to stop again while three men checked the truck and contents. We were stopped at two other bridges before reaching camp.

When we arrived at camp, one of our company men was guarding the entrance. We went through the same routine as at the bridges, only this guard did not recognize my name and wouldn't give us the order to advance. The mess sergeant told me to pull up to the entrance. When we moved, we heard another "Halt!" We heard a shell go into the chamber of the rifle and were afraid our own man was going to shoot us. I asked the mess sergeant to give his name, as everyone in camp knew his name. This he did and the guard gave us the orders to enter camp.

We spent one week in camp working on the railroad, then the first platoon of Co. A was sent to Ft. Kamehameha to build ammunition dumps and gun mounts for Coast Artillery. This trip took me back the same road we had driven nine days before, and we couldn't believe the changes in Pearl Harbor. We could no longer see ships, except for the mast of two that had been sunk. Hickam Field was a mess! The PX and mess hall, where we lunched, was bombed and burned to rubble. We were told that more men lost their lives in that mess hall than any one place on land on December 7.

We worked from daylight to dark building ammunition dumps for coast guard guns. These guns were already in place, but ammunition was stored in a warehouse and had to be hauled to the guns by truck. We built underground bomb-proof storage. This required excavating down to water level, then pouring a waterproof slab. A box form was set up with reinforcing walls. There was an entrance way with baffle doorway poured all at the same time. The baffle doorway made it impossible for a direct hit. After the walls dried, we set up support beams inside, strong enough to hold the 12-inch ceiling with reinforcement. When the ceiling was poured and dried, the cement building was covered with sand, 6 feet on top, and slanted off to appear from the air as sand beach.

All companies of the 34th Engineers returned to Schofield for a Christmas Eve turkey dinner. Gifts from home, which had been kept in the supply room, were given out after dinner, and we sang Christmas Carols. Christmas Day was our first day of leisure after the war had begun; Saturdays and Sundays were work days the same as other days. On December 26, we resumed our assigned duties at Ft. Kamehameha.

We built eight ammunition dumps, then four more gun mounts for 155-M guns, which were in storage at the ordnance depot.

We built revetments around some large railroad guns. All of these guns were covered with camouflage made from chicken wire and dyed burlap so as not to be visible from the air. Four men were sent to Ft. DeRusse to bend reinforcing rods to build gun mounts and ammunition dumps in back of Ft. Shafter and on Waianae Range. We were in Ft. DeRusse for two weeks but did not get to see Waikiki Beach which was only one-half mile away.

We joined the rest of our company at Camp Malakole and built gun mounts and ammunition dumps along the crest of the mountain of the Waianae Range. One evening several of us were tossing a baseball around. One man threw the ball wildly, it glanced off the glove of another, and caught me flush on the side of my nose. My nose was broken and seemed to be under my right eye. One of the medics took me to Schofield Hospital, over an hour's drive. A doctor had to be called, as there was none in emergency. This doctor did not give me a sedative. He put me on a hospital table, strapped both arms and legs to the table, placed his thumbs on each side of my nose, and pushed it back in place. A medic helper put a splint in each nostril, then taped my nose in place. My nose was no longer numb from the blow of the ball; tears and sweat rolled from my eyes and forehead.

The doctor gave me the choice of staying overnight in the hospital or going back to the company and doing light duty for a week to ten days. The feeling toward that doctor made the decision easy—I went back to the company. The medic gave me two pain pills for then and two more for the night.

We moved from Camp Malakole back to Ft. Kamehemeha. This move made it closer for our next job of building portable pillboxes for outlying guard posts. These pillboxes were built by setting forms to pour concrete over a network of reinforcing rods with 1 by 2-ft. windows on three sides. The closed side would be dug into the side of the mountain with a window view from three sides. When the concrete was set, we took off the forms, then a crane would lift them on to a truck to haul to their destination. We built these on land between Hickam Field and Honolulu Harbor, which is now Honolulu International Airport.

Our next project was building reserve gun mounts between Tripler General Hospital and Ft. Shafter. That was a nice place to work as we could see from Pearl Harbor to Diamond Head. While on this job, I was asked to consider taking a job as clerk at a training depot. This depot was training recruits who had not been in service over three weeks. They were given basic training in Hawaii.

The following six weeks we were in Headquarters Basic Training Center at Schofield Barracks. This was a drastic change from the beautiful scenery we had been enjoying. We were working in tents setting in a gulch between two mountain ranges, with sunshine only a few hours each day. The good part was that we could visit with men fresh from civilian life, and they gave us the scoop about what was going on back in the States. We couldn't believe women were actually working in factories, and the prices of everything was going higher! Gasoline and food rationing didn't make sense to us. We spent most of the evenings in the muddy company streets talking with these recruits.

Upon returning from the training camp, I became clerk for Co. A, 34th Engineers. I was responsible for service records of all enlisted personnel of the company. My duties consisted of posting medical information in service records, changing work assignments, hospital stays, furloughs and special assignments, special schooling, scores from rifle range and court martials. The changes in pay scale through promotions and length of service were recorded. The company payroll of enlisted men was one of the major duties. We wrote letters to the Red Cross, pastors, priests, family, and lawyers for enlisted men who were having family or marital problems. We made out applications for Officers Training School and aviation cadets, transfers and discharges. For most of the 160-170 men in my company, the work was routine. Ten percent of the men seemed to require 90 percent of my time. I sometimes felt like a chaplain to some of these fellows.

I was able to attend several USO shows. Some of the stars were: Bob Hope, Francis Langford, Jerry Colona, Artie Shaw, Claude Thornhill, Boris Karloff, Helen Hayes, Maurice Evans. We saw a lot of major league ball players at Honolulu Stadium. The better known ones at the time were Al Kaline, Walt Judnick, Joe Gordon, Darlo Lodejohni, Bob Kennedy, Vince DeMaggio, Special Delivery Jones (a football player that was a top-notch baseball player). We were fortunate to see President Roosevelt when he visited the island in 1943.

In April, 1944, I was transferred to H & S Company, 1334th Engineer Combat Battalion, and put in charge of personnel, with all new clerks. Some of these clerks had no training and we were facing combat duty. We spent several nights training new clerks; then I had to do a lot of studying to learn how to meet my responsibilities. I had to take extra combat training, including rifle range, which I had not taken for over two years. One advantage for us was that personnel was put on rear echelon and did not ship out until six weeks after the advance units left.

The advance units left Hawaii on June 1, 1944, for a 17-day voyage to Saipan. Our battalion was given the duty of organizing the beachhead, selecting sites for supply dumps, and providing security for the beachhead. The rear echelon of the 27th division was stationed at Ft. Kamehameha. The personnel of our little battalion was moved into one corner of a large tent, which housed all the personnel sections of the 27th division. Communications from advance units were relayed daily to us at this tent. We, in turn, made formal reports of casualties and recorded same in service records and files of individuals affected. Fortunately, our battalion had very little work. We could take care of casualty lists in an hour most days. We spent the rest of the morning studying procedures and further training our clerks. The afternoon was free for my clerks. This gave me a chance to meet members of the 27th division and pick up pointers that we could use.

The rear echelon left Hawaii in convoy for Saipan on July 15, 1944. We were a part of the convoy from Hawaii to Eniwetok, Marshall Islands, where we were one of four ships dropped off. The other ships in convoy were joined by another convoy that was headed for the Philippines.

We spent ten days on ship at Eniwetok, and then were sent, with a destroyer on each side, to Saipan. We joined our home unit, the 1341st Engineers, in Saipan some time in August.

The heavy fighting was over by the time we arrived. There was some sniper fire and a lot of bombing at night. Most of the enemy left were in caves and hide-outs. Our biggest threat was their coming into company area at night, trying to get food. Those captured were contained in two large camps, built with chain link fence. One camp was for men, both civilian and military; the other was for civilian women.

Our first day after landing was spent receiving all the information regarding: morning reports, casualties, hospitalizations, additional shots for tropical fever, field promotions, transfers, and men on detached service to other units. All this information was to be recorded in service records as soon as possible.

Clerical personnel decided to work up to 10 o'clock P.M. until we had records up to date. The first three nights we were interrupted by Japanese air raids. Lights were turned off and we headed for trenches. These Japanese planes were small bombers and dropped anti-personnel bombs that weighed about 65 pounds. They did not make large craters but threw shrapnel over a large area. One of these bombs hit a supply tent filled with picks and shovels, which was about 100 yards from where we lay in a trench. We were stunned from the concussion, but it didn't last long and we never had any after effects from the blow.

After three nights we decided that our trying to work then wasn't practical. We put in full days and were caught up in a short time. The bombing continued almost every night. One night we watched as coast artillery put their powerful lights on some of the incoming planes and the artillery started firing. Two enemy planes were brought down and the others turned back. Later on, navy fighter planes intercepted the Japanese planes before they flew over land.

Our battalion was attached to the 4th Marine Division for landing operation on the island of Tinian. Tinian is off the south coast of Saipan, with a small body of water between the two islands. None of the people from our office were on the island of Tinian, but the majority of our men were in the landing. We could see from Saipan the full-speed operation. Large guns from ships fired on Tinian for some time before the landing forces were put into operation. It is amazing to watch the navy, marines, and army work as a unit. Our casualty list had no loss of life but actually had more minor injuries from Tinian than were recorded on all of Saipan. Our unit later was awarded the Presidential Unit Citation for Tinian Operation.

All personnel on the island of Saipan were hit by Dengue fever. We were given shots, but sooner or later everyone came down with it. The hospital was full of more serious cases, so every man with fever was instructed to stay on his bunk with a mosquito net over him. All my clerks were bedfast at one time or another, as was I. A patient just lies on the bunk shivering and sweating. We were told to drink lots of water and eat.

Once the Dengue fever was over, we had to make a payroll for four months. This was a tough job, as some men had been promoted in the field, others had drawn supplemental pay on passbooks, and others had charged for PX books. We had men who had been put on hospital ships and sent away without records; some men were lost in action. We were required to put every man on payroll, regardless of status. We encouraged the men to send most of their pay home to their bank or put it into soldiers' savings. We sent the payroll to the 10th Army financial office for approval and payment. That was the largest payroll we were involved with, and it came back in Japanese invasion money. There were no coins; everything was in paper. It took ten yen to make a sen; one sen was worth one penny. This made for large stacks of paper money. Each company commander brought his first sergeant to battalion headquarters to help clerks count each man's pay and put it into envelopes. That night there was one big poker game in the mess hall! Some men actually lost every piece of money they earned in four months of battle.

The army made plans in October, 1944, to rotate men back to the States for rest and relaxation. All men in our battalion were eligible for rotation. However, the men who came to Hawaii in October, 1941, had more time overseas. Our battalion was short on men, as we had not received any replacements since leaving Hawaii. The decision was to send ten men per month until all men had been rotated; if replacements arrived, a larger number could be rotated. Ten were sent in October, ten in November, and ten in December. Yours truly was pulled for the December quota.

There were planes taking men and cargo to the Philippines and making stops at Saipan on the way back. These planes would pick up men going on rotation. The ten of us were taken to the airport to wait for a plane. The first plane through picked up men from the hospital in Saipan to go to Hawaii for further treatment. There was room for eight of us on this plane. A sergeant from Company B and I volunteered to wait for the next plane, making it possible for the other eight to leave. We waited all night for another plane. The plane we left on was a C-55 transport and had only ten men on board, besides the crew.

We left Saipan as day was breaking. It was a pretty morning and the view was wonderful. Within an hour, it was blue in every direction. Occasionally you could see white waves on the water below.

We landed on Kwajalein Island and had a good meal at the army mess. This island had been captured by American forces about a year previously and still showed the effects of heavy battle scars. The palm trees were split in half, some cut off at ground level, and others cut off higher. There were still craters in the sand from bomb blasts during the invasion. There were a few goonie birds along the beach.

The plane left Kwajalein around nine o'clock P.M. with a full load of mail and men from all branches of service. One motor on the plane burned out and we made an emergency landing on Johnston Island. Circling it before landing put fear in my soul. That island looked like a match box! The landing strip ran from shore to shore. We came in low over the water, and just before hitting the strip, the pilot gave the three motors full throttle. We hit the water at the end of the landing strip. The water splashed the wings and there was a lot of yelling. There were over 100 people on board who thought, the same as I, that we had landed in the ocean.

All personnel ate at one mess hall on Johnston Island and it was open 24 hours each day. While the mechanics on the island repaired the engine, we walked over for breakfast. Within two hours, we climbed aboard, and were headed for Hawaii.

That night, after landing at Hickam Field, we loaded on the Luraline for the trip to San Francisco. The Luraline was a passenger ship from Matson Ship Lines that made regular trips from San Francisco to Honolulu. There were soldiers, sailors, marines, coast guard, and civilians on the liner. Women and children were on top deck, service nurses below. Officers of all services next; enlisted men were on all the lower decks. In fact, there were bunks three tiers high put into cargo space.

Merchant Marines operated the ship and the Marine Corps was security. There were marine guards at all steps going from one deck to the other. We were not allowed above fifth deck. The food was excellent and the galley was clean. There was a ship store, open two hours in the morning and afternoon, that sold magazines, playing cards, toilet articles, cigarettes, candy, and other small items. The Luraline had no escorts as it traveled so fast that the fear of submarines or any type of enemy ships' attack was unthinkable.

On arrival at San Francisco we were taken by ferry to Angel Island. This ferry took us around Alcatraz so we got to view that island from three sides. We were given lectures on how important it was for us to keep warm. We also were given the usual lectures on sexually-transmitted diseases and how the army dealt with soldiers contracting these diseases. Special care was taken when fitting the newly-issued winter uniforms to make a good impression of the armed services.

From Angel Island we were taken by ferry to Oakland, California, for loading on a troop train. There were ten coaches on this train, with a kitchen, dining and baggage car. Each coach was loaded for a different destination in the States. Our coach was the last one and was assigned for Jefferson Barracks, St. Louis.

We left Oakland that evening and the next morning woke up in Idaho. The snow was three feet deep and the natives were wearing snow boots, fur-lined coats and heavy hats and gloves. The train stopped on a siding in a small town. There were soldiers running all over town in shirt sleeves. We came to the conclusion that the lectures about keeping warm were not heeded. We were of the opinion the lectures on sexuality would be remembered about the same way.

There were three or four Military Police on the troop train and they had a hard time rounding up soldiers. Our coach set on a siding in Kansas City to be picked up by a mail train running from Kansas City to St. Louis. We were given breakfast at the railroad terminal in Kansas City and given box lunches for the noon meal. Some army men, carrying box lunches for our evening meal, met us at St. Charles, Missouri.

Our coach was dropped off just before entering the St. Louis Union Station, and another engine pulled our coach and four box cars down to Jefferson Barracks. We were taken from the warm coaches to a cold, wooden frame barracks with no heat and only one blanket for each bunk. We put on all the clothes we had and crawled under the blanket. We were processed and given our furloughs at 2 o'clock P.M., December 20, 1944.

When reporting back on January 19, 1945, for our return to the South Pacific, we were given another ten-day leave. On January 29 we reported again and were given a five-day leave. On February 4, 1945, we left in a pullman coach attached to the rear of a fast passenger, direct to Des Moines, Iowa, where our coach was transferred to the rear of a troop train. We had to walk through all the other coaches on this troop train to a dining car near the front of the train. The men on this train had completed basic training in Texas. When they learned that we were Pacific veterans, they questioned us as we walked through their coaches. It was interesting to see their reactions.

This train took three days going from Des Moines to Seattle. While setting on a siding near Portland, Oregon, we could see men, with long poles with a spear on the end, pushing logs away from the piling of a railroad bridge. We watched these men jump from log to log, pushing other logs around to keep them moving past the bridge. One of the men on our coach said he felt safer in the war zone than being on those logs.

For five mornings in Seattle, while waiting for shipping orders, we answered roll call. We were given passes to go downtown Seattle for the evening. There were a lot of women working at Kaiser Ship Yards from all over the United States. They lived with three or four in one-room apartments and ate all meals at restaurants. The night spots were filled by 3 o'clock P.M. and were still jumping by 3 o'clock A.M. At one club we had to wait in line to enter at 7 o'clock P.M. When one party left, the doorman would let that same number enter. A friend and I were standing at the front of the entrance line when a girl came to the doorman and said she had room for us two at her table. He informed her that two people had to leave before we could come through the entrance. She stood beside the doorman until we were allowed to enter and led us to the table. Her roommate was holding the table.

These girls were from a small town in Washington and were sharing a one-room apartment with kitchenette. They had worked at Kaiser for over a year and had boyfriends in the service. They usually ate their evening meal and then came to this night club to dance. By coming around 6 o'clock P.M., they could get a table before the crowd arrived. This gave them the opportunity to choose their dance partners. They insisted on buying the first round and would drink only one alcoholic drink. They were to report to work at 11 o'clock P.M. Their policy was never to give out their phone number or address, either at Seattle or at home. They were good dancers and wonderful hosts. They bid us goodbye at 10 o'clock; we stayed until midnight and danced with other women. The line at the door was longer at midnight than when we arrived at 7:00. Other night spots we attended were not as well organized and were infested with prostitutes and other people of questionable character.

Upon arrival at Ft. Kamehameha in Hawaii, I received orders to stay there to help process records for men in transit. Some of these men were headed for the States and others were headed for the war zone. We were present when the Japanese Americans returned from serving at Anzio Beachhead in the invasion of Italy. These men were in bad shape, missing arms and legs and had other scars. Most of them were sent to Tripler General Hospital for rehabilitation and receiving artificial limbs. Many of these men's records were missing and very few records were complete. We had to get a ruling from the Attorney General's office to admit some to the hospital.

In April, 1945, 140 of us left by ship for Okinawa. We crossed the International Date Line on May 8, going from May 7 to May 9. It so happened that May 8 was V-E Day. When the news came over the radio on May 9, there was a lot of hooping and howling—lucky there were no arms available to fire. A few days later we heard of discharges being given to those men with over 85 points. Most of us had well over 100 points. We tried to turn the ship around and head back to the States, but it continued to Guam.

Our company unloaded from the troop ship to a small LST (Landing Ship Tank). The landing ship took us from Guam to Saipan, where we joined about 50 LSTs, a flag ship, and a host of destroyers for convoy to Okinawa. The trip took 11 days. On the sixth day we noticed all the LSTs were scattered, and we couldn't see the flagship. We were told there was a typhoon coming and these ships scattered to keep one ship from hitting the others during high winds.

Raymond Poppe, Courtesy *The Sidney* (Ohio) *Daily News*

The typhoon hit about midnight. Within a short time all hatches were closed and fans circulated air throughout the living quarters. Waves raised the front of the ship up high, then it would slam down on the water. There was a sudden jar, then the whole ship would vibrate. Our cargo was ammunition, with large racks of projectiles stacked in the tank bay. Needless to say, we didn't sleep, and there was a lot of praying.

The next afternoon, when the hatches were opened and all casual troops were brought top deck for roll call, we had to hold to each other to stand up. Waves were still coming overboard at times, getting us wet. For the balance of the trip to Okinawa we played cards at night and slept most of the day. We landed from the China Sea on the western side of Okinawa.

A truck from our battalion picked up 14 of us returning after an absence of five to seven months. Upon arrival we were informed that one-half of the original men had been rotated to the States; replacements had been added for the Okinawa operation. We were no longer attached to the 27th Division but working under the island command. Our battalion was located just north of Naha Harbor, and a lot of ships were still in the harbor.

We saw a Japanese Kamikaze, in a glider pulled by a plane, make a hit on the harbor. At a certain point the glider, loaded with explosives, was released from the plane and the Kamikaze nose-dived the glider into the harbor, just missing a battleship. The explosion was worse than any single bomb. The blast threw water and debris high in the air.

Our battalion was moved to the north end of the island. We had a few bombings there, but most of the Japanese planes were going for ships and more concentrated places in the southern part. The original members, who did not have leave, were ordered back to the States for discharge. Our unit of 650 men was losing over 200. This put our unit at two-thirds strength. Those 200 plus service records had to be updated to ship with the men leaving in August, 1945.

On September 10, 1945, we received orders to ship to the States all men with 85 points or over. This included yours truly as well as all men with the original 34th Engineer regiment. We heard on the radio of the truce being signed on the Battleship Missouri on September 2. There was no jubilant celebration but a good feeling—no more air raids, and we were making ready to go home.

We boarded a ship for the happy journey home on September 21. We arrived at San Diego and were put on a troop train for Camp Atterbury the following day. I was discharged from Camp Atterbury, Indiana, October 12, 1945. It took me four years, three months and ten days to fulfill one year of selective service.

ROSELYN (Ross) PRICE

SIDNEY, OHIO

Photography Lab Assistant, Map maker, Cpl., WAACs, 1943-45
Basic Training: Ft. Oglethorpe, GA
Duty: March Field, California; Pentagon

I joined the WAACs (Women's Army Auxiliary Corps) which was later changed to the WACs (omitting the Auxiliary), hoping to go overseas; however, I was sent to California to mix chemicals for a photography lab. From there I went to the Pentagon and prepared maps for military planning.

My fondest memory is of President Franklin D. Roosevelt, and his dog, Fala, coming to the base to review the troops. The order, Eyes Right, at that time was the thrill of a lifetime.

I was the youngest non-commissioned officer in our company and was pleased to be voted as the prettiest non-commissioned officer on March Field, which was published in the field newspaper.

RICHARD W. RICKEY

SIDNEY, OHIO

Gunner, M/Sgt., Air Force, 613th Bomb Squadron, 1940-63, WW II

Basic Training: Ft. Knox, KY

Duty in Europe

I was a gunner for more than seventeen years, starting in 1941, on an O-47 observation plane. There had been a notice on the bulletin board asking for volunteers. We trained by shooting a water-cooled machine gun mounted on a tripod. This shooting was done from a prone or sitting position.

On this O-47 there was a pilot, a photographer, and the gunner. A single .30 caliber machine gun, mounted on a track that formed a semi-circle around the rear seat, was the only defense. To use the gun, the canopy was opened and the weapon maneuvered into position.

I flew a few flights in the front turret of two B-10s. Then on to an AT-6. To fire from this plane, you opened the canopy, ignored the air blasts and prop wash, and cut loose. I moved on to A-20s and A-24 dive bombers.

My first combat mission (B-17) was on January 6, 1944, in Germany. We returned after six more; but on the next one, March 2, 1944, we were returning from a raid on Frankfurt when, over Belgium, our tail gunner called out, "Five fighters at 6 o'clock!" Incendiaries hit the primer system near the copilot, setting the cockpit afire.

With the cockpit blazing and the fighters pressing their attack, the pilot ordered us to bail out. Those still alive bailed out, the pilot and I exiting through the bomb bay. No jumping practice had been given, but we really didn't hesitate. I wasn't as scared then as later. We went out at about 23,000 feet. The P-51 that was our escort flew along beside me and helped to protect me as I fell to the ground.

As I got near the ground I could see a group of people staring up at me. My chute caught in a tree, leaving me hanging a couple of feet off the ground. Helpless and scared, I prepared for the worst as the people came running toward me.

Seven or eight civilians started babbling to me in French and then one man spoke up in English. He explained that they could not help me because they thought the Germans had probably seen me coming down, too. They gave me a bottle of coffee and a sandwich. Then they quickly disappeared and left me alone in enemy-held Belgium.

Confused and frightened and with my face badly burned, I knew I had to move quickly. I guess I did everything wrong, according to survival experts. I lost my gloves on the way down and my hands were frozen. Luckily, I was wearing the English-type quick-release harness. I slipped out of it easily and dropped to the ground. My chute was stuck in the tree, though, and I couldn't shake it loose. So I left it there. I also left my other gear, including my wool flying boots. This was a mistake because I was really cold, and there was snow on the ground, but I could make better time without them.

Not knowing which way to go, I headed toward a woods and walked from about 2 o'clock until dark. I hiked on the next day, but saw no one 'til about dark, when I spotted an old man collecting wood in the forest. He saw me, too, and we just stood staring at each other for a couple of minutes. He was probably just as scared as I was.

I took out my phrase book from my survival kit and stumbled through some phrases. He couldn't understand, so I pointed to the phrases in the book. This old man helped me get in touch with the underground, and I started a clandestine life that lasted for the next six months. Having been given civilian clothes and counterfeit credentials, I passed from one underground cell to another. Plans were made many times to slip into France, but something always happened to stop them. My face became infected and sometimes I could hardly see through the slits formed by my swollen eyelids.

As I moved from place to place, I ran into our bombardier and pilot who had also been picked up by the underground. Eventually there were four of us. We were turned over to a farmer who found a small cave for us to live in. We ate well, at least better than if we had been prisoners. Some things the family had plenty of and others they didn't; but they shared everything with us, although they were risking their necks just to keep us.

Our cave was only a few miles from a German air base and we watched the Me110s and Fw190s scramble to intercept Allied bombers.

On one occasion, while eating dinner with friendly Belgium farmers, three German soldiers suddenly knocked on the door. I and the other Americans darted out the back door and took cover in the woods. Later we learned that the unsuspecting Germans were merely begging food and did not know of our presence.

Finally, the underground informed us we should move westward where the Americans were advancing. With four new German bicycles, we left on a 72-mile trip. For us, who were quite out of shape, it was difficult trying to keep up with our underground escort. As we rode our bikes we passed some Germans, but they didn't pay any attention. They were as scared as we were because they were in retreat at that time.

When we arrived at a barn within earshot of a German army encampment, we found fourteen other downed airmen. After a week there, the entire group one night was moved into the Ardennes Forest to a four-hut camp where we joined twelve more Americans. We were practically under the nose of the Germans.

The Germans had been retreating down a nearby road so we had to be careful when wandering outside the camp. One day another fellow and I were out on a food pickup when we heard voices. Someone shouted, "Chicago." We held our breath and the same thing was repeated. Deciding that the voices must be Americans, we walked out of the brush and right into Rangers accompanied by an underground worker.

On another occasion we had to cross a bridge guarded by German soldiers. I approached the guard and showed him my forged identification papers, complete with the Swastika stamp; he waved me through without a word. Any questioning meant certain capture because I could not speak the language except for one or two words that I had tediously memorized.

We went to Paris on a truck, where we were put in a stockade with German prisoners of war until we were debriefed. We were out of uniform, of course, and had no papers at all to tell who we were. When they questioned me and I said I was from

Sidney, Ohio, the officer in charge asked how far it was from Sidney to the next biggest town. I said it was eight or nine miles to Piqua. He replied, "You're okay. I'm from Piqua."

When they decided we were okay, they put us up in a hotel and gave us some money. We didn't get our clothes replaced, however, until we were back in England. We were still in the underground clothes. And we still were not to contact anyone until we had more clearance. We were sitting in a bar saying how we would like to let our wives know we were alive, because we had been listed as Missing in Action. A foreign correspondent happened to be there in the bar and heard our conversation. She came up and said: "Give me your names and hometowns and I'll put in the paper that I talked with you. Probably somebody will call your wives and let them know you are okay." Sure enough, our wives received many calls and many newspaper clippings.

We were returned to the United States and remained there until the end of the war and my discharge. After two and a half years as a civilian, I returned to the Air Force. At that time, the Strategic Air Command (SAC) was the thing, with its B-29s. I was put on these Superforts as a scanner. Then I moved into B-36s in 1949. These planes would run forty-two hours without refueling. The world record was set for flying without refueling. We were on photo reconnaissance, flying a lot over England, Italy and and North Africa, and practicing in the United States. These B-36s became obsolete and were replaced by the all-jet B-52s.

We weren't sent to Korea because we were the only ones that could go to Russia, if need be, so they reserved us for that. SAC had bombing competitions with B-36s and B-29s, and my group won. We were in photo reconnaissance at the time, and as Gen. LeMay handed me the winning cup, he said, "I congratulate you men, but bombing is my business."

With gunnery, I think much of the adventure has gone out of it. There used to be a closer association between man and weapon. The repeated jolts of the .50s as they roared their defiance and the pungent odor of burnt gunpowder stirred men's instincts. Modern-day remote control turrets guided by radar impulses are far more accurate and deadly, but you lose the personal feel. (In later model B-52s, the tail gunner was up with the pilots and controlled the gun through radar—had a closed circuit TV.)

We were in an alert squadron, stationed in Amarillo, Texas. The crew members slept underground; when the buzzer sounded, we could be airborne within six minutes in our B-52s. Nuclear missiles were kept in them. All we knew was what we needed to know; we didn't even know our target. So if we were shot down, we couldn't disclose anything. I was the tail gunner on the last plane to have a tail gunner.

We had 24-hour missions, flying to New York, to the Atlantic Ocean, across Canada as far north as possible. Canada didn't like us flying over with those bombs, so we had to fly up north as far as we could.

There were always so many B-52s in the air at all times. They refueled in the air. There were three pilots; six bunks so we could sleep. Had a two-or-three burner stove so we could cook; had an oven with places to put six or so lunches, similar to TV dinners. Sometimes we had cold sandwiches, which were packed in dry ice. There was a bathroom with a little stool, similar to what is used in campers now. No one on board had medical training, but we did carry morphine. It was checked out just before takeoff and then returned immediately after landing.

Richard W. Rickey

B-17's Courtesy Richard W. Rickey

The plane's cruising speed was around 450 or 500 miles per hour, at a height of 40-50,000 feet. Got better mileage up there; tried to hit a tail wind.

All crew members but the tail gunner had an ejection seat. We pulled a lever and the whole tail jettisoned from the aircraft. The tail gunner unbuckled himself from the seat and stepped out. The parachute opened automatically at about 12,000 feet. Rafts hooked on to the parachute.

At the time of the Cuban Crisis, we were called out by President Kennedy. I was at home but on alert. When we got in the plane, we never knew until we were in whether it was real or practice. But this time we stayed up for hours and then were called back. The alert planes were loaded with two hydrogen bombs all the time.

One time while sitting in a bar, a guy was bragging because he flew 4,000 miles without an accident. After a while I got tired of listening to him so said, "What's so great about that? I flew more than that in the last couple of days."

ROGER ROESSER

SIDNEY, OHIO

Construction, Co. D, 34th Engineers; 476th Maintenance unit
Duty at Pearl Harbor; European Theater

Just fresh out of boot camp, Roger Roesser had no idea what was happening when he saw planes with a funny red insignia on their wings buzz over his primitive Army camp near the Kanoehe Naval Air Station as Roesser was walking to breakfast that fateful morning 50 years ago.

"They had that big ball on the wings," Roesser said. "I asked my squad leader what they were and he said they were new Navy planes." Roesser said his squad leader was usually wrong about things and such was the case with his guess about the low-flying planes.

Roesser and others in his camp had no way of knowing that history was unfolding just over a mountain ridge as those odd-looking planes, flown by Japanese pilots, were pounding the air station and other military targets in Hawaii as the attack on Pearl Harbor threw the United States into World War II...

Roesser said he heard machine guns blasting but he thought it was just US planes making practice runs. "Until we heard the bombs, we thought it was just maneuvers." When the bombs hit the air station, thick clouds of black smoke rose up over the mountain ridge that separated Roesser's Army camp from the Kanoehe Naval Air Station.

Although the attack on Pearl Harbor was by far the most devastating, bombs dropped by Japanese planes also left death and destruction in the wake at Kanoehe and other military installations on the island of Oahu. "It (the attack of Kanoehe) was just a drop in the bucket," Roesser said. "We knew something was wrong, but we didn't know what it was. We didn't think it was anything serious. We went on over and ate breakfast."

It wasn't until the commander of Roesser's company... drove into the camp some three hours after the attack that the terrible news hit home. "When we heard it, we were all ready to fight the Japs." he said.

And they thought they would get their chance to battle the enemy..."They (commanders) told us that they were going to invade. We were told that they would be wearing blue dungarees and red arm bands."

Roesser's company was not a fighting unit, but rather was sent to Hawaii to do construction work. When the word of the Japanese attack reached the camp, the soldiers scrambled for their .30-caliber rifles. The only problem was, they didn't have ammunition clips for the rifles. Roesser said they had to feed one shell in at a time.

Roesser's unit of about 120 soldiers quickly made the approximate half-mile journey to the air station. When they arrived, some of the Navy men who survived the aerial assault wanted to know why the Army soldiers took so long to show up. "We told them 'we couldn't have done you any good, anyhow, we had rifles and no ammunition.'"

The soldiers quickly dug foxholes along the coast line and braced themselves for the rumored invasion. By evening they had received ammunition clips they needed for the new rifles.

"I don't think anyone slept that night." A few days later the imminent threat of invasion had passed and more information about the destruction at Pearl Harbor began to flow to units in other areas of Hawaii. He later received a special detail assignment at Pearl Harbor, but did not have time to see the full scope of the destruction.

Roesser and others serving in the military quickly realized after the attack that their one-year stint in the service would be much longer. "We were told that we were in for the duration plus six months," Roesser recalled.

What he had thought would be a one-year tour in the Army when he was drafted on July 3, 1941, turned into four years, three months and 15 days...

In the months folowing Pearl Harbor, Roesser was transferred to the 476th Maintenance unit at Schofield Barracks. Roesser worked in a machine shop that made parts for heavy equipment, such as bulldozers and graders.

Before his time in the service was up, Roesser was assigned to the European Theatre, as well as the Pacific. When the war ended in 1945, Roesser was serving with a unit in Austria...

Reprinted with permission from *The Sidney* (Ohio) *Daily News* and Tom Millhouse.

MARION RUSSELL

SIDNEY, OHIO

Sgt., U. S. Army Air Corps, WW II
Duty in Africa, Sicily, Italy

...One of the features of overseas life I shall always remember were the almost nightly gatherings we fellows had in our tents after darkness had enveloped the airdrome. Even during the off-duty hours our lives had sort of a routine. We would inevitably shed all burdensome clothing, get out our pipes and cigarettes, make coffee, and then sit around talking about everything from sex to senators.

And in those most informal of all conversations there were usually several remarks about our respective hometowns. There might be a man from Iola, Kansas, or New York City, or Follansbee, West Virginia, or Sidney, Ohio, and to each representative of a particular town it was always *the garden spot of the world* to him. That hometown occupied a special place in his heart, memories of it influenced his dreams, some of his hopes were based on its progress.

It really doesn't matter if a hometown is big or small. In many cases it is no more than a word. But the things contained therein are what really count. It is wonderful for me to visualize the thousands of American hometowns and the infinite influence they hold for millions of men and women scattered over the world...

When I stepped down from the bus last Thursday evening and felt the firmness of Sidney's streets under my feet for the first time in well over two years, I felt no emotional exultation like you read about in a make-believe story. I was happy to be back, of course, but instead of showing an outward jubilance I felt an inward feeling of reverent thankfulness. I was humbly grateful that Destiny had permitted me to come back again for a little while.

As I strolled slowly along toward my home on Maple Street, gawking at all the once-familiar places with hurried glances, I must have resembled the country boy arriving in a big city for the first time. My first impression was that my hometown hadn't changed. It was the same. But then I became practical and realized nothing is changeless. Then I forgot all about Sidney for several minutes and my pace quickened as I came nearer home. I could think only of meeting Mother and Dad and I hoped I would be able to say the right things.

Mother's embrace was warm and tender. She was smiling just as when I left her on a bleak March day two years ago. Dad and I clasped hands more firmly than ever before and in his wind-tanned face I could see a quiet happiness. I prided myself that in their eyes I could detect a joy and satisfaction which came from the realization that "that boy of theirs had come home."

...I got a big kick out of meeting all those with whom I once worked. Some faces have gone and added work has been placed upon the shoulders of those who remained. All of which is an accepted part of war-time business; everyone must do a great deal more than was usual in those halcyon pre-war days.

...There in the popular confectionery, where I used to drink scores of cokes, about the only change I could notice was in the display cases. They weren't so full as when I left; but here again the reason was all too obvious.

...It was during my conversation with the Papas family that I began to realize what the biggest change in Sidney was. It's the absence of young men and women who have entered the armed forces, many of whom I used to pal around with. I feel a touch of nostalgia when I walk down the street and the old familiar faces fail to appear. I miss the old-time friends when I see so many girls walking along without male escorts. But the empty feeling doesn't last long because somehow you know that someday they'll come back and you'll meet them again.

Aside from the changes mentioned, the old hometown is just about the same to me. Of course, if I were to be here for a long period of time and learned to think of things from a civilian standpoint again, the number of changes would become more numerous I suppose. I have come to look upon things more casually since being overseas and I am unable to grasp the significance of the events which have occurred here since I left.

I shall always remember how courteously and pleasantly everybody has treated me since I arrived...renewing acquaintances with relatives and old-time friends with whom I had spent so many happy moments in the past...feeling a gentle tug at my heart strings as I looked into cradles and beheld newly-arrived babies...of how my sister Wilma started tussling with me about fifteen minutes after we met again...and learning more and more that in friendship, love, and sincerity you have indestructable qualities which wars and rumors of wars can never take away.

I shall return to the army routine on June 1st. It will be hard leaving all this. I suppose there will be many lonely moments where my next assignment takes me, but just having been here for a few days will enable me to combat them most readily. I wouldn't be surprised if a tear appeared in my eyes when I remember the happy moments I spent here.

Sidney will always occupy a special place in my heart. I sincerely hope and pray that her wandering service men will soon be back. And I shall always be grateful if Sidney will permit me to come back at different times as I travel along the highways of life—just for a few moments of relaxation, companionship and a renewal of my appreciation of the things in life that really matter.

Reprinted with permission from an article. Marion wrote for *The Sydney* (Ohio) *Daily News, June, 1943.*

JOHN SEARLE

PERRYSBURG, OHIO

60 mm Mortar Squad Leader, T/5, Third Army, K Company, 355th Infantry Regiment, 89th Division, 1944-46, WW II
Basic Training: Ft. McClellan, Alabama
Duty in Germany

As we loaded up that evening, many of us said for the umpteenth time, "This is it!" I looked around at our platoon in that truck and thought any one or all of us could very well get killed in this. I don't believe it had really dawned on me up until then that we might actually lose some of these men.

When we finally arrived at the edge of the village where the other company was dug in, our trucks slowed down to a crawl. We could see even in the dark that the ditches alongside the road were full of GIs. Out of the darkness someone said, "Go get 'em, K Company. It's your turn now." Nobody ever talked like that before and I don't remember anyone ever talking like that again. I felt, for the first time, real fear.

We got out of the trucks fully equipped. I had the barrel and two legs of my mortar buckled up and in my right arm. Over my right shoulder, but slung on my left side, was a large canvas pouch in which I carried the base plate. The entire weapon weighed forty pounds! I have checked on that. We had dumped our packs and sleeping bags in a company truck. I had the usual stuff around my waist, my pistol belt, gun, knife, canteen, first aid kit, plus those extra clips for the pistol. We walked to the north edge of that village and saw tracer bullets ricocheting up into the cloud cover. They came from a German machine gun. I wondered why someone didn't order us to drop a few rounds on it since we could plainly see its muzzle flash.

Orders were whispered along our line and we filed off into a field, down what would pass for a lane on a Wood County farm, and out into the fields east of that little village. We were in extended formation, five yards between men, in double column. Once in a while a jeep would be seen slowly moving between our moving lines. We walked all night. The night was fairly bright, some ground fog. All night long there were explosions going off several hundred yards ahead and on both sides of our moving column. I thought it was from our own 81 mm. mortars. The diary says it was from our artillery. Their fire protected us all night long. We walked for fifty minutes and rested for ten. As the hours wore on, my shoulder got sorer and sorer with the weight of that mortar. All my ammo bearers were loaded down with shells, so they couldn't spell me. My shoulder hurt, my arms ached. I tried shifting that thing from one shoulder to the other; I tried carrying it under my arm, anything to get some relief. It was a long night.

Finally, we detected that faint lightness which precedes the dawn. About this time we came to the edge of a wooded area. We were still following a country lane which took a sudden right angle turn and began to descend. We went several hundred yards on a downward slope when abruptly the lane made a sharp hairpin turn and descended some more in the opposite direction. It had become extremely foggy! In fact, the lighter the day got, the foggier it became. We could see but a few feet in front of us. Finally, our officers called a halt. A jeep pulled up and a forward observer from our artillery got out and spoke to Captain Brown. The jeep had a radio which explained how that friendly artillery fire followed up so well all night.

The officers knew in general where we were. They ordered us to set up our three mortars along that lane and aimed in the general direction we had been moving during the night. We set our aiming stakes, got the weapons lined up on them, and waited. Our asistant gunners had already pulled the safety pins on one round each. On command we all three fired. There was a loud whump, and then we waited. We had fired at a range of well over 500 yards, as I recall. Incidentally, a mortar shell goes like a punted football... way up, turns over, and comes down. I have no idea what we thought we were shooting at. We had been so quiet all night except for the artillery fire that it seemed odd that we were about to announce our presence loudly, if not accurately.

The Company was sprawled along that lane trying to get some rest. I still recall the absolutely startled look on our faces when that explosion of three mortar shells, all going off together, came thundering back at us. It echoed and re-echoed up and down... what turned out to be the Mosel River Gorge! We had fired down into a wide, deep, long river valley. As soon as that first reverberation stopped, one of the riflemen back down the line was heard to shout, "Reveille, you Kraut bastards!"

We fired three rounds each, all in unison. After announcing our arrival to every German who lived up and down that river valley, we continued to walk the rest of the way down those switchbacks until we got into the little town of Ernst. It had 500 or 600 inhabitants, I would guess, no more than a thousand. The town seemed empty of people. We put out outpost guards, got ourselves situated in certain buildings, got as familiar with the place as we could while moving around in dense fog. Meanwhile, it was getting on toward sunrise. As the sun warmed the place, it lifted the fog. And suddenly it became clear that we were stuck in Ernst. German gun emplacements were scattered all up and down the east side of that gorge! We could not get out at least until dark and no one could get in to us. The switchback road we had used was now in plain sight to anyone looking from the other side of the river. We noticed that we had gone down through huge grape arbors from which Mosel wine was made in that area. After the fog lifted, we could not move around openly in those streets. Whatever we had brought in with us in the way of jeeps, ammo, food, and medical supplies would have to do us until we could get out or some trucks could get in.

A German machine gun began firing into our town. The streets in Ernst all pointed from the hill toward the river. Thus only the alleys were safe from German observation. That machine gun caught Jim Hensen on a street and in the open. The rest of our squad was in an alley. We heard the gun begin to shoot, Jim begin to swear, and then the sound of his boots as he raced ahead of the bullets. He came running toward our alley, skidded around the corner into safety, banged up against the building, and with chest heaving and eyes wide as saucers, he blurted in shocked amazement, "Why... that sonofabitch tried to *kill* me!" We laughed ourselves silly. Strange how it took a while for the seriousness of all this to soak in.

Lt. Adams yelled for us to come along with him. We realized we were about to get in our first fire fight. I felt... not fear, but... exhilaration. We put our mortar in a fairly open space within a combination grape arbor and orchard, making certain no tree limbs were immediately overhead. That German machine gun had been joined by several others. Then we began hearing our own guns. We got set up and were ready for firing data, range, etc., when one of our riflemen gave out a yelp, swore, and loudly proclaimed he had been shot in the neck and wanted a medic as of right now! I heard Chuck Lichwald growl, "If he's shot in the neck, how come he can still make so much noise?" He actually was grazed by a bullet, but it did not hurt him seriously, just burned him good.

We could see little spurts of dirt flying up around our gun. The realization that we were being shot at came to us all at once. We moved in a hurry to better cover. We were in fire fights the rest of that day, stayed awake a good part of that night, and had more fights the next day. Only by now, some German guns were firing on us from our side of the river.

In late afternoon word came down that second and fourth platoons were to load up on what jeeps and trailers we had and get back up that switchback road and work our way south and occupy the next two small villages along the river. We all understood we would be under German fire all the way up, from the moment we cleared the buildings on the edge of town until we got safely around the top of the hill and hidden in those woods.

We dumped our mortar somewhere, I don't remember where, and climbed into a trailer. There were at least six or eight of us. This whole line would be composed of ten or twelve jeeps, each pulling a trailer—sixty or seventy men in all.

That ride was exciting to say the least. Our driver kept that little jeep in second gear all the time, with the engine howling away. I wanted to crawl up under my helmet. Every other switchback I was on the outside of the hill, nearest to the Germans firing at us. We could hear those snapping sounds as bullets went by us. The Krauts must have had what we would call a "shooting gallery" view of us, with the targets going back and forth as the road switched back and forth. I suppose it was only a few minutes, five at the most, that we were under that kind of fire, and completely unable to shoot back. Finally we turned into the woods, ran several hundred yards farther on to be certain the tail end of the column was clear and well protected. Then we piled out to take stock of the damage. There were a few shot-out headlights, as I remember, a couple of flat tires, two or three busted windshields, even though they were folded down on top of the jeep hoods, three or four slight wounds... and one very dead soldier, Herman Casey, a rifleman from Salem, Indiana. He had taken a bullet in his head. He probably died instantly. I have thought several times since then that I might go see his folks. But what could I say? I have not gone to see them. Then our column moved up river to the village of Ellenz.

Sixty or seventy days later the war in Europe ended. By then my outfit was near Dresden on the Mulde River, running patrols east to meet the Russians. All our combat days were in General Patton's Third Army.

John Searle

OLIVE M. (Ferguson) SHEAKS

SIDNEY, OHIO

Clerical, Yoeman 1st, Navy, 1944-45, WW II
Basic Training: Bronx, New York
Duty in Washington, D.C.

My basic training was at Hunter College in New York. That sounds fine, but it wasn't. I caught duty the first night and had to make an officer's bed. I did not know how; it was a little scary, and after a few days, I was ready to go home.

We made a lot of nice friends all the way through. While at New York, they brought Frank Sinatra out for a performance. This was when he was just getting started.

After six more weeks in Iowa, I was sent to the Bureau of Personnel in Washington, D.C. I had never been there, so I enjoyed seeing all the places.

I was also in D.C. on V-E Day, so we went in town that evening after work. Our barracks was just across the Potomac River. We went to the park across from the White House and saw President Truman come out and wave to everyone. It was rather exciting. We were in our barracks when it came over the radio. We were shampooing our hair, so we couldn't wear our uniforms and went in wearing our navy slacks and white blouses. This has always stuck with me because we weren't allowed in the service club out of uniform. They were very strict about that. I even had to get permission to wear my wedding gown.

I also saw Gene Kelly while in D.C. He performed on stage at one of the theaters.

My husband was a Marine. He was in the first division on Guadalcanal. I had a brother in the Navy, and we had a son in the Marines, who was in Vietnam. I also had a brother in the Air Force. He was a lieutenant on a fortress and was killed over Germany. So my family knows what war can mean.

I was in only a little under two years. The food could have been better, but when we were in D.C., we ate out most of the time until just before payday; then we had to eat at the barracks. They didn't pay much in those days.

Olive M. (Ferguson) Sheaks

DONALD J. SLOCUM

HAINES CITY, FLORIDA

Rifleman, machine gunner, truck driver, bulldozer operator
Private, Marine Corps, 1941-45, WW II
Basic Training: Parris Island
Duty in Pacific Theater

I was one of the first Marines on the beach at Guadalcanal. Japs overran our position—scary as hell, but exciting. Your range of fire was in front of you. You couldn't get too far back cause you'd hit your own men. I was a machine gunner, 30-caliber. I was just glad to get through it, get out of there. A lot of my buddies didn't. I didn't want to talk about it or even think about it. This is the first time I've talked about it at all.

The river got so high in our gun emplacement I was standing in water up to my waist. My assistant gunner was feeding the ammunition to me. Japs were piling up in front of our gun, and I pulled them out so he could get a line of fire. They were coming across the mouth of the river. The BAR gunner stood up and the Japs were coming so fast they over-ran him—hit him with a bayonet that stabbed him right in the jaw. The blood was pumping right out of him. He just stood there.

A sentry was out on the river. In our position, we are back probably a thousand yards from the river. The guy on the radio was talking to us and everything went dead. The commander said, "Open fire!" By that time the Japs were already overrunning our positions.

One guy got back and the other three didn't—114 bayonet wounds, but the corpsmen saved his life. He was like a sieve. He was joking about it when the corpsmen took him to the rear position—still awake; said he had to put his fingers in the holes.

We were only supposed to establish this beachhead and be there 72 hours—we were there 90 days before the army got in. The Japs were cutting off the transports, patrolling so heavily that the army couldn't get in.

We used to sit up on the hill and watch the sea battles. The subs would come up and fire a torpedo. You could see it in the moonlight. It made a great colored light—beautiful! Everyone would yell "torpedo, torpedo" and we'd run from the beach to get up on the hill. The torpedo would come right up on the beach; didn't hit anything; didn't explode; guys disarmed it.

One night an English transport (or one of our own ships) was sunk. It was in the harbor and they couldn't see who it was and they sank our own ship.

I didn't have a family, no one to write to me. I never got any mail. I figured I'd never come out alive, so I just volunteered for everything. Those other guys with families needed to live more than I did.

If the Japs had known about it the first 72 hours we were there, they could have wiped us out. We had no ammunition left, no food. We ran them into the sea; had the island secured. But had to live on Jap rations that we confiscated from their food dump. It had worms in it. We'd boil and boil the Japanese oatmeal until the worms were dead, then pick them out and eat the oatmeal.

We ran out of drinking water, so had to use river water. Dead Japs were floating in it. So we took our helmets off, took the liner out, pushed the Japs out of the way, scooped the water up, and drank it out of our helmets. You do anything to survive. We got diarrhea.

We made spears out of the coconut trees, sharpened them to a point, and buried them in the river bank because the Japs were coming in behind their tanks. The tanks came across the sandbar with the Japs lined up right behind them so we couldn't get to them. We were trying to demobilize the tank so the Japs would be out in the open and we could get to them. They'd come up over the bank and we'd have all these spears sticking up. The tanks would keep bucking up against them. Our 37-mm cannon would try to hit them and detrack them as they backed up, trying to get a run on them. They were standing still in the water. The Japs would come pouring out of the tanks like bugs and we could just pick them off. If a guy would get a good aim, he'd try to catch them inside. When you stop to think about it today, it is just not right to take a human life, no matter what nationality they are.

We were sitting on the beach sunning ourselves in a pair of cut-off dungarees—all we've got for gear now except maybe a pith helmet. The gung-ho guys like me would wear twin 45 pistols and an old pair of shoes that we cut the top off of and made moccasions.

When the army supply ships came, I had a work party on the beach one night unloading a ship, canned Spam. The officers got beer, 3.2 beer. We'd hustle it off and take it out in the jungle somewhere. We'd eat Spam and peaches. Peaches would come in those gallon cans.

At Guadalcanal every night a little single engine plane would come and he'd drop one bomb over the mountain. We'd all run and get up on the ridge. He'd go down in the valley and drop this bomb. All of us would sit up there with a rifle, hoping somebody could hit him with the rifle. Called him Washing Machine Pete.

When we ran out of ammunition, we had enough to get one plane up. He'd get up there and get in a dogfight. I don't know how many pilots flew that one plane, but there were some aces. They did a lot of damage; the Japs never got that plane.

Finally we did get some supplies. Henderson Field got fixed up; the Japs had bombed hell out of it. We got the field lengthened cause that's when the P-38s came out. The first day there were six of them came in in pairs. You should have heard the Marines—it was like Homecoming! Those were fast! F4F Gremlins when we first started. These pilots would do barrel rolls and loopity loops when they were coming back. If they had a good flight and had knocked down a few Japs, they would really show off when they got back.

We had a guy that was a real card on the patrol. Everyone thought he was coming and he wasn't. The rest of the squad got wiped out. All those men were depending on him, and he wasn't even there. He ran and got back to his outfit. They were out there naked—no rear guard—and they didn't know it. The Japs just sneaked up on them and wiped them out.

Our ammunition dump was on fire and shells were going off all over the place. This officer wanted someone to help him. I said I'd go. "Grab the hose!" I laid on the fender when we went into the ammunition dump. The thing didn't have a cab or anything. I said, "You run it and I'll use the hose." We stopped in the middle and he stood up to tell me where to run the water. A 37-mm shell went right through him. He just stood there with blood pumping out. I crawled around and when I got a fire out, I'd get up in the truck, lay down on the seat, put it in gear, steer it, look up and stop it, put more fire out. Nobody came out to help. I got the fires out—that was all the ammunition we had. If the Japs had known that, there would have been nobody left. We were lucky!

I never saw a snake on an island, and I was on Guadalcanal, Guam, Okinawa, Iwo Jima. Altogether I was in the South Pacific 38 or 39 months. I had several attacks of malaria and they sent me back to the States.

I carried a machine gun and the gunner carried the tripod on a 100-mile march. The company commander had a bet of a hundred dollars that I could make the hundred-mile-march and never have to have a relief. We marched an hour and 10 minutes, then rest; an hour and 10 minutes, then rest, for the hundred miles. I did it! You know enlisted men don't associate with officers, but we sneaked off one night and he spent fifty dollars on me.

EDGAR R. TEETS

SIDNEY, OHIO

Driver in Supply Squadron, Sergeant, USMCR, 1942-45, WW II
Basic Training: Parris Island, SC
Duty in San Diego and Honolulu

It was August, 1942, when I was sent to Parris Island, SC, for Marine Corps basics. Little did I know then that for the next twenty-two months I was to live in an all-male society. It would be nearly two years 'til I'd see my family and friends again. It's hard to imagine how all alone you can feel among hundreds of other men.

Consequently, I turned to reading, a lot of reading. There was a rainy day when four of us were holed up in the motor pool shack with nothing but a deck of cards and an old copy of Reader's Digest. When I chuckled over something I'd been reading, the other guys got curious. At their request, I read the anecdote to them. They asked for more. Such was the beginning of a new diversion from boredom.

While stationed at Miramar near San Diego, I was assigned to the motor pool of the Supply Squadron. During routine landing and take-off practice, this one particular four-engine bomber apparently developed engine failure just above tree-top level after take-off. It crashed less than two miles from the runway. Of course, by the time we arrived on the scene with firetrucks and ambulances, it was already too late for the crew. The plane burst into flames on impact. The whole crew died instantly, literally cooked by the intense heat. As we pulled the bodies from the wreckage, some of them came apart at the joints, like dismembering a roast chicken. Others were split open like a well-grilled hotdog. Sleep didn't come easy that night.

The storage area covered acres and included all kinds of rolling stock, equipment on wheels—trucks, bulldozers, jeeps, weapons carriers, cranes, field equipment. Periodically we would go around starting up all the engines to make sure they were in working order. When equipment was needed in the South Pacific, we would take it to the ship, or the plane, depending on how quickly they needed it. Someone else would load it and get it on its way.

One day I was pulling, in a convoy, a portable machine shop, a trailer almost the size of a room. We ran into a traffic problem. I hit the brakes and almost lost the thing.

One day we took some equipment up into the California mountains to help fight a forest fire. I had a flat-bed semi with a bulldozer on the back of it. Up in the mountains we turned on a back road into the forest, and the road was so narrow that I had to back that semi about two miles into where the fire was. We bulldozed the brush out so the fire couldn't get across.

The overall experience of military life led to the development of a wreckless, careless, devil-may-care attitude which manifested itself one night on leave in San Diego. After bowling and drinking rum and cokes for a few hours, we just barely managed to catch the last transport truck back to camp. The truck was so packed with care-free Marines that a couple of us had to ride the front fenders, astraddle of, and holding on to, the headlight. That late at night the fifteen-mile ride back to camp was a sobering experience.

On another late-night occasion I came into the barracks after lights out. I knew laundry pickup was early next morning, but how was I going to get my dirty socks and skivvies, etc. together in pitch blackness? So, feigning a severe case of inebriation, I stumbled around my bunk and locker, making enough noise to awaken my bunkey, Steve Walkowiak. After slamming the locker door a few times, falling against his bunk, and using a few well-chosen expletives, good ole Steve found a flashlight, got up and helped me stuff my laundry bag. He was more than a little upset when he realized the ruse.

Steve was also there when I had my first experience with body lice, more commonly known as crabs. Coming back to the barracks from the shower house, I was standing at my open locker, getting into some clean skivvies, when I noticed a couple dark gray spots clinging to the hairs on my chest. Was I developing skin moles? The barracks lighting was poor. I picked and dug at the spots. They clung tenaciously. Finally I picked one loose. Holding it up to Steve's face I asked him what it was. Instead of answering my question, his eyes about bulged out of his head as he exploded, "Get the hell away from me!" As you might have guessed, I itched and scratched all night and went to sick bay as soon as I could get there the next day.

Following San Diego, I spent 14 months in Oahu. I think this was the last part of 1943, and, while we were restricted mostly to the base and seldom got leave into town, we saw very little evidence of the Pearl Harbor attack. Everything seemed to be in good shape; the harbors were in use. We got up to Hickam Field, Army Air Force Base, and it was in good shape. Occasionally we got permission to use a truck and took a bunch of guys and gals (female marines) to the beach at the other end of the island.

After getting out of the marines, I married, had a child, and started to college on the GI Bill. Some young fellow I was riding with convinced me to join the army reserves. Then the Korean Conflict broke out; I was called. I went to Camp Stoneman, California, and was about to be shipped out when my wife, who was pregnant with the second child, went to the Red Cross. They arranged a hardship discharge for me. At that time they weren't drafting people with kids, so I wouldn't have had to go if I hadn't been in the reserves. Another fellow with the army engineers got called the same way. When I got out, he was sitting on his bunk crying. A month or so later, though, he got out, too.

We must find a way to develop a world-wide, non-violent brotherhood among all the earth's peoples! Amen!

RITA (Aselage) THOMA

SIDNEY, OHIO

Operating Room Nurse, 1st Lieutenant, ANC, 1944-46, WW II
Basic Training: Ft. Benjamin Harrison
Duty in Ashford General Hospital, White Sulphur Springs, WV

I was stationed at Ashford General Hospital in White Sulphur Springs for my entire service. Before the war it was the Greenbriar Hotel and since the war it is again the Greenbriar Hotel. The hotel itself was made into a hospital and we lived in the cottages surrounding it.

We were a neuro-vascular center and that was the type surgery we did. I was instrument nurse to the Chief of Surgery, Col. Elkin. He was a professor of surgery at Emory University in Atlanta, GA, prior to his service, and would be going back to that position after his service. Consequently, we filmed many of our surgeries for his use in civilian life, and I would help edit these films.

We had many dignitaries come to White Sulphur Springs upon their return from overseas: Gen. Eisenhower, Gen. Wainwright, Gen. Bradley; and I got to meet them all.

I enjoyed my time in the service and learned a lot about surgery which helped me when I returned to civilian life.

MARGARET VOLENS

PRESCOTT VALLEY, ARIZONA

WAVE Beauty Shop, 3/Class Petty Officer, Navy, 1943-45, WW II
Basic Training: Hunter College, New York City
Duty at Cleveland, Ohio, and WAVE Barracks, Pearl Harbor

The training at Hunter was very vigorous and a few didn't make it; they were just sent home. I was wondering why I ever left Sidney, but it didn't take long before I loved it. I was there in the summer, so we wore the grey and white uniforms. We were measured and the uniforms fit well.

After training, I was sent to Cleveland, where all pay records are kept. We lived in a hotel which the Navy had taken over. And the food was good, but I wanted to move on. I had joined the Navy to see the world and then they sent me to a place three hours from home!

We were sent to California and on to Oahu on an old tanker ship, with WAVEs only on board. The bunks were seven high. We had to keep the quarters clean and be on watch duty. Our ship was alone, no convoy.

Margaret Volens

By this time things were pretty normal at Pearl, except where the Arizona had gone down. I was put in the Mess Hall and liked it. The floor had to be swept and mopped, sugar, salt and pepper containers filled, trays and silverware separated and ready to run through dishwasher. The shifts were 5 or 6 hours, but when the work was done, you could do what you wanted until time for the next meal. There was a great cook and food was good.

But they needed beauty operators and I had been one for seven years, but didn't want to do that work in the Navy. However, I was put in the shop in the WAVE Barracks, which was only for women from any of the bases.

WILLIAM (Fred) WAGNER
SIDNEY, OHIO

Bombardier, Navigator, Tech. Sgt., Marines, 1942-46; 1951-53,WWII, Korea
Basic Training: San Diego
Duty in Pacific

In June, 1942, I applied for Naval Aviation School, passed everything, but was not accepted—had an overbite. Enlisted in Marines in July, but there were so many enlistments that I wasn't sworn in until December 3, 1942. My preference was the Paramarines or the Raiders, but was put in aviation.

I volunteered for bombardier school, but while waiting for one to be set up, I was sent to aerial gunnery school. After I went to the first class of bombardier school, they realized they didn't need bombardiers and sent me to navigation school.

After 291/2 years of training, I was shipped to the South Pacific as a bombardier-navigator in Squadron 443, Group MAG 13, on a coral island, Emirau, off the north coast of New Guinea. Our aircraft were PBJs, the Navy version of the Airforce B-25 Billy Mitchell Bombers, equipped with a Norden bombsight, a drift meter, sextant (never used because of short flights and the plane was equipped with a radio compass).

When I joined the Group (four squadrons with a maximum strength of 12 planes each) one assignment was to harass the Japs on various islands around the eastern end of New Guinea. My first bombing raid (four planes from our squadron) was an airdrome on the island of New Britain at 10,000 ft., with no resistance.

The Group's main assignment was training for the invasion of the Japanese mainland (Honshu), scheduled for November 1, 1945. Our training entailed making low level flights, simulating diving on a target at an angle of 45 degrees and launching 1000-pound rockets. The rocket racks had been placed on our aircraft, but no rockets had been delivered by the end of the war.

With no reasons given, the Group was ordered to cease all bombing and training flights. Many rumors were going around the island. Then came the dropping of the atomic bombs and the end of the war, V-J Day.

The dropping of the bombs and V-J Day were greeted with mixed emotions: joy that the war was over and the fact that an invasion would result in 65-85 percent of the Group's planes being lost. Many of us were sorry, though, because we had trained for many years, the Marine Corps way, the hard way, and we were cheated out of contributing to the downfall of the Japanese Empire.

In August we left Emirau for the Philippines. Upon arrival at an abandoned airforce base on the southern tip of Mindanao, we, the flying contingent, began setting up camp near the metal airstrip. Since I always enjoyed mess duty and not guard duty, I volunteered to help establish the kitchen, chow tent, and cook.

On the first day a detail of men went into the heavily-wooded area (jungle) to cut trees for poles used to support the tents for our living quarters. The next morning the detail returned to cut more trees. They were surrounded by small-in-stature Filipinos, Moros, carrying machine guns, bandoleers of ammunition, revolvers and machetes. Nearly each one had the full complement of weapons. At their request, the senior officer of the detail was taken to meet their chief, who informed him that the detail had cut some of his trees and he wanted paid for them. Our officer apologized but advised him that payment couldn't be made until the commanding officer arrived by ship. The chief did show him an area where free trees could be cut.

Things were going great; we dealt with some of the natives, buying pineapples, bananas, coconuts, and vegetables. But at night while we slept, small items—clothing, blankets, chow equipment—came up missing. With arrival of the ships and remaining members of the Group, including the commanding officer, who was briefed of all that had transpired, especially of the night before—one of the cooks was awakened and saw someone trying to take his footlocker. He yelled, the footlocker was dropped, and the culprit grabbed the blanket off the cook's bed and fled. The commanding officer met with the chief and informed him the request for payment for his trees would have to be turned over to the officials in Manila and, due to the excessive thievery, no trading would be permitted. A guard detachment would be placed on the perimeter of the camp. The chief was irate—he declared war.

The commanding officer returned to camp and ordered a survey of all weapons and ammunition on the base. All flight crew members had been issued 38-caliber revolvers when they joined their squadron and there were 30- and 50-caliber air-cooled machine guns mounted in the airplanes, and a few carbines. All the ammunition was collected and redistributed equally. A few of the 30- and 50-caliber machine guns were set up in sandbag bunkers on the perimeter and manned with a couple of guards.

The first night the camp heard the chatter of a machine gun, a young Marine challenged a noise out in the woods. He fired at the noise, then silence. Next morning it was found that he had shot one of the chief's cows. More tension hit the camp—we didn't know what might happen.

When the ships arrived, bringing the remainder of the Group, the camp was wired for electricity. Night lights were placed on poles along the backside of the camp, shining toward the river. Three nights after the cow incident, a Moro was observed crawling up the river bank toward the camp and was challenged by the guard. As he started to run, he was hit in the shoulder. The Moro was placed in sickbay; the doctor cleaned and dressed the wound. Next morning the chief came to see the patient. The boy was from town, not of his tribe, but he was seeing after him. After about a week, the boy was released to the chief, who took him back to his people.

During our brief stay, we learned the Moros, natives, were not too far removed from being cannibals. During the war they had been supplied by American submarines with munitions and medical supplies. They were guerrillas, ridding the area of Japs. A bounty was collected from the Americans for each captive; not quite as much for ears of a dead Jap.

Our planes were R5C, Navy version of the C-46 Curtiss; RY3, Navy version of B-24 (Liberator bomber converted to a transport); R4D, Navy version of C-47 (Douglas); and a rehab R5D, Navy version of C-54 (Douglas).

(See remainder of story in Korea section.)

Next page—clockwise, from top: William Wagner, C-47-R4d, B-25-PBJ (Billy Mitchell Bomber), C-54-R5d cargo workhorse, C-46-R5C.Courtesy William Wagner.

石橋
螢ヶ池

56517

44

KENNETH WALTER

JACKSON CENTER, OHIO

Civilian coppersmith, U.S. Navy, 1940-45, WW II
Duty at Pearl Harbor, Hawaii

December 7, 1941, has remained in the national consciousness as, in President Franklin D. Roosevelt's words, 'a day which will live in infamy.'

Kenneth Walter... was working then at Pearl Harbor for the U.S. Navy, but as a civilian. He worked on naval ships as a coppersmith, repairing and refitting copper piping and units aboard various ships.

Despite being a civilian, though, Walter experienced all the dangers and horrors of the battle. He was fired upon by the attacking Japanese aircraft, worked to put out fires aboard ships which had been hit and tried to save sailors who were victims of the only time since the Civil War that war had been fought on United States soil.

"No one ever thought the Japanese would be dumb enough to hit Pearl," said Walter.

He acknowledged that work was already underway to prepare the U.S. armada for the event of war, but no one believed it would be forced upon them, or their efforts set back by the surprise attack. He said people at Pearl Harbor at the time were unaware that the Japanese were moving their warships east to position themselves for what they would unleash shortly before 8 A.M. that December morning.

Walter was age 27, working as a coppersmith in a shop in Bucyrus when a government representative arrived from Cincinnati in the fall of 1940 to see if he would be interested in working for the Navy. He was making 65 cents an hour at the time, and the government could guarantee him $1.65 if he took the assignment. A bachelor who liked to *gadabout*, Walter agreed and found himself leaving by train on October 4, 1940, bound for the West Coast and later to Hawaii on the USS Grant.

Working on ships was something that he had never done before, but he found it to be work that he enjoyed and was good at. Walter worked on all kinds of ships at Pearl Harbor, submarines, battleships, destroyers, cruisers, carriers, even merchant ships.

Weighing 145 pounds, Walter was a relatively small man who could find his way into close quarters on ships that other men could not hope to reach. His foreman was a Chinese man named Henry Chang, who Walter described as "one smart cookie."

The eve of the attack was like any other evening at Pearl. No one suspected trouble. Walter said there were about 60,000 sailors on liberty in Honolulu.

Walter worked on the USS Ogalala until late the night of December 6. He had no way of knowing that the minelayer ship would be hit by a torpedo and capsized during the attack.

He left about 11 P.M. for home which was about 13 miles from Pearl Harbor. On his way, he ate a late supper at a Japanese restaurant.

"I used to like sukiyaki," he said. "I don't like it anymore."

The morning of the historic attack started off relatively uneventful. Walter donned a new suit and planned to go to the doctor at the base hospital at Pearl Harbor to have an eye examination. He started driving toward the base.

Before reaching the base, on a Honolulu street, Walter said he heard an explosion. That was shortly before 8 A.M., the time when the first torpedo was believed to have been dropped by a Japanese warplane and hit one of the ships docked at Pearl Harbor.

"I just happened to stick my head out the car window," said Walter, "and saw this plane flying low overhead with a big red ball on the wing."

He then heard on the car radio that an attack was in progress and that all Navy yard employees were to report to the base. It was at around 8:15 A.M. when Walter reached the shipyard gate and was waiting in a line to go inside.

"I heard the sound of a plane screaming down," he said, "I shut the car off and got out the passenger side, and rolled down into a ditch. Three planes came down, strafing machine gun fire."

He said Marines manned guns near the entrance in an attempt to return fire. Walter would see later that some 50 holes and dings had been put into his car during the strafing run. He had no time to check the car out then, however. Walter said he followed the ditch around the gate, showed the guard his employee badge number and hopped into a truck which took him and others to his shop near Dry Dock No. 1 at Pearl Harbor.

In Dry Dock No. 1 there were two destroyers, the USS Cassius and USS Downes and the battleship USS Pennsylvania. Each had been hit by enemy fire. Walter worked with others to extinguish the fires aboard the ships.

Walter said the enemy pilots would drop their torpedoes, then return to the same area and strafe with machine gun fire. He noticed that when a Japanese plane would drop a torpedo, it would rise several feet quickly, evidently due to the loss of significant weight of the torpedo.

Fighting the fires aboard the ships was not the most vivid recollection that Walter has from his experiences during the attack. Those most profound memories actually were from his work after the attack.

He said a friend and he were trying to get some lunch at around noon that day when a man who identified himself as a doctor came into the restaurant saying he was seeking volunteers. Walter and his friend really didn't know what they were getting themselves into, but wanted to help out in any way they could.

They left with the doctor, who led them out on the docks. He pointed out into the harbor where a wall of flame was rumbling over burning oil which had drained into the water from sinking ships. The doctor told them they were going out to pull sailors from the harbor...

"... as we were going into the harbor he said a prayer," said Walter. "We prayed for the safety of the boat." They were approaching intense fire and the launch was made of wood.

As they were heading toward the burning oil, Walter said he could hear men yelling. He said their launch went right into the flame. He and the others started pulling sailors from the water. To pick them up, Walter said he had to pull them up at the armpits. Due to the burns some had received, to grab their arms and pull, he said, risked pulling off burned skin.

"Some of the sailors were just barely alive," he said. Other sailors were injured beyond help. Walter said 18 sailors died in his arms that day.

"I was 28 and these kids who were 20 years old were dying," said Walter as tears filled his eyes. "They said, 'Tell Mom I love her.'"

"One boy said, 'write my mother.' It was hard to take." The doctor told Walter that he would help write the letter.

Through the difficult, emotional work to rescue sailors, Walter believes that a religious experience helped him find strength to complete his task. Walter... (145-pound man) estimated the injured sailor to weigh well over 250. Walter wondered how he would lift him into the boat. He said that as he was trying to lift the man, he felt a hand on his shoulder. He somehow had the strength to lift the sailor. Walter looked around for the person who had touched him, but others in the boat were busy about their task, unaware of what he just had to do. He said he never felt fatigued throughout the rest of his work that day, efforts which continued from I to 10 P.M.

"I believe God touched me," said Walter.

... he worked three days to find survivors. His later efforts were directed at trying to rescue sailors from the many ships which had been hit. He said they would move along behind someone who would rap SOS on the bulkhead. If they heard a tapping response, Walter would use a torch to try to cut through the metal. Others behind him would go in to try to rescue sailors, while he went on to cut through other wall sections.

... Walter said he continued to have disturbing dreams years later, up until about three years ago when he said he started to attend church.

In his dreams, Walter said he "would see that red ball on the wing."

"Sometimes I would sit straight up in bed..."

Reprinted with permission of *The Sidney* (Ohio) *Daily News*, and Dan Liggett.

Left: USS West Virginia, Pearl Harbor, December 7, 1941.
Right: Kenneth Walter. Courtesy Kenneth Walter.

WILLIAM R. WEIGAND

SUTTONS BAY, MICHIGAN

Heavy Equipment Driver, Cpl., Air Force, 1938-45, WW II
Duty in China, Burma, India (Flying Tigers)

After landing in Bombay, went across India on the narrow gage railroad, and then a flat-bottom riverboat to Calcutta, taking about a week altogether. Ate K-rations for breakfast and lunch; stopped at some British camp for dinner or where Indians would feed us.

Flew the Hump in a C-47 to Kunming, China. There was no oxygen in the plane, and parachutes only for the pilot and co-pilot—they sat on them. Many C-47s crashed flying the Hump.

While in Kunming I drove one of two 21/2 ton semi-trucks, with wenches on the front and a boom that we used to lift. They were the heaviest equipment we had. We hauled everything from soup to nuts, mostly gas and oxygen, to outlying bases from Kunming. Lots of nights I slept under my truck, awaking to find myself surrounded by staring Chinese. The Japanese were bombing the Burma Road as well as Kunming.

One day I arrived at the railroad to get a load of bombs and the Chinese were rolling them off the car on to the cement—I took off running.

Once a B-24 crashed before getting off the runway. Of the twelve people aboard, one in the tail section was the only one to get out alive. The plane was going on a bomb run, so there were bombs all over.

General Chennault, a very nice, friendly man, was our commander. He was the kind to get a job done.

LINCOLN WICAL

BOTKINS, OHIO

Carpenter's mate, Chief Petty Officer, Navy, 1940-45
Duty at Pearl Harbor

Lincoln Wical was an eyewitness to the Japanese attack on Pearl Harbor which started the United States' involvement in World War II 50 years ago... Later he also watched from a ship in Tokyo Bay as the peace treaty was signed which ended the war.

"It was one of the happiest days of my life when it was over and I was alive," Wical recalled of watching the activity aboard the USS Missouri during the treaty signing in 1945.

His thoughts were much different on Dec. 7, 1941, as he sat reading the Sunday newspaper aboard a US repair ship in the Hawaiian harbor. "It is hard to explain," Wical said of that day. "You thought the world was coming to an end."

Wical was a carpenter's mate on the USS Rigel and an early riser. He went for a newspaper and was sitting on his workbench, which doubled as a bunk, waiting for breakfast. It was a few weeks before his 26th birthday.

"You could hear the planes. They were so close—that was pretty unusual. I stuck my head out the porthole and saw them dive and turn a bomb loose."

The bomb hit an airfield and Wical went running topside where an excited chief warrant officer grabbed him and sent him back below deck to look for the only gunner in the crew. Wical noted there were only a couple of pistols on their repair ship.

As he went down, a bomb hit near their vessel "and the whole ship rocked to beat hell," Wical said.

The seaman ran back up and saw planes turn more bombs loose. "You could see them hit and everything just blew up. I think they hit the (USS) Oklahoma."

Lincoln Wical

The battleships, which were the main targets of the Japanese air attack, were docked across the bay from Wical's ship.

"It was all right in front of your eyes," Wical said. "You couldn't help but see it happen." His own ship had two near misses with bombs, causing 213 holes in the ship. Thirteen of his shipmates were injured but none killed.

Wical saw a buddy "tumbling down all bloody" from a shrapnel wound and helped his friend down to his workbench where a make-shift hospital was being set up. Wical was not injured.

There was a break in the bombing and Wical and others from the fire and rescue party of his ship were sent with tools to try and help the battleship Oklahoma which he had seen take a bomb in the side. "At the time it was still all ablaze and we couldn't even get close to it. We saw guys swimming out through fire from it," he said.

After helping some sailors get out of the flaming water, Wical and his party were sent back to their ship temporarily.

After about 45 minutes, there was another wave of aircraft bombers in a second Japanese attack. "It seemed like it lasted forever. It was not like bombing raids that lasted four or five minutes," said Wical from later experience. "They (Japanese planes) stayed and hammered."

"They kept coming until they ran out of ammunition."

The noise of that gun firing repeatedly within 40 feet of him "was enough to drive you nuts," Wical said.

When the bombers finally left, "I looked over before the sun went down. We thought we had a good navy and it was sitting on the bottom."

"However, it was the next morning that really presented the worst sight." He walked past the hospital where fatalities were placed in rows outside. "Body bags were piled up like cord wood, stacked seven to eight feet tall on top of each other."

After the attack, Wical was part of the rescue crews. After the fires were out, Wical returned with a relief crew that Sunday afternoon to the USS Oklahoma to try and free trapped sailors. He was among those who rescued 11 people alive. The work continued through Tuesday and some people who were rescued did not even know they had been bombed, he said.

As the rescue crews quit work because they were not able to go any further, they could still hear sailors pounding on the bulkheads, trapped inside the ship, seeking to be let out, Wical said.

After the attack, a blackout was imposed. "The first four or five days, no one could light a cigarette in the open—you might get shot," Wical said. "That was just how nervous and itchy everyone was. When you have laid there and got hammered for three hours, it affects you."

As for the family wondering about him back home, Wical was able to send a telegram to his fiance. However, censorship was in place. Mrs. Wical still recalls the words: "Don't get excited. Everything OK."

But it would not really be OK for quite a few years.

Reprinted with permission from *The Sidney* (Ohio) *Daily News* and Christine Henderson.

THOMAS C. WILCOX

FT. MYERS, FLORIDA

Radio Operator and Gunner on B-26 Marauder, 344th Bomber Group, 496th Bomb Squadron, Sgt., Army Air Corps
Duty in Europe

"Shot down behind Nazi lines in German occupied Holland, Thomas Wilcox recounts this significant time in his life. Anti-aircraft flack struck his B-26 Marauder while flying deputy lead on his 67th bombing mission over Europe, the day before a replacement crew was scheduled to take over. It became his longest mission."

...'Come quickly!' she said, and hurried us down the hall and through the door that led to the bedroom over the milking room cook stove. Nico sneaked out a side door and disappeared into the night.

We hurried in and she got down on her knees in front of the panelled wall at the end of the room facing the outside of the milk barn. She pulled three boards loose and told us to get in. Mac and I crawled into what was a small compartment between the roof and wall.

There was a small hiding place there, about five feet wide, ten feet long, and four feet high. This was where Cisca kept some of the treasures she didn't want the Germans to find. On the door to the bedroom there was a sign which read: Warning! T.B.C. (Tuberculosis). The Germans were deathly afraid of that disease and didn't like to go near any place that might have the germs.

The word had come to Cisca from Hanna that the Germans were searching for men to dig tank traps in the roads to slow the advancing American and British soldiers. The situation became very dangerous because the next day the Germans moved into the farm to cook food for the front line soldiers.

Hanna then came to Swolgen in her nurses uniform and told the German Captain that it would be very dangerous to stay in that room, the room in which we were hidden. She said that a few weeks earlier one of the servants had died from open T.B.C. The Captain thanked Hanna for that information and her concern for the health of his soldiers.

Mac and I spent a very uneasy night in our small hiding place. We could hear the Germans talking in the room only a few feet from where we were hiding. We took turns sleeping in case one of us might snore and give away our hiding place.

The next day, a little before noon, we heard voices and footsteps coming up the stairs toward our room. They paused before the door, then we heard a man speaking German. The door to the room opened and two people entered. Mac and I held our breath. Would they find us?

There was a window directly above where we were hiding. The footsteps came over to the wall where we were and, looking through a crack where the boards were put together that covered our hiding place, I could see a pair of black boots just inches away. My heart was pounding so loudly I was sure he would hear me. He said something in German, turned around, and left the room. We could hear clump-clump down the stairway and out. It was the Captain, with Cisca, checking to see if Hanna was telling the truth about the room.

Several hours had now passed since Mac and I had gone to the toilet. We had crawled into our little room around 10:00 P.M. the evening before, and it was now about 5:00 P.M. the next day. I thought my bladder was going to burst. Mac was in the same condition. We were afraid that if we went on the straw upon which we were lying, it would run down through the ceiling and the Germans would see it and come to investigate. The cook stove was almost directly beneath where we were lying. I got the bright idea to let it go in our flannel shirts. Mac agreed, so we slipped off our shirts, rolled them in a ball and relieved ourselves ever so slowly. Later that evening, shortly after dark we heard someone opening the door and ever so quietly tiptoeing toward where we were. It was Cisca. She had been waiting for just the right time to slip up and bring us some food and a thunder mug (an old-fashioned pot) to relieve ourselves. She handed in a beef stick, some black bread, a hunk of cheese, a couple bottles of wine, and the thunder mug. By peeking through a crack where the roof met the wall, we could watch the Germans coming and going from the parking area right below us. We found out later

Thomas Wilcox

that it was a German cook unit using Cisca's place to prepare food for their soldiers fighting on the front.

We were into the fifth day now and getting awfully cramped up, since we could only raise up on our elbows. The highest spot in our little room was only about four feet; the ceiling sloped down to just a few inches where the roof met the wall. About every evening, Cisca would slip up to our hiding place, bring some food and drink, and swap the thunder mug for a clean one. An hour or two after dark, on the fifth day, we heard planes coming. There was some loud talking, men scurrying about, then Cisca came opening the boards to our hiding place. She told us that the German soldiers were very much afraid of the bombers, so when they heard them coming, they ran out of the house to their foxholes. This gave us time to get out of our hole. 'Come quickly!' she said, and we got out as fast as we could and followed her down the hall to her bedroom.

That night, Nico slipped into the room and said that it was too dangerous for us there and we would have to leave in the morning. At about daylight, we got up and dressed while Nico checked out the situation as to which Germans were there and moving about. He was back in a couple of moments and said, 'Let's go—only three of the cooks are up and they won't pay any attention to us, but don't say anything; remember you are deaf and dumb.'...

We were about halfway down the stairs, when one of the soldiers came through the kitchen area with a towel over his shoulder and his shaving kit in his hand. My heart skipped a beat, but he waited until we cleared the stairs, said, 'Gute morgen,' and clumped on up to the bathroom. We tried to act cool and followed Nico through the dining room, living room, and out the front door. We walked in quick time, down the road and back to Tienray, hoping that we wouldn't encounter any curious German soldiers.

In a little over an hour, we got to the Van de Voort house in Tienray without incident. When we arrived, we were introduced to Hanna's brother, Theo, and sister-in-law, Trina. They had three little girls... from about four to eight years of age. They told us that the fighting had moved into their town and they had to evacuate to a safer place.

Hanna managed to find room for us, and I had fun playing with the little girls... The family then moved on to another relative's home, even farther from the fighting. Two elderly aunts were then brought in because their home was also destroyed by the shelling.

The next day, the British began shelling our village, trying to hit a German headquarters unit a few blocks from our house. The first two rounds landed in our backyard with an earth shaking explosion. Mac and I tore the carpet back from the living room where earlier we had been shown a trap door. It led to a hiding place dug under the floor some months earlier. It was used to hide some of the things that the family didn't want the Germans to find. We jerked open the trap door and dove in just as another round exploded nearby. The shells continued to whistle and whoosh over for what seemed like hours. We could hear the rest of the family scurrying about and running to the cellar. Mac and I finally looked at one another during a slight lull in the shelling, and simultaneously decided to crawl out of our hole to see if we could be of some help.

The first shell, as I said, landed about twenty feet from the rear of our house and knocked several holes in it. The other one hit near the neighbor's house and killed a young man who was in the back yard, and his seven year old sister. It wounded another sister who was hanging up clothes.

Mac and I felt quite ashamed when we found out that Hanna and Virrie had run out into the yard immediately after the first shells hit and carried the young neighbor girl into our cellar. After crawling out of our hole, we joined the rest of the family. We found Hanna and Virrie dressing her wound and giving her comfort. She was about thirteen years old and had a piece of shrapnel lodged in her back. We watched Hanna and Virrie remove it, then stitch up the wound.

The shelling continued for over an hour and then let up. Under intermittent shelling we spent another day-and-a-half in those cramped quarters with eight other people, and were then greatly relieved to hear the all clear.

We assessed the damage to the house and found that it wasn't serious, so things went back to normal. Mac and I told Hanna and Virrie we were sorry that we weren't of more help and were quite impressed by their bravery in the situaiton. They said that they had had much practice living with tragedy, ever since the Germans had invaded Holland, and would only be happy when they were gone.

A couple of days later, we were again given a start when Nico burst into the house and told us the Germans were coming, looking for workers to dig tank traps. We were rushed up the stairs to a closet off the hallway. Hanna jerked the door open and then pulled the back wall of the closet open and motioned us in. We squeezed into the small area at the rear of the closet and very quickly she shoved the door shut. None too soon, because we heard a loud pounding at the door followed by some loud talking in German. We heard footsteps come up the stairs and doors opening and closing. After a while the footsteps went back down the stairs, then silence.

In a few moments Hanna opened our closet door and we squeezed out and hurriedly scrambled down the stairs. We ran out the back door, across a small creek, and crawled into a haystack much like the one we first hid in when we landed in Holland. We stayed there until dark, then Nico came for us. We walked quickly to a Convent only a short distance from Hanna's house.

We were introduced to the Mother Superior and two of the Sisters. None of them spoke very good English, but we could understand their signs and followed them to a bedroom in what looked like, and we found out later, was a small hospital.

Mac and I were well taken care of by the Sisters for two or three days. Then one night, we had just gotten into bed when there was a hurried knock at our door. We said, 'Come in,' and in came the Mother Superior in her black gown and with a very serious look on her face. She motioned us to hurry, so we jumped out of bed and, pulling on our pants and shirts, we followed her down the hall.

She took us down a back stairway to the first level of the Convent. There we met two more Sisters who went with us to a back corner of the Convent. They led us to the front of a large oven and motioned us to climb a small ladder over the front of it to a window located about halfway back. Mac and I crawled over the oven, through the window and into a room that, we found out later, was a fruit cellar. The Sisters had plastered shut the door to that room which was a little to the right of the oven. The room contained some of their valuables hidden from the Germans, also canned fruit and vegetables.

The reason for the hurried exodus was that, in the middle of the night, the Germans came to check out the Convent. The next morning they moved in with a medical unit to take care of the wounded soldiers from the front. Later, Nico laughingly told us how embarrassed the Mother Superior had been, because we had seen her in her underclothing. We honestly didn't know that because her long black nightgown looked much like what she wore every day.

Nico would come by every couple of days to tell us what was going on with the war. In that room there was no electricity, only candles and no toilet, so the Sisters had to take care of our toilet needs in the old-fashioned way, with a portable pot.

One morning we were startled when two German soldiers pulled the straw bales from in front of the window of our room facing the street, and crawled in behind them. Mac and I fell flat on the floor beside our cots and waited. Soon, there was an earth-shaking explosion. The soldiers then got up, put the straw back and left.

When Nico came, we told him about it and asked him what happened. He told us the Germans had blown the steeple off the church so when the British got there it couldn't be used as an artillery observation point. He said the soldiers were probably the ones who set off the explosives.

The next day we heard the wailing and crying of people coming from the street in front of the Convent. Later that evening Nico told us that the Germans had sent two soldiers to get a cow from the farm located a short distance from the Convent. It was the only cow the farmer had left, as the Germans had already taken the rest. He told them that they couldn't have the cow because he needed the milk for his grandchildren who were living with him, along with their Mother.

An argument ensued and the old man went in the house and got a pistol which he had hidden there. He came out and told them to leave, which they did. It wasn't long though, until the soldiers came back with several others who then shot down the farmer, took the cow, and set fire to the house and barn, burning them to the ground.

...We were in our third week at the Convent, and the gunfire which we had been hearing off in the distance for several days seemed to be getting closer.

We hadn't heard from Ben for several days and asked Nico on his next visit what happened to him. He said that the British troops were beginning to move in now and it wouldn't be long before they would be here. He said that the last he saw Ben was in Meerlo. The British were on one side and the Germans on the other, with shells exploding everywhere. Ben got on his bike and said he was going to try to make it through to the British side. He rode off, zig-zagging into the town of Venray between explosions. 'I hope and pray he made it,' Nico said.

That evening, the Germans began firing a type of cannon that we had not heard before. It was in a wooded area about a quarter mile from the Convent. Nico said it had six or eight barrels and looked and sounded more like a rocket launcher than a cannon. Later we found out that is what it was. The

Germans would shoot off several salvoes and then tow it to a different location before the British could locate it and fire back. The firing was getting closer every hour, and the word came from Nico that the Germans were moving out and, hopefully, we would be able to make a run for it in a day or two.

The date was November 22nd, not long until Thanksgiving. Mac and I were praying that we would be out before then and back with our outfit...

Reprinted from the book, *One Man's Destiny,* 1992, with permission of the author, Thomas C. Wilcox, and Telcraft Books.

GEORGE J. YOUNG

HAINES CITY, FLORIDA (DECEASED)

Radar Operator, Petty Officer, Navy, WW II, Korea
Basic Training: Great Lakes
Duty in Pacific Theater

After our basic training at Great Lakes and three weeks of Radar School, it was on to the LCI-L 738 (Landing Craft Infantry-Large). There were 20-40 in our crew; the ship was 120 ft. long, 26 ft. wide, flat bottomed, and bounced like a cork. We were part of an amphibious force but carried no troops.

Oftentimes we were used as an errand boy, carrying messages between ships. Our buddy ship, the LCI 598, traveled with us most of the time. We carried fire and welding equipment, tools, and a machine shop especially designed for ship repairs.

The LCI 738 was in convoys (as many as 25 ships) most of the time and escorted by destroyers. Radar was used for spacing to keep the ships from ramming.

Our ship was involved in the invasion of Leyte (Philippines) when General MacArthur returned. The Philippines were in bad shape; the Japanese had sent everything of value to Japan.

I was at Okinawa on the first commissioned ship of the U.S. Navy to enter and tie up at the docks in Naha harbor since the day of Admiral Perry. One evening five or six Jap suicide planes were coming in and there I was on the bow gun (20mm). Between my gun and another one, we knocked one of the planes down. The army knocked a couple down, and the navy got the rest. Our ship was part of the picket line there. The army and marines were still fighting just over a ridge from us.

I still recall the beautiful sunrises and sunsets while in the Pacific.

After V-J Day (Victory in Japan) our ship returned to Manila and pulled shuttle duty to some of the outer Philippine Islands.

Top: George J. Young. Bottom: LCI (Landing Craft Infantry) Courtesy George J. Young

TATIANA A. BARCHENKOVA

RUSSIA

Telephone and Telegraph Technical Expert, Senior Lieutenant,
Army, 36th Regiment, Western Front Forces

Before the war I lived in the town of Smolensk, Russia. I worked at the local telephone and telegraph exchange as a technical expert, responsible for maintenance and operation of telegraph equipment of the BODO system.

I was returning home on a bus from a city bath-house when I heard for the first time that Germany had invaded our country—war with Fascist Germany had begun. It was one o'clock P.M., June 20, 1941.

I did not feel any specific worry or anxiety about the news. I remembered words from a popular song often broadcast over the radio during the pre-war years: "We do not need other nations' lands; however, we won't let anybody claim even a small piece of our territory!" I strongly believed that my country was powerful and the Germans would be defeated in no time.

On June 26, 1941, the company where I worked delegated me, with my telegraph equipment, to a military unit of the 36th Regiment, which was part of the Western Front Forces. The unit was located in the village of Gnezdovo, about 500 kilometers outside of Smolensk. There I was registered in the unit and was issued a military uniform. I was never to return to my telegraph company in Smolensk.

On July 15, 1941, I was directed to the unit at the new front line near the town of Vyazma (in the direction toward Moscow). On July 16, 1941, the Germans occupied Smolensk.

Till the end of September, 1941, our military unit was in defense. Germans started an offensive attack in the direction of Moscow on September 30, 1941. The attack was given a code name of *Tayfun*. Germans broke through the defense line of the Western and Reserve Fronts on October 2, 1941.

The attacking forces of the enemy were rapidly moving ahead, surrounding the Western and Reserve Fronts near Vyazma from the South and North; by October 6, 1941, Germans encircled the major part of our military units to the west of Vyazma.

At the same time, Germans made an air attack on the headquarters of the Western Front forces where my friend, Anya Gromovich, and myself were on night duty operating the telegraph equipment at the signal office. The next morning when we went off duty, we saw planes diving very low above us, reminding me of a flock of crows over prey. The bombers circled several times, then formed a straight line and left in the direction of the Western Front headquarters.

It would have taken just one bomb to demolish our ten trucks and kill all the personnel. Fortunately, the pilots of the bombers obviously had a different assignment, which saved our lives.

We did not wait till darkness. We got into the trucks and started moving along the highway in the direction of Moscow. It took us about three-four hours of driving to get out of the enemy's encirclement. On our way we were several times attacked by enemy planes. Every time we would hear bombers approaching, the trucks would stop and we would immediately jump out, run as far from the highway as we could, and drop onto the ground. When we were approaching Moscow, we had to turn onto a dirt road, as the highway was already occupied by the Germans. It was dark by that time and that is probably why we managed to break through the enemy's encirclement. We could hear German soldiers talking and German tanks moving along the highway that ran parallel to our dirt road. But fortunately, we managed to escape.

While working at the signal office, I often saw General Zhukov, who was appointed Chief Commander of the Western Front on October 11, 1941. He would come there every time he needed to communicate with his troops. He never came alone; he was always accompanied by comrade Bulganin, Member of the Military Council. Whenever they visited, the signal office would be surrounded by special security officers.

I saw General Zhukov at a very close distance. Here is one recollection of him. A telegraph operator was transmitting information from Zhukov to his troop commanders. She did not understand the name of an inhabited area and asked Zhukov to repeat the name. Zhukov got outraged. He got up from the chair and ordered that Psurtsev, Head of Communications of the Front, be called in. Psurtsev was at a significant distance from the signal

Tatiana A. Barchenkova

center, so he ran as quickly as he could and was quite out of breath when he stood at attention before the General. Psurtsev was ordered to provide another telegraph operator. Now there were only two first-rate telegraph operators cleared by KGB and authorized to work with General Zhukov. So it took quite awhile to get the second one to the signal center. During all this time of waiting, Zhukov was standing on his feet, never taking a seat until the second operator arrived. Then he proceeded with the communication.

During these communication sessions, Zhukov would normally sit on a chair, unbutton his tunic, and sometimes curl his foot up under him. He always seemed extremely tired. Bulganin would always be standing next to the telegraph machine. He never said a word.

In March, 1942, I was promoted to the rank of an officer, junior lieutenant. By the end of the war I was senior lieutenant and was awarded the Order of the Great Patriotic War, Medal for the Defense of Moscow, Medal for Seizure of Kenigsburg, and several others. When the war was over, I was in Eastern Prussia. I was demobilized from the Army in 1946.

DORIS M. BOBLIT
SIDNEY, OHIO

Resident of London, England, during WW II

I was seven years old when the war began, and the first thing I remember is being fitted for a gas mask and having to carry it wherever I went.

My brother and I were evacuated, along with thousands of other children, from London. We spent three months in the countryside and hated it so much that our mother brought us back and we stayed in London for the duration of the war.

We got used to the rationing, doing without fresh eggs and butter, fresh fruit, etc. I cannot remember how much of each staple food we were allowed, but do remember Mother saving up her coupons so she could have enough for a cake or pie for a special occasion.

My grandparents' house, which was five down from ours, received a direct hit from a bomb; their house and four other homes were destroyed. Luckily, none of the residents were hurt—they were in the bomb shelter—but four people who came running out of a pub across the street were injured when the front walls collapsed.

After a while we got tired of getting out of bed to run to the shelter in the basement, so we just made it into a regular bedroom. The Council had built these shelters in a lot of the homes. Between each house there was a steel door that slid up so people could escape should their house be hit, and they did not have to go into the street, just into the next house.

A friend of the family was getting married, material for a dress was unattainable, so she got a parachute, nylon, and had her wedding dress made from it.

My mother, brother, and I would spend two or three nights at the pictures just to get our minds off the bombing. We knew all the big American film stars.

I also remember the black cloth we had to put up at our windows to prevent any light from showing through, and the watchman yelling at anyone forgetting to do so.

I also remember the barrage balloons floating over London, put there to try to stop the planes or buzz bombs. (If they came in low, they would get entangled in the cables.) The buzz bombs were the most feared. You could hear them coming, then suddenly the noise stopped, and you knew they were dropping somewhere.

The celebration when the war was over was something I'll never forget—the dancing in the streets and the parties.

BERNICE CAIN
CONOVER, OHIO

Civilian Worker, Washington, D.C., 1941-45

The organization I worked for in Washington was the BAS-BSM (British Army Staff and British Ministry of Supply), headed by a British Brigadier General. Our job was to find out where military supplies could be purchased and arrange for their transport across the Atlantic.

Before you were employed, you had to have security clearance and be photographed for a pass, which you had to present when entering the office.The passes resembled today's drivers'license photos—awful! I was wearing a striped blouse in mine, which made me resemble those post office pictures of characters in "unlawful flight to avoid prosecution."

I was put into the registry office and a supervisor showed me the ropes. Every letter was numbered, summarized, and passed to the correct person to deal with it.

The staff was a mixture of nationalities. Most of the typists were Canadian and American, since Canada, New Zealand, and Australia, were now at war against Hitler. Our head honchos were: A British professor of economics; a former teacher in a British boys' school; a lady who had been in the British Civil Service; a young Canadian banker; and the American girl in charge of the registry where I was assigned to work.

Some of the letters were in code, and these were promptly dumped on the desk of a retired British army officer. As a child he had traveled with his father in the foreign service and was fluent in languages. He was on active duty in WW I, was shot in the spine and told he'd never walk again. He did. Confronted by a pile of coded messages, he would swear in one of his languages, dig the code book out of the safe, and go to work.

About a month after I arrived, the girl in charge of the registry got ill and left. I was in charge. By now I knew MS meant medical supplies, SPA was self-propelled artillery, 20M was anti-aircraft—the expert on this was the British Civil Service lady. But now we had a new expert, a young Dane who had escaped with his wife and child past the occupying Germans who were after him. He had stowed away on a ship and landed in England. He was our expert on small arms and small arms ammunition.

Security was tight. If a document was missing, everything stopped 'til it was located. Liquor was served at rare office parties, but if you got drunk, you were fired. Top secret papers were locked in the safe. You did not write down the combination; you memorized it. To complicate this, the combination was frequently changed. The files were locked and a steel bar attached to the handles. There were also bars over the windows, with a device that triggered an alarm, if touched. Security people dropped in from time to time to test the alarm. The din was terrific, and usually came on just as you were trying to talk on the phone. I could see the need for security—the location of a factory where war supplies were produced would be a boon to the saboteur.

Also at that time there were groups of Americans opposed to any American participation in the war. Their argument: "We have two oceans to protect us." Apparently, they had not heard of the submarine. Charles Lindbergh said the German air force could not be defeated.

Through the U.S. were organizations called German American Bunds, composed mainly of people of German descent, preparing for a Nazi takeover in the future. They met for military drills and were arming themselves. Stalin had by now joined Hitler and Mussolini in plans to divide Europe, while Japan was to control Asia. The Communist newspaper, *Daily Worker*, kept joining with the America Firsters in protesting any American aid to the British.

The FBI was keeping close check on the German American Bunds, and after Pearl Harbor, gathered them in.

Pearl Harbor put an end to the America First movement. A number of young American pilots were already fighting in England, flying Spitfires, then the fastest combat aircraft around.

On Pearl Harbor day I had turned on my radio to a station that broadcast opera and settled down for a peaceful afternoon. The music suddenly stopped. The announcement came. Two U.S. civil service workers and a young navy man dashed in, asking, "Did you hear it?" The main reaction was disbelief. Then reality set in.

One of the most entertaining things to happen was when Hitler turned his army on his supposed partner, Stalin, leaving the Communist *Daily Worker* with nothing to say. They suspended publication. There wasn't much to laugh about those days, but practically all of Washington found their predicament funny.

We had a new lady in the typing room not long after Pearl Harbor, a lovely competent Jewish lady, who didn't really need the job. "I had to do something," she said. "My son was on the battleship Arizona."

HELMUT MEKELBURG

SIDNEY, OHIO

Child in Province of Prussia, Germany, at time of WW II

I was 14 when WW II was over. Before the war, we lived in the town of Loetzen (or Lotzen, with an umlaut), the Polish name being Gizycko. This was in the Province of East Prussia, just north of Poland, about eighty kilometers from the Polish border. The main part of Germany and East Prussia were divided by a portion of Poland. It was called the corridor. This is not the same corridor going into Berlin. This was prior to WW II. East Prussia was cut off from the main part of Germany by part of Poland. The way German propaganda told it, the reason for WW II, and Poland was the first to be taken by Germany, was that somehow Poland harassed the traffic on the highway joining E. Germany to Prussia.

Since the second WW then, Poland got the southern part of East Prussia and Russia got the northern part. Russia and Poland were allies, sort of, at the end of the war, but at the beginning of the war, Russia fought on the side of Germany. When the war ended, Russia decided they wanted part of the eastern part of Poland, annexed it into Russia, and then moved Poland west into eastern Germany. The eastern part of Germany was divided twice, the part to Poland and the other part remained with Germany and became known as East Germany.

In 1940 probably, Germany and Russia got into it. The German army marched into Russia and went as far as Stalingrad. Around 1942 the Russians began to get the upper hand and the German army retreated. Early to mid 1944, the Russian army was really advancing swiftly and by the end of 1944 they were getting close to where we lived.

German troops were in our town all the time, for recuperation, for R & R. A lot of the units got decimated or whatever and came back to regroup. We were the closest German territory to Russia. So when they came back, they'd stay here a while and then leave again.

As Russians were proceeding westward, pushing the German army back, and getting close to where we lived, we began to make preparations to leave, to get away, because they were considered to be a bunch of barbarians. We had no experience with them before, but word was that they were very nasty with Germans, and, as it turned out, it was true. And, of course, they were getting even, too, for things the Germans had done.

The U.S. and the Allies had already landed in Normandy and were advancing into France. By the time that we left to get away from the Russians, I think that France and part of western Germany were already in allied hands.

We were country people. When we tried to escape, our only transportation was horses and wagons, but people from towns and cities didn't even have that kind of luxury. They had to make their way however they could: baby buggies, wheelbarrows, and whatever, to transport their goods. There was no organized train or bus or any kind of transportation at that time. We didn't have that much transportation in peacetime, and now what we had was used to move troops. Families that could afford a bicycle had one; some families might have had two.

We made preparations for this trip west for some time. In the spring of 1944, things weren't going too well for the German army, and we knew eventually we'd have to leave. So we put a roof on top of the wagon. When the Russian army got so close that we could hear the artillery fire, we packed up and left, January, 1945. We had staples, like flour, bacon, potatoes. Later on, these ran out. Our aim was to get to West Germany or wherever we could meet the western Allies. We had heard that they had a lot nicer disposition than the Russians.

Dad and my granddad worked as farm hands for very large landowners, so we were at their mercy. If they wanted to take us with their horses and wagons, we were okay. If they didn't, it was too bad, we would be left. A lot of the people who worked for this landowner were left. Out of the 10 or 12 families working for them, they just took a few that were their favorites, and we just happened to be included.

We headed west, and in seven weeks we probably traveled 150 miles. Never got out of our clothes. The people from the cities didn't have the amount of food that we had and many didn't make it. A lot of them starved or froze to death. Once you get hungry, it doesn't take much to freeze to death. It's colder there than in Ohio, 25 degrees below zero. Ice on those lakes would probably freeze 3 or 4 ft. deep. And it lasted a long time.

There was my mom and 3 boys; then on Dad's side (Dad was in German army) there was Dad's only sister, his father and Grandma; then my Grandpa and Grandma on my mother's side. We were three separate families, but we were pretty much together. I was 13 at the time; one brother was 11; my youngest brother, 6. Some people had babies or gave birth on the way.

We headed west under most dire conditions. As long as our food lasted, we were okay. Everyone survived on whatever they could—horses that died provided meat. Once you get into situations like we were in, it's only human nature to look out for number one, so there wasn't that much neighborly love shown. There wasn't stealing. If you made it, you made it, and if you didn't, you didn't; you died.

Trying to avoid the Russians coming through Poland, we went in a northwesterly direction, and started our crossing of a frozen body of water just before dark. As many refugees as possible got on that ice to cross to a strip of land which had just one little dirt road on it. We stayed on the ice all night, moving with our horses and wagons. It was human masses as far as the eye could see, black with people. That ice was thick enough to carry all those people, plus all the horses and wagons and everything.

We were fortunate that the next morning we could leave the ice and get on the strip of land next to it. People who had lived west of us were probably on the move, too, all on a very primitive highway system, so we only moved maybe 200 yards a day; some days maybe not even 100 yards.

What a lot of people did was stay on the edge of the ice and head the same direction we were. The Russians would strafe civilians with machine gun fire or shoot artillery in, and when a shell knocked a hole in the ice, it just kept on breaking. So a lot of these people on the ice just broke right through and drowned.

A lot of people lost their lives. Along the edge of that water quite often the water was deep enough to drown horses. And if a horse in harness gets into a situation where it can't get out, it will start to scream. A horse's scream, when it's in pain, is a horrible sound. A lot of time their heads would be sticking out; they couldn't drown and they couldn't get out, either.

A lot of people, in the pitch black night, got separated from their families. Some drowned, some didn't. It probably took a month for everyone to cross while the ice was strong enough.

We didn't get out of our clothes from the time we left home until we finally ended up stopping, seven weeks. We had disease, lice, fleas, we stunk. There was a lot of diarrhea, and you know what happens when you can't control that. We were cold, hungry, and just everything imaginable, we were.

Our lady ran the show for the families she took along. If anyone could find out anything or make connections, she could; she was a very influential lady and could get information that we peasants couldn't get. Her husband had died during the war, so she was the boss.

When we were in what I think was the Gdansk area, we were told we would have to leave our horses and wagons cause the Russians had moved north and the only way we could get out was by train. The boss lady's influence got us a spot on this freight train.

The train began to move west. One other thing was that while we lived and farmed in East Prussia, we had French prisoners of war. These prisoners of war were with us all this time while traveling. They could have left us, but for some reason, they didn't. They stayed with us. Before the lady got us on this train in Gdansk, she told the French prisoners to join the other prisoners there and start making their own way. (There were many there.) She felt they could make it easier on their own than having a bunch of civilians along.

Our moving train stopped, set there for hours, and then, with no explanations, the train moved backwards and we ended up where we started. After staying there a day or two, we were told to get back on the train. The second time the same thing happened—it stopped, stayed maybe four hours, and then backed up. We were cut off and couldn't go any farther. So we made our way up north of Gdansk and were told there was no way out; that we were on our own and to do the best we could.

You can't picture some of the places where we slept, or some of the things we did to feed ourselves, or some of the things we did, like going to the bathroom. There wasn't a conductor saying "All Aboard!" If you had to do something and you didn't make it back to the train, it was just tough. You were lost. Naturally, everybody just relieved themselves right along the train out of fear of not getting on it if we started to move. So we weren't very modest, out of necessity. Same thing on the train. You either held it or found a corner some place. It wasn't pleasant. There were no bathrooms; this was a freight train.

Somehow we got separated from the boss lady when we arrived at this little town. However, all my family and another family—a lady with 5 kids—managed somehow to stay together. This was early March, 1945. All this time we could hear the war, all the shooting, artillery, mortar. We saw the German front maybe a half mile away.

We began to walk, carried what few belongings we had, and wound up in what is now called Pomerania in English. Then the Russians came into this little town. The first Russian soldiers I saw were in a buggy with one Cossack horse in front of it. Three or four drunken Russian soldiers came busting through that town. At that time the German army was practically nil. They were either taken prisoner or they surrendered, or they died or were shot up, or whatever. There wasn't any evidence of any German army left.

When the Russians came, it was pretty much true what we had heard. They killed, they raped. Most of the time they were drunk, and when they were drunk, they were highly dangerous.

A lot of people, half grown boys or young grandpas, were made to work for the Russians. The Russian army plundered wherever they went, and everything they felt was of any value, they shipped to Russia. A lot of people were taken to drive cattle to railroad yards. Those people they took just never came back again. They took women for their pleasure and they never came back again. One time this lady had a little baby. Russian soldiers wanted the woman. They yanked the baby out of her arms, handed it to somebody else, and took the woman.

This area was all rural, mostly farm land, and some livestock was still there. Some of the farm people wouldn't leave their farms. Others left maybe weeks before.

We stayed in a grocery store. The front door was right on the sidewalk. The people that owned the store were still there and lived upstairs, used the back door, but they allowed us to stay in the store.

We threw some straw on the floor, making a long community bed. There were 14 of us sleeping in a row. Because my aunt was only 4 or 5 years older than I and the age the Russians would like, we'd hide her in the straw when we saw a Russian coming. The women used old garb and babushkas and made themselves as ugly as possible so the Russians wouldn't take them. If the Russians were drunk, they'd take almost anything. The folks often hid me in the straw, too, cause I was almost grown and they'd want me to go on one of those cattle drives.

As time went on, the Russians calmed down somewhat. We were there from early March, 1945, to early November. We didn't have the means to go anywhere. It would have been foolish to try, with Russian soldiers all over the place. They didn't lock us up; we weren't prisoners, but we couldn't escape. We weren't informed enough; we had no communications. We knew nothing. The only thing we could do was stay put.

We stole grain; we had some potatoes; grain and potatoes were our staple foods. There was no electricity. We didn't even know the war was over. The Russians told us it was over, but we didn't believe them. We were proud Germans, and there was no way the Russian army could defeat us. That was the German thinking. It was stupid, but that was the way it was. We had all this pride.

When it came harvest time, the Russian soldiers had settled down considerably, and my mother and Grandpa would go help with the harvest. When the Russians butchered some cows, the people that helped with the harvest would get a couple pounds of beef. Things were looking up then. I would still stay hidden because of my size and age. I didn't venture out. My younger brothers could pretty much move around.

Going back, before the Russians came in, Grandpa on my mom's side was under 65; the German army drafted him into the people's army. (We did hear from him after the war, through the Red Cross.) My grandpa on my dad's side was a little older, so they left him. One grandma was by herself, and in fact, she died in that store, later on.

Later in 1945, and remember all this time we had no communication, the Russians started bringing in Polish civilians. We didn't know what was going on—why or what for. As they moved into the territory the Russians gave them, the Russian army disappeared. So then we were under Polish rule.

Toward the fall of 1945, the Poles wanted some of the German people to sign some documents and stay there and work for them. I felt they had the power to keep us there without asking, but apparently there was a formality they had to follow, and so they asked us. We were pretty proud Germans and my Grandpa on my dad's side was a real proud German. In peacetime the Poles and Germans would swap cows across the border or dogs or whatever. But still, the Poles, in our eyes, were second class. That's the way the Germans felt about them. They actually weren't, but that's the way we felt. So when the Poles moved in where we were——.

Grandpa treated me like the head of the family. He didn't talk or negotiate with my mom, or even ask her opinion. He talked to me because my dad wasn't there, and I was the oldest. Believe me, when I was 14, I was grown, very mature because of all of this. So Grandpa said, "We're going to have to talk this over. What do you think we should do?" I said I certainly didn't want to stay here and work for the Pollacks. This was below our dignity and just out of the question. He said, "Well, that's just the way I feel about it. So we're not going to sign these documents to stay here. What's the worst thing that could happen if we don't sign?" We had no idea, but decided to take our chance and see what happened.

So a little time went by and the Poles rounded up certain German civilians, which we were part of, and loaded us on a freight train. By then we were getting into probably November, 1945. The train left at night and, not being Boy Scouts and not having any training in telling directions or reading stars, we didn't know which direction the train was moving. Now I realize that you can look at the moss on a tree and know that is the south side, but at that time, we didn't know that. Everybody had a fear of Siberia; that was the place people claimed the Russians would take a lot of Germans. It was rainy, cloudy, nasty weather; we couldn't even see the sun; once daylight came, we still didn't know what direction the train was going.

I don't know how many days and nights it took on the train—3 or 4 days or so. We still had no food or anything to drink. We were diseased, sick, skinny. We just couldn't sleep. We had lice and fleas, and some kind of an itchy skin disease. We had no way to wash our clothes; we had no soap. With this skin disease, we got big bubbles of pus on our skin. The brother 1 1/2 years younger than I, got all this stuff on his head and it was a solid scab. Pus was running down. Mine was mostly on my arms, shoulders, legs. We have no idea what that stuff was.

Anyhow, we were moving on this freight train that the Poles put us on. One morning we came to what looked like a big pile of rubble. You have to remember that we didn't know what had happened to the cities in the west, that they had been bombed by Allied airplanes. We didn't know the war was over.

This rubble looked like it used to be a city. The only things cleared were the streets and the railroad track; there were some church steeples standing and some walls. We had no idea where we were. The train slowed down, and as we looked out the door, it seemed like we were coming into a railroad yard.

Sure enough. We pulled into a railroad yard and there were strange-looking soldiers with odd uniforms and they had these round caps. We wondered who they were. We were told pretty quick then that they were British soldiers. The train had stopped in the British sector. The British soldiers took us from the Poles and put us in some bombed-out building. About that time we were beginning to find out that the war was over, but we still didn't know what the British soldiers were doing there; didn't know what they had to do with us.

They put us in a building that had nothing but walls. They gave us a bowl of soup and a slice of bread once every day, so that was a pretty good treat, as starved as we were. However, it was still like a drop in the bucket, hardly enough to keep us alive, but the British didn't have anything, either. We didn't speak English, and the British didn't speak German. We were still scared, didn't know what was going to happen to us. We didn't know why they were there, that they had supervision over part of Berlin.

Little shops were springing up in Berlin. People would nail up little huts and maybe they'd start baking bread. They would sell it to fellow Berliners; even though money wasn't worth anything, human nature is to make money. We didn't have any money, but Grandpa and I would go into these little shops, some not any bigger than an outhouse. We'd beg for bread, and sometimes people would give us a little bit; sometimes they wouldn't. We weren't too proud at that time because we were hungry.

Anyhow, my grandpa was a very resourceful old cuss. He said to me one day, "You know, (of course, we knew by that time we were in Berlin) there's bound to be a lot of farm land around Berlin. I'm pretty sure these farmers raise potatoes, and they probaby do the same thing we did in East Prussia, load the potatoes and everything they raise on trains and take it to the city so city people will have things to eat. It's harvest time and those farmers are bound to be bringing those potatoes to some of these railroad yards. Tomorrow morning we're going to take one of Grandma's pillowcases and see if we can find something to eat."

So Grandpa and I took off looking for a railroad yard with potatoes. We walked the biggest part of the day. The Berliners had gotten the streets cleared off; everything else was rubble. With my Grandpa, it didn't matter how bad things got. He had a handlebar moustache, a crooked pipe; he had no tobacco to smoke, but he always had dried leaves. It didn't matter what variety, but he preferred cherry tree leaves; he'd burn whatever he could find and have that thing hanging out of his mouth. He walked a little bow-legged, and he hummed. It never got so bad that he wouldn't hum.

It was getting pretty late in the day and we saw this street go up a rise a little bit; it looked like a bridge. So we walked up that rise and, lo and behold, there was a railroad yard right beneath us. Grandpa was right! There were cars there with potatoes on them, open cars and cars with tops on them. Grandpa said, "Son, we're not going to enter this thing from the front, we're going to the back. There's some trains over there that don't have any potatoes. (The potato trains were in the middle.) We're going to come in from the back and maybe no one will see us."

When we were up on that bridge, we saw a tower right in the middle of the yard, and there were some people in it. Had no idea who they were. We might have been in the Russian sector. We didn't know it was divided into sectors, and we had walked a long time. So we entered from the back, and I climbed up on one of the open cars. Grandpa told me to throw the biggest potatoes down. I was throwing the potatoes down fast, and he was raking them into that pillowcase. All of a sudden somebody yelled, and I thought it was coming from that tower. He no more than yelled than this machine gun fire started coming right at me, down the cars. It was just following the cars. The last thing I saw was that it splattered some of the potatoes on the car I was on. By then I was hauling tail. I slid on my belly right down the side of that car, and Grandpa and I took off. We went under a couple of trains, and Grandpa didn't lose one potato.

When we got back to camp, we found some tin, punched holes with some old rusty nails, and made a grating iron out of it. We grated those potatoes and made a little stove out of brick and another piece of tin. We put that potato dough on there and had potato pancakes; everybody envied us something fierce. All the people we knew at that time, all the people we had any connection with, ate good that night.

At this camp, there were probably a thousand refugees crowded together. This fine-looking lady—you could tell she had been someone of standing at some time—was in the same boat we were in, but she had a little dog. And when the British fed us the soup, she spoon-fed that little dog. She'd take a spoonful and then give a spoonful to the little dog. People were so hungry there that if she had ever let that dog away from herself, someone would have skinned it. They were eyeballing that dog all the time.

Remember a few years ago when that airplane went down in South America and there was some cannibalism? Everybody was so outraged. Well, I tell you what, when you get that hungry and see some of the things people eat, you could understand why cannibalism was absolutely possible. I didn't hear or know of anyone that killed to get food or water, but hunger hurts. You might be in an awful lot of pain and you might do a lot of things you wouldn't do, otherwise.

After being in Berlin maybe two or three weeks, the British loaded us on another freight train. We still didn't hear anything about the zones, had no idea. They sent us to what they called Germany. Well, we thought we were in Germany! We disembarked from the train in the province of Oldenburg in West Germany. Later on we found out that was called the British sector, and there was a French sector, an American sector, and a Russian sector. Once we got there and got our feet warm a little bit, we found out what had happened.

They dropped us off at a farm. We found out later that the West German government (even in late 1945, W. Germany was governing itself) more or less forced these people, if they had the means and the facilities to take in refugees, to do so. This farmer gave us a couple of attic rooms, and that's where we lived, my mom and us three boys. Grandpa and Grandma and my aunt went in another direction; the British separated us; we had no choice. They took us where they had the room for us. Grandpa and Grandma and my aunt ended up in Hanover. We were separated again without communications. Once we got to Oldenburg, we lost contact.

We were expected to work for this farmer for our food and our quarters. All this time, my dad wasn't with us, I was the oldest. My younger brother worked, but he also went to school there. The school had been disrupted for a long time, but by this time, it was in operation. This was a rural area and there wasn't any damage. In 45 churches and schools, things were already fairly normal. Law enforcement was in operation. German policemen weren't armed, but they had authority over the civilian population. The British army was there in that area, also.

All this time, since he had been drafted (age 43) we didn't know what had happened to our dad—didn't know if he was alive, and he didn't know if we were alive. The way we got together again: My dad was one of seven brothers. His two oldest brothers, being young and adventurous, didn't want to work on the farm, so they went clear across Germany into the Ruhr valley, before the war. We communicated then so much that we didn't need their address written down; we remembered it. So at the first opportunity to send mail, we wrote to my dad's brothers. We knew that area had been bombed and wondered if they were still alive. Wrote to Uncle Gustav. Didn't hear for a long time. Finally we did hear, and it was from a different address than the one we knew. Their home had been bombed out, so they lived somewhere in the same area but not the address we knew. The Red Cross found them for us. Before we had written, my dad had gotten in touch with them, saying he was in the British POW camp in Yugoslavia.

My dad, when released from the POW camp around 1947, came to work for this farmer we were with. By this time I was 15 and really grown! I was smoking and was a macho cat (so I thought). I got a job on another farm and made my own way.

Money reform took place in Germany, I think, in 1947. What's called the Deutsch mark today came into being then. Up until that time, money was worthless. Inflation was probably several thousand percent. You had to have a wheelbarrow of money to buy a pack of cigarettes.

I need to back off and talk about food and hunger. Of course, we were on farms and food was more available. City people would get on trains, or whatever transportation they could get, and go out to the country and trade for food, whether it be fruit, grain, potatoes, or a little meat. Food was rationed and scarce, during and after the war. Transportation was poor, and the food couldn't be distributed; so people in cities were hungry a long time after the war. The Berlin Airlift didn't start until maybe 1948. Anyway, people flocked into the countryside bartering for food, trading rings, other jewelry, clothing, watches, fountain pens—anything that some farmer might want. A farmer wouldn't sell anything for that worthless money. There was a constant trek along the roads of people with their sacks, etc., almost like Pilgrims trading with the Indians.

Our food on the farm wasn't too plentiful cause the farmer would rather get some goodies from the city. We hadn't had much food in our bellies for months, but it was still a heck of a lot better than what we had previously..

So money reform came and so much was distributed per head. We could use it as we wanted. We could begin to buy things; things began to be manufactured. Before, we couldn't even buy bicycles, but once the money gained some value, industrial production started up and things began to move. People began to work for money and to buy and sell for money.

Once this money reform came, my dad decided that he wasn't making anything on the farm and he was going to quit. He found a job with a general contractor in the city nearest us and got paid well. I was finally beginning to make some money and saved enough for a bicycle. The other brother had left and gone to another farm.

This contractor my dad worked for would build a barn, put drainage tile in a field, or whatever you wanted done. In wintertime they would be unemployed. We had unemployment insurance (as we had before the war) as soon as things started to get organized. My dad had to report to the unemployment office for benefits. He saw this poster in the office that asked for displaced persons—the people in Oldenburg called us Damned Refugees. We were considered scum. A lot of people from the Balkan countries like Yugoslavia, Czeckoslovakia, countries that came under Russian control during WWII, those people didn't like the Russians any better than we did, so a lot of them made their way into West Germany. So talk about a melting pot, we had Russians, Poles, every country represented east of France. Our chances of ever getting anywhere economically were slim. So my dad saw this poster and it told displaced persons from the eastern parts of Germany to sign up to emigrate to either Canada, United States, New Zealand, or Australia.

One weekend when my brother and I were home, Dad brought this up. We talked it over and decided to register to emigrate. This was probably in 1951. Sometime, maybe in the spring, we got registered mail to report for processing. We went to a camp run by Americans and British, and somehow we got into the American part of it, and they began to process us for emigration. After staying in this camp for 4 or 5 weeks, they told us to go home and we would be notified what to bring, what to do, and to be prepared the next time to be loaded on a ship and leave.

We got to the New York harbor, knowing nothing about the U.S. We had no dealings with Americans at all because we had been living in the British sector. The only thing we remembered about the Americans was that the German propaganda said they were nothing but scum. You would assume we knew all about the U.S., but we didn't. We were still apprehensive. And we didn't know where we were going now that we were in the U.S.

In fact, when we got to New York City, Church World Services told us they didn't have any place to put us. Now what would we do? We were told that if we had gotten there in the summertime, some farmer in the western states wanted us because we were farm hands. Anyway, we had no place to go. Church World Services said they would give us some money and put us in a hotel until they found some place for us. This was panic time, too. We were in a strange place, didn't know the language, didn't know anything from Adam—country people in New York City!

We walked a number of blocks, keeping in touch with Church World Services. Three weeks later they loaded us on a Greyhound bus, practically putting address stickers on us and shipping us to Piqua, Ohio. We wondered where on earth Ohio was.

Going to a hotel in Piqua on the circle, as instructed, we had difficulty communicating who we were, but they finally gave us a room. The bus didn't get there 'til late and it was dark. While we were on the bus trip, all the Americans went to machines and got food, but we didn't know how to operate the machines. We traveled a long time. We watched how people operated those machines, so I think we finally bought some candy bars.

When we got to the hotel in Piqua, Dad said, "Let's go and see if we can find a restaurant." I asked him what he was going to do when he got to a restaurant. He said, "Well, you remember that Americans call wieners *wieners* just like we do." Mom was scared to death to go out. So Pop and us boys took off and found a little hole-in-the-wall restaurant, a beanery, had 2 or 3 tables. There was a bar and bar stools, and we had no idea what those were for. If you went to a restaurant in Germany, you sat down at a table. We sat down and a big guy with a white apron came up and started to talk. My dad said, "wieners, wieners," and tried to explain with his hands. The old guy said, "Huh?" He couldn't understand any of this. So he talked and my dad talked and then he left. Pretty soon he came back with four bowls of bean soup and some Saltine crackers. We ate that and filled up, all but Mom. She was still in the hotel room, hungry.

We decided there must be a grocery store some place. We saw some in New York City where all we had to do was walk in, help ourselves, walk up to the counter—didn't have to say a word, just handed them the money. Didn't have to know English. Dad figured if they had those in New York, there must be some around here. You understand, we didn't buy groceries that way in Germany. In our stores, if a guy wanted a pound of sugar, the worker got the sugar out of a sack and weighed it for him. We had no idea about self-service. We scouted around Piqua and sure enough, we found a grocery store, bought some food, and went back and fed Mom, and ate some more ourselves.

The next morning we went out again, cause you talk about hungry! Even when we were in West Germany, our food was more or less rationed. Anyway, we were still in that hotel and didn't know what was supposed to be happening. I don't recall having anything to show anyone except our immigration papers.

A lady who spoke German and a Mr. Petersimes from Gettysburg, Ohio, visited us shortly, and she explained, in German, that he was a staunch member of the Church of the Brethren and was going to be our sponsor. At that time we were smoking—my dad, my brother, and I. The first thing the lady told us was to please put out our cigarettes because Mr. Petersimes was a member of the Church of the Brethren and they do not tolerate smoking. We had bought cigarettes with some of that money the church gave us.

She explained to us that we were going to go, once our house was ready, to a farm that was owned by a friend of Mr. Petersimes, an attorney from Cleveland, Ohio. At that time, though, our house wasn't ready to be moved into, so they were going to take us to a Church of the Brethren church camp.

This church camp happened to be on Rt. 47, east of Bellefontaine, a place called Mountain Lake. Mr. Petersimes and the woman (by the way, she was a Lithuanian lady, also a refugee, and they got her the job of being Mr. Petersimes' secretary) loaded us into their car and drove us to Bellefontaine and put us in the first cabin. They said that while we were here we could do this and that work, cut weeds, clean out the big building, and what not. They would bring us groceries once a week. We could pay them back once we started to work. They would keep track of all the money spent.

The first morning, all of a sudden, we heard this shooting, and cars drove by. Whenever a car drove by, we'd run and hide cause we didn't want anyone stopping and trying to talk to us since we wouldn't know what they were saying. So it took us a while to figure out what was going on, but it was people duck hunting. Well, in Germany we weren't allowed to own guns, and we had no idea that ordinary people were allowed to have guns here. But they were blasting away! We were scared to death with all this shooting and stayed in the cabin.

Betty and Mr. Petersimes would bring us groceries, but we could eat a lot more than they brought us. We started hoofing it into Bellefontaine and buying more food, and cigarettes.

I knew how to snare rabbits. We did that in Germany—it was illegal here, but I didn't know that. I'd snare rabbits and once in awhile I'd supplement our table. I made some snares from some thin wire I found in the big building there at the camp. One day I went out to look at my snares to see if I caught anything, and I saw the biggest white rat I ever saw in my life caught in one of my snares. When I got close, that thing was hissing at me. It turned out it wasn't a rat, it was a possum. We didn't have those, so to me it looked like a big rat. The snare caught him around the belly. The head and everything was in good shape and that thing was alive and hissing at me. How could I get it out of there? It was trying to bite me. I had the snare tied on to a stick, so I pulled the stick out trying to get away from it and I broke the stick and somehow the wire loosened up and that thing took off. It still had the wire on but was in good shape.

Finally Mr. Petersimes and Betty came back and said our house was ready; took us to a farm at Webster, south of Versailles, Ohio. Another man was already managing the farm for this lawyer from Cleveland and he was our boss. We were obligated to work there for one year, the minimum. I worked there for a little less than a year, but I got hurt and then it took me a while to recuperate. The attorney came down from Cleveland one weekend and I asked if he would let me go to work in town because I could make more money. By that time I was learning English and could get along pretty well. He agreed to it, so I started to work at Copeland in Sidney in January, 1953. My dad and my brother stayed on. My youngest brother was going to Versailles H.S.

Within six months after arrival here, I had to register for the draft, but couldn't even speak English. They wanted to send me back to Germany as an interpreter. I spoke German and Polish, and if you speak Polish, you can also talk to a Russian.

Once they found out that I could do this, they really wanted me for an interpreter, wanted me to volunteer. I was still the subject of another country and they couldn't draft me, but I could volunteer. The Korean War was going on at the time, and you have to remember, I didn't trust the Americans that much at that time, and when they said volunteer, I said to myself, what if they lied to me and they send me to Korea. I'll be right in another war. I told them that I just came out of one war and I didn't want to go into another one. He said he'd guarantee that I wouldn't go to Korea. But I said I didn't want to go back to Germany, either.

EMILY MAY MILLER

SIDNEY, OHIO

Civilian Administrative Librarian for Air Force
Duty in England and Japan

I was in Honolulu with my sister in 1960 when the Air Force asked me to be a librarian in Japan.

While in Honolulu I knew the wife of the Japanese Consul General did not speak English. I wrote a note to the Consul General and offered to teach English to his wife. He asked me to come to the Consulate and talk with him. After that he invited me to his house for luncheon. That was quite an honor because normally Japanese do not entertain in their homes. The home was the new consulate palace; they were the first people to live in it. Contrary to Japanese custom of sitting on the floor at that time, they sat on chairs at a dining room table. The little girl spilled her milk, just like any other little girl.

At a later date, the Consul General invited me and my family—5, sister, brother-in-law, and children—to a dinner party. In Hawaii most things are quite informal, so we dressed casually. Ambassadors were there, the Honolulu symphony was playing, and women were dressed in their fanciest kimonos. And, to my great surprise, I learned I was the guest of honor and was seated at the Consul's table. He asked me to decide whether or not the symphony should go to Japan. I didn't think it was that good and told him my opinion.

The wife took everyone through the house, opening cupboards to show bedding because she was so pleased and proud of it. Later my sister invited them to her house for dinner. The children got along fine. While Helen was cooking, the wife wanted to see the bedrooms. She opened closet doors and dresser drawers, wanting to see everything. Helen was so embarrassed because she wasn't expecting anyone to be going into the bedrooms, and with children, many things were just thrown around.

The family brought gifts to all of us. We hadn't realized when we went to the palace that the Japanese custom was to always take gifts, so again, we were embarrassed.

When I was leaving for Japan, the Consul's wife came to the airport to say goodbye.

The Air Force had libraries at all bases for the troops. We also had Japanese cadets at our base studying for civil defense and they had to learn English. They were using textbooks and grammar books from the beginning of the 20th century, British. All but the captain were too bashful to try to talk. He, or any Japanese, couldn't pronounce his "ls" so my name came out more like *Murrer* than *Miller*.

While stationed in Japan I attended a Fertility Festival. The Lt. General, a woman, made arrangements for the staff to go to this festival. She made reservations at a hotel which had been built and occupied by the British, but upon our arrival, we were told there was no reservation. With her clout, she managed to get us in, but there was no question about the fact that they didn't want us there for the festival. No one at the festival, however, mistreated us.

There was so much to see. Everything there was related to the penis or women's parts. Sexual parts were identified in everything, even to the crotch of a tree; it all had some reference to fertility. The lady that took us said that all the men carry a replica of a small penis. Childless people went to the temple and asked the priest to pray for children. Many grandparents went to ask for grandchildren. The Japanese people also post prayers on buildings and posts.

In the library at the base we had a flower arranger come three days a week with fresh flowers for every table. The Japanese workers paid for those flowers.

At the Cherry Blossom Festival, everyone was happy, having picnics, and drinking a lot. I noticed one family of three generations had spread their lunch out on a cloth on the ground (which all of them did—no picnic tables). The older couple was in kimonos and did a lot of bowing. The teenagers were in modern clothes.

There was much evidence of these changes in Tokyo—many older people with their kimonos and right beside them were younger people in western-style clothes. Standing at a railroad station were senior citizens all in dark gray kimonos watching for the train. All were stoop shouldered from carrying babies on their backs. These people waiting for the train had been provided tours by the government, their way of giving them a pension, taking them places they should see.

The Japanese way of bathing was different from ours. Of course, they had public baths, but whereas we get in a tub and put a lot of soap all over ourselves, they sat at the side where there was a spigot of water. They used their cloth and soap and washed themselves all over from their bath pan. There was a drain and they changed their water. After they had cleaned themselves all over, then they got in the hot bath. And they still had baths with men and women together. At the hotel where we stayed, the management found another private place for us to bathe.

MacArthur had insisted on everyone getting an education, and they were wild to read! The base was outside of Atachikawa. To go into Tokyo you took a commuter train, without air condition or any amenities. As soon as the Japanese men got on the train, they took off their coats, shirts, and pants. They would play a game called Go. They would play it all the way into Tokyo, and then quickly put their clothes back on and get off.

Tokyo was not clean nor very sanitary. Far out from the base was a good seamstress. Her house was a small cubicle right next to the street. You passed the toilet on the way into the sewing room. The honey wagon would come every day or so and dip the remains from the toilet. The clothes that the seamstresses made for us were uncomfortable because Americans are shaped differently than the Japanese.

While on a bus trip, there was a rest stop. There was a little stream where the men urinated. The women had to squat over holes in the ground. In Tokyo a woman squatted in the middle of the street.

On the day before Christmas, I was transferred, by military plane, to Akata, near Fukuoka, in the southern part of Japan. The base commander met me, and we went directly to the Christmas party that the whole base was having. There I met commissioned and non-commissioned people. Later they took me to my residence, where my bags had already been unpacked and things were put away. The next day I had Christmas dinner at the home of the base commander.

The base commander was black and had family there—wife and two high school boys. They were ostracized by air force people. The wife volunteered to come to the library and help. I had the shoulder the wife needed to cry on.

While in Japan it was difficult for American women to go out on a date. The Japanese system was for men, and they didn't want women around.

I took my car to Japan with me, red, eight-cylinder. The Japanese thought the authorities would not give me a license because only fire engines were red. As I drove around, men swarmed around. They talked about how I could speed up faster than anyone else could.

ERNST SCHMIDT

SIDNEY, OHIO

U-Boat Commander, Germany, WW II
P.O.W. in England May 13, 1945-July 14, 1948

May 1, 1945, North Atlantic, south of Iceland, a German U-Boat plowing steady westward. The lookouts on the bridge, waiting for their relief after their four-hour watch, were eager to go down and change into dry, warm clothes. The ocean was still cold at this time of the year. A top secret radio message was just received and, since the sun was coming up, it would soon be time to dive in order not to be surprised by the patrolling planes.

The skipper deciphers the message. As he reads, his face grows pale, his hands are shaking. *Is this the end? Now what?*

He withdraws to his bunk, draws the thin green curtain, and stares at the curved overhead ceiling and dripping pipes. *I must collect myself, I must be strong. Give me time and the right words to tell the men, my crew.*

The crew assembles in the forward torpedo room; they squeeze together in the already-overloaded room, where the reserve torpedos are laying on the floor plates, where food and provisions for seven months are stored; hams and sausages are dangling from pipes and ceiling. It is hot, sticky, and uncomfortable.

The skipper climbs through the round hatch. The First Watch officer reports to him the crew is assembled, except for those needed in the electric motor room and those who are on the diving watch in the control room.

The words come out slowly and hesitatingly as he reads the message from the Grandadmiral Doenitz, Chief of the German navy and father of the U-Boat forces: "May 1, 1945, radio 0900 hrs. Our Fuehrer, Adolf Hitler, fighting to his last breath, fell for Germany in his headquarters in the Reich's Chancellery on April the thirtieth. The Fuehrer appointed Grandadmiral Doenitz to take his place."

...Silence... only the electric motors hum and move the boat, now at 600 ft. down, further west towards the coast of

America. Stunned faces all around; eyes, some moist, hanging on the lips of the skipper.

"Men, the war will be over soon, a matter of days or weeks. Berlin is conquered by the Russians; Germany is split in half in North and South; Germany is overrun in the East by the Soviets, where terrible things are happening to the population; and by the British and American troops in the West. But we are here, thousands of miles away and cannot help. We must wait for further orders and instructions.

"And you, my crew, must continue to trust me, since my first duty is to bring you all safely back home from this patrol. We had good and bad times together. And... "

He was interrupted by the rumbling of depth charges and explosions, which could be heard clearly on the port side. Still far away and not an immediate threat for the boat. Calm and composed, he gave the order to the Chief Engineer, who had watch in the control room: "Stay on 600 ft., change course to 315 degrees, and hold her steady. Let's get away from here. They won't spot us; they are too far away."

He looks into the faces of his men, clears his throat. "Comrades, you see, the war is not over yet. The enemy is still fighting. I hope the poor fellows out there are holding out and get away. It would be a pity if they do not make it, now, just a minute before closing.

"As for now, as our original orders indicate, we must reach our patrol area. Therefore, nothing has changed in our daily routine on board. At night, when we are surfaced and charge our batteries, I urge the lookout and the watch to stay especially alert, so that the enemy does not surprise us. Remember, we want to stay alive, and when it is over, we want to go home.

"Are there any questions? Anything? Well, then, you are dismissed to your stations... and I thank you!"

It takes awhile before the men begin to move and return to their places. They are silent and slouch as they wind themselves through the boat. They carry a heavy load and are in deep thought.

Somehow relieved, he checks the control room. The chief engineer, the two sailors on the diving plane controls, the helmsman, and the two control room mechanics perform their duty in silence. The mechanic's mate looks up from his log book and tries to smile at the skipper. With that, the skipper turns and goes back to his bunk.

The depth charges can still be heard. He enters his report into the war log. He does not draw the curtains this time. When the men see him sleep, they think that everything is all right, at least for the time being. He tries to sleep. You never know how long you will have to stay awake.

In the next days no specific orders are received. The official reports state only that the fight goes on and heavy resistance is put up by the army against the advancing Soviets in the East, whereas heavy bombing of cities in the West by superior Allied airplanes continues. Rescue operations are going on to transport soldiers and civilians across the Baltic from the eastern provinces.

A depressing situation for the crew, but they take it and bear it in silence. Their thoughts and fears are with their families. And still the patrol must go on... *Is there any hope of victory as the Fuehrer promised?*

Finally, on May 4, 1945, the radio message and order came: "All U-Boats. Attention all U-Boats! Cease fire at once. Stop all hostile actions against Allied shipping. Remain on stations. Do not proceed further west! Doenitz"

With later communications it was learned that negotiations were progressing between the Allies and German leaders.

With a heavy heart, the skipper announced this news over the loudspeaker. He could not quite collect himself to tell the men this discouraging news to their faces.

Dutifully he enters the proceedings in the war log and orders the Officer of the Watch and the navigator to reduce speed and steer in a wide circle in order to stay on the spot, the final position of this patrol.

He is not ready, just now, to answer any questions which show up in the faces of his men. He feels for them and would like to do something to ease the unbearable situation. To come up and surface and see the daylight, maybe the sun would do wonders. But then... if the enemy, a plane or a destroyer, would spot them and did not have the information, and they would attack, it could mean almost certain death for the boat, as they would not have manned the anti-aircraft guns and it would be too late to dive. It is too risky.

So he tells the cook to prepare a good meal and issue a candy bar in the meantime. Why not? There is plenty of food on board; who will hold the skipper accountable for lost or spoiled food? The enemy? The base in Germany, if they make it back?

Early in the morning, while still on the surface, another message is received:

"May 9, 1945, 0140 HRS. Attention all U-Boats! My U-boat men. Six years of war lie behind you. You have fought like lions. An overwhelming material superiority has driven us into a tight corner from which it is no longer possible to continue the war. Unbeaten and unblemished, you lay down your arms after a heroic fight without parallel. We proudly remember our fallen comrades, who gave their lives for Fuehrer and Fatherland. Comrades, preserve that spirit in which you have fought so long and so gallantly for the sake of the future of the Fatherland. Long Live Germany! Your Grandadmiral."

More radio reports followed to inform the boats at sea what had happened in the last few days—the negotiations and signing of a partial surrender in the West with the Allied forces at the headquarters of Field Marshal Montgomery in Reims, the continuation of rescue transports of soldiers and civilians in the East, and that finally the senseless fighting had stopped.

(Later the U-Boat surfaced and was surrounded by British navy. All taken as British prisoners. Eventually Ernst had opportunity to apply for entrance to the U.S. and ultimately became American citizen.)

Ernst Schmidt,
P.O.W Camp, England

RENATE SCHMIDT

SIDNEY, OHIO

Child in Germany (part that is now Poland) during WW II

Mother was an American citizen, born in Milwaukee, Wisconsin, took a trip through Europe, met my dad, married, and they decided to stay there. The part of Germany where I was born is now Poland.

At the time of the war I was six years old. The Nazis just came in and took over. Dad was a pure German, dating back to 1492, but since he was married to a foreign-born and an American-born person, that made us second-class citizens. We were not considered the pure Germans. We were the mixed breed. Mom found a letter in Dad's trousers that read: Mistakes are made but they can be corrected, so if at any time you feel you would like to get rid of your mistakes, all you have to do is let us know.

My mom was more or less, I can't say under house arrest, yet she was not allowed to move about. She had to have a permit or be accompanied by a German, even to go to the movies. And she couldn't go whenever or wherever she wanted; maybe she could go once a month. They forced my mom and dad to sign off the white brick company they owned. My mother refused. Finally they took our whole family, pushed my mom about, and she was forced to sign because they threatened to take the children away. My dad and grandpa, who was part owner, had already signed.

One day my dad came home very upset and forbid me to talk to or go into anyone's house. He never told me why until many years later. The pure Germans felt so bad and thought maybe Dad didn't have the nerve to get rid of us. They were going to help or make it easier on him, so they got a petition with signatures to have us removed out of his life so he could lead a clean Nazi life. They thought they were doing him a favor. We were very lucky—nothing happened. So in our lifetime during the war, for every bad thing, there was always one voice or person that would help us out, save our life.

Our lives did hang on the life of my father. If Dad had been killed on the Russian front, and they did take him into service, I would not have been here today. We wouldn't have survived.

They did take me to a camp, not a concentration camp, but a camp (I found out later. I was watching a program on TV one day and there it was) for mixed breed children, from mixed marriages. This was in the wintertime, because at that time they had more control; in the summertime you would have a good time. This was cold, so we slept in a cold room, unheated, under one blanket, on straw, on real rough kind of beds, and we stayed there 'til Christmas the first time—November 'til Christmas. The idea was to find out whether we were being indoctrinated in the wrong way by our parent of the other nationality or whether we were being raised as good German citizens.

My mom, being an American, I always said was such an intelligent person, and she truly outsmarted all three governments. She was always ahead. If you got a notice from the Gestapo and it said to take a change of clothing, then it meant you were coming back. If there was no change of clothing mentioned, then it meant you would be gone forever. So in my case, there was a change of clothing to be taken along. That meant I was returning, so my mom said, "When you're writing, do not complain. Don't ever criticize or complain; don't let anyone know you're sick unless you drop. Do not let anyone know anything. And when you write home, write good things, happy things. I will understand and do the same. Never, never give any secrets away." So I remembered and did exactly that.

We had to write home every other day; that was part of our curriculum. However, my mom never did receive a letter and neither did I receive one from anybody at home. She had to take her letters to the Gestapo office and they said they would forward them to wherever we were. Even I did not know where we were staying. It was a farm house, but to this day I don't know where it was. We were taken in the evening in a military truck. Everything always happened at night. When the people disappeared, it was at night time. You did not dare to ask because by asking that meant you were a friend and therefore were also guilty of what they were charged. Ninety-nine percent of the time it was treason and that gave the right to do whatever they wanted to, mostly execute, or the people would just disappear. It was all a very big secret. So if someone disappeared, you just had to pretend it didn't happen.

I returned home for Christmas, and the second time they took me, in the same situation, they did say "Go home. This is the last time you will be at home with your family. When you return in January, you will not go home again." I did not tell this to my mom. My dad was on the Russian front at that time. The Russians were advancing cause this was in 1944. For some reason, and here again I don't know whether it was done on purpose or what, but my name never came up, and I didn't have to go back. So when the Russians came in, more or less, we were liberated of that kind of situation.

TONY VANDERSTRAATEN

SIDNEY, OHIO

Resident of Holland during WW II

Although I was only five years old when WW II ended, let me try to give you some impressions of the general living conditions in Holland during 1940-45.

In early May, 1940, the German army attacked both France and the low countries. After a five-day struggle, and the destruction of most of Rotterdam, the Dutch gave up and the German occupation came into being. In the nick of time, the Dutch government and the Royal Family escaped to England. From there an active campaign was started to assist in the eventual defeat of the occupying German forces.

During the early years of 1940-42, life did not change all that much in Holland. Everyone cooperated as best as possible. In order to keep up the spirit and show a respect for the Royal Family, orange flowers were grown by many citizens. I remember my parents were busy in the spring planting orange flowers. Everyone in Europe knows the official colour of Holland is orange. In fact, the last name of the Dutch Royal Family is Van Orange Nassau. This goes back to the sixteenth century.

The Germans knew, of course, the true meaning of the orange flowers and proceeded to march over the many flowerbeds, crushing the orange flowers underneath their boots. However, every time this happened, mysteriously the orange flowers always came back in full bloom.

Around 1943, slowly but steadily, life became more difficult. Jewish people were forced to wear the yellow star and the first shipment to the concentration camps were taking place. Approximately 300,000 Dutch Jewish people did not survive the week.

Through the centuries the Dutch have shown a live-and let-live attitude. It came, therefore, as a shock to most people, realizing what the Germans were up to. By the middle of 1943, the resistance movement became better organized and went over to the offensive. Many well-thought-out attacks were undertaken against the German forces. Particularly, the county record centers were blown up as much as possible. This was done to make it very difficult for the Germans to find out exactly all the names of the Dutch Jewish citizens. The problem was, however, the bolder the resistance movement became, the harsher the

German reprisals grew against prominent local Dutch nationals.

By 1944 life became even more difficult. Our own family had to give up the house we lived in. We moved away with relatives in the countryside. The German army took over our house and placed heavy AA guns in our backyard. Luckily, after the war was over, most of our house was still in decent shape.

By early September of 1944, the Allies had liberated the southern part of Holland. This area is located south of the big rivers. The big cities, though, and about 75 percent of Holland was still in German hands. It would take another seven months before finally the main part of Holland would be free again.

Due to the fact the Allies under-estimated the strength of the Germans (Battle of the Bulge), the Dutch population suffered terribly in the winter, 1944-45. Unfortunately, this winter happened to be a very severe one—I would say similar to a strong winter in Ohio. In most of Holland food became very difficult to come by. Particularly in the big cities, thousands died due to starvation. Through all of this, the German army was still fighting the resistance movement, practically to the bitter end. Many Dutch people either rotted away in prisons or died from malnutrition. Miraculously, some survived.

In March, 1945, the Swedish Red Cross was allowed to parachute foodstuffs into Holland. English planes were used for this purpose. The German High Command, who knew, of course, the war was lost, thought to buy goodwill. However, this was to no avail. In September, 1945, the German commissioner of Holland was hanged in Nuremberg. By late April the war was finally over and the rest of Holland was liberated by the English and Canadian forces.

There are a couple of interesting points I should add: Even today there is no great love between the various European countries and Germany. This is particularly true in Holland.

Each year at 8:00 P.M. on May 4, all traffic stops in Holland for one minute. People walking in the street stand at attention to pay respect for those who did not come back.

Once every five years each major town in Holland holds an evening candlelight people's walk to the various monuments within the city limits, paying respect to the war's victims.

Up to 1986, three German generals were still in prison in Holland, a fact which was known by most knowledgeable people of Europe. Keep in mind since 1956 there were no more German prisoners left anywhere in Europe except for Hess in Berlin and the three generals in Holland. In 1986 one general died in prison, the other two were then allowed to go back to Germany. Both were in their late 80s.

This last story particularly illustrates the point of how severely the Dutch population still shows their disrespect for anything German.

As in the case with later generations worldwide, the young people growing up today in Holland are barely aware of what happened 50 years ago. In order not to forget, a number of museums have opened during the last five years. I have visited two of the main museums and found them most interesting.

In conclusion, of the many American service people killed in WW II, approximately l2,000 are buried in Holland.

VICTORY C

END OF JAPANESE WAR---Ser
Philippine Islands.

LEBRATION

adron Ten Anchorage, Leyte Gulf,

Printed aboard U.S.S. AJAX

KOREA

SYNOPSIS OF OUR INVOLVEMENT

Five years after the close of WW II, on June 27, 1950, with our military branches diminished, neglected, inadequately trained and equipped, President Truman, without a declaration of war, because he thought it would be a small short skirmish, pledged our support to South Korea. Two days earlier, 90,000 North Korean troops pushed across the 38th parallel into South Korea, surprising everyone and meeting little, scattered opposition. Seventeen other nations joined the U.S. in the cause, with General Douglas MacArthur, well-known from WW II, appointed as Commander in what was to be called a *police action*.

Awareness of this small Asian country started after WW II, when defeated Japan was required to give it up, a territory they had occupied since 1904. Korea wanted its independence, but the feeling was that a colonial people would not be able to rule themselves. So the two super-powers, the United States and Russia, agreed to divide the country at the 38th parallel, Russia taking the North and United States the South. An election was to be held later determining the path of the

Korean War Memorial, Dayton Ohio.
Courtesy James W. Snyder, President, The Korean Veterans Memorial Association

country, but agreement there could not be reached, even when the United Nations intervened.

While Russia fought with the Allies against Hitler, as soon as the hostilities ended, differences again surfaced, beginning with the Wall (the Iron Curtain) in Germany. America and the Free World were fearful of a world-wide Communist takeover. Along with Russia and now North Korea, China had become Communist when Mao's army defeated Chiang Kai Shek. Rushing to the aid of South Korea was the move to indicate that the Free World was ready to repel any Communist attempts.

North Korea is located between Manchuria and Japan, the North having most of the minerals and heavy industry, the South most of the agricultural lands and ice-free ports leading to world trade.

Starting in 1945, the United States occupied South Korea, giving them financial aid, helping to establish their own government, and attempting to form and train their own army and security force. Realizing they were not making much progress toward establishing a democratic country and that the people were wanting their own self-rule, the bulk of the American forces left in 1949, with just a 500-man assistance and training group remaining.

On July 1, 1950, less than a week after the North Korean troops crossed the 38th parallel, additional American troops arrived at Pusan, but North Korea's superior, motivated, and well-equipped forces were not to be detained. UN forces, including naval and marine air support, were pushed farther and farther, almost into the sea. Many of the South Korean soldiers just disappeared. More countries were sending help while the United States was calling in reservists and national guards and rushing draftees through training. This, to go to a land where the troops couldn't understand the language, the people, or the customs. They looked at the situation with hate, not being sure why they were there and wondering why there wasn't more military there to help them. "After the creation of the mightiest military machine ever forged on this planet the United States dismantled her military might with incredible vigor, utterly emasculating her armed forces after 1945. Intelligence hardware went the way of the rest, to the scrap heap."[1]

A colonel remarked that his *kids* (half being under 20) had plenty of guts and were willing to fight, but they didn't know their weapons and hadn't had enough training. And besides that, shells, ammunition in general, and equipment was in short supply. There were times when there was incoming fire for hours but there was nothing to fire back. After WW II, inventories of these things were neglected. Ammunition industries had been discontinued. Hospitals were short of supplies, not even having enough plaster to put a cast on a soldier's arm.

With the situation looking bleak in the Pusan area, MacArthur decided to make a landing at Inchon, behind enemy lines, cutting them off from their supply lines. Regardless of many obstacles and against all arguments, MacArthur forged ahead, and with the Navy being in better shape than the other forces, the landing was made. Eight LSTs unloaded tanks, trucks, supplies, and Americans scrambled up the high seawall, to the Communists' astonishment. MacArthur's plan had succeeded. With much hard fighting, the Marines reached Seoul and raised the flag on the Capitol ten days later.

People at home seemed to support the Administration's action to combat this aggression, thinking our forces could defeat the aggressors quickly and the fellows would be home in time for Christmas. But that was not to be.

After the invasion at Inchon and the capture of Seoul, North Koreans moved farther and farther above the 38th parallel, being chased by the South Korean army, with the American, British, and other UN forces not far behind. These countries had hesitated about crossing the 38th parallel, debating whether Russia and China would interfere, but deciding that was not probable.

Sporadic fighting was encountered, but when reaching the Yalu River, on the border of Korea and China, October 25, 1950, the situation changed. Chinese troops seemed "'... to arise right out of the ground,' advancing silently through the chilly mist to attack the astounded United Nations forces."[2]

The Chinese had slipped 350,000 men into North Korea without our military leaders suspecting a thing. They came into North Korea silently, at night, on foot, hiding in the forests during the day to avoid observance by the soldiers or the UN aircraft. On November 1, 1950, before dawn, the Chinese, accompanied by drums, whistles, and bugles, attacked, using machine gun and mortar fire, and many grenades. Approaching suddenly, killing and wounding, they would then withdraw.

Men died by the hundreds.There was mass hysteria among UN troops; it was each man for himself. One infantryman said, "'There's no end to them—the more you kill, the more they come.'"[3] Many of the men withdrew to the coast, and the Navy, who cruised and fired on the shoreline, transported them to the South. Planes did their part with bombing and strafing.

Some men were caught in their sleeping bags, bayoneted before they could unzip them.Thereafter, some officers forbade the men to zip the bags. Few men took off their boots at night.

"... a host of ingenious and intricate devices had been created and deployed to break the momentum of an assault: wire, minefields, trip flares, booby traps, and a few uniquely Korean innovations, such as barrels of napalm or white phosphorous that could be unleashed and ignited by a wire pulled from a foxhole."[4]

American prisoners were shot by the roadside, their hands tied behind their back with barbed wire. They got kicked a lot if they didn't keep up in the march. If they couldn't go on, they were shot. Because of this, many soldiers, when the situation looked bleak, bolted.

One prisoner inferred that Geneva Convention rules about treatment of prisoners were completely overlooked. They were packed into cold, damp, lice and rat-infected places, so tightly that they each had to lie on their side on the hard floors. As one of the many types of punishment, a prisoner was made to stand, with shoes off, on a frozen lake for as long as two hours.

As they walked faster and faster in their withdrawal, to miss being cut off by the Chinese, some of the guys' thighs became raw with the constant rubbing of cold wet pants; one being in permanent misery from diarrhea. They discarded gear to lighten their loads, even down to sleeping bags. With no supply system, the men were hungry. Two soldiers found "... an bandoned, half-empty can of peas coated in days of dust. They simply scraped off the dust with a bayonet and wolfed the remains."[5]

Many of the men were upset about withdrawing, but it saved many lives and left them to fight another day.

"The battalion (Marines) divested itself of all but the most essential heavy gear... Individuals were left to decide about what food to carry, but all the men were admonished to carry at least one full canteen of water. Most of the troops chose to subsist upon fruit cocktail and syrupy peaches and the like. By carrying such sugary canned foods close to the skin, they could rely upon having a quick energizer in reasonable condition for bolting down during brief breaks or on the move."[6]

"There was the soft crunch of rubber-soled feet on the hard-packed snow. The soft jingle of metallic equipment. The soothing shirring sound of cloth-encased thighs rubbing together in mindless rhythm. The muted oaths and sighs of tired, struggling men. The labored, whistling rasp of breath drawn painfully between clenched teeth. The freezing saliva upon the roof of the mouth. The burning of cold-numbed ears. The painful clenching of fists and toes. The boring, mindless pace. The heightened sensation of imminent danger and the progressive grip of underlying terror. The throbbing discomfort of overtired eyes darting swiftly upward to check progress. The bobbing gait of seven hundred frozen men struggling against the worst nature could hurl into their faces."[7]

Most of the American men in the North were wearing all their available clothes: long woolen underwear, two pairs of socks, wool shirt, wool trousers, cotton trousers over the wool, shoe pacs, pile jacket, parka with hood, and trigger-finger mittens. They were still cold.

They would also have "... a steel helmet with liner and camouflage cover... and a normal load of web gear and pack, with all sorts of pouches and pockets crammed full of oddments and ammunition."[8]

These pockets usually carried the essential things, ones they didn't want to trust to a backpack or duffel bag in case they got lost or left behind. There was probably a pocket knife, which could be used in many different ways; maybe nail clippers, although the knife could also be used for cutting fingernails; a bar of soap, razor, toothbrush and paste, all of which most likely were in a shaving kit, but which did not get much use when men were in a combat area. Water for brushing teeth or for their two canteens, which they always carried, came from melted snow. A Zippo lighter was common for smokers and was handy for lighting fires, when permitted. Some carried a durable rubberized flashlight; two or three large handkerchieves; maybe a compass; maybe a pen and small notebook; almost certainly an extra pair or two of wool socks.

Dry socks were a safeguard against frozen feet. The men were warned repeatedly that wearing dry socks and having their weapon in good condition were two essentials. In sub-zero temperatures it was difficult to wash and dry socks. However, they could be changed, with the dirty ones possibly being carried against the body or put in the sleeping bag, allowing the perspiration to dry out. Even though still dirty, they could be reworn, cleanliness not being as important as keeping dry.

Rations may have been in the pockets or in the backpack or duffel bag, depending on the circumstances. The C-rations came with a small candle-like heating element. There was probably a blanket or sleeping bag, a change of clothes, a rain poncho, probably airmail paper and envelopes, a book, maybe a small Testament, a deck of cards.

A watch was probably being worn, preferably one with a luminous dial that could be seen at night, and maybe an I.D. bracelet. The wallet may have been wrapped in a plastic bag.

These items could usually be replenished except in immediate combat areas. Many of them, however, were mailed lovingly by families and friends. Packages from the Red Cross were also welcomed.

Two dog tags were always worn around the neck, their being two different lengths to avoid the sound of clinking together. In case of death, one tag was left on the body; the other given to officials.

There was little enemy activity during the day. So our men, black and white together, always before segregated, rested, read their mail if they had any, put their sleeping bags out to air, cleaned their weapons.

Later in the day the men might eat a ration can of lima beans and ham and try to get themselves prepared mentally for whatever the night might bring.

The cold was numbing to body and mind. The men stomped their feet on the hard ground to keep the blood circulating. The simplest tasks became difficult. "The jeeps were kept running continually. In some cases their headlights were run on cables into key positions such as the sick-bay and operations tents to supplement the feeble Coleman lanterns. To start an engine required hours of work—thawing its moving parts, persuading its frozen oil to liquefy. Blood plasma froze."[9] Rifles and carbines sometimes failed to work.

"For many men the greatest fear was that when the moment came, when the Communist wave broke upon their positions, the cold would have jammed their life-saving weapons."[10]

In some places they had warming tents where every two or three hours the guys could go and thaw themselves out. With their fingers and bodies so numbed by cold, it was difficult to fire a gun or even move. Their hands were always chapped and sore, cracked and bleeding. Many developed rheumatism from sleeping on the cold ground. Many had toes or fingers that had been frostbitten. Many had colds, sore throat, flu, but they took aspirin and went on.

The terrain was mostly mountainous with few trees. Therefore, battles were fought on hillsides. "Coping with the hills is more exhausting to fighting forces than meeting the fire of the enemy."[11]

Most of the farm area, which is only about one-fifth of the country, is used for rice paddies and thus, is under water. In the winter roads are muddy; in summer, dusty, except at times of monsoons.

Vehicles couldn't travel over these mountainous, dusty, or snowy trails, so the men had to carry more than their share. More than 100,000 South Korean men were enlisted, with American pay, to carry supplies and needed equipment to the fighting men. "Again and again as the infantry met Communist attacks and approached their last reserves of ammunition, they were saved at the last moment by resupply from the patient files of Korean porters trudging up the reverse slopes, their backs bent over their A-frames laden with ammunition. 'We couldn't have fought the war without those Korean litter bearers,'"[12] said one GI. Sometimes, because of these Korean porters, the men, not caring what it was, were treated to a hot meal.

Because of the terrain and the guerrilla-type fighting of the enemy, the United States was at a disadvantage, not being able to use more sophisticated equipment. The Chinese used grenades, rifles, tommy guns, and mortars, and captured and used American arms and supplies whenever possible.

Much of the fighting was hand-to-hand. There were no paved landing strips for planes. Planes from Japan bombed main routes, but the Chinese stayed off those routes. They moved at night, staying out of sight of the bombers. Or they were in their underground garrisons, under the mountains. Planes bombed rail lines and bridges, also, but then the Chinese brought out retractable bridges. The Navy, deploying aircraft carriers and other ships relatively close to shore, used as much ammunition as against Japan in all of WW II.

At the start of the war the air force units were stationed in Japan, average missions lasting around eight hours, and with a big mission having as many as 72 aircraft. But after Inchon, many units were based in Korea. Using more planes than those on bombing missions, transports "carried troops on regular runs, dropped paratroops in assaults, evacuated wounded, and provided rotation service; they also carried supplies and equipment, from much-needed ammunition for local shortages to the famous dropping of the bridges for the Marines..."[13]

Helicopters, used extensively for the first time in war, proved their worth by carrying men into fighting areas and quickly getting the wounded to hospitals.

Troops were sent home after accruing 36 points. "A soldier earned four points a month for front-line service, two a month for service in Korea but not in the combat zone... the drawback to it was that at any given moment, lesser or greater numbers of seasoned soldiers were going out of Korea and raw replacements were coming in. It took time for these to get acclimatized, to find their way around a battlefield, and to become useful soldiers."[14]

"...November 1, 1950, an Air Force plane encountered a Communist-manned jet for the first time. Then eight days later a MIG-15 was shot down by an F-80, the first jet-against-jet duel in history... On January 23, thirty-three American fighters engaged twenty-five Chinese fighters near the Yalu and shot down three of them. This was the first great jet battle in any war..."[15]

"The Air Force dropped 450,000 tons of bombs and fired 183,000,000 rounds of heavy machine-gun ammunition in Korea... lost 1,000 aircraft of all types... "[16]

With the Chinese entry into the war, the MiG appeared and gave the UN some troubles, but the development of newer jets again gave the UN the advantage. The F-84E and F-86 jets seemed to be superior to the Soviet-built MIGs.

"If an American aircraft was hit, in winter the pilot would try to bale out overland, for the sea was too cold to offer much prospect of survival. A pilot who ditched in the winter months could last three minutes in the water before reaching his dinghy, and seven minutes thereafter before his saturated flying suit froze. But in summer he would always opt for the sea if he could, where the huge and efficient rescue organization might reach him..."[17]

Much debate was going on with MacArthur, American government officers, and the UN. It was a period of mixed signals from Washington—whether to back off, hold, bomb China (even with the atomic bomb), or what. After these defeats of the UN forces, "The Administration was now willing to consider a peace proposal based upon restoring the prewar status of Korea, divided at the 38th Parallel."[18]

But MacArthur still wanted to bomb bases in Manchuria and was making such unauthorized statements in public, which Truman felt were injurious to the UN cause.

Because of this disagreement, MacArthur was dismissed from his duties April 11, 1951. So arose the oft-heard phrase, *Old soldiers never die; they just fade away.*

Cease-fire negotiations began on July 10, 1951, but became an on-and-off thing as "... the Communists did their best to make the United Nations look like losers."[19] At the meetings they placed UN representatives where the sun would be shining in their eyes, provided low chairs for UN delegates, facing north, and high chairs facing south for themselves. With this arrangement they could look down on the others, and in Asia, traditionally the victor faced south, the defeated, north.

When Eisenhower took over the helm as President in 1953, China and Russia, fearing he might use nuclear weapons, allowed peace talks to become more serious. On March 28, 1953, they agreed on what became known as *Operation Little Switch,* an exchange of sick and wounded prisoners.

The Western World was extremely upset when seeing the gaunt UN prisoners with untreated wounds and hearing their tales, but thought the end of the conflict was at hand. But still the talks dragged on. Americans felt they could not forcibly repatriate people who did not want to go home, and the Chinese did not agree with this at all. Heavy fighting continued all the while the peace talks dragged on. "The UN suffered 17,000 casualties, including 3,333 killed, in the twenty days between agreement in principle being reached between the delegations at Panmunjom and Syngman Rhee (South Korea) acknowledging his readiness to accept it."[20]

"On July 10, 1953, two years from the hour when truce talks were begun, the delegations reconvened at Panmunjom, this time to work in earnest... documents were signed at 10 A.M. on July 27. Twelve hours later the firing ceased."[21]

The peace papers were signed with neither general speaking to the other nor offering to shake hands. "They got up, looked coldly at each other, and walked out."[22]

When the cease-fire came into effect at 10 P.M., "a sudden deafening silence fell upon the line... (A Lt. commented that) 'There was no rejoicing—we were just sad and quiet. This was the first time Americans had ever accepted a no-win war... So many people had died, for what?'"[23]

At dawn soldiers from both sides were slipping out to look with curiosity at those of the other side. Some Chinese "... passed over beer and bottles of rice wine. UN troops offered chocolate and cigarettes."[24] When the Communist prisoners were being trucked north to be released, many cut their fatigues into shreds, threw out cigarettes, toothpaste, chocolate, threw away their clothes and boots and returned naked.

The final prisoner exchange was called *Operation Big Switch*, with 3,597 Americans being returned. UN prisoners returning from the North returned gaunt, broken men. One private remarked that "'The average POW was not really a human being when he was released... he was a wild animal.'"[25]

Twenty-one Americans chose to stay with their Chinese captors. Two-thirds of the Chinese did not want to return to their country.

"The war itself never ended... there may never be anything better than an armed truce."[26]

"Given what the war had cost, it seemed as if the result ought to be more than that."[27]

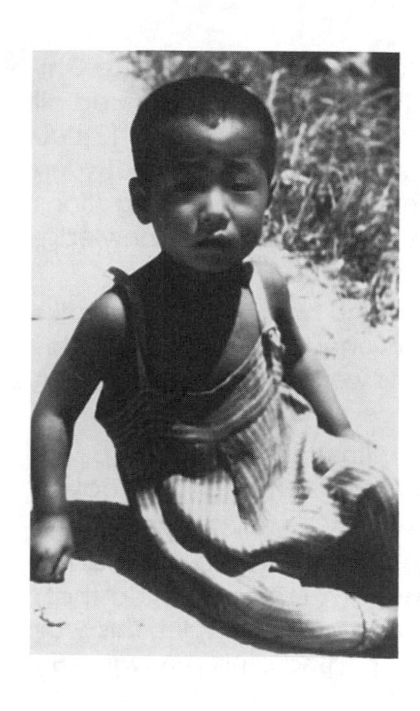

Courtesy Herbert Young, Sidney, Ohio.

KOREA

THE HOMEFRONT DURING OUR INVOLVEMENT

The early 1950s was a time of Communist Mania. Communism was viewed as a perpetual threat to the American way of life. World War II had not long been over when the Soviet Union again started using its muscle power in Europe.

When the Soviet Union blockaded West Berlin as a result of disagreements over the zones in Germany, the Allies started the Berlin Airlift, June, 1948. The American air force, using 150-300 C-47s and C-54s, carried 1,500 tons of supplies daily into Berlin. Ultimately, over 2 million tons of food, petroleum, and other supplies were delivered in more than 250,000 flights. Britain was also involved, using civilian, as well as military, aircraft. The Soviets were forced to lift the blockade by May, 1949.

In 1949, China was taken over by the Communists. In August of the same year, there was news that the Soviet Union had the atomic bomb. Immediately President Truman authorized the go-ahead on the hydrogen bomb. Julius and Ethel Rosenberg were executed for passing atomic secrets to Russia.

Also contributing to the Communist mania was the crossing of the 38th parallel in June, 1950, by the Communist North Korean troops. President Truman quickly sent American troops, as did other countries.

"On July 10 (1950) the first draft calls went out, greeting 50,000 young men with news of their impending induction... factories began to retool to meet the military's wartime needs. By early 1950 draft calls were running at 80,000 per month; by midyear l.8 million men, including 609,000 reservists called up to active duty, had been added to the armed forces..."[28]

College students received deferments until after graduation. In April, 1951, Truman recalled General Douglas MacArthur, who had been serving as the Commander of unified UN forces in Korea, because of disagreements about the conduct of the war. General MacArthur felt the war in Korea should be taken as far as the China border, and possibly into mainland China, and did not hesitate in speaking his thoughts aloud. President Truman and other UN delegates generally felt this idea could lead to much trouble. MacArthur came home amidst much hoopla and ticker tape parades. To his tearful, admiring followers, he said, *Old soldiers never die; they just fade away.*

With this Communist mania in the country, Sen. Joseph McCarthy fueled the fire with his accusations. "And by 1953, as chairman of the Senate Permanent Subcommittee on Investigations, he (McCarthy) would be conducting sweeping witch-hunts through the State Department, the army, and other institutions of government looking for evidence of Communist 'subversion.'" [29]

McCarthyism dominated the news. His suspicions were of people in all walks of life, declaring they were aiding the Communist plot to take over the world. His bullying was finally ended in 1954 when the Senate voted to censure him.

The presidential race between Adlai Stevenson and Dwight D. Eisenhower also claimed much news time. Between McCarthyism and the presidential race, there was very little news time for the war in Korea.

In January, 1953, Eisenhower was inaugurated with promises that he would go to Korea and see what could be done toward ending the war. Also aiding his victory over Adlai Stevenson was the fact that the Republicans hammered on the idea that Stevenson was *soft on communism*. People had been building bomb shelters in backyards and in basements, stocked them with food, medicines, and bedding, in case of nuclear attack from Russia. They were tired of thinking of war and wanted reassurance that America was safe from Communism.

The 50s were bountiful years. Americans found themselves better off than ever before and they wanted to buy. Companies learned that advertising paid off; the amount they spent doubled between 1949 and 1957. And the use of credit expanded. By 1955, three out of five cars were purchased on credit. But with all this spending power, prices and wages moved upward. To combat inflation, the government imposed a price-wage freeze.

The Baby Boom was in progress. People were buying homes, many in the newly-created suburbs. Mothers had to have station wagons to haul their children, and those of friends and neighbors, to Scouts, ball games, and the many activities. Dads started riding the commuter trains. Managers of downtown stores decided it was too inconvenient for suburban residents to go shopping—thus, the emergence of shopping malls.

Backyard barbecues became the social outlet. It was a good way for neighbors to get together. And then if the parents decided to go out for an evening, the teenage neighbors might look after the small children. This *babysitting* was a new concept, a way for them to make some money, and the idea caught on fast. Fast food restaurants had not yet appeared, so most teenagers did not have jobs.

And along with these new houses in the suburbs came the novelty item, television. Sales of television grew in leaps and bounds—from the approximate 7,000 sets sold in 1946 to more than 7 million per year by 1953. By 1960 it was estimated that at least one TV could be found in 86% of all American homes. While Uncle Miltie and Sid Caesar and Imogene Coca furnished humor, and Edward R. Murrow the news, family shows, such as "Leave it to Beaver" and "Ozzie and Harriet" thrived. Religious programs with leaders such as Billy Graham, Bishop Fulton T. Sheen, and Norman Vincent Peale, seemed to hold great appeal. "Church affiliation grew from an estimated 86.8 million in 1950 to 109.6 million in 1958."[30]

College enrollment shot up from 2.1 million in 1951 to 3.6 million in 1960, due to a flourishing economy and more federal, state, and private scholarship and loan programs. This was stimulated after WW II by the GI Bill. College was no longer just for the elite. "... a college education came to be regarded by the end of the 1950s as a virtual necessity for anyone hoping to climb the American social ladder... (now) the mission of higher education was not to cultivate scholarship for its own sake, but rather to serve the practical needs of society at large."[31]

In the 1950s there was a marked rise in juvenile delinquency. It was thought "that the increased hostility of youth reflected both the rise in world tensions and the glorification of violence by the mass media... (or) the 'decay of moral and spiritual values' brought on by excesses of materialism... (or) 'lack of love and care and attention' in the home."[32]

Rock 'n Roll took over the music world with Buddy Holly, Jerry Lee Lewis, among others; later, with Elvis Presley becoming the idol. Elvis and his gyrations annoyed parents while teenagers loved him.

A new way of thinking was initiated in 1952 when Christine Jorgenson had the first publicized sex change.

Ninety West Point cadets were expelled for cheating on an examination.

Black Americans began demanding equal rights as citizens. Under President Eisenhower, the government and armed forces were desegregated, but not much was done otherwise at that time. The Reverend Martin Luther King, Jr., led the battle during the 50s.

Because of the technological revolution, output of America's farmers increased 84 percent. So that the farmers' products wouldn't flood the markets and cause them to receive only token prices, the government bought and put huge amounts in their storehouses.

The television bonanza caused the film industry to go into a slump. To compete with this new entrant in the entertainment world, the movie industry came out with 3D and Cinerama. James Dean was a favorite of the young movie-goers and, upon his death, wearing leather jackets became the fad.

The Catcher in the Rye was the popular book in 1951. *The Old Man and the Sea* brought a Pulitzer prize to Ernest Hemingway in 1953. "The King and I" opened as did the movie, "An American in Paris," with Gene Kelly and Leslie Caron.

The New York Yankees were having phenomenal success. The 50s saw the end of Joe DeMaggio, Jackie Robinson, and Roy Campanella, but the beginning for Mickey Mantle, Willie Mays, and Hank Aaron. And, as golf appeared on TV, Arnold Palmer became the star.

Rocky Marciano held the heavyweight boxing title for five years; Sugar Ray Robinson, the middleweight title.

Dr. James Salk developed an anti-polio vaccine and, with a nation-wide immunization program, polio was on the decline.

England's George VI died and Princess Elizabeth became the Queen in February, 1952. In 1953, John Fitzgerald Kennedy, then a member of the U.S. Senate, married Jacqueline Lee Bouvier.

Wernher von Braun, in charge of the U.S. Army's ballistic weapons program, said that scientists should start working on a vehicle that would carry man into space. In 1957 the Space Age began with Russia launching Sputnik, the first earth-orbiting satellite.

BEN J. CUNNINGHAM

TEMPLE, TEXAS

Flight Operations, S/Sgt., Air Force, 1951-55, Korea
Basic Training: San Antonio, TX, and Wichita Falls, TX
Duty in Eniwetok (Marshall Islands)

When I went over, they were getting ready for the atomic bomb tests. They had done some tests two or three years before on Bikini, but the operation wasn't nearly as big. They had all the planes, air force, and everything else on Eniwetok. Then they did drop the bombs on Bikini.

During the year I was there, they dropped several atom bombs and the one and only Hydrogen bomb. The Hydrogen bomb was a lot bigger than they thought. They dropped it from a B-36 and when the plane came back, there was a bunch of sheet metal hanging on it and one engine out. It was a pretty good-sized blast! That was the first and last Hydrogen bomb ever dropped.

They had taken off early in the morning—it was a beehive at daybreak. One hundred planes—little, big, all kinds. Navy guys were out there in ships all around. When they all flew back in, they had to be washed down. Washed all the stuff off.

Eniwetok was 186 miles from Bikini. I remember very vividly when that Hydrogen bomb went off because I had gone back to my quarters and it was still semi-dark. The explosion lit the whole sky up—just a weird orange. Was almost 20 minutes later when the blast came. You didn't hear anything or see anything except the orange color. And then KABOOM! The canvas sides on our tent started shaking. It was like a 70-mile gale hitting.

During the next two or three months, they had senators and important people visiting for a week or so. They fed us the best food there could be while those visitors were there—huge T-bone steaks! One would go end to end on that metal platter! I had a private working for me, big redheaded kid—he'd wait until the end of the line was there and then he'd go and get two or three of those big steaks.

Eniwetok is only 15 ft. high at the highest point and these tidal waves don't affect the island because there is not a sloping shore line where the water builds up. The water just goes around the shore. So that blast didn't affect it. Some tidal waves are only six inches high from what I understand. But when they come in to land, they build up to where they are 20-30 ft. high. The water stacks up.

Eniwetok is an atoll. This is the outer rim of a former volcano, 50 miles across. The island was 2 1/2 miles long and 1/4 mile across. There were no natives, all military, no other foreign countries.

They set off a small atomic bomb about seven miles away. I was lying on the runway when that thing went off. It was a pretty good-sized blast. We wore radiation badges during this time. Had special glasses. I often wonder if we were affected in any way. They told us we wouldn't get enough to affect us, but, of course, we don't know. There was a questionnaire from the air force about a year later—that's been it.

In the mess hall I noticed all these marks on the wall—they were for days until people were going home. Guys put the marks there while waiting in the long lines. There were no women on the island. You can't get off to go anywhere. There is no R & R. (Rest and Relaxation). All they talk about is women. They had movies; beer was a nickel; you could play cards. You had a lot of leisure time.

The ocean was absolutely clear. You could see the ocean underneath the ship when we came in. In the center part it's green and out where the water was deep, it was blue. The island is gorgeous; no trees except for a few coconuts. Coral is beautiful—they didn't want us walking on it—wanted to protect it. At some of these other islands, there were LSTs rusting away (from WW II).

There were a few civilian contractors out there that did construction work. They drove these jeeps, castoffs from the army and air force. No windshields. They were almost rusted away. There were still engines and running gear and seats. The guys wore beards, weird hats, cut-off pants. It was so funny seeing them drive down the road in these rusted-out jeeps.

Once in a while a plane would go to Kwajalein. So if you knew the right people, you could get on the plane and go down there for a little R & R. It was a navy base—fairly close—also part of the Marshall Islands. It had a better PX than we did.

The army had these L-19s, small single-engine planes. I got a chance to go with the pilot to another island—little runway! Was all he could do to get the plane stopped when it got to the other end of the runway.

JOHN E. LAWS

SIDNEY, OHIO

Radar Navigator/Electronics, AT 1, Navy, 1951-55, Korean War
Basic Training: Great Lakes, IL
Duty in Naha, Okinawa

During the Korean War we were stationed in Okinawa, back pretty far from any fighting. We lived in quonset huts which weren't the best, but they were much better than tents. Our showers were the kind with buckets of water hanging overhead. The sun heated the water somewhat. A little Okinawan boy, whom we called Boysan, did our laundry by jumping up and down on the clothes in a bucketful of hot water. We marked our clothes with numbers.

Our job was to monitor and chart all shipping in the area. Our IFF equipment sent a signal out; if it came back, the ship was friendly; if it did not, we knew it was an enemy. We could tell if it was a troop ship, supply ship, or even a submarine. We had a lot of anti-sub equipment, so that even if a sub wasn't running the engine, we could detect it.

Radar equipment was invented during WW II but perfected during the Korean War. The old horizontal scan was hit and miss, but our equipment locked in on the target and we could dive down and find it. The old P2V aircraft was slow but accurate. Our squadron only lost one aircraft, shot down.

We flew on patrol to Atsugi, Japan, and one or two other places there, a minimum of ten or fourteen hours' flight time, stayed overnight and then flew back. The Japanese worked really well with us, helped us get fuel and repairs. Patrols were completed every day, 24 hours a day, by one of our aircraft.

We initiated one rather exciting rescue. We detected a Japanese fishing boat, the Skoshi Maru, with 20 or 30 men aboard, in a typhoon. And when there is a typhoon, the water really rolls. We made a 10 1/2 hour flight into the eye of the storm. It was rough getting there, but when we reached the eye, it was rather calm. We steered a U.S. ship to them and they made the rescue.

One time when we knew a typhoon was coming, we threw everything we had in planes and flew up to a large air base at the other end of the island, seventy or a hundred miles away. There we had some rain but no bad storm.

In late 1954 and early 1955 we assisted the Chinese Nationals in their departure from the mainland to the island of Taiwan (Formosa then). They went on ships, which we escorted, from the Tachen Islands, right off the coast of China. As they left, they dynamited the islands so there would be nothing left for the Communists. They were so poor and brought nothing with them. After landing on the northern part of the island, some were taken to Tainan in the southern part, so our air force pilots could train them to fly jet aircraft.

In April, 1955, our squadron was the first Patrol Squadron to circumnavigate the globe and finish with our entire flight crew intact. We went from Naha, Okinawa, to the Philippines; on to Singapore; to Ceylon (now Sri Lanka); to Saudi Arabia; some place in what is now Iraq, I believe; to Naples, Italy (the Royal Air Force base); to Port Lyautey (Kenitra), Morocco; to Lajes, Azores Islands; Quonset Point, Rhode Island; Hutchinson, Kansas; Naval Air Base at Whidbey Island, Washington (Ault Field). The reason for the circumnavigation was to prove that a whole squadron (12 aircraft, each with a 5-man crew) was mobile enough to go around this way and that the engines could keep going for that length of time (941.2 hours' actual flight time).

One sad experience was when my squadron was returning from deployment and stopped at Hickam Field in Hawaii before returning to Whidbey Island, Washington. A member of one of the crews was killed when he stepped from the curb in Honolulu.

I think there are times when the news media interferes too much. There are many times when the type of missions must be kept secret to protect the servicemen in performing their job.

I am proud to have served my country and believe anyone who will not stand up to serve should not be allowed to live in such a free country.

Top, left: John Laws. Top, right: P2V. Bottom: Quonset hut.
Courtesy John Laws

RALPH E. MONROE

TRABUCO CANYON, CALIFORNIA

Pilot, Colonel, USAF, 1941-63, WW II, Korea
Basic Training: California
Duty in European Theater; Korea

...(Two years after his 1948 retirement, Monroe) was recalled to active duty for the recruiting of pilots into the Air Force from colleges.

On June 25, 1950 the Korean War began. 'The next day I was on an airplane heading to Korea and the next day I was in combat,' Monroe recalled.

Flying from Japan and later Korea, Monroe piloted the Douglas B-26 Night Intruder, a twin-engine bomber that mostly attacked at night.

On one memorable mission, Monroe was in charge of organizing the dropping of flares onto targets deep within the enemy lines so the accompanying smaller jets could see to drop bombs.

Lighting was essential for the night missions because of the hilly terrain, Monroe explained. At times the Koreans would even string lights on hillsides to entice pilots, who would then crash into the mountainsides.

...The air war was different in Korea from World War II, Monroe said. In World War II the pilots flew at 23,000 to 27,000 feet at high altitude. In Korea there was low-level flying, carrying rockets and machine guns to shoot at targets. The pilot would fly low to shoot even small boats and ox carts believed to be loaded with weapons.

Monroe is one of the Chosin Few for his assistance to the Marines trying to evacuate from the Chosin Reservoir under heavy Chinese and Korean fire in 1950. Monroe was returning from a mission when asked to assist with air support for the badly-outnumbered U.S. troops. He dropped his remaining bombs and fired off his machine guns to help hold back the attacking enemy to give more time to the Marines. 'I was proud of that attack,' Monroe said.

Returning from Korea in 1951, Monroe was assigned to the new field of air research and development at a command in Baltimore, MD. He served as aide and pilot to three generals and often was there for top secret meetings.

He was then transferred to Europe near Paris for a troop-carrier group that provided support for the troops all over Europe.

About 1959, Monroe requested and received a transfer to the Strategic Air Command and began as a crew member and worked up to squadron commander of KC 135. He eventually was commander of the 916th Air Refueling Squadron in Travis, California... He retired from the Air Force as a colonel in March 1963.

Reprinted with permission of *The Sidney* (Ohio) *Daily News* and Christine Henderson

(See WW II section for Monroe's experiences there.)

RICHARD NEER
SIDNEY, OHIO

Aircraft Maintenance, T/Sgt., USAF, 1944-67, Korea
Basic Training: Chicago

While fighting in the Pusan perimeter of Korea in 1950, our fighter bomber squadron had an urgent need for additional napalm fire bombs.

We had hundreds of 150-gallon fuel drop tanks which were unassembled in wooden crates. The crates were just the right height to assemble the tanks on. We set up 15 to 20 crates in an assembly line. The drop tanks came in two parts, a bottom shell and a top shell. A large rubber seal was placed between the two shells and then several metal clips clamped the two shells together. We had about 15 to 20 men assembling these tanks and were able to build one tank every fifteen minutes.

At the very end of the assembly line were men who loaded the completed tanks on to the aircraft as they taxied to our assembly area. The aircraft would then taxi to the area where the napalm and gas mixture were poured into the tanks and the detonator installed. Then the aircraft would taxi out, take off, fly over the mountains next to our base, drop the napalm and come back in to land, rearm and out they went again. That's how close the enemy was in those desperate days.

WELDON W. OAKLEY

SIDNEY, OHIO

Corporal, Army, 58th Engineering Treadway Bridge Co., X Corps, 1949-52
Basic Training: Ft. Knox, KY
Duty in Korea

I was testing 100-ton bridges for Sherman tanks in Virginia when Korean War broke out. Our unit was immediately sent to Yokohama, Japan, and waited there for our engineering equipment to arrive. Trained in what was an American prison camp during WW II.

Landed in Inchon on October 3, 1950, and was sent immediately to Seoul—had just been taken. All the bridges had been blown. My company was a specialty one, not attached to any one unit; we were never all together but went here and there putting up temporary bridges (pontoons).

I was moved to Hamhung; the Chinese were not there yet. Americans were dropping leaflets trying to get North Koreans to surrender. Headquarters were needed in North Korea; since we had engineering equipment, they loaded our ten 21/2 ton trucks with pre-fab quonset hut material and, along with four Brockways (6 tons with big wenches and things to lift with), we headed north to Hagaru-ri. I drove a 21/2 ton truck. There was only one mountain road at that time. We went clear up to the Yalu River and past the reservoir.

The Chinese, estimated to be 110,000-120,000, came out of hiding, blowing bugles, and overwhelmed our 15,000 Marines and soldiers, pinned us down. Most of the fighting was at night; planes from carriers would make air strikes at night. Little air force planes, P-51s, would come through the mountains in the daytime and strafe. There were a lot of Corsairs that had proved themselves against the Japanese Zero in WW II. Everything we had was left over from WW II: trucks, tanks, artillery, even C-rations. Didn't have anything at the beginning that would knock out a tank. Later they developed a 3.5 bazooka.

The Air Force dropped rations and medical supplies to us, but, because of wind shifts, the Chinese got many of them.

Most of the time food was frozen; sometimes we couldn't even get the cans open. We had enough food to get by on, but really, food wasn't our main concern. It was so cold, - 30 degrees and more, with wind chill factor, -70 degrees; so much death, much frostbite; many lost toes and feet. This winter of 1950 was an extra cold one in Korea. In fact, I've been told that it was also extra cold in Ohio that year. We were not to zip our sleeping bags after incidents of Chinese slipping up and killing men, not even having time to get out of the bags to defend themselves. There were warming tents at the perimeter where severe cases could go. The Chinese were even worse off, not prepared for the cold.

The engineers were issued carbines and they didn't freeze. Marines and infantry had M1s and they did freeze.

Being surrounded, troops had to fight their way down the mountain to safety. On December 7, in Koto-ri, with no air support because of a snowstorm, the Chinese were expected to take over. Many were praying to see a star in the sky, indicating that the storm might be over. That night a star appeared, then the sky brightened, more stars appeared, and the snowstorm ceased. The next morning our aircraft arrived and helped the forces get down the mountain to the coast. That star on the night of December 7 is well remembered.

The Chinese had blown out a bridge on the southern end of this mountain—our only way of escape. The only way to get out was to airlift a bridge and drop sections of this steel treadway at Funchilin Pass. It was a miracle that we had those engineering trucks with those big booms. We used Chinese prisoners to help build the bridge.

At the end of the evacuation, engineers destroyed anything the enemy could use. Bridges, roads, tunnels, railroad cars, piers, retaining walls were blasted. And the final blow was blowing up the harbor.

A poem called "The Ballad of Chosin" was written by one of The Chosin Few while recuperating in the Philadelphia Naval Hospital. This poem is to be permanently included in the Archives of the Valley Forge Historical Museum because of its similarity to the spirit and the endurance of the men who fought at Valley Forge.

I'm proud that it was my company's treadway bridge at Funchilin Pass that helped the withdrawal and ultimately saved many, many lives. I'm honored to be considered one of *The Chosin Few.*

(Land area in Korea is the size of the state of Kansas.)

Weldon W. Oakley

WILLIAM E. OGLE

SIDNEY, OHIO

Platoon Leader, Company Commander, 1st Lt., US Army,
1947-52, Korean War.
Basic Training: Lackland AFB, TX; Ft. Riley, KS; OCS, Ft. Benning, GA
Duty in Korea.

I went to Pusan in 1952, so the war had been going on for awhile. The troops had been to the North and were driven back to the 38th parallel. We went on a train to Inchon, but this was two years after MacArthur's landing there. We were in more of a holding action rather than battling back and forth. We did mostly patrols into enemy territory, going out at dusk and coming back the next morning, spying on the enemy—reconnaissance patrols. This was around the 38th parallel.

I was in the Heartbreak Ridge area. We had fields of fire between us and the enemy; between our trench to their trench artillery and tanks firing back and forth. Two times we had the enemy come to our trench line, especially at night. Of course, they were held back.

We were always on the move and always relieving South Korean forces. They would come out of the trench and we would go in. One time we were moving in, which was always at night, and the next morning we saw all these dead bodies that had been there for several days. The Chinese had attacked when the South Koreans were on duty, and there were all these bloated bodies, infested with rats. There was a terrible smell. When the fog lifted and the sun came out, we identified them as Chinese by their suits. We took flame throwers and incinerated the bodies rather than picking them up. We had rats in our trenches almost as big as cats. It was a disease-ridden situation where the rats would be out biting those dead bodies at night and then come back and bite us. So those bodies had to be disposed of as quickly as possible.

The bunkers where we stayed were just part of the trench. The trench went clear along the 38th parallel from sea to sea. Every squad or squadron had its own sandbag bunker built right into the trench, just like a little room, and maybe five or six guys would sleep in it. Trenches themselves were sandbagged.

I think maybe these bunkers were unique to this war because, at this time, it was a stationary war. The Chinese had their line, the South Koreans had theirs, and they were separated by maybe a mile in between. This was where the action took place. We had artillery fire, rifle fire, whatever.

We were pulled back to a rear company, a resting area, for maybe three or four weeks and then moved back to the line, relieving the South Korean troops. The South Koreans had their own army, the ROK, their own chain of command, and they stayed to themselves, didn't mix in with our army. But their esprit de corps was different than ours. They conscripted people right off the street and gave them a couple weeks of training. At the first sign of serious trouble, many of them took off and ran.

As to all the comments that have been made about lack of cohesiveness in the Korean War, it may have started there, but there was comradeship. Many of us went over together and stayed together for our whole term. The first time you are fired upon, cohesiveness develops immediately between those two or so people.

Pusan had been liberated for maybe a year and it was a devastated city—mud streets, huts, and everything very dirty. They had a single railroad going north and we took it to the 38th parallel, right up to the rear area of our regiment, the 45th infantry. The train was very crude, very slow, went through every little town.

We arrived in the springtime, but were there a year, so we experienced the extremely severe winter—lots of snow; very mountainous territory. Slept outdoors in sleeping bags with our rifles in the bag right up against our bodies. Kept it functional that way. One morning I woke up and it looked like mounds in a cemetery—snow on top of everybody in their sleeping bags. But it was really, really cold, but beautiful country and particularly so with snow. There were lots of fir trees; lot of pine trees, not many deciduous trees.

Many people might not realize that you can see tigers there. A friend of mine was out walking and shot a huge one; brought the skin back, 8 ft. long.

The Chinese would blow bugles. They had a loud speaker system and all night long, in broken English, they would say things like, "Hey, American GI boy, why don't you go back home?" They'd play modern American music, then break in and say "Wonder what your girlfriend is doing now."

They also tried to get prisoners to come to their side. They'd say, "Come and join your brother. Come to our country—live a good life. Live in peace with us."

Also, with artillery shells they would shoot propaganda leaflets over to our side. The shells would break up in the air and the leaflets would come flying down. There were all kinds of propaganda to try to demoralize our guys.

Many times when we replaced the ROK troops, we opposed crack Chinese outfits. The Chinese were poorly equipped. They used what we called a Burp gun. It fired so fast that it sounded like somebody burping. The range was not good but the ammunition was deadly. When we would find Chinese, they would have food packs on them that would last many, many days—lots of rice cakes. The ROK troops lived on kimchi, a sauerkraut type of thing with fishheads in it; they carried it around in a big metal bucket.

On our front lines, they tried to bring in one hot meal a day by truck. The guys would come out of the trenches and line up with their mess gear. The rest of the time they ate C-Rations. It was dangerous standing in line because those snipers were very accurate. I saw two guys standing in line ahead of me get shot right through the head. About two months afterwards I got a package of cookies from my wife. They were wrapped in newspaper, The Cleveland Plain Dealer. When I opened it up, there was a picture of this one boy and a story of his being killed at Heartbreak Ridge, Korea. He was wearing a steel helmet and the bullet went right through it and emasculated his brains.

Chinese snipers tied themselves up in trees and perched there for all night, maybe 12 or 14 hours. They were extremely accurate and would shoot only one time so we couldn't range in on them.

Going out on patrol could be a hair-raising situation. You were going from the so-called protection of your front line to the enemy's no-man's land. You were in the pitch black of night and there was radio silence. You could walk into a land mine; anything could happen. Our patrols always had 8 to 12 men and included a medical corpsman with a stretcher (folded up). Our goal, of course, was to be as quiet as possible.

One night we set up base on a hill. The patrol leader is usually in the center and the others make a perimeter or a fence around so they can see in all directions. This corpsman thought he saw the trees starting to move and got panicky, started throwing grenades right and left, boom, boom, boom. There was nothing there; he was just jittery.

All of our equipment worked pretty well once we got it, but it was in short supply. We had to wait a long time to get it. The M-1 carbine was the workhorse of the infantry. You could depend on that thing. You're trained to know that your weapon is your best friend; you sleep with it, you live with it, you work with it. It will serve you if you serve it. You don't go anywhere without your weapon.

I'd say that 95 percent of those guys in Korea were there proudly, with a sense of pride and duty. Most of the lower officers felt the same. There was a job to be done and they were there to do it. Maybe some of the higher officers were there for personal gain, to further their careers. After about the second year, this became rather a safe war to be in. At this time talks were going on and there was fire, but it was rather a static situation.

Once a week or every ten days you could leave the front lines on a truck, go back to battalion headquarters where they had a portable shower. You could throw your clothes in a pile, wash, and then get a new set of clothes.

In spring when the rains came, it was a sea of mud. No concrete; sandy, mud roads. Trucks got stuck everywhere. Tanks were scarce because of extreme weather and mountains.

WILLIAM RICKEY

SIDNEY, OHIO

Radio Repairman, Sgt., US Marines, 1952-54, Korea
Basic Training: San Diego
Duty in Korea

I tried to enlist in 1951, but they wouldn't take me because of my eyes. A year later I was drafted into the Marines. I was the youngest of five boys and all of us served in the military between 1940 and 1962.

With almost no training other than boot camp, I went to Korea. It was kind of a Last In, First Out thing. Because I was the newest one in this stateside group, I was chosen as the one to go to Korea. I had no training as a radio repairman. The only thing I could do was put radios in the airplane and take them out.

We went across on a merchant marine ship—3 weeks to get there, with a typhoon. Immediately I was put on a transport aircraft to another base and then on to a sea plane to a carrier. We got into an armada that was the diversionary force that went on the northeast shore of Korea. (We were out far enough that we couldn't see the shore.) We were there to distract attention from the invasion of Seoul. Hundreds and hundreds of ships. I was on a CVE, escort carrier, one squadron-type carrier, about 30-33 planes. Small group. Two destroyer escort. This was our group. We patrolled in the North Sea. The squadron I was in was the VMA312, made famous in World War II by Pappy Boyington. There was a television series about it, WW II aircraft, old Corsairs. The checkerboard was their logo, so to speak, and they painted this on the planes.

We flew close air support for the troops on Korea. Each day when the planes came back, the pilots would go on the loud speaker and tell what their accomplishments were, how many oxcarts they got. No matter what their goals were, they always managed to get some oxcarts, which carried food, supplies, ammunition to the Korean people. All propeller planes. They flew down low and in between the mountains.

The navy would change ships every six weeks, so I was on five carriers. We would go to shore and take all the planes and supplies from one carrier and put them on another. The first one would go back to the States and we would go out for another six weeks.

I was aboard carriers for the first eight months. We'd go out three weeks to patrol and come back to Japan for resupply, one week.

Japan was rebuilt on the southern island where we were. The town was Sasebo, not too far from Hiroshima. The Japanese liked the Americans and the American dollars. When the fleet came in, they took good care of them. We were allowed to mingle with the Japanese. No hard feelings. Could buy things very cheap. Never saw MacArthur.

Our equipment, and even the aircraft, was old. It had all been used in World War II. At first we were just busy taking radios out that didn't work and putting ones in that did. Then the guys that had training would do the repairs.

One of the most traumatic things in my life was my first day in boot camp. We took a train across the U.S. and stayed on the car, never got off. The first day in San Diego was really traumatic; everything very disciplined. And there were ten weeks of that. Some guys just deliberately goofed off to get out. They were given a rough time, and sometimes physically mal-treated by the other guys, but then they were discharged. When the guys finished, they were a polished group, mentally and physically, had discipline. If you were told to do something, you did it.

Wherever you go you have a rifle, not a gun. One time I called it a gun and got chastised. Had to stand at attention for several hours.

In San Diego there was an exchange depot for B-36s. My brother was flying on a B-36. He flew into San Diego when I was in boot camp there. We happened to be out at the rifle range. They notified me and I went to the guard house. He was standing there waiting, but I couldn't speak to him. I had to go through certain things, certain formalities, with the guards before they would acknowledge that my brother was there to visit me. My brother saw all this and said, "You know, you wouldn't have to do all that to see the President of the U.S. if you were in the Air Corps." There's just a difference in the training in the Marine Corps and the Air Force, or any other branch of service.

In town before my brother came to see me, he asked what he could bring me. Some Marines there said to take him a candy bar. We never had candy or pop, only went to one movie in ten weeks, so he sneaked in some candy bars for me, and we lived it up in the tent that night.

It changed after boot camp. We had candy on the carriers. But I think the discipline was good—it hangs on for the rest of your life.

After eight months on the carrier, the squadron was sent back to the States, but I didn't have enough time in (12 months) so was sent to the mainland of Korea, K-9, in the South. I was connected with a night fighter squadron, 2-engine jets, Nighthawks. Still was a radio repairman. There was an air strip here, and the Seabees were constantly there with their heavy equipment, bull dozers etc., improving or expanding the length of the runways. Our aircraft were small support type and couldn't fly long distances. This base or complex had army troops, marines, and probably some air force. Spent four months there and was there when the war ended.

It was announced that the war was going to end in so many days. We emptied the barn. We had airplanes going all the time, dropping and shooting as much as they could in those two or three days. The planes would come in, they'd load them up again, and send them out. Then the war ended.

There were rice paddies all around this base. Some of the guys, being very lonely, would sneak out there where there were prostitutes and all kinds of people like that. There was a lot of VD and they warned the troops not to go out there.

We stayed in framed tents, eight-ten guys, wooden floor. We pried up the floor between my bunk and another guy's, dug a hole, and made a little refrigerator. We could keep stuff a little longer there than in the tent cause it was so hot.

There was a lot of rain. I couldn't get any boots to fit me and got trenchfoot. The structuring there was very bad. The latrine was on top of a hill; the mess hall was at the bottom of the hill. I got trenchmouth—similar to pyorrhea. It's gone now.

The dirt was red, sticky clay. I don't remember seeing any trees. No birds. Lots of dogs. Troops used the dogs to smell Koreans that tried to sneak up. There was no real threat of sniper fire—we were not that close. About every evening a little North Korean plane would come by, the air raid sirens would go off, he would throw out a couple of hand grenades, and then leave. The guys called him Charlie; didn't shoot him down.

Since I wasn't trained, I was very lucky to get the job of being on the flight deck as the planes took off and landed. If a radio didn't work, a repairman would be called to fix it.

There were quite a few crash landings. I heard a lot of pilots say it was the equivalent of landing on a postage stamp.The planes would get in what they called a dog pattern. The aircraft carrier would be going south and, if you looked to the right side of the carrier, the plane would be going in the opposite direction. It would make a circle around and come up to the back of the aircraft carrier. They always hit the aircraft carrier into the wind, going as fast as they could. There'd be a guy on the back using lights as directional signals. He had a microphone, too, and could talk to them as well as give them signals. I've seen them make ten approaches before they would be allowed to land because they were not in the right position. Sometimes they'd run out of gas and have to dump the planes in the ocean; the pilot would bail out. A whaleboat or helicopter would be sent to pick the pilots up.

The front third of the flight deck is where they take off from, and there is a thing called a catapult, similar to a slingshot. They would hook this slingshot to the bottom of the plane. Like when pulling a slingshot back, it would be full of tension. They would rev up the engine and at the moment when the pilot was ready, he would give a signal and the catapult would shoot the plane into the air, within a few yards of the front of the carrier. They have to be going very fast, very quickly, to take off on such a short space. Sometimes the plane wouldn't be going fast enough and the plane would nosedive right into the water.

The back two-thirds of the carrier is where planes land. The plane has a tailhook that is dropped behind the tailwheel. Across the deck are big iron cables. They are hooked to some kind of shock absorbers. The tailhook would catch one of these cables and stop the plane. There's a barrier that came up out of the floor and stopped the plane if the tailhook didn't catch and the plane crashed. That barrier kept the plane from crashing into the other planes or going off the front (bow).

One plane hit that barrier when it landed, caught fire. The fellows got the pilot out and shoved the plane right over the side.

The planes were kept on what is called the hangar deck, beneath the flight deck. They put them on an elevator and roll them up to the flight deck.

Before they can land planes, they disarm the plane of any bombs, rockets, or whatever they didn't use; they'd drop them into the ocean. Machine guns had to be put on safety. In one case I went to check some radio equipment on the flight deck and a fellow was trying to put the machine gun on safety and it shot off a burst of fire right over my head.

It took hours and days to load supplies on board the carrier. There are eight or ten decks on a carrier, and the food and other supplies are on one of the bottom decks. The ship had fresh water available, to a degree. As long as it could produce fresh water, you could take fresh-water showers. Toilets were always flushed with salt water.

If they were loading gasoline or filling an aircraft, they would announce: "Smoking lamp is out." When done, they would say, "Smoking lamp is lit."

When the war ended, we were sent back to Japan, where we waited for six weeks for transportation to the U.S. On the ship, officers got 50 percent of the space and enlisted men got 50 percent; there were ten times the number of enlisted men as officers. Took three weeks to get back.

WILLIAM (Fred) WAGNER

Sidney, Ohio

Bombardier, Navigator, Tech. Sgt., Marines, 1942-46; 1951-53
WW II, Korea
Basic Training: San Diego
Duty in Pacific

Recalled to active duty in November, 1951. Enrolled in a refresher course of Navigation, where I was known as the *old man,* age 27.

Assigned to VMR352 Barbers Point, Hawaii, with a forward base airfield at Itami, Japan. Our planes were R5Ds, the Navy version of the Douglas C-54 Transports. One R5D our squadron received in 1946 was still in service in 1952. These R5Ds were equipped with Loran, an electronic receiver; the readings, when plotted on a chart, would establish a line a known distance from the point of transmission. The other standard eqipment was a sextant and drift meter.

Our assignment was to fly airplane parts, mail, and personnel to various bases in Korea and return with mail and personnel for R & R (Rest and Relaxation). Nearly all our flights originating at Itami stopped at K3 Pohang on the east coast of Korea.

Several times when approaching K3, I saw two or three men throwing a baseball. I learned they were probably Lloyd Merriman of the Cincinnati Reds and Jerry Coleman of the New York Yankees, both stationed at K3. Ted Williams of the Boston Red Sox, K6, occasionally flew in to work out. Later, both Williams and Coleman flew with us to Itami for R & R.

When in October, 1952, the squadron office in Hawaii had a request from the Marine Personnel Headquarters for a civil engineer with surveyor schooling, they cut my orders for detached duty. I was to complete the final layout of a compass rose, used to set the plane's compasses on true north. I used a transit to take some shots on the sun, calculated the azimuth, which is the number of degrees from the true north the sun was at the time of each shot. Then at night I shot a couple of stars and Polaris for checks.

In December, 1952, the squadron headquarters sent two extra planes to Japan to help carry the Christmas mail. Since morale on the front lines was low (the Chinese were harassing our troops across the demilitarized zone), the services requested the people back home to help cheer the boys up with mail and packages. You never saw so much mail in your life! Our planes flew every day and we finally had to get some help from the air force. To get their Christmas mail to them on time, we had the air force bring our mail from Toyko to Itami, and we delivered it to the various airfields in Korea. I flew every day from December 16 through December 23, except for two days. Each flight averaged six to ten hours' flight time, including fueling, unloading, loading.

It was mandatory that each crew member return to Hawaii for a period of time at least every month. When I was making my trip for the month, we left Atsugi Air Base on Christmas Eve, flew to Midway Island, as we always did to refuel, then flew on to Barbers Point, Hawaii, and landed there on Christmas Eve. Just before we crossed the International Date Line, we had 1½ hours of Christmas. Also on this trip we had four passengers going home on Emergency Leave (death in their families). As we landed, these men were loaded on a plane to the States. Two of these men who lived on the West Coast were home for Christmas. They happened to fly with us back to K3, recognized me, and thanked me for my part in getting them home on Christmas.

Had 1670 hours' flight time combining both wars, but the world I got to see, even though war-damaged, was great and wonderful.

(See first part of story in WW II section.)

ELZA WILLIS

SIDNEY, OHIO

Aircraft Refueling, Seaman 1st Class, Navy, 1950-54
Basic Training: (Boot Camp) Great Lakes Naval Training Center
Duty in Malta

Young, eager, adventuresome, at age 20 the world is a challenge. My challenge was the U.S. Navy's slogan of "Join the Navy and see the world through a porthole (window)."

I began my enlistment by becoming a near casualty in Boot Camp. It didn't take long to realize that those superiors meant business when they yelled a command. At the very first morning wake-up call, I leaped out of my bunk into the bunk near me and almost dislocated my shoulder.

One night I witnessed a near murder. The guy who slept in the top bunk was given to strong drink. One evening, rather late, he wandered into the wrong barracks and, while there, proceeded to urinate on a heat register that was being used to ease the chill. My friend Higgins did not really appreciate this intruder. In the meantime, the drunken wanderer came up the backside of the barracks and climbed through the window, pushing my locker onto the floor. Through the door burst Higgins, flipped on the lights, and said "Where is that——?"

By this time the drunken one had gone to bed. Higgins was carrying an empty quart glass beer bottle. I said, "Higgins, put it down. You may kill him." About this time the drunk raised his head. Higgins dropped the bottle and knocked the guy out. Needless to say, he was very quiet the remainder of the night.

Most of my naval experiences were routine, I suppose. You know, ship life could get a bit boring. I kept trying to get an assignment overseas where things were, or I thought could be, much more exciting.

I finally made it into the Mediterranean Sea to the small island of Malta, maybe seven by twelve miles, and being about sixty miles south of Sicily. Surrounded by some smaller islands and with a very pleasant temperature range, it was a paradise compared to the USS Mindoro CVE 120 aircraft carrier.

Malta was once a British crown colony. In 1964 it became an independent country. Valletta is the capital and chief port. With a population of 356,000, it was indeed crowded.

People (Maltese) were friendly, English-speaking, a lot of influence from Italy. The island was originally a rock. Phoenicians brought over dirt and built rock walls around the place and filled in with dirt. They created for themselves an island that they could produce food on. Built plots of land encircled by rocks. When you fly over, it looks like a checkerboard, with each one having his own little parcel. Then they got involved in a lot of fishing; have a lot of natural ports for the British navy.

Unique on Malta were the catacombs, the burial grounds for early Phoenicians. An adult Phoenician was very small, less than 5 ft. These catacombs during WW II were used for protecting themselves from the Germans who bombed them from both directions as they came across N. Africa to England. So these catacombs saved the Maltese people.

My first revelation of change came when I was assigned, along with others, living quarters with the British Royal Air Force (RAF). All but the equipment was theirs, even the buildings.

We ate with the British and paid them so much per day. They used British money, the pound. We couldn't drink the water, drank wine instead. The final showdown of culture: breakfast with Cornflakes, no sugar, and warm milk!

We had a service contract with the British government, a protectorate of Malta. Our attachment there was a repair garage for the fleet in the Atlantic and Mediterranean. Pilots would fly the planes, single engine Corsairs, (props; the wings folded up over the top) into Lucas Field, Malta. Our unit of mechanics would repair the planes, the test pilot would test them, and then the pilots would fly back to the fleet. This was a commercial airstrip.

We had a permanent fleet in that area but there was an increased fleet during the Korean War. We were on alert for anything and everything going on anywhere at that time. Even though we were not involved, we were always aware of the fact that any number of our personnel might be transferred into the Korean conflict.

We picked up gas, which was stored in large tanks, from the British as we needed it, hauled it in 1200-gallon tankers.

We measured with large dipsticks. Most of the planes we'd top off with 200 to 300 gallons of gas. I never filled one that was empty, so I don't know how much it would hold. Always kept them topped off.

Fire trucks were always on patrol on runways and on ramps during refueling. Before we were permitted to take the nozzle out of the truck and mount the wing of the plane, we had a four-point grounding procedure: First we had to ground ouselves by laying the palms of our hands on the ground to take the static electricity off of us. Then we grounded the truck to the ground. Then grounded the plane to the ground. Then grounded the truck to the plane. Especially was that true if you were loading a plane that contained loaded missiles. Then you always had a guy with a carbine rifle watching you ground all this before he would allow you to touch a nozzle. He was ordered to, if necessary, pull the rifle on us and force us to do it. We were subject to disciplinary status if we made any mistake or any snotty remark to him. But I agreed with him because I knew what those missiles could do.

The navy had an interesting maintenance program. As soon as the ship would leave port, you would be issued a metal scraper, a wire brush, and a gallon of paint and shown an area that had to be painted. When the Chief Petty Officer came by, I said, "There's nothing wrong with this paint. It's clean; there's no rust on it or anything." "Now," he said, "I'd throw your paint over the side a lot quicker than I'd throw you, but I'll consider the whole crew if you don't get busy! You lie right there on your belly and take every bit of that paint off!" So we painted the ship to stay busy, to keep from going crazy. We used taxpayers' dollars to scrape new paint off and put new paint on. It wouldn't matter if we were out to sea every other month—we'd still have to scrape all the wall down and paint it.

When you and your buddies went out to sea, you worked it out so that every once in awhile a case of tuna would have to be slid off the conveyor belt and carried up alongside the ship on the flight deck level. There'd be little holes or places that you could get in and smoke and tell jokes, or take a nap sometimes. But you put that tuna in there so that when you're out to sea, you can steal some crackers from the cafeteria and then you can go up there and have tuna and crackers at times. It was like a squirrel stashing stuff away—part of the game.

For relaxation and enjoyment, some guys made raisin jack. They got the raisins from supply department, took them down to inert room (souped up ventilation system, I guess) and got a crock or barrel or something and put the raisins in it. We had guys that almost went blind from that raisin jack. Several guys got in trouble over that.

Space on the carrier is like going into your closet during a nightmare and not finding your way out. The rudest awakening I had was when I went aboard the carrier the first time and laid down on my cot and looked over at the carrier wall. There was a place on the side, probably about 25 ft., that had been welded. When asking about it, I was told there was a torpedo that went through there! That reminded me that I was not at home any more!

Gasoline was stored in the middle of the ship in case a torpedo came through and it was also away from the boiler room.

We had our own dentist, doctor, medical facilities, food, communication, transportation system. The hangar deck was quite an elaborate place where the planes were readied for the flight deck. Had an elevator fore and aft. As the planes came in, they would be taken down on the fore elevator as one was coming up on the aft elevator. The savior for the pilots was the LSO officer (Landing Signal Officer).

I was also land based in N.W. Africa, Port Lyauty, which was also an aircraft repair station. Fueled navy planes. Very little flying went out of there other than the testing of planes and sending them back to the fleet.

We were near the Sahara Desert, so we picked up sandstorm residue quite often. We'd find it in the food, silverware, plates, etc.

The people here did not speak English, so we didn't know what they were up to. The first time I was on guard duty, after midnight, when they started their prayer tower calls in the early hours of the morning, I had goose bumps.

If there was a lot of rain, we guarded our 30 planes, which set on a steel ramp, so they wouldn't sink into the ground.

The Moslems worked on the base; drove some of our vehicles. We hired as many of them as we could. It was interesting working around Arabic, Moslem people. One of the most comical things was when we asked an Arabic guy if he had any children. Yes. What its name? Mohammed B. Mohammed. He had four kids and all he did was put one more B. Mohammed to each one.

F-86. Courtesy Delbert Yoho

DELBERT M. YOHO

SIDNEY, OHIO

Jet Fighter Pilot, 1st Lieutenant, Air Force, 1948-52, Korea
Basic Training: Randolph AFB, TX
Duty at Otis AFB, Cape Cod, Massachusetts

In June, 1950, when North Korea invaded South Korea, I was a jet fighter pilot, flying F-86s, and stationed at Otis Air Force Base on Cape Cod, Mass. Our government was very unsure of what the Russians would do since they had exploded their first atomic bomb in 1949, and they were supporting North Korea.

We were immediately put on continuous early morning patrol at 35,000 feet, a few miles out over the ocean, to intercept a possible Russian attack with atomic bombs. No one knew how many more of this type of bomb the Russians had or how or where they would deliver them. But, with big cities like New York and Boston in the area, everyone was kind of nervous.

We intercepted all aircraft entering the U.S. that were not identified by ground radar controllers using flight plans given by the aircraft home country. We were to intercept, following directions by ground controllers, fly close enough to read any identifying marks on the craft, and wait for instructions from the radar station whether to shoot it down or not. Fortunately, all turned out to be friendly.

The hierarchy decided we needed some guidelines on what to do if we did intercept an aircraft heading inland that was known to have an enemy A-bomb on board. The directions were to exert every effort to shoot it down, but if that failed, to knock it down by ramming. In the operations room when that announcement was made, you could have heard a pin drop. No one knew if an atomic bomb could be set off in this manner.

VIETNAM

SYNOPSIS OF OUR INVOLVEMENT

At the time of World War II, France was one of several nations that had colonial empires. Vietnam, Cambodia, and Laos, making up what was then called Indochina, was claimed by France. Although most colonies were being given their independence by the end of WW II, France, because she felt she needed the empire's wealth to rebuild her country after the war, was willing to fight in order to keep Indochina.

And fight she had to do. Ho Chi Minh, who called himself a democratic leader but was really a communist dictator, led Vietnam in guerrilla warfare against France. The United States, under Truman's leadership, contributed money and supplies to France, hoping to prevent a Communist takeover of Southeast Asia. But when Eisenhower was in office, France asked for American air strikes, which Eisenhower refused for fear of getting the United States involved in a war for years. Without help, France could not hold Indochina.

Vietnam Memorial, Bellefontaine, Ohio. Doris Eggleston.

In 1954, an International Peace Conference in Geneva, Switzerland, decided to divide Vietnam at the seventeenth parallel, leaving a strip of land on each side of the line where no troops would be allowed, a demilitarized zone (DMZ). Ho Chi Minh's government was given control of the territory north of the DMZ; South Vietnam, south of the DMZ.

After two years there would be an election to see if the people wanted the country reunited and what kind of government they wanted.

The President of South Vietnam refused to have elections because he felt the people in the north would not be free to vote as they chose, and also that some of the people in his territory might vote to join the North.

The United States continued to send food and military aid to the South. America's idea was to train and equip South Vietnam and eventually turn the whole job over to them of defending their country, with only American military advisers.

But the North started guerrilla action in the South and those guerrillas became known as the Vietcong. When President Kennedy took office, he sent the Green Berets, who were trained in anti-guerrilla warfare, to Vietnam, along with armed helicopters piloted by Americans. These men were not to take part in actual combat because we were not officially at war. Kennedy said in 1963, "'In the first analysis... it is their war. They are the ones who have to win it or lose it.'"[1]

After John F. Kennedy's untimely death, Johnson came into office, promising "... to meet the danger of Communist aggression, while affirming his intention not to escalate the war in Vietnam."[2]

When there was an incident in the Tonkin Gulf regarding some questionable firing on two U.S. destroyers, President Johnson asked Congress to pass, which they did, the Tonkin Gulf Resolution, giving him authority "'to take all necessary measures to repel any armed attack against the forces of the United States and to take all measures necessary, including the use of armed force to assist South Vietnam.'"[3]

This took the place of a declaration of war. The first Marines landed in South Vietnam on March 8, 1965, and by the end of that year the number was up to 200,000. One source says that almost 3 million Americans fought in Vietnam.

A Seabee commented about his landing at DaNang, "As we got off the plane... the hot humid air hit us in the face like a slap... the sweat was running down our bodies... how can human beings stand this heat!... Every day was 95 to 110 and humid. The only exception was the monsoon season—the temperature went down, but it never stopped raining for six weeks, day and night."[4]

The war in Vietnam was not fought with a front line; it was *grunts humping the boonies*. "A grunt is an infantryman, the guy with the rifle in his hand out humping the boonies... Going out on patrols..."[5] or search-and-destroy missions. "If they (grunts) knew an area, knew what to look for, knew who was friendly, they could keep alive."[6]

"The simple physical weight of his load, combined with the heat, humidity, and the fact that most of the time he won't have any spare water to wash in, is immediately going to cause the grunt's skin to start breaking down. Soon he will have jungle rot, open sores on his legs, on his feet and ankles, between his toes, on his groin, under his arms and the straps to his pack. These sores will scab up at night and break open every morning."[7]

The grunts were out carrying 75 lbs. on their backs. They carried "...an M-16, web gear (those belts over the shoulders and around the waist to which all the other stuff is hooked), a steel pot, a combat pack, a protective mask, four fragmentation grenades, two smoke grenades, a claymore, two pop flares... Three hundred fifty rounds of M-16 ammo... (some) a fifty-foot coil of rope for crossing rivers... three days' C-rations... an entrenching tool, too, and two canteens of water."[8]

Claymore mines are "... the ones with 900 double 0 buckshot in them along with glass, cut-up wire, steel chips and anything else they can put in them."[9]

The grunts waded through rice paddies, being chest deep in water; walked through thick, sharp elephant grass and had to stop every so often to pull off leeches; they coped with dust, mud, mosquitoes, red ants, spiders, snakes. And then their success was not in how much territory they gained but in body counts.

They carried M-14 rifles at the beginning; later received M-16s and M-79 grenade launchers. A point man always led the way. They walked slowly, noticing bent grass, fresh footprints, smells, movements of any kind, listening for any sounds, communicating only with hand signals.

"One of the loneliest and spookiest jobs in the world was walking point in Vietnam."[10]

"Armored personnel carriers (APCs) and tanks gave the grunt a lot more protection and firepower, although even the tanks were vulnerable to mines and antitank weapons."[11]

It was difficult to distinguish the enemy, often called Charlie by the grunts. He was not in a front line, could be anywhere. A friendly looking farmer, dressed in black pajamas, or women or kids, might suddenly become the enemy. Because of this, certain areas were named Free Fire Zones. All people were to know that if they were in that area, they would be shot, machine-gunned, or bombed by artillery or aircraft. The trouble was that all farmers did not realize this. As a result, many of the unaware, plus their animals, were killed.

But, the Americans brought medical assistance to the sick and injured and stopped epidemics through vaccinations.

And, as in every war in which the Americans have been involved, the soldiers received special joy from the children.

Commanders also established the Strategic Hamlet program. Farmers were moved in to these areas where they could be fed, protected, taken care of by the Americans and not bothered by the Vietcong. However, because of the strong ties of the people to the villages of their ancestors, they hated this arrangement.

It was another case of the Americans not understanding the culture, the thinking of the Vietnamese people. Personal associations ran deep. Many families had known one another for generations; it was a world of tradition. The culture is based on Confucianism, with one of the most important elements being faithfulness. If he forgets this, he loses honor, face.

Agent Orange was used to kill jungle foliage so that the Vietcong could not hide there. This and other chemicals killed not only the leaves on trees but also crops growing in fields. It is also thought to have caused cancer and other diseases in the people it fell upon, as well as birth defects in children.

"... our men faced people who... skinned people alive, cut out their eyes, and made 'Christmas trees' out of them by slitting open their bellies and pulling out their intestines and draping them all over the place, leaving them to die slowly."[12]

"... I found one of my Vietnamese friends' heads cut off and put on a bamboo stake just for being my friend. The VC were merciless."[13]

The enemy dug tunnels. "...an artillery shell with a pressure detonator could be buried at the entrance... Inside the tunnel poisonous snakes might be hung from the ceiling. A pit might lie beneath the floor, lined with sharpened stakes—perhaps with poison on the tips. Or men might be inside—men with rifles, knives, grenades, or even spears—waiting for the marine who would come groping around a bend in the darkness, helpless."[14]

"Our technology, our air superiority, our firepower, all were useless... We fought a darkness we could neither penetrate nor understand."[15]

"He was out on a death detail, assigned to truss a rope around the NVA corpses festering in the hot morning sun and flip them over one by one from a distance in case they had been booby-trapped with grenades. He tossed one body, then came close and started going through the pockets. The head came off and cracked open. The brain spilled out onto the ground."[16]

Those of our men who were taken prisoner had to endure isolation, no windows in their cold, damp, and dark cells, not being able to see other humans; there were plenty of rats, roaches, vermin of all kinds, many times covering the little food that was set on the floor for the prisoners; they endured beatings, torture, endless interrogation. Everett Alvarez, Jr., prisoner for eight years, said in *Chained Eagle* that any kind of communication with the other American prisoners gave such a lift to their spirits, kept them going, whether it be by tapping on the walls with a code system they developed, sign language from afar, singing songs loudly. A British officer said he thought that was what made American soldiers unique: they gained strength through sharing their pain, their jokes, their food, whatever.

Drinking and smoking pot by the servicemen was common. It was a way to forget where they were, what they were seeing and doing.

Many men came down with dengue fever, similar to malaria. In one particular case a commander ordered all men to stay and fight unless their fever was over 103.4 degrees, and he stayed when his own hit 104.5.

Many of the troops in Vietnam were support personnel, doing jobs like building bases and roads, airports, driving and servicing trucks, cooking the food, sorting the mail, jobs which might be considered safe. But in Vietnam, everyone was subject to rocket or mortar attacks; there were no safe jobs.

Helicopter use became widespread in Vietnam. Not only did they carry troops to needed positions (outmoding paratroops), but they evacuated the wounded, quickly getting them to a field hospital or to a hospital ship offshore. They used Huey transports with M-60 machine guns; CH-34s and OH-23 Ravens; OH-6s and H-13s; also CH-46s.

As to planes, Americans were flying F-4s and F-105s and B-52s, C-130 cargo planes, among others.

Huey HU-1. Corpus Christi, Texas. Doris Eggleston.

By early 1972 Nixon reduced the number of troops in Vietnam from 500,000 to 160,000. But he stated that there would continue to be American troops there until all American prisoners were released.

Peace talks, which had begun in 1968, began to break down and the Communists refused to return to the table. President Nixon ordered what became known as the Christmas bombings. Starting December 18, 1972, American B-52s bombed Hanoi for twelve days in the largest single bombing campaign of the war.

"Between February 1965 and October 1968 American aircraft dropped 1 million tons of bombs, rockets, and missiles on North Vietnam."[17] This was "... more than three times the tonnage of explosives that were dropped during all of World War II in military theaters that spanned the world."[18]

But Hanoi was largely undamaged. The city had clearly been spared by our B-52s. "Bach Mai (dispensary) had the misfortune to lie across the street from a military airfield and petroleum storage depot, and it had paid for this by absorbing a string of bombs... It had not taken the North Vietnamese long to determine that we were deliberately sparing the (Red River) dikes, and they reacted by emplacing mobile antiaircraft batteries in their shadow to secure them from attack... cowering citizens of Hanoi and military convoys filled the streets outside the Hoa Lo prison (the 'Hanoi Hilton')... (knowing) that the raiding B-52s could and would avoid bombing our own captured aviators."[19]

After the Christmas bombings, peace talks resumed. "The Americans' demands were... a cease-fire, the return of prisoners of war, and a guarantee that Thieu's (S. Vietnam) government would endure."[20] Saigon also wanted a promise from North Vietnam that their military activities would cease in South Vietnam, but that promise was not given.

"In the interim, Hanoi ordered its soldiers and cadres in the South to seize as many hamlets as possible prior to a cease-fire..."[21]

President Thieu continued his opposition to the agreement, but Nixon told him that he had decided to go ahead with the treaty and if Thieu didn't approve, relations between South Vietnam and the U.S. would be severed.

B-52 courtesy Air Force

"On January 27, 1973, a peace agreement, the Paris Accords, was signed. By that spring all the remaining U.S. troops had returned home from Vietnam, with only a few hundred Marine guards left on duty at the U.S. Embassy in Saigon. The draft officially ended in June 1973."[22]

In exchange for the repatriation of all American prisoners, the U.S. had agreed to a total military withdrawal within 60 days of a cease-fire (January 27, 1973).

"The period of cease-fire began not with the hoped for silence over the battlefields but with renewed skirmishing as both the Saigon regime and the Communists strove to bring more territory under their control."[23]

Fighting continued for another one and a half years. "The first year of 'peace' (1973) had cost the lives of 57,000 Vietnamese combatants... By the end of the Year (1974)... the only unanswered question concerned the timing of the impending Communist victory. How much longer could the South Vietnamese stave off the inevitable?"[24]

"In January of 1975, the North Vietnamese army began the final assault that brought it total victory in four months. As the Communist army raced southward, South Vietnamese soldiers and civilians alike fled before it in panic and disarray. They fought and killed each other to get aboard planes and ships that would get them out of the country."[25]

In the final days, a native North Vietnamese, acting as senior interpreter and special assistant to our American Colonel, wrote a plea for help to the U.S. Congress. Part of it read: "You are responsible to yourselves if you want to remain a—if not the—big power; for big power comes in the same package with big responsibilities, and you will cease to be a big power if you refuse the big responsibilities. You are responsible to the world, for just as each effort makes the next effort easier, each failure makes the next failure easier; by failing to stand up to the challenge here you are actually paving the way for many other Vietnams to come until you are backed into another world war which will destroy it... I regret having to say that you didn't seem to know what you were doing when you first got into Vietnam and now again you don't seem to know what you are doing when you try to get out of it."[26]

A South Vietnam general said, "'... you insisted on doing things your way... And then in the end you wouldn't stand with us... You made us dependent, and then you abandoned us to our fate.'"[27]

The final offensive progressed rapidly, taking only 55 days until the fall of Saigon (April 30, 1975). "The thirty-year war waged by the Communists for control of their country had come to an end."[28]

During early April Operation Babylift evacuated some 20,000 Vietnamese orphans to the U.S. Adult Vietnamese were sent to the Philippines in this process.

On April 30, 1975, the day Saigon fell, U.S. helicopters landed at the embassy to rescue U.S. officers and Marine guards, as well as the American Ambassador, and to carry them to U.S. warships located offshore in international waters. Around 7,000 people were evacuated. American ships waited offshore to receive those refugees who found the means to reach them.

With the take-over of Saigon by the Communists, it was renamed Ho Chi Minh City.

"For millions of Vietnamese who fought on our side, the end of the war meant suffering, imprisonment, exile, even death."[29]

In the spring of 1976, after the formal unification of the two Vietnams into one country, more than a million people fled the country. Many escaped in fishing boats, hoping to be picked up by the U.S. Navy ships and other free vessels. They were called the *boat people*.

"... whatever the price of winning the war—twenty more years of fighting, another million dead, the destruction of Hanoi—the North Vietnamese were willing to pay it... North Vietnam had no threshold it would not cross. The war was a battle to the death. They had no compunction about mobilizing their whole society, about absorbing terrible destruction, about losing hundreds of thousands of lives. For them this wasn't limited war—it was total war."[30]

"A North Vietnam general later said: "'We did not have to defeat you; we had only to avoid losing.'"[31]

"The lesson we should learn from Vietnam is that if we are going to get involved in a foreign war again, let's make up our minds as a country that the cause is worth fighting for, then let's go in and do it right and win. Otherwise, we shouldn't get involved in the first place."[32]

VIETNAM

THE HOMEFRONT DURING OUR INVOLVEMENT

One commander, as his group was leaving Vietnam, told them that each one of them would have to decide for himself whether we belonged in Vietnam and whether we did any good.

"The essential morality of the soldier is that he is willing to give his life for something larger than himself. The principle that some values are worth dying for is what finally underlies patriotism... But if the war had no value, then what were the men who fought it worth? Too many American veterans thought of themselves as losers... They blamed everyone: protestors, the government, the media... Or they blamed themselves and wallowed in guilt."[33]

Veterans were told before they deplaned not to expect a welcoming party. Some veterans say they were treated badly by some people but warmly by others. Some were spat upon; pointed at; laughed at; had eggs, tomatoes, vegetables thrown at them; called pigs, monsters, baby killers, murderers; bombarded with expressions such as: *You ought to be ashamed! Go back to Nam! We don't want you here! You deserved to die!* O'Hare airport was one of the worst places for slurs; one veteran said that walking through the rice paddies and jungles of Vietnam was not as stressful as walking through O'Hare airport.

There was no one segment of society that handed out the slurs and physical abuse; it came from representatives of all classes. People didn't want to sit by them nor speak to them. They treated the soldiers as though the war had been their fault.

Many veterans learned to never wear their uniform while traveling and not let anyone know they were in the military.

One GI said that they had changed but so had the country, that it was not what they left.

Guys couldn't get dates if the girls knew they had been in Vietnam. Nineteen-year-old veterans that had been living in the worst possible conditions, killing and concentrating every minute on not getting killed, came home and couldn't buy a beer, couldn't get a driver's license without his father's signature. Those who went back to school were outcasts. If they did wish to go to school, benefits were very small. Regulations required that they go full-time, not leaving much time to earn extra money. They needed to work full-time; being 22 or so, they were ready to get married. Then, too, in the early 70s there was a glut of people with college degrees.

"... he had been too far and seen too much and had come home too fast, a stranger. 'One day you have a license to kill... The next day a cop pulls you over for speeding.'"[34]

The journey home "...was a journey without transition for most of them. American dog soldiers in past wars had come home together in troopships and had had time en route to sort things out among themselves—to swap stories and discover that no one of them was alone in his anxieties or his guilts. But the one-year rotation policy in Vietnam meant they came out singly from the war to The World without company or time in which to decompress. Fewer than seventy-two hours passed between... departure from the jungle and his arrival in his parents' front parlor... it struck him that the Army had given him a week to acclimate to the heat in Vietnam and not even three days to readjust to the alien psychic climate awaiting him back home."[35]

Some of the veterans, still having time to serve, decided to go back to Vietnam rather than stay and take the verbal and mental abuse in their own country.

Jobs were difficult to find. A year of college or job experience was more valuable to employers than a year in Vietnam. "Nearly one-half of all blacks reenlisted, most because they found few employment opportunities in civilian life."[36] Adjustment in the U.S. was particularly difficult for blacks. While he could fight and die beside a white buddy in Vietnam, he could not live with him or get the same respect from the commanding officers in the U.S.

Somewhere between 250,000 and 500,000 of these veterans needed physical or mental help in order to live a happy, productive life. Many couldn't sleep, were nervous, had chest pains or dizzy spells, deep depression, all common reactions to the stress of battle.

There was no recognition of psychological conditions until the 1980s—shell shock, combat fatigue. The army said that any such problems had been present before going to Vietnam.

Shamefully, for all those wounded returning to Veterans Hospitals, the facilities were poor, as was the care. Military men have said the treatment of the returning Vietnam veterans was disgraceful.

Why was Vietnam different from WW II? The men in WW II were older, the average age being 26, in Vietnam, 19. In WW II, people from all social and economic classes served; in Vietnam, "... people with money dodged the draft, and you had to explain why you did serve."[37] College students were not subject to the draft.

In WW II, men trained together in the States and went overseas together. They became buddies and depended upon one another. The officers were with them the whole time, knew them, knew what they could do, had faith in them. In Vietnam, it was a constant come-and-go situation. The tour of duty was one year for the grunts; usually only six months for officers. This caused resentment on the part of the enlisted men, and the frequent changes hurt morale. It was also ineffective in that as soon as they learned the country and how to operate, they were sent home. The one-year tour was to brace morale and to diffuse pressure in the States to bring the boys back home, but the gains were negligible.

WW II was a declared war; Vietnam was not. There was a definite enemy in WW II. During the Vietnam war, most people were not sure what we were fighting for, and as a result, servicemen did not have the support of the people at home. The men thought it was useless and senseless. "... an after-the-fall survey of the 173 surviving army generals who had managed the war disclosed that 70 percent of them had been uncertain of what they were fighting for."[38]

In August, 1963, Dr. Martin Luther King, Jr., gave his I have a dream speech in Washington, D.C. More than 1500 chartered buses and trains had carried people there for the march for freedom. School desegregation and the Civil Rights Movement, under the leadership of Dr. King, gained momentum. Americans were becoming convinced that blacks should be given the same rights as whites.

President Kennedy was assassinated on November 22, 1963, while deliberations on the civil rights bill were in progress. Lyndon B. Johnson immediately took over the helm as President.

Johnson wanted to spend money on his Great Society program, but he also believed that we couldn't give up on Vietnam.

He attempted to do both while trying to convince the American citizens that we were not actually engaged in a war. He stressed that we should not send "'... American boys... to do what Asian boys ought to be doing to protect themselves'... (and not) 'yield to Communist aggression.'"[39]

By 1964 animated rallies and political debates over issues were becoming popular, demonstrations with sit-ins, folk songs of protests put to music, slogans, arrests. A lifestyle known as the counterculture was the result with not only rock music and radical politics, but drugs. Woodstock in August, 1969, with between 300,000 and 400,000 in attendance, was symbolic of the times.

There were also the flower children, in the mid-60s who "...rejected politics ...and wanted to 'transcend' the ugliness of contemporary society..."[40]

The first anti-war demonstration was held at the University of Michigan in 1965 with maybe 100 protestors. Four years later there were 100,000 demonstrators. In these student demonstrations, law enforcement agencies were being called in and students were being wounded and killed.

The American economy in 1966 was in the midst of one of the biggest booms in the nation's history. American industry was at nearly 90 percent capacity. But by the end of 1966 inflation was at three percent and continued to rise.

In order to raise support for his policies, in August, 1967, Johnson started a huge propaganda effort to make the American people believe we were winning the war.

By October, 1967, polls showed that a majority of Americans believed that we should never have sent troops to Vietnam. People began to think that all of America's problems were worsened by the war. If we got out of that, then the other problems would certainly go away.

Johnson realized he did not have the support of the people and announced he would not run for reelection. The Democratic political convention in Chicago in August, 1968, was one of the most violent and disruptive demonstrations. More than 600 protestors, out of about 10,000, were arrested by some 20,000 law enforcement officers. Richard Nixon was elected and promised to end the draft and bring home the troops. A commentator said the task of the President would be to "'heal a nation.'"[41]

In November, 1969, more than 500,000 people marched on the capital demanding an end to the war. The FBI and the CIA began investigating protest groups, suspecting that Communists were behind them.

Besides demonstrating and marching, many protestors burned their draft cards and American flags. "By the late 1960s some 35,000 young Americans had been prosecuted for draft evasion. (Statistics vary on this number.) ...perhaps as many as 100,000—fled to Canada or Sweden to avoid conscription. After the war President Jimmy Carter declared an amnesty for all draft evaders who had fled the country during the Vietnam War."[42]

"At the peak... an American soldier was going AWOL every two minutes and deserting every six minutes."[43] During the conflict, more than 50,000 men deserted, many of them fleeing before being shipped to Vietnam.

"Drug use... Over 40 percent of the troops based in the U.S. or Europe used marijuana... 50 percent usage estimated for Vietnam... The use of drugs contributed to an increase in crimes—both on and off base..."[44]

On April 30, 1970, when the announcement was made that the American and South Vietnamese troops had invaded Cambodian territory, trouble erupted on many college campuses, the worst being Kent State in Ohio. The National Guard was called in; nine students were injured and four killed.

News coverage of the war, not because of reporters but because of official information given them, was overly optimistic, not accurate. How deceived the American people had been was not known until the Pentagon Papers were published, which led up to Nixon's resignation. Daniel Ellsberg, who worked in the Department of Defense, gave to Defense Secretary Robert S. McNamara a complete history of the U.S. involvement in the Vietnam War and showed how much was kept secret from the American public.

Although this was classified as secret, it was leaked to the press. In trying to discredit Ellsberg, several of Nixon's aides broke into Ellsberg's psychiatrist's office in Los Angeles. This group was called the *Plumbers Unit*. Then when Nixon was running for President in 1972, the national headquarters of the

Democratic Party in Washington were burglarized and this became known as *Watergate.* When it became known that Nixon was aware of both of these burglaries, he was threatened with impeachment by the Senate and chose instead to resign.

"My feeling is that North Vietnam had the capability to outlast Washington and its South Vietnamese ally just as it had outlasted the French before us... I believe that, by 1975, continued aid at the levels Congress might underwrite would have been matched or exceeded by Hanoi's allies, which would have delayed the inevitable at a great cost in human lives."[45]

Americans were deceived also by North Vietnam concerning POWs and MIAs. In exchange for the repatriation of all American prisoners, the U.S. had agreed to a total military withdrawal. The country returned what it claimed were all of the U.S. prisoners of war, but many think there are still more. "According to the Pentagon, more than 2200 servicemen remain missing in Indochina (May, 1993)."[46]

Many Amerasian children (American servicemen and Vietnamese women) still roam the streets. They have not been accepted by the rest of Vietnamese society. They are outcasts and are forced to beg in the streets. Some have been reunited with their American fathers, but many still remain.

Veterans of the War in Vietnam organized as the Vietnam Veterans Against the war, with their goal being "'to tell Americans what their country was really doing in Vietnam.'"[47]

The response was not what they had hoped for. But they continued on with "a five-day 'invasion' of Washington, D.C."[48] With all their attempts at protests rebuked, upon the final day they came up against a barrier on the Capitol steps. "They halted and one by one hurled medals they had won in Vietnam over the barrier onto the steps of the Capitol Building. One vet explained that returning his medals was 'the final act of contempt for the way the executive branch is forcing us to wage war.' Many of the veterans embraced each other and broke into tears."[49]

"As the U.S. headed into the presidential election year of 1972 the problems of veterans, however, were largely ignored by the public. Indeed, even the Vietnam War had become a secondary concern."[50]

The Vietnam Veterans Memorial was dedicated in 1982, with the names of more than 58,000 American dead and missing. Another sculpture was added in 1984. More than two million visitors a year go to see the Memorial. It is the most frequently visited monument in Washington. "They come silently, reverently, many bearing flowers."[51]

"John Wheeler, a leader of the veterans' organization that made the memorial possible, commented about the wall's effect on veterans visiting it. 'The actual act of being at the Memorial is healing for the guy or woman who went to Vietnam. It has to do with the felt presence of comrades.'"[52]

"The somber black wall, with its grim honor roll of those who gave their lives in Vietnam, has become a symbol of the nation's binding up its wounds and coming together again so many long years after the end of that terrible conflict."[53]

On November 11, 1993, the long-overdue Women's Memorial was dedicated.

MAX CLELAND

ATLANTA, GEORGIA

Platoon Leader, Signal Battalion, Captain, First Air
Cavalry Division
Basic Training: Ft. Benning, GA
Duty in Vietnam

I jumped to the ground, ran in a crouch until I got clear of the spinning helicopter blades, turned around and watched the chopper lift.

Then I saw the grenade. It was where the chopper had lifted off.

It must be mine, I thought. Grenades had fallen off my web gear before. Shifting the M-16 to my left hand and holding it behind me, I bent down to pick up the grenade.

A blinding explosion threw me backwards. The blast jammed my eyeballs back into my skull, temporarily blinding me, pinning my cheeks and jaw muscles to the bones of my face. My ears rang with a deafening reverberation as if I were standing in an echo chamber.

Memory of the firecracker exploding in my hand as a child flashed before me.

When my eyes cleared I looked at my right hand. It was gone. Nothing but a splintered white bone protruded from my shredded elbow. It was speckled with fragments of bloody flesh. Nausea flooded me. I lay where the blast had flung me for a moment, fighting for breath. I found myself slumped on the ground.

Then I tried to stand but couldn't. I looked down. My right leg and knee were gone. My left leg was a soggy mass of bloody flesh mixed with green fatigue cloth. The combat boot dangled awkwardly, like the smashed legs on the dead soldier after the rocket attack.

What was left of me? I reached with my left hand to feel my head. My steel helmet—now gone—had apparently protected it. My flak jacket had shielded my chest and groin from shrapnel.

Intense pain throbbed my body with each heartbeat. I seemed to be falling backwards into a dark tunnel.

I raised up on my left elbow to call for help. Apparently, surrounding troops had mistaken the blast for incoming rocket fire and frantically scattered. I tried to cry out to them but could only hiss. My hand touched my throat and came back covered with blood. Shrapnel had sliced open my windpipe.

I sank back on the ground knowing that I was dying fast. A soft blackness was trying to claim me. *No! I don't want to die.* The words burned through my head. I fought to stay alert to what was going on around me. If I gave in now, I knew I would never regain consciousness.

"Somebody call a medic!" screamed a GI. The men slowly emerged from hiding. "Get a med-evac in here—right now!" someone barked.

Men stood over me, their faces white. One began cutting off my fatigues. I felt naked having my uniform ripped off in such an unceremonious fashion. I clung to consciousness as they worked.

"Hold on there, Captain," said a young man as he carefully wrapped my arm stump with his T-shirt. "The chopper will be here in a minute."

Time seemed suspended. Powerful waves of pain now surged through my body. Every fibre of me seemed to be on fire. I couldn't look into the men's faces as they worked feverishly over me. I stared into the clear blue sky that I had welcomed so gratefully that morning. One aching thought spun through my head: *God, why me?*

A familiar roar tremored the ground. Prop blast from the incoming med-evac chopper billowed dust into my face.

Two medics leaped out with a stretcher and helped ease me onto it. I was lifted into the helicopter. As the engine roared into takeoff, someone yelled, "You're going to make it, Captain. You'll be okay."

I tried to answer but could only hiss the words through my cut windpipe. "Hell, yes, I'm going to make it."

As I lay on the chopper floor, the pain flooding through me, I looked up at the medic as he stuck an i.v. needle into my left arm.

"Have I lost much blood?" I croaked.

"Well, not much, Captain," he said, steadily hooking the needle tube to a plasma bottle.

The chopper landed at the division aid station. I was hurried into a bunker and stretched out on a table where medics worked on me.

Someone asked: "Name? Rank? Service number?"

Is he serious? I'm dying, and this guy is asking me questions.

Angry thoughts pounded in with the pain.

With all the defiance I could muster, I tried to shout. But I could barely whisper, "Cleland, Joseph M., captain, service number zero... five... three... two three... four three six."

Fear invaded me now. Every nerve cried out as I struggled to breathe. I shrank from looking at my mangled body. Instead, I stared up at one of the medics working on my arm stump with surgical scissors.

"What do you think?" I wheezed. "Am I going to make it?" He continued snipping.

"You just might," he murmured, keeping his eyes on his work. He stuck a needle in my arm and pulled it out.

"What was that?"

"Morphine."

Suddenly, a familiar face appeared over me. It was Captain Barry. He was ashen. "What happened?" he asked softly.

I tried to tell him about the grenade. "It blew up... it... just blew up."

The medics hurried me out to a waiting med-evac chopper for a flight to a surgical hospital at Quang Tri, 40 miles to the east. All through the 24-minute flight I was conscious, trying to understand what happened, trying to make the chopper go faster. Lying flat on the floor, I thought about potential snipers below and that I had more of my body exposed than was necessary. Then I realized that snipers couldn't do much more to me than already had been done.

At Quang Tri, attendants at the 38th Surgical Field Hospital rushed to the chopper, grabbed the stretcher and, hunching under the blades, whisked me into the surgical quonset hut where I was lifted onto a litter bed. They rolled the bed directly into the operating room where a team of four doctors began working on me immediately.

I tried to concentrate on their low voices. "He's bleeding badly now," said one. I learned later that flash burns from the exploding grenade had seared my flesh, slowing the immediate bleeding. But now the wounds were hemorrhaging freely.

I fought the drowsiness that was overtaking me. I knew I might not make it back. I was also choking, and I pointed to my throat. A doctor grabbed my slit windpipe and held it open with his finger so I could get more air. He said they would perform a tracheotomy so I could breathe better.

"Please save my leg," I gasped to another physician.

"We'll do all we can," he said reassuringly.

I seemed to be sinking down and down into a dark, deep vortex as the anesthesia took over. My last thought was amazement at how many limbs I had lost in so short a time.

Groggily, I tried to make sense of my surroundings. I was in a bed somewhere, and I could dimly sense the presence of another person sitting nearby.

Time passed and then I was able to comprehend that the person was a girl—a young girl. She was either a nurse or a Red Cross volunteer, I couldn't tell which.

I tried to speak but could hardly make a sound. She looked up and stepped over to the bed.

"Have—have I got my leg?" I whispered.

Her eyes moistened. "No," she said softly.

Oh my God! Both legs gone! I wanted to bury my face in the pillow but couldn't move. I lay there for a while looking into her stricken face. Pain still pounded through me. How much else was gone? At first I was afraid to look.

Then, unable to raise my head to see, I tried to move my left arm. But it bristled with so many i.v. needles that I could hardly budge it. Then I tried to flex my leg muscles.

Nothing happened on the left one, but I felt something on the right! My spirits surged. I could move a muscle in my right leg—the muscle that I knew controlled my knee.

"I've got my right knee," I whispered excitedly.

She shook her head sadly.

"I'm sure," I argued. "I can move it a little."

She put a cool hand on my forehead. "It's only the muscle" she whispered. "Now try to get some sleep."

Her face wavered through my tears. I didn't even have a knee left. I lay there staring at the ceiling.

Then I noticed my right arm in a sling. The forearm and hand were gone. She saw me looking at it and volunteered in a small quiet voice, "It's kinda like traction. It works to pull the flesh down over the elbow bone so the end can heal."

She told me that I had been in the operating room for more than five hours the day before. They had given me 41 pints of blood. "You can thank God," she added softly. "It's a miracle you're alive."

I shut my eyes and winced. *Thanks for nothing,* I thought.

I looked up at her again. "I'll get artificial limbs, won't I?"

"Sure," she said soothingly. "They'll fix you up."

I tried to drift off into sleep to escape the pain and misery of knowing what had happened to me. But I could not. My body seemed aflame with fever.

"Water," I whispered.

The girl bent over me, her eyes pained, and said that I couldn't have anything to drink. I didn't realize that my body fluids were being carefully monitored and controlled and that if I took any extra liquids it would flush the remaining vital fluids from my body. I continued to plead for water.

Finally, she moistened a small piece of cotton and put it on my cracked lips. I sucked the cotton, then begged for more.

She shook her head. I thought of all the iced tea and lemonade I used to have at home. Still working on the dry cotton, I finally slipped into unconsciousness.

It was sometime the next day when I woke up. I was told I was going to the naval hospital in Danang for an overnight stop, then to an army field hospital further south. I slipped in and out of consciousness as I moved from plane to plane. After a trip in a C-130 cargo plane down the coast, a helicopter transferred me to a small army hospital in the Vietnamese village of Thuy Hoa.

It was little more than a hut—and it was steaming hot. Two small air-conditioning units vibrated vainly against the heat. And the stench was almost unbearable. There were about 30 patients in the hut. I was the only American. The intensive care unit was used for both allied and enemy casualties. On my left was a silent North Vietnamese prisoner, to my right a glaze-eyed Viet Cong.

At night, the hut temperatures plummeted to an icy cold. The swing in temperatures raised my continuing fever. At 4 A.M., following my arrival, the attendants decided to try to bring it under control with an alcohol rubdown. Convulsing with chills, I thought I was about to die.

Morning brought a little relief in the form of fresh air. This was possible only during the cool, early dawn hours when the end doors were opened for a few minutes to dilute the stench.

None of the pain I experienced was as intense as when a doctor decided to change all my dressings at the same time shortly after my arrival. Just touching the bandages sent agony flooding through me. Both thighs were as open as a slab of raw beef and my arm still had the bone sticking out of it. After a shot of Demerol, the doctor pulled away the blood-encrusted bandages one after another. It reminded me of a movie I had once seen when a cowboy was given a bullet to bite and a slug of whisky while his trusty buddy amputated his leg.

Despite my continued agony and the frequent drifting in and out of consciousness, I soon realized how strange this hospital was. The medical staff walked around like zombies and seemed far removed from what they were doing. Then I began to understand why. They had become casualties of the war just as we had. After breathing blood and death for months, they were victims of "psychic numbing."

It had particularly affected one of the day-shift nurses. One morning I had been helped painfully onto the bedpan by an attendant. But he was gone, and I was ready to get off.

The day-shift nurse was with another patient across the ward. I called to her for help.

"Do it yourself," she shouted angrily. "I'm busy."

Supporting myself with my left arm, I somehow inched off the pan.

By Easter Sunday, April 14, 1968, the infection in my body was full blown. Six days had passed since the accident but my legs and arm stumps were still raw and open. My lungs were filling with fluid, and my windpipe had to be suctioned every few hours to keep the fluid from drowning me. When my fever reached 102 degrees, I felt that either it would break or I would die in this miserable hut.

Max Cleland

When a Vietnamese nursing aide took my blood pressure, he was alarmed that it had dropped so low and reported this to the physician on duty. An order was placed for blood plasma.

Unfortunately, the nurse I had shouted at from the bedpan was responsible for setting up my i.v. feeding. Through an oversight she failed to turn on the mechanism that would allow the plasma to drain into me when she left to attend another patient. Burning with fever and my strength ebbing fast, I called out to her: "Come over here and turn this damned thing on."

Her head shot up and she wheeled on me: "Shut up and take a tranquilizer."

"The hell I'll take a tranquilizer," I spat. With low blood pressure and fever, I didn't think I could stand one.

The nurse stood, hands on hips, and froze me with one of her looks.

I fell back on my pillow and reached for the tranquilizer. Someone eventually turned on the i.v. feeder, but my fever soared higher. Other attendants aimed electric fans at me. Finally, they gave me an aspirin.

I floated in and out of consciousness throughout the nightmarish experience. Desperately grasping for something to hold onto, I fantasized a congressional investigation into this hospital. I'll have this whole hospital blown right off the map, I dreamed.

After a week I began to reason more clearly and thought of calling Mom and Dad. I knew by now they had received the standard telegram sent to families of the wounded. *(The Secretary of the Army has asked me to inform you...)* telling them I was on the "seriously ill" list.

As yet, I did not want them to know my real condition. But I had to talk to them.

It was a weird conversation. Using a regular overseas telephone in this little, outpost hospital was out of the question. But thanks to a radio patch hookup through MARS (Military Affiliate Radio Station), manned by a volunteer ham operator in California, I reached home.

Though still foggy under the Demerol, I was thrilled to hear Mom in the receiver which they brought to my bed.

"Mother, this is Max. Over."

Each statement had to end with "over" so the short-wave operator could switch his transmitter to the other person.

"Hello, Max. How are you? Over."

"Fine, Mom. I hope to be seeing you and Dad soon. Over."

Back and forth it went. A crackling hum filled the airways as our voices traveled 12,000 miles. But thanks to some unknown person on the West Coast of the United States, a son could tell his family he would soon be coming home.

Reprinted from the book, *Strong at the Broken Places,* (1986) with permission of the author, Max Cleland, and Cherokee Publishing Company, Marietta, GA 30061.

E. W. CRUSE

BACLIFF, TEXAS

U.S. Marines, Vietnam

Lots of people drop by the office to chat, and last Wednesday afternoon was one of those days. My good friend Robert Russo sat in front of my desk, and somehow the subject of Vietnam came up. "So, Robert," I asked, "when did the last major ground combat involving U.S. troops happen in Vietnam?" "1973," Russo said, after thinking a minute.

"No, you're not even close," I said.

"Well, when?" he asked.

"October 8, 1971," I said, grinning.

"What?" he asked, increduously.

Then I pulled out the source of my information, the March issue of Veterans of Foreign Wars Magazine. In one of its best issues ever, VFW Magazine chronologically listed the beginning and ending dates of the United States' involvement in that highly emotional war where 58,000 Americans died.

For years now I have been contending that all U.S. troops were out of Vietnam by 1972, but no one has been listening. The major television networks have brainwashed nearly three generations of Americans that the U.S. lost the war when Saigon fell in 1975.

How could the U.S. have lost if its troops weren't even in the field of battle after October, 1971? You figure that out. The media (this generation) has been putting out wrong information, and doesn't appear willing to correct it.

In February a dear niece looked me square in the eye and said: "You all lost that war in Vietnam." That cut nearly as deep as when I had to listen to others defend "Jane Fonda's right to her opinion."

This niece had just graduated from Texas City High School. My friend Robert thought our last battle there was in 1973.

Network television still shows the U.S. helicopter hovering over the U.S. embassy in April of 1975 as frantic Americans and South Vietnamese struggle to get out of the country.

We lost the Vietnam War in 1975?

No, no, my friends.

Then, just about three weeks ago, two high school students, researching the abortion issue, came by our office. We asked them what they knew about the war. Both were in agreement that the U.S. had *lost* the Vietnam War.

"No," we explained, "we did not *lose* it."

"Well, if we didn't lose it, how did we win it?" one of them asked.

Shocker!

Taken aback for a few seconds, we had to think—think hard. "Well, while the U.S. troops were there, we were effective in restricting the advance of communism," was the best answer we could come up with.

Back to my friend Robert, who faced the pressure of the draft in the 1960s. He had a brother who was a combat photographer for the U.S. Army in Vietnam. On the advice of that brother, Robert did not relish the idea of getting drafted, or serving in the military.

He opposed the war, as he says did many of his friends. Then, another friend dropped by, and he jumped into the Vietnam conversation. "Just a minute John," I said, getting hot under the collar, "if you can tell me when the last ground combat, involving U.S. troops in Vietnam, happened, then I'll listen to what you have to say."

"1975," John replied.

"Wrong, wrong." And then we showed him the article in *VFW Magazine* had the accurate date: Page 32—"Operation Jefferson Glenn. Final major U.S. Operation in Vietnam is concluded by 8 battalions of the 101st Airborne Div. It began Sept. 5, 1970 and lasted 399 days."

I went on to show him where VFW Magazine reported that U.S. ground troops begin a "defensive role," in November 1971.

But, this is not the story Robert said we should write about.

He was flabbergasted when I told him that I was drafted into the U.S. Marine Corps on January 10, 1966, even though I had three dependents, two sons 4 and 2 and a daughter 3.

"The Marine Corps didn't draft people," Robert said.

"Yes, they did starting in 1965," I said. Then I told him how it happened. After dropping out of Alvin Junior College in October of 1965, and a messy divorce in July of 1965, I received a pre-induction physical notice from the Galveston County draft board, headed by Elsie M. Thrash.

Funny thing, I told Robert, is that on the day of my divorce in July, 1965, I walked from the Galveston County Courthouse to the Army, Navy and Marine Corps recruiting offices and tried to join either of the three services. They flat turned me down. Too many dependents (3) they said.

So, on December 7, 1965, I and about 50 or so other Galveston County men were bussed to the induction center in Houston where we were paraded around in shorts, given physicals, and written tests of some sort (like the scene in Alice's Restaurant).

That afternoon two guys in front of me were classified 4-F for declaring themselves homosexuals. Another guy in front of me could swivel his knee in four directions and he was classified 1-A.

Me?

"You are hereby declared 1-A and have 20 days to get your business and personal affairs in order," said the Army guy sitting behind the desk.

"With three dependents?" I asked.

The guy behind the desk got angry. "Three dependents," he said. "Is this some kind of a joke?"

"No," I replied. "Talk to that big fat air force sergeant. He already knows about it."

The fat air force sergeant said "Yes, he did fill out the information sheet and listed three dependents."

"He's probably lying," said the fat air force sergeant, "and when we draft him, if he doesn't have three birth certificates, he's going to Leavenworth."

So, on January 10, 1966, at age 23 and with three children, yours truly went off to Marine Corps Recruit Depot in San Diego, along with about 80 other men from Texas, New Mexico, Oklahoma, Arkansas, Louisiana and Georgia. And four Peruvian sailors. The Peruvian sailors, three enlisted and one officer, are another story.

But at least I didn't go to Leavenworth. Or to Russia, like Bill Clinton, where that country provided most of the bullets, rockets, and hand grenades, that were used to kill American boys in Vietnam.

I saw my children only 3 days during the next 26 months and missed two Christmases at home.

This was not written to whine, or get sympathy.

Because that then was life in the Bean Patch.

So, here's the story, Robert.

• • •

The 1968 Tet offensive Veterans, family members and guests attended the 25th Anniversary Reunion of that battle in Galveston (Texas) on January 29-30 (1993). The Tet Offensive began January 31 1968, and involved about two months of close and brutal combat in which about 81,000 lives were lost, including 3,895 Americans. The Communists lost an estimated 58,000 troops and the Viet Cong were destroyed as an effective fighting force.

Retired U.S. Marine Corps Major General W. H. Hardy was the guest speaker at the buffet dinner... "The next time the U.S. Congress wants to tell the military how to fight a war, they (the Congress) should shoulder the arms, and the military should tell them how to fight it," Hardy said to loud applause...

Reprinted with permission from *The Eagle Point Press* of Galveston Co., Texas.

KENNETH (Mike) KRUEGER

SIDNEY, OHIO

Scout Dog Handler, Spec. 4, U.S. Army, 1967-69, Vietnam
Basic Training: Ft. Jackson, SC
Duty in Tay Ninh Province, South Vietnam

I volunteered for the draft. At that time in 1967, the war in Vietnam was well entrenched. We had a good number of troops in southeast Asia, and it was escalating month by month. Just waiting to be drafted and not knowing how far I wanted to commit myself financially in the buying of a brand new automobile or perhaps any burden of that nature, I decided to volunteer for the draft, a two-year commitment in the U.S. Army. I had a brother two years older, who in June, 1966, was seriously wounded in the Vietnam war, serving with the U.S. Marines, near the Chu Lai area. For that reason and the fact that I had been raised as a loyal American, I felt a duty to serve my country in the military. At the same time, I think I was somewhat naive as to knowing what war was all about, and within a year from the time I went in, I had quickly learned.

As I waved goodbye to my folks, I realized this would be the first time that I was ever away from home for an extended time; and even the first time I would have flown on any kind of aircraft.

Upon my arrival in South Carolina, Ft. Jackson, which is outside Columbia, my eyes were being opened very quickly. When we arrived at the airport about four o'clock A.M., there was a large number of people from every walk of life, black, white, Hispanic. I recall looking at all those people. Many of the black people wore afros, many of the Caucasian folks had the long hair. Poor, to probably upper middle class, young men waited with anticipation for the military buses arriving to take us to the training center at Ft. Jackson.

The drill sergeant, with a stern voice, quickly commanded everyone to *fall in* and board the bus in an orderly and reasonable manner. It wasn't until we passed through the gates and I stepped off that bus that I knew perhaps how stupid I was. As we departed the bus, we were told immediately to knock off all the noise. The drill sergeant did not want to hear a whisper. All he wanted to hear was "Yes, Sir!" and "No, Sir!" He indicated to each and every one of us to fall in at the appropriate alphabetical designated sign that corresponded with our last name. We were tired, and yet everything, at the same time, appeared to be somewhat unorganized. Many of the people now in the military had difficulty even finding their correct alphabetical designation.

After being tested, inspected, and medically checked and retested, finally the following day at three or four o'clock in the afternoon, having had no sleep, they marched us off to our temporary barracks. On that particular post, those waiting for the final destination were on what was known as *The Hill*. In fact, all the military cadre would refer to *The Hill* as the area where all the military trainees would be broken into soldiers.

Strong regimentation and strict discipline was the order for the day, long hours of training, with very little sleep or rest. Appeared to me that the military always had you marching or running to wherever you were going, whether it be to the post office or to the mess hall, never walking. Perhaps that's the reason I was in pretty good shape after the eight weeks.

Kitchen police, or KP, meant long hours of duty in the mess hall where, basically, you were kept under the watchful eye of the mess sergeant and ordered to do tasks that were long and tedious and very tiresome: cleaning the tables, carrying the food, doing the dishes, mopping the floors, cleaning the walls, and making the mess hall spotless. That was for three meals a day. If we were assigned KP, we were up at about two or three o'clock in the morning and generally didn't finish until the following evening at approximately 9:30 or 10 o'clock. So that was a good many hours with no rest in between.

Shortly after my eight weeks of training, we fell out on graduation day, anxiously awaiting our orders for our next training center. Many of the people were hoping they would get into the medical field or perhaps be a clerk or a driver in a motor pool. Unfortunately, most of us, probably 80 percent of the 230-man Charlie company, 9th Battalion, Second Brigade, went to the infantry. I was one of the individuals selected for the infantry.

My next duty station was Ft. Polk, Louisiana, for eight weeks of advanced infantry training. About two weeks prior to my duty station at Ft. Polk, I got leave to come home. It was around Christmastime, and returning back, leaving on the plane out of Columbus again, the weather was extremely bad and they diverted my aircraft, originally scheduled for Houston, to Atlanta, Georgia, and I spent three days in Atlanta air terminal due to the inclement weather. Eventually I cashed my airplane ticket and obtained a bus ticket into Leesville, Louisiana. It took two days to get to camp. I knew I was going to be late and was afraid the military was going to hang me up by my thumbs or put me in front of a firing squad for being AWOL. However, when I arrived, I was only

Kenneth (Mike) Krueger and Brute

one of about eight thousand troops that were late, due to the inclement weather.

I was assigned to Bravo company, 4th Battalion, 5th Training Brigade, and it was kind of a rehashing of my basic infantry training, a lot of weapon training, marching, bivouacing, spending time in the field. We actually only went off the post one time, going into the little town of Leesville. That was my first exposure to the GIs, a few of them, getting a headful of liquor, getting stupid, basically, and the hustle of prostitutes. Again, for an old country boy, I was taken aback somewhat by this. I only spent about two hours in Leesville and went back to the post. The bus we were on was checked by the military police at the main gate. They were looking for someone who had apparently robbed or assaulted one of the prostitutes in one of the local bars in that little town.

I developed two very close friendships at Ft. Polk: With James Penuchi from New Jersey, and Herbert Francisco from Bluefield, West Virginia. Our records were lost in Ft. Polk, and we were placed in a hold-over company for an additional four or five weeks until they cut us new orders or new records. In the meantime, we were able to obtain orders for 12 weeks' training in Ft. Benning, Georgia, which is known as the Scout Dog School.

I didn't even know what a scout dog was. I felt it was 12 more weeks in the States and, what the heck, I'll try anything. Surprisingly enough, I was one of the few draftees with the infantry MOS specialty ever offered that particular training. Most of them were regular enlisted army personnel.

Jim, Francisco, and I left in April, 1968, by bus for Ft. Benning, Georgia. Once we arrived in Georgia, things were looking up—the weather was great, the city of Columbus, Georgia, was just on the outskirts of Ft. Benning, the people seemed very friendly. It was definitely a post where the military was well thought of.

They put us in the old OCS (Office Candidate) barracks. We were a specialized unit, commanded by a major, and no more KP, due to the fact of our exposure to dogs. We could not work around food products. Therefore, we had civilian cooks that prepared our meals. The barracks were modern, three floors high. The Scout Dog training program involved, not only army personnel, but marines, and a couple of squads of navy Seals. It was a 12-week course and a relatively new program that the U.S. army and marines were using in Vietnam; it worked similarly to the bird-dog concept. The dog, with his extra-sensory perception, sight, smell, and sound, could detect enemy presence for the handler. Then the handler would advise the main body or the commander of that particular patrol of enemy movement, the distance, the direction, and possibly even the number of people involved. The dog alerted, and it was up to the human handler to be able to read that specific alert, and from that alert to be able to make those judgments. It was the most interesting training I've ever been through.

I became very attached to my dog, Caesar. The dogs came from good homes; they had to meet certain criteria in order to be accepted by the military. Most dogs were between 12 and 15 months of age, had to be of good health, and have good features. They had to be robust, a good worker, very attentive, very perceptive; physical characteristics were very important, such as the length and size of the ears. Most of the dogs we worked with, probably 99 percent, were of the German Shepherd breed.

My first dog became my guardian, and I became his guardian, as well. We went through basic command training every day for a minimum of six to eight hours. We trained in the field, learning how to detect the distance, the windage involved, the direction in which the alert was given, and being able to determine, based upon the degree of alert, how strong an alert it was.

I was with my old friends, Jim and Francisco, in twelve weeks of training, and we knew that we had a 30-day leave coming up, in which we could go home to our families; then we would be assigned to duty in Vietnam. The dog I trained in the States went directly to Vietnam to be assigned to another handler.

As I got on the airplane after my 30-day leave, my thoughts went back to my family and whether I would ever see them again, the experiences I had growing up, the people I loved. As to the state of affairs of the country, I was as confused as anyone else as to whether I was doing the right thing. But I still held to that notion that as an American I needed to serve my two years to show my devotion and commitment to living in this country. I still feel that way today.

I flew to Oakland Army Terminal in Oakland, CA, and there, after two days, I met Jim and Francisco. At this stage we didn't know whether we would be assigned to the same unit or not in Vietnam with 350–400,000 military personnel in the country. We made a pact that we would try to stay together, fall out at the meetings at the same time, etc.

The day we left Oakland Army Terminal, our destination was Long Binh, South Vietnam, on the outskirts of Saigon, basically a reception center for all military personnel. We flew on a large aircraft, held approximately 350 passengers, all military personnel.

When the pilot indicated we were breaking cloud cover and below was the Republic of South Vietnam, my first impression, probably from 10-20,000 feet, was how green it was, just really a lush, brilliant green. The countryside, from the aerial view, showed large craters, just literally thousands and thousands, that kind of looked like the surface of the moon. Unfortunately, those craters were formed by bombs that were dropped.

Arriving in Long Binh, once we touched down and got off, I thought how intensely hot it was. The heat just seemed to really take my breath away.

I noticed all the military personnel had rifles across their backs, and jeeps had 50-caliber tripods on them. I knew now that this was real and everything I was trained for would be coming into play.

Once we were in Long Binh, they broke us down into smaller groups, but Jim, Francisco and I pretty well stayed together. They gave us a sheet and a pillow and assigned us to a barracks. There were sandbags all around the barracks, about five feet in height, from ground level. I was wondering what they were for, around all these barracks and little frame constructions. Later that evening I found out.

I was on the top bunk looking out through the screen of the barracks. I thought I heard a whistling sound passing overhead and all of a sudden, a tremendous explosion! I saw this large fireball! I was stunned by it, having no idea what it was. Then someone yelled, "Incoming!" Everyone immediately hit the floor and started scrambling, in a reclining position, to the front door of the barracks into an underground bunker complex. It had been a large enemy rocket fired into the American military installation.

There were approximately eight or ten more rockets within two or three minutes. Immediately the sirens would sound, and about ten or fifteen minutes later the sirens would resound, indicating an all-clear alert. It was kind of a welcome-to-Vietnam situation!

About our third night in Vietnam we had a large gathering, and they started calling out our serial numbers and names and assigning us to our specific units. Jim and I were, fortunately, able to stay with the 25th infantry division; Francisco went to the Americale division, which was hundreds of miles away from where we would be. So we bid him goodbye and good luck, embraced him and hoped to see him back in the States in a year. It was a sad parting.

We were assigned to the 25th infantry division, 46th IPSD (Infantry Platoon of Scout Dogs) and our working area would be out of the Tay Ninh Province I Corps, which is about 85-90 miles northwest of Saigon.

At Bien Hoa I met my new dog, Brute, Serial #3330 Mike. Brute was a beautiful dog, part German Shepherd and part Husky, kind of a blondish-color dog with beautiful ears. His snout was a little black on the upper portion near the nose. First meeting I had with the dog didn't go so well. In fact, he turned on me and tried to engage me. I was able to correct him and punish him in the way we were taught, and later he definitely knew I was the master and he was the one being mastered. He was by far the best dog I've ever had in my life. We worked extremely well together.

After two weeks of getting to know the dog and training in the field, on a limited basis, by convoy they took Penuchi and me up to Tay Ninh Province and to the 46th IPSD.

The 46th was a platoon of 28 scout dog handlers. We served five-day commitments, five days in the bush, or jungle (in the field), and one day back. One day back means we were able to come back to our base camp, which was Tay Ninh, and rest our dog for that one day. That didn't mean the handler got to rest. It only meant that the dog got to rest. Keep in mind the manner we worked with infantry units was on point, which was generally 50-75 meters beyond the main body of the patrol. I had a shotgun man or another infantry rifleman that accompanied me on point. He basically watched my security as far as snipers and things of that nature. I was constantly watching the dog's ears, his nose, and his gait, as he was watching or scouting. My full attention was kept on the dog and not on the surrounding area or what may have laid ahead for the main body of the patrol. I carried a double canteen, one for the dog and one for me.

The C-Rations they served us weren't really that bad. Probably the worst of the lot was the lima beans, or the egg and ham.

By far the best eating was the beef, chicken, or turkey. They always gave us a roll that, if you put a little water with it and heated it, it wasn't bad. We'd use C4, which was composition 4, an explosive, and we'd burn it to heat our food.They had peanut butter or jelly with the roll. Maybe there was a little can of fruit cocktail or pears or peaches; maybe three cigarettes; and a little package of toilet tissue.

Probably the biggest problem I had was lack of sleep. Whether sleeping inside a bunker or out in the open, we were constantly pestered with mosquitoes and bugs.

With the bunkers, I almost developed a fear of claustrophobia because the rats would walk around inside the bunker and sometimes the sand would drop down on my face; I knew the rat was walking up above me. Or I could hear it and feel the sand dropping down in my face from that little rodent's tracks. I had a difficult time sleeping the entire time I was in Vietnam. Of course, there was always the sounds of war, the rockets, the bombs, the exchange of weapon fire, so that was ongoing, non-stop day and night.

Another problem was the lack of bathing water. We washed from our steel pot or helmet. That's not a lot of water to bathe a human body, but occasionally I went back to base camp after my five-day commitment and did have a good shower. It was a makeshift shower in the field, but yet it was plenty of water, and I always felt sorry for the foot soldiers that I left after my five days. Those fellows, I tip my hat to them, they lived in the bush 365 days a year. At least I got a break every sixth day.

Dry season was hot and dusty, extremely hot. During the rainy season, wetness everywhere. Everything was always wet, boots, clothing, fatigues, our entire body. Just an immense amount of rain fell in a short period of time, and it would actually even get a little cold. Trying to live out of a bunker with water in it was a little difficult at times.

My first view of a dead North Vietnamese army body was signaled first by a distinct and putrid smell. A body of an NVA soldier had fallen three or four days prior to my discovering it. It really hadn't even sunk in yet as to what was going on here until then, and I don't think it actually set in until I saw my first American soldier that was killed. A young man fell screaming into a bunker that we were in; we pulled his fatique shirt away from his back; the shrapnel had literally severed his spine, in the mid-section of his back. He died within just a short period of time. I tried to block it out of my mind, but I think most people that came in contact with death and anything associated with it, tried to repress it; that seemed to be the best way to deal with it.

For our ambush patrols, we left early evening, having a rendezvous point with a squad of men. We'd set up our claymore mines out in the bush or in the jungle along a trail that we knew, or suspected, was heavily traveled by enemy soldiers. A 12- or 14-man squad always went on, grouped in twos. While one individual tried to catch a little shut-eye, the other would use starlight scope, infra-red starlight scope, in order to detect human movement in the evening. When we got confirmation that it was human, we'd blow our claymores, which were 50 yards of total death and destruction, shot thousands of little ball bearings with a terrific force. Claymores would, in fact, totally destroy human flesh. We'd blow our claymores and then commence, on a dead run, to our rendezvous point, take a head count of our squad, and then move back to our fire support base, which might be a couple thousand meters away.

I was detached. Some of the commanders I, and my dog, worked with were: Captain Hiromoto; nickname was Humpin' Harry. Hiromoto was of Japanese ancestry and the guy enjoyed walking, and I mean hoofing it. To go 20 or 25 clicks in a day was not unusual for Humpin' Harry. And that was about equivalent to ten to fifteen miles. Humpin' Harry served many times as body guard for me when I was on point. Harry was always good about requesting Specialist Krueger and his scout dog, Brute, to be with his company on his search and destroy missions or his reconnaissance enforced missions.

Another officer I met, 1st Lt. Pritchard from Texas, one that everyone dearly liked and really loved, a very friendly sort, always smiling, always had a good outlook on life, was killed on his last day in Vietnam. The good people die from strange circumstances.

Sgt. Francis Smith—one specific time we got mixed up as to the commitment we were supposed to be out on; I went with Charlie company and he went with Delta company, and later on my good friend, Penuchi, told me our platoon commander was concerned about me when he heard that the scout dog handler from Delta company was seriously wounded. He thought it was me and was relieved when he found it wasn't. Unfortunately, it was Sgt. Francis Smith, who used to be a policeman in Boston, and he was wounded quite seriously and sent home.

Black Virgin Mountain, known as Nui Ba Dinh, located just outside the provincial city of Tay Ninh, about 20-25 miles, was controlled by the Americans on the top and bottom, but the North Vietnamese regulars controlled everything in between. Many times during noon hours we'd be at the base looking up into the rock caves and seeing NVA troops through our binoculars, and they'd be looking back with their binoculars.

It wasn't unusual for us to sit around plucking bananas from banana trees, watching the NVA troops and hoping within a few hours that we would try to extricate them from the caves. It never made too much sense, but occasionally we'd start from the bottom and work our way up to the top of the mountain and next day come down the mountain. It always seemed we took casualties, and yet we never controlled the middle of the mountain. We had a communication center on the top of the mountain and it was just a matter, from the military perspective, I think, to do this a couple of times a week to keep the NVA off guard. We lost a lot of good people for something I never understood.

One of the things I enjoyed was getting letters; they were extremely important. And anyone that got a package from home was the most important guy in camp.

I look back and think about the people in Vietnam. I think of the old people and the kids in the villages as we passed through, the look of despair and terror, the look of uncertainty in their eyes and their faces. That's the devastation of war.

Went on many, many air assaults from helicopters, Huey UH1s. Perhaps the closest I ever came to actually thinking I was going to die, was when a helicopter I was riding in dropped out of formation, hit an air pocket, and we dropped about 7,000 ft. in about 45 or 50 seconds before the pilot was able to pull it out of its uncontrollable pattern.

I visited my brother. My younger brother was in the Marine Corps, serving with the 3rd Marines, Mike Company, in Quang Tri Province, which was near the DMZ, about 350 miles north of my work area. I got to visit him on Mother's Day of 1969, and probably my only thoughts of wanting to go AWOL entered then when I was leaving him. He was married at the time and had a baby. He was serving in the field, much like an infantry unit, and I told him we could both hang together if we decided to go AWOL cause maybe this war wasn't what it should be. We both thought it over and came to the conclusion that we didn't want to bring dishonor to our family and to our good name, and we knew it was just a thought in our head and we weren't that serious about it. So we departed, hugged, said we loved one another and that we'd see each other back in the States.

I came home the first of June, 1969, and my younger brother came home in a box, September, 1969. He was killed in Vietnam. That's my one regret. It will forever more be entrenched in my thoughts and feelings.

The abrupt adjustment to civilian life was extremely difficult. I think it took a couple of years for me to get readjusted and to try to understand what happened in Vietnam. Perhaps we'll never understand. I have different attitudes today about war. I think war hurts children and old people. I think war is, in fact, senseless, unless we have a situation where our boundary of the continental U.S. is threatened by a military force. Then I feel we have the duty and the right to defend our country. But I have a lot of feelings that we should never have been in Vietnam, 10,000 miles away, and not clearly understanding what our purpose was in being there. I went there under the impression, as President Nixon said, that we were there to stop Communism, and that obviously was not done.

I have a sincere appreciation for life, and thoughts of war's devastation upon our children and upon the old folks of this world scares the hell out of me. I was glad to hear that we were able to get in and out of the Persian Gulf situation the way we did, but I was very, very concerned about how sincere the American people would be if we started bringing home our boys from the Persian Gulf in body bags in the thousands. I've often wondered what our attitude would be then. As human beings we need to learn to live together and weigh all the consequences of any armed conflict.

RONALD LATHAM

URBANA, OHIO

Rifleman, E5, Army, 1969-70, Vietnam
Basic Training: Ft. Jackson, SC
Duty in Vietnam

It was the only war the United States ever lost. It was a war the nation never intended to win, according to Ronald Latham, a Vietnam War veteran...

"That war was run strictly for money," said Latham, who has co-authored a new book, *The Heart of the Country*... "I thought this book would go a long way in proving that."

... To avoid having to serve in combat in Vietnam, these men paid money to other military men who were in a position to help them. Latham paid $500 to get out of combat. Not only could soldiers buy the relative safety of duty behind the lines in Vietnam, but they could also buy rank, according to Latham. He said he paid $250 for his sergeant's stripes.

... The Big Red One was the division of the U.S. Army in which... (Latham) served. Of the 20,000 GIs in the Big Red One, one fifth of them were told about the cash or combat deal: for a price their orders could be changed and they could be reassigned to another company. Four-fifths of those soldiers had no idea the option was possible.

Those who did pay money were reassigned to a company in the Big Red One known as the First Administration Company. Latham said his job with that company was to be a driver for a first sergeant, driving him to Saigon three or four times a week.

After he paid the $500 to avoid combat, Latham said he is unaware where that money went afterwards. He suspects, however, that it filled the pockets of military people and the civilians involved with them to organize a black market of sorts in Vietnam. The book claims that 3,000 soldiers in the Big Red One division alone paid their way out of combat. If each paid $500, as Latham said he did, combined with other paid-for privileges such as rank, reassignment and R & R, the book asserts the potential income during 1969 for those involved in the alleged organization was $1.6 million.

..."They were sick," Latham said of those who knowingly operated this scheme while tens of thousands of the nation's young men fell in combat.

Latham is someone who finds it difficult, if not impossible, to trust anything the government tells him. He is frustrated that apparently people of influence in the current government evidently do not wish to tackle the issues he raises through the book.

"All the politicians avoided me," Latham said of persons he has approached to try to get his story out... "It's something they don't want to touch."

Reprinted with permission from *The Sidney (Ohio) Daily News* and Dan Liggett.

Ronald Latham and friends

FRANK E. MILLNER

DELRAY BEACH, FLORIDA

Aviation, Colonel, U.S. Marine Corps, 1958-88
Basic Training: Pensacola; Duty in Vietnam, Korea

Upon arriving at the Naval Air Station, Pensacola, for flight training, I scaled the steps with my suitcase in one hand and my tennis racquet in the other. As I reached the top step, I was met by a Marine Corps drill instructor. It did not take long before I was persuaded that I really had no use for the tennis racquet and probably not the suitcase.

After receiving my naval wings and a commission in the Marine Corps, my helicopter squadron HMM-264 (flying the UH-34 helicopter) spent much time aboard helicopter carriers, exercising in the Caribbean and participating in hurricane relief operations in Belize, British Honduras, and Freeport, Texas.

In late September, 1962, now attached to HMM-261, we found ourselves, along with the rest of Marine Air Group 26, in Memphis, Tennessee, as a result of the James Meredith integration crisis in Oxford, Mississippi. Our mission was to transport federal marshalls in case riots broke out. Fortunately, our services were not required.

In October, when President Kennedy took a stand against Communism in the Western Hemisphere, HMM 261 was again called on, with the rest of the units in the Second Marine Aircraft Wing, to participate in the Cuban Missile Crisis. We deployed aboard the helicopter Carrier USS Thetis Bay and sailed to an area off Eluthera Island in the Bahamas and awaited further developments. Our briefings on our proposed mission, needless to say, got our attention as we learned how well the Cuban coastline was fortified. It was estimated that the first few assault waves would take heavy casualties. As history knows, the blockade served us well and the crisis subsided.

In June, 1963, HMM-261 deployed to the Far East and our first area of operation was out of Danang, Vietnam, in what was then called *Operation Shu Fly*. While home on leave prior to departing the U.S., I learned that few people had any idea that we had military units in Vietnam or even where Vietnam was located.

During our first four months in Vietnam we often found our helicopters loaded to the hilt with such items as pigs, ducks, goats, chickens, cows, rice, fish, and a hundred other things that no one could imagine would be essentials of war. We also evacuated Vietnamese soldiers wounded in action and supplied them with ammunition and medical supplies necessary to conduct the war against the Communist Vietcong guerrillas. We also flew strike missions, carrying Vietnamese soldiers in to various Vietcong controlled areas.

The news media did not really focus on Vietnam until the buildup began in 1965; however, the conflict was real, as were the bullet holes in our helicopters.

Upon leaving Vietnam in early October, we spent the next six months aboard the helicopter carrier USS Iwo Jima. Our home port was the Naval Air Station Cubi Point, located in Subic Bay, Philippines. During this phase of the cruise, the squadron participated in two large-scale amphibious exercises in Taiwan. It was during one of these exercises, while the ship was docked in Kaoshung, Taiwan, that early one morning we were awakened to the news that President John F. Kennedy had been shot. We spent the rest of that day trying to find out what had taken place and the President's condition. Also of concern was the world-wide implications and the impact on military readiness and deployment. During this period, the squadron stood ready to support any crisis that might arise in the Western Pacific area.

On a sad note, the squadron lost seven of our crew members as they were returning to the ship from Clark A.F.B. As we prepared to depart the Philippines for Hong Kong and then Okinawa, all were aboard a squadron helicopter and, in an attempt to traverse a mountain pass in marginal weather, they became disoriented and crashed in a dense jungle area. Squadron aircraft searched all day on Easter Sunday before the wreckage was discovered.

In June 1964 I reported for duty with Marine Helicopter Squadron One (HMX-1) at Quantico, Virginia.

September 1957 marked the beginning of a mission which made the squadron truly unique. While vacationing in Newport, Rhode Island, President Dwight David Eisenhower was required to return to the capital on short notice. He flew the first portion of that trip, from Newport to the air station at Quonset Point, aboard an HMX-1 UH-34, thus marking the first time that an American president had flown in a Marine helicopter. With this first flight, President

Eisenhower realized the usefulness of the helicopter and continued to fly with HMX-1 for the remainder of his term.

Having established a record of safety and reliability, HMX-1 continues to provide helicopter transportation for the President and Vice President, as well as for cabinet members and foreign dignitaries, as authorized by the director of the White House Military Office.

The critical nature of these missions require highly qualified and experienced pilots to fly HMX-1 aircraft. For assignnment to the squadron, all officers are carefully screened, both for aeronautical ability and for superior military performance. Each officer must also have completed a significant amount of training within the squadron as a co-pilot prior to becoming a White House helicopter aircraft commander. Crew chiefs and other maintenance personnel are also selected for assignment to HMX-1 based on exceptional performance and integrity while with squadrons of the fleet Marine Force.

My first tour with HMX-1 lasted from June 1964 to November 1967. It is a humbling and exciting feeling when a new pilot joins the number one helicopter squadron in the Marine Corps. The tour was three years and the squadron had over 50 pilots and 500 plus enlisted personnel, as well as technical representatives for the various aircraft in the squadron inventory. Presently (1993), the tour is four years and the squadron has over 70 pilots and 700 enlisted.

After training in the aircraft and learning the many facets of the White House Support Mission, the pilot is ready to participate in presidential flights.

President Lyndon B. Johnson, after assuming the presidency upon the death of JFK the previous year, was in the process of running for reelection. We learned early on that when we were on call for any presidential flight that we kept a bag packed at all times. This was particularly true with LBJ.

One time when, as the commanding officer's designated copilot, I was at home having dinner when the call came that LBJ was going to Texas the next day. In order to arrive in Austin, Texas, before Air Force One landed, we had to launch our flight of helicopters that night. This included having a fixed wing aircraft to transport advance and support personnel to Austin. When Air Force One arrived, LBJ transferred to the helicopter and was flown to his ranch. This was about a 30-minute flight. Once there, we kept one helicopter and crew, plus security personnel, at the ranch for evacuation or to respond to any on-call mission. The helicopter was parked on an apron to the rear of the house, with an old hangar nearby. The flight crew stayed in a trailer near the helicopter.

LBJ and his friends used to enjoy going to the Haywood Ranch, where they had access to a lake and could go boating and have a good time. He was not especially known for his sense of humor when dealing with support personnel and the Secret Service. However, after returning from the lake late one night, he poked his head into the cockpit with a big smile on his face and thanked us. This was one of the rare times I remember this happening.

One of LBJ's favorite tricks was driving his golf cart toward the helicopter. We would dash out as soon as we got the word he was on the move. Not knowing if he was heading out for a flight or not, we would start the engines to await further instructions. As he drove up to the helicopter this time, he looked up at the cockpit with a big smile on his face and headed off in another direction.

We were at Camp David and it was time to return to the White House. The weather was not very good, as well as being on the warm side. As we departed Camp David, we were having a problem with the helicopter's air conditioning system, and the crew chief was working on it. About five minutes into the flight, LBJ came up to the cockpit, brushing the crew chief aside, and shouted at the commanding officer, who was concentrating on the flight instruments, due to the bad weather. The C.O. did not hear him, and the next thing I knew, a very large hand slapped my shoulder. I looked around and the President's face was glaring down at me as he let loose with a few well-chosen words about the air conditioner not working. My first thought was to tell him that if he had not disrupted the crew chief, it would probably be operating by now. However, discretion prevailing, I said, "Yes, sir. We are working on it." The system was back on line by the time he got back to his seat.

During the Pope's visit to New York City, the President arrived at JFK International airport where he boarded our helicopter and we flew him to a landing site at the base of the Statue of Liberty for a ceremony. Prior to the trip, there was confusion as to how Vice President Humphrey was going to get to the site. We thought he would go by helicopter, but much to his consternation, he ended up going by ferry. When we landed and the helicopter door opened for the President to depart, the Vice President was standing at the bottom of the stairs with a big smile and handshake for his boss. The Vice President was a real trooper and a class act.

We had the opportunity to transport Former President Eisenhower on several occasions from his Gettysburg, Pennsylvania, farm to the Pentagon helicopter landing pad, and then return after his business was completed. When he flew with us, he liked to be referred to as *General* rather than *Mr. President*. We also put his five-star plaque on the helicopter. He was very gracious and would stop by the cockpit before departing to have a short chat with the crew. It was evident that he was a military man at heart.

As my tour with HMX-1 came to a close in November 1967, I was promoted to Major and had orders to transition from helicopters to the KC-130 aircraft.

The KC-130 is a four-engine transport which was introduced into the Marine Corps inventory in the early 1960s and is still a workhorse in the 1990s. The primary Marine Corps mission of the KC-130 is aerial refueling. Other missions included cargo and personnel transport, aerial resupply, paratroop drops, airborne command and control, and night flare drops to assist troops on the ground and helicopters flying into night landing zones. There were other missions assigned as required, such as we did in Vietnam when we were tasked to evaluate the feasibility of dropping large bombs out of the aircraft at various altitudes and weights to clear jungle landing zones for helicopter operations. These flights were directed to various sites under radar control.

After joining the squadron in April, the in-country (Vietnam) operational training phase started with on-the-job experience. The squadron was located in Okinawa, but the aircraft and crews were deployed more than half of the tour. A permanent squadron detachment was set up at the Danang Air Base. The aircraft and crews cycled in and out on a somewhat regular schedule. A normal detachment for a crew began with an early launch from Okinawa with cargo and personnel for Vietnam. Many times the route to Danang would vary if requirements dictated picking up or unloading cargo/personnel at other air fields enroute, such as Taiwan, the Philippines and Hong Kong. The crew would land at Danang in the afternoon and be assigned to one of the three primary missions the squadron supported.

The first mission was aerial refueling and supported Marine Corps and Navy aircraft wherever required. A normal refueling track was flown in the Danang/Hue area so that aircraft enroute to or returning from missions could take on fuel to give them a longer range and time on station. We also supported missions in the Gulf of Tonkin, mostly at night, working with carrier and land-based aircraft. Shortly after I arrived back in the states, the squadron lost an aircraft in a mid-air collision during a refueling evolution. The co-pilot of the ill-fated aircraft was also my co-pilot during my last flight in Vietnam.

The second mission was cargo/personnel transport to and from air fields throughout South Vietnam, but mainly in Northern I Corps. I joined the squadron shortly after the TET offensive. During TET, squadron aircraft were heavily involved along with air force C-123S and Marine and Army helicopters in resupplying the area of Khe Sahn. The airstrip was a lifeline to the base and the resupply aircraft had to contend with poor weather, anti-aircraft fire, and mortar attacks on the ground while evacuating casualties, insert replacements, and drop off supplies. Pilots had about three minutes to land, unload, and take off, due to the heavy mortar fire. On February 10, the squadron lost a KC-130 to enemy gunfire while approaching the Khe Sanh airstrip, loaded with bladders of fuel, and began to burn. As the plane slid along the runway, crash crews covered it with foam. The pilot and co-pilot escaped; however, several others inside were killed. After that the KC-130s were restricted from landing, but continued to fly supplies into Khe Sahn, using parachute drops or a low altitude parachute extraction system, which would enable the pilot to extract the load while flying low over the airstrip without having to land, thus keeping their exposure to enemy weapons to a minimum. The squadron flew many resupply missions into airstrips such as Hue, Quang Tri, Phu Bi, and Dong Ha, among others.

The third mission was night-flare drops. Upon arrival, the crew was briefed and went to bed to be ready to launch that evening and fly for eight to ten hours. After takeoff we would be directed to a holding point until a mission was requested through the controlling agency. When a call came, we were briefed and radar directed to drop flares over the coordinates assigned. A mission length would depend on whether it was to illuminate the area for a helicopter medical evacuation, ground troop requirements, or other scenarios. Most nights were busy, but you also had an occasional quiet one when most of the time was spent orbiting the holding area. The local weather was always a factor. One night we were called to support a ground troop operation, and we spent several hours bouncing around in a thunderstorm, dropping flares. However, it is worth it when you hear the voice on the ground thanking the crew and knowing you were able to help make their job a little easier.

In the later phase of the Vietnam War, naval aircraft executed the most extensive aerial mining operation in history, blockading the enemy's main supply routes. This action may well have been the deciding factor in bringing the hostilities to an end.

Upon joining Marine Air Group-36 (MAG-36) in Okinawa in May, 1973, I was assigned as the Assistant Group Operations Officer. With the drawdown of the Vietnam Conflict, U.S. forces were committed to the clearing of minefields in the North Vietnam coastal areas. This was known as Operation End Sweep. In 1970 the navy formed a minesweeping squadron (HM-12) with RH-53 aircraft home based in Norfolk, Virginia. However, the navy airborne mine countermeasures (AMCM) forces were not sufficient in quantity, and Marine Corps helicopters were utilized to support the navy minesweep operations during late 1972/early 1973.

This was a busy year with the uncertainty of the truce with Vietnam. The Navy and Marine Corps commands had to ensure that all of the required units were in place to respond in the event that the truce broke down. Also, planning at all levels within the Marine Corps was required to ensure a smooth transition from many years of focus on Vietnam to the redeployment of assets and personnel in a new era.

In 1976 I was selected for assignment to a second tour of duty with Marine Helicopter Squadron One in Quantico, Virginia, as the Commanding Officer Designate. I arrived in June and served as the Operations Officer and Executive Officer prior to assuming the duties as Commanding Officer and Presidential Helicopter Pilot in June 1977.

When I rejoined the squadron in 1976, President Ford was in office and the presidential campaign was well underway. The outcome of the election is now history, and Governor Jimmy Carter assumed the office of the Presidency and Commander in Chief of the Armed Forces.

During the 25 months that I commanded HMX-1, I was only home for seven weekends. President Carter's travels took him virtually around the world, along with our helicopters and numerous other support units and agencies.

Some of the major trips abroad on which we flew the President during this period were: downtown Paris to Normandy Beach; around the Panama Canal; in Japan, Korea, Mexico, and Egypt.

The types of trips that we flew him on in the continental United States were varied: Some were political; some, vacations; some were to military installation/institutions or universities; some were official visits to disaster areas; and some were just to get a feel of the grass roots.

Camp David originated with President Roosevelt and was called *Shangrila*. President Eisenhower renamed it Camp David in honor of his grandson. Most presidents have spent much time there as it is very restful and one of the few places where news media can't catch up with them. When President Carter took office, he had a study done to see where cutbacks could be made in support personnel/equipment and facilities; the camp was one of the areas under study. However, after he had been there a couple of times, he didn't care what the study said because he enjoyed it and had come to understand why it was necessary.

The camp was one of President Carter's favorite places, as he could reflect and relax with his family and their guests. The First Family had a nice cabin (called *Aspen*) with a beautiful view. He was very good to the support personnel and staff who accompanied him during his camp visits. On occasion he would invite some of us to join the family for an evening movie at Aspen. He was very active while there with tennis, swimming, bowling, running, hiking, biking, and fishing, not to mention having time to prepare for, or rest from, exhausting trips and events. He was determined in whatever task or sport he was engaged in.

One day the President and I played tennis against the President's physician, Admiral Lukash, and one of my pilots, Ken Fugate (who had played on the Marine Interservice team). The President could tell that Ken was not playing as hard as he could and allowed as how he should. Well, they beat us, and I reminded Ken that he was in trouble as he not only beat his commanding officer but also his Commander-in-Chief.

Camp David was also a wonderful place to hold top level meetings, such as the Camp David Summit, which turned out to be historic in nature. The squadron was very busy during the 3-day evolution of the Summit, with transporting members and staff of the delegations from the U.S., Egypt, and Israel, as well as courier flights and press, when required. Being there, we knew the Summit was having ups and downs throughout the period. However, when it came time to amass the helicopter transportation for the trip back to Washington, we still did not know for sure who we would take and where. As we discussed the success or failure of the meetings, I felt that if President Carter, President Sadat, and Prime Minister Begin all departed together on my helicopter, it was good. If not, it was back to square one. As we all know, it turned out good at the last moment.

We had a 30-minute flight back to the White House. Enroute President Carter, President Sadat, and Prime Minister Begin all talked to Former President Ford, who was in Palm Springs, through the helicopter communications system. After landing on the south lawn, they departed for a news conference.

President Anwar Sadat, Egypt; President Jimmy Carter;
Prime Minister Menachem Begin, Israel.
Courtesy Col. Frank Millner

President Carter was a big fan of former Vice President/Senator Hubert H. Humphrey and relied on his counsel in many areas. When President Carter learned that Humphrey had never been to Camp David, he invited the senator to join him for the weekend. We departed from the White House lawn on a Friday evening.

The weather was a little on the grim side, with a strong westerly wind. As we approached the camp for landing, we had gusty wind and turbulence as we entered the landing zone (completely controllable, however). Even though it was a bumpy ride, the senator departed the helicopter with a big smile (He may just have been happy to be on the ground). During the weekend Senator Humphrey and the President had time to get together one-on-one to exchange views. The senator stayed in one of the guest cabins and ate (if not dining with the President) at *Laurel*, which is the lodge where guests and support staff eat. There is also a large conference room and casual area with a fireplace and television. After Sunday brunch at Laurel, a couple of my pilots and I had an opportunity to sit and visit with the senator for over an hour. Though he was very frail, his mind was quite sharp. He told us many stories about his past that were extremely interesting. I had the chance to recount the time I was the co-pilot on the flight that landed LBJ at the Statue of Liberty during the Pope's visit to New York. This is when LBJ made then Vice President Humphrey ride a ferry boat there to meet him.

Weather and Camp David did not always mix well. If the weather was questionable when the President was going to the camp, we would have another helicopter in the area to give us reports. If it was too bad to get into the camp, we would go to an alternate zone and he would ride up the mountain by car. One morning as we were preparing to return President Carter to the White House, the weather was socked in, and we could not see the trees a short distance in front of the helo pad. We had been watching the weather move in and out for several hours and noticed that about every 45 minutes or so it would be good enough to depart. The military aide called down to see if we could go, and I explained what the weather pattern had been. He said to give a call on the next occurrence. I told him that by the time they got here from Aspen that it would be bad again. The President decided to come down and wait on the helicopter. When he boarded, I discussed the weather with him and that it was too bad to go now. He said he understood and went to his seat to read. We waited for about ten minutes before we were able to get airborne, and then with radar direction, made an approach into Washington National Airport and then across to the White House lawn. It was at this time I felt that we had an agreement that he would not tell me how to fly the helicopter, and I would not tell him how to run the country. We were also on a first name basis—he called me *Frank* and I called him *Mr. President*.

The President loved fishing. During visits to Camp David, he and the First Lady frequently fished at Hunters Creek, which was a short ride down the mountain from the main security gate. Other fishing side trips from the camp were made; however, his favorite spot appeared to be Spruce Creek, Pennsylvania. I recall the first trip well. One evening I was told that the President was going to Spruce Creek the next day, by helicopter, of course. I had no idea where it was, so we started pulling out maps and found it was not far from College Station, Pennsylvania. The next thing we did was call our advance officer in Quantico and tell him to head out to the area and get in touch with a contact we were given and scout out a suitable landing zone. The next morning he contacted me with the information that we would be landing in a cow pasture right beside Spruce Creek. It was a 40-minute flight and, upon arrival, we were guided to the zone by our advance officer over the radio. It took some time before the press knew about the trip.

One of the most interesting trips we made was the President's vacation trip to Idaho and Wyoming, just prior to the Camp David Summit. He arrived in Boise, Idaho, where the First Family stayed overnight. The next morning we flew them to Indian Creek for the start of a three-day rafting trip on the Salmon River. During the trip we had an advance officer on one of the rafts with a radio, in case we had to evacuate the presidential party for any reason. When they reached Colson Creek, we picked the party up and flew to Jackson Hole, Wyoming. It was a 2-hour and 15-minute flight at an altitude of 10,000 ft. As we approached the Grand Tetons, we were up to 12,000 ft. It was a magnificent view as we started our descent into Jackson Hole. We set up a camp for the helicopters in a somewhat wooded area north of town.

Our first local flight was to take the President to an isolated area of Yellowstone National Park to fish. We were to also have a helicopter for the press, a large Marine CH-53 transport, to accompany the flight. After we prepositioned all the helicopters in the pickup zone, we had a problem with the press helicopter, and it could not make the trip. While enroute to Yellowstone, the President came up to the cockpit, and I related the problem with the press helicopter and that they would not be joining us on the trip. The President looked at me, with a big smile from ear to ear, and said, "That is too bad!"

After they had enough fishing, we took off to sightsee parts of the National Park. Enroute the aide said that the park ranger, who was with us, wanted the President to see a herd of buffalo that was just ahead. He asked if we could go lower for a better look. I asked, "How low?" He replied, "As low as you want." The President got a real good look!

One of the hardest trips we made was to Egypt. I received a call from the military office in the White House to see how long it would take to be ready to go to Egypt, if it became necessary. At ten o'clock A.M. they called back to confirm that the President was going. The first concern was getting our advance officers to Cairo to coordinate with all of the other units and agencies as well as finding a hangar, hotel rooms, transportation and coordination with the embassy for required flights. They were airborne before the day was over. In the meantime, we had to get shots, pay for 75 officers and troops, and give them time to get their personal items. Also, we flew four helicopters to Andrews Air Force Base to prepare them for loading on an Air Force C-5 transport. We had two larger helicopters which had to have the rotor blades and engines removed as well as some smaller jobs. This was all accomplished and we were airborne before daybreak the next morning.

Upon arrival we then had to reassemble the helicopters and fly them for a period of time to ensure no problems. We finished just in time for the President to arrive on Air Force One. We had several flights during the trip. President Carter went to Alexandria and stayed at the RAS-AL-TIN Palace. We flew him to President Sadat's home a few miles away for an evening function. The next day we flew both presidents back to Cairo. When President Carter finished his business, he headed to Israel to visit Prime Minister Begin. We had prepositioned two helicopters there for emergency purposes. President Carter returned to Cairo prior to departing for home. Most of the business conducted was a continuation of the Camp David Accord. After the dust settled, we again had to ready the helicopters for our C-5 flight back home. All hands did a superior job on very little sleep.

This was just a sprinkling of the many trips we supported during the 25 months I commanded the squadron. As the old saying goes, "You are only as good as the people that work for you." I can assure you that I have been very fortunate to serve with this squadron of real can-do professionals at all levels.

When President Sadat was assassinated, it was a sad day for many of us in this country. I had the honor of flying him on several occasions and he was always a very gracious gentleman. I had received a personal letter from him, thanking me and the squadron, for the helicopter support during the Camp David Summit. I will always cherish his thoughtfulness and his letter. President Reagan sent a delegation to his funeral, which was headed by former Presidents Nixon, Ford, and Carter, as well as many other dignitaries.

Prior to the trip, the Egyptian Embassy had requested my boss, Mr. Ed Hickey, to help them acquire a protective vest for President Mubarak so it would be available for the funeral. Ed Hickey was a former Secret Service agent who later worked for President Reagan while he was Governor of California. After the election, President Reagan asked Ed to take over the military office and he became

Frank E. Millner

the director of the White House Military Office, as well as White House contact with the Secret Service.The vest was obtained and after Ed's discussion with their Embassy, I was designated to hand carry and deliver it directly to President Mubarak and to ensure he had no problems using the vest. I flew to Egypt on the delegation's backup aircraft. Upon arriving at our hotel, I was contacted by President Mubarak's brother-in-law, a general in the Egyptian armed forces. He later picked me up outside the hotel and we proceeded into downtown Cairo by way of at least three roadblocks. On arrival, we entered a well-guarded door, walked through several passageways before entering a dimly-lit room where President Mubarak and his bodyguard/security man welcomed me. I assisted him with the vest, he thanked me, and the general and I retraced our route back to the hotel.

After the funeral was over, former President Nixon proceeded on his own itinerary while Former Presidents Ford and Carter returned on the delegation's aircraft. I also traveled with them and had an opportunity to reminisce with President and Mrs. Carter. It was the first time I had seen them since they returned to Georgia.

Later in June 1983 I reported to the First Marine Aircraft Wing on Okinawa, Japan, and assumed command of Marine Air Group Thirty Six. Our first large exercise was a month and a half deployment to a small airfield called R-228, which was about seven miles south of the DMZ.This was an excellent training area and we learned much. One of the real pluses was the cooperation and friendship forged with our Korean counterparts.

During March 1984 the group took part in the largest exercise of the year, Team Spirit-84, conducted in Pohang, Korea. We had the largest part of our group assets committed to this exercise. It was a three-week operation which included the highest level Marine Corps organizations, the third Marine amphibious force which encompassed a Marine air wing, and a division. The Republic of Korea forces were also heavily involved.Team Spirit is a yearly exercise that always gets close North Korean attention.

It was a very busy year with units and aircraft participating in 22 joint, or combined, operations in Korea, The Philippines, Guam, and Okinawa.

Marine Air Group 36 has a long, 32-year history and its motto is Subsidium Peditatus, which translated means: In support of the foot soldier.

DONALD B. PARDUE, JR.
ATLANTA, GEORGIA

Inf. Platoon Leader, 1st Lt., Army, 1966-69, Vietnam
Basic Training: Ft. Benning, GA
Duty at Loc Ninh

One of the first areas of concern for the combat soldier is his daily rations. During my tour in Vietnam in 1968, the food that we ate was either in the form of canned C-rations, which we either carried on us, or air-lifted into whatever area we were working in that day. The C-rations got old very quickly, but they were supplemented by hot meals which were provided by Chinook Helicopter to our temporary camps wherever we were in the jungle. The hot food was not too bad, if you could keep it dry long enough to consume it, between the monsoon rain storms that occurred periodically throughout the day. Between the hot meals, which came in insulated metal containers, and the canned fruit that was occasionally provided in the C-rations, overall I would say that the provisions, the various rations that were provided to the combat soldier, were at least adequate, if not slightly above standard, certainly in comparison with other armies in other parts of the world.

Equipment that was utilized by the combat soldier was judged to be, in my opinion, of the highest calibre of any standing army at that time. Our primary weapon was the M-16 rifle, although it had its malfunctioning problems in adverse environmental conditions. Overall, the weapon, if it were cleaned every day, did perform fairly well.

Auxiliary small arms equipment, M-60 machine guns, M-79 grenade launchers, LAW rocket weapons, etc., all functioned for the most part, in a very adequate manner. Personally, I preferred the standard issue AK-47 Assault Rifle. Other auxiliary equipment that was supplied to us was of equally high standards, and ammunition and small arms parts were readily available and easily replenished in a short period of time.

My thoughts on engagement with the enemy came primarily in two different formats, depending upon who the aggressor was: the enemy either was Viet Cong, local citizenry that had converted into very astute fighting soldiers; or, the one most feared by American soldiers, at least on my team, the North Vietnamese Regular Armies, known as the NVA, which came down through Cambodia, along the Ho Chi Minh Trail, and were at various points slowly injected into the southern sections of South Vietnam.

The Viet Cong were more of a nuisance and harassment factor which impaired our operations, not daily, but at least every second or third day. We had to contend with small bands of VC taking advantage of our more regimental and conventional form of running a war. Usually a small group of VC could tie up an entire company for a morning or an afternoon, in which case we would normally take some type of casualties, either in the form of killed immediately or wounded categories.

Our contact with the VC was usually when our commanders had decided to initiate what was then known as the Search and Destroy Mission. This was simply to identify the enemy and eliminate him as quickly, and inexpensively, as possible.

As for the North Vietnam army, I must admit that they were the most fearsome fighting element. Their discipline, training, motivation, equipment, and desire were unprecedented. They used excellent tactics for the terrain in which they worked, and when we were forced to fight them, either through ambush or search missions, it was always a level above anything else we had ever experienced in terms of challenge. The NVA were the true element that turned the war from an unacceptable situation to victory and, eventually, of course, caused our departure of South Vietnam in 1973.

It is interesting to note that not only did we have to contend with a combination of the North Vietnamese, the Viet Cong, and in some instances, even our own allied South Vietnamese troops, we also had to contend with our own ineptness in jungle warfare. The first confrontation I had with the enemy resulted in a tremendous disaster to my own platoon. My artillery forward observer had called for howitzer cover to help neutralize the enemy that was bringing fire upon my command. As the first round was fired in the conflict, it fell short of its forward target and landed in immediate proximity of my platoon. The results of that tremendous explosion, which not only knocked me down, and my radio/telephone operator standing next to me, it also killed my medic and wounded two of my enlisted men seriously. Those three men, that were either killed

Donald B. Pardue, Jr.

or injured by our own artillery battery, never returned to my platoon after that day. Ironically, it was my very first day with my command in South Vietnam.

Another area of somewhat concern to me personally, was becoming a casualty in and around the Cambodian/South Vietnam border. I was shot in the left shoulder and left lung on August 23, 1968, near a village known as Loc Ninh, III Corp. Not only was I critically wounded, but some of my men were also wounded or killed in that early morning conflict. This was almost an inevitable conflict because it took place in a rubber plantation, which although very shaded and cool to maneuver in, was also very hazardous, as the enemy knew.

The advantage that the Communists realized early in the war, in working in the rubber trees, was that the American forces could not call for any air support, indirect fire, or artillery assistance because of the high canopies of the trees. No helicopters, no gun ships, no attack jet could be utilized because nothing could be seen from the air, and nothing could be detonated through the deep triple canopy that the rubber tree plantations afforded the enemy.

We, as small unit commanders, first and second lieutenants, who were for the most part highly trained prior to taking command in South Vietnam, realized very quickly that when we had to traverse the old French plantations, many of which were formerly owned by the Michelin Rubber Corporation, we knew that trouble would always ensue and prevail for the most part. That was certainly the case on that August day back in the late '60s.

As to hospitals, I can only give you a brief schedule of what my own personal experience was and that of some of my men, who I later ran into as they would become casualties of the war. As I mentioned, I was critically wounded on the Cambodian border and was med-evac'd later that day to the 93rd evacuation hospital in Long Bihn, South Vietnam, and was operated on that afternoon. After an unsuccessful operation on my left lung and shoulder, I was placed in intensive care for approximately two weeks, on the critical list.

After recovering from that particular flash point, I was then transferred to a regular seriously-wounded ward, which was certainly a positive move for me. After staying in the ward at Long Bihn, I was later transferred to Camrahn Bay.

While at my latest hospital, which was located on the coastal area of South Vietnam, I had a chance to convalesce and was ambulatory at that time. I remained in a sling and was constantly monitored for my respiratory problems that were inflicted from an AK-47 round in my left lung.

After diagnosis at Camrahn, I was transferred to Japan for further evaluation. Upon arriving at a northeastern suburban hospital from downtown Tokyo, I was further evaluated as not being able to return to normal duty and was then sent back to the United States for an extended tour of rehabilitation in a U.S. hospital. After a total of nine months under hospital care and physical therapy, I was returned to limited duty prior to being discharged from the military.

As far as hardships were concerned, the fear of death on an hourly basis was always apparent, but then that was not new to any soldier since the beginning of time. The most disappointing thing to me, however, was not having the confidence of the fellow Americans at home and trying to psychologically keep my command in a positive attitude throughout each day. It was very difficult to work with some of the men who became depressed with the attitude of their fellow countrymen and an obvious lack of support in what we were trying to accomplish. It, therefore, became an extremely challenging psychological game that we, as young lieutenants, had to successfully pursue at times on an hourly basis.

The most peculiar thing was that during a conflict, when small arms firepower was exchanged, keeping the morale of the men high seemed to be the least of my worries. It was the aftermath that was so demanding on me at 22 years old.

The other disappointing thing was that we never saw any senior officers. My company commander was a captain, one grade higher than myself. As far as our battalion commander, or anyone higher than the grade of captain, we never saw them. They never came to the field where we actually lived and died. I think that the reason for their absence is quite obvious. We never went to a place, and we never ran a mission, that didn't have the word hostile built into the environment. So, I think it was disappointing as a junior commander, to not have someone, a senior officer, occasionally visit the men and help with the morale situation.

As for my remembrance on coming back to the United States, I was technically transported by an Air Force C-141 medical aircraft. This particular jet was specially designed to function as an airborne hospital, and those of us that were in a certain level of impairment, were required to come back on this medical airship. I remember very distinctly the inside, which had no windows, but took the form of a miniature hospital in itself, complete with doctors, nurses and supporting staff. Operations could be performed in the air for those men who were in even more critical shape than I, and it was actually an extremely amazing thing to witness our modern technology. I don't recall if we lost any of the wounded patients on that trip, but I am sure that if we had, we were not to be notified directly of that event.

After my assignment back in the United States, another new bed in another new ward, I was awarded a 30-day convalescent leave to go back to my home in Atlanta, Georgia. It was at that point, I think, that the true attitude of the country towards our effort came to my realization. With the exception of my mother and father, my girlfriend, who later became my wife, my brother, my immediate family, and a few very close friends, no one really gave a damn. It was extremely disappointing and depressing to walk into a public facility, whether it be a restaurant, bar, shopping center, or theater, and have people look at you a very odd way, knowing that with that extremely short haircut, you were certainly of military status. I still feel very angry about the lack of empathy that was placed on the American fighting soldier. The commanders such as myself that had to deal with, not only the enemy, not only the adverse terrain that we were not familiar with, but with the disgusting attitude of our countrymen in what we were trying to accomplish.

An American mother of a son sent to Vietnam

SIDNEY, OHIO

I have to say that I will always be furious about the Vietnam War and forever grateful to my God that he sent our boy back to us. I have difficulty wondering how those who lost one can endure normally. May be that time helps!

Our son was in college but wanted to get it behind him, so dropped out and, of course, was picked up. I didn't think he would pass due to his eyes, but a gas mask can go with glasses.

We got through the first weeks and went to visit him at Ft. Knox, Kentucky. He was in great shape, so we had hopes that it wouldn't be so bad.

Eventually he was sent to Vietnam with five other boys with whom he became friendly. We sent six letters a week from here, cookies, etc. I did not let myself feel any more than I could help. The days were easier as I felt with the time difference, he would be sleeping. Little did I know.

One of our local boys was badly wounded and little buckets were put out around town for donations. As we all put in money, I wondered about those in places like inner city, so I wrote my congressman and asked if money couldn't be put aside for a mother or someone else to go to the hospitals in the States to visit the boys, at least a telephone call. He wrote that the people would not stand for another tax for this. Shortly, he, his wife and several others went to India to look at something. I wrote again, but this time he didn't answer. Why?

So few people really seemed to care, and I had to miss some things as I couldn't keep still.

We slept little when he first came back as we knew a noise or sound could make him upset and didn't know how he would react. He slept in the same room with his brother, and we worried a lot. Also, his table manners were terrible. He forgot how to use his fork, spoon, etc. It took much understanding, and, at times, we didn't know the right way to treat him.

One thing I'll never forget. One early morning (about two A.M.) he woke me after he had been out. It was pouring, and he heard the kittens crying and the mother wasn't with them. He was so very upset that I went down. We brought them in and I dried them, heated milk, etc. Our son said, "I knew you'd take care of it," and went to bed. This I still kid him about.

Last spring I saw the memorial. I could not believe the size and how many were mourning there. I cried for all of them.

This doesn't tell of the pain, the prayers, the sadness of an empty mailbox, but maybe it will do some good.

DESERT STORM

SYNOPSIS

On August 2, 1990, Saddam Hussein sent 140,000 of his Iraqi troops into Kuwait, meeting only sporadic opposition as they moved eighty miles into Kuwait City. There his men beat, raped, shot Kuwaiti people; looted and smashed contents of businesses and homes. Within twelve hours Saddam had control of "...a fifth of the world's known oil reserves."[1]

After Saddam's becoming head of state in 1976 and then leading Iraq into an 8-year war with Iran, the country's economy was hurting. He wanted a bigger chunk of the oil-producing desert. Also, by acquiring Kuwait, Iraq would have better access to the Persian Gulf.

President George Bush immediately condemned Saddam's actions and asked the U.N. Security Council to demand that Iraq withdraw. The Council gave unanimous approval. President Bush also ordered an embargo on all trade with Iraq and froze Iraqi and Kuwaiti assets in our country. Removal of Kuwait's oil from the market, plus the possibility of an invasion of Saudi Arabia and possession of their oil wealth, was a serious threat to the world.

Saddam stated publicly that he intended to hold foreign nationals, particularly Britons and Americans, as guests of the state, or in other words, as hostages. He planned to house them in strate-

Sidney, Ohio. Doris Eggleston

gic military locations so that these sites would be protected from Allied attacks.

Looking toward the possibility of Saddam invading Saudi Arabia, the United States, plus a number of other nations, acted upon the request of Saudi Arabia to come to their aid and began to assemble a military force.

Other countries that deployed military forces were: Argentina, Australia, Bangladesh, Canada, Czechoslovakia, Egypt, France, Great Britain, Saudi Arabia, Oman, Qatar, UAE, Bahrain, Kuwait, Honduras, Italy, Morocco, Niger, Pakistan, Senegal, Sierra Leone, Syria, and the Soviet Union.

Financial and other contributions were made by: Korea, UAE, Germany, Japan, Kuwait, Saudi Arabia, The Netherlands, Turkey, (with a small amount from others).

Deployment of aircraft, troops, equipment, and supplies began on August 7, 1990, upon order of President Bush. The massive buildup, the largest transport effort ever undertaken, was called Desert Shield.

The military, including General Colin Powell, Chairman of the Joint Chiefs of Staff, and General H. Norman Schwarzkopf, Commander in Chief of the U.S. Central Command, the multi-service headquarters, believed that if our intent was to drive Saddam out of Kuwait, then it should be a full-scale effort, not a half-hearted one like Vietnam.

Congress argued for three days about whether to approve force. But after the vote was taken, Congress, as well as the American people and the U.N., backed the President.

Green Beret, DELTA forces, and Navy SEALS started their reconnaissance in August to learn about enemy defenses and their movements, their mission depending upon their not being detected.

With an American troop strength of 240,000 at the end of the first ten weeks, the Pentagon decided to increase it by 200,000 more. Since the United States was in the midst of downsizing its troops, equipment, and funding, the supply within the country was becoming depleted, so they took those stationed in Europe. The National Guard and Reserve units supplied 49,703. By the end of the year over a half million allied troops, including air and navy, would be in and off the shore of Saudi Arabia.

Since 1949 the U.S. has had ships in the Persian Gulf, so when Iraq invaded Kuwait, the warships were already in the area. By the start of Desert Storm, there were approximately 65 warships, with six aircraft carriers that could carry 5500 people each, two battleships, and other supporting craft. Besides these there were ones from other countries.

Sealift was used for transporting heavy equipment. Cargo ships were taken from the mothball fleet and then crews had to be found for these not-recently used ships. At the busiest time, 172 ships were at sea each day.

Troops and light equipment went by air, using the C-5 Galaxy and C-141 Starlighter as well as commercial airliners with reinforced cargo decks. These commercial airliners were part of the Civil Reserve Air Fleet, activated by the Defense Department. Some of these

Aircraft Carrier. Courtesy U.S. Navy and Robert F. Dorr.

C-141s, which had served since the Vietnam era, had already flown 38,000 hours or more, with a predicted 45,000-hour lifetime. The C-5 Galaxy could "... carry four M551 Sheridan tanks, a Humm-Vee battlefield vehicle, and seventy-two soldiers."[2] At the peak, there was a plane landing every seven minutes in Saudi Arabia. The planes were in the air so many hours that there was hardly time for routine maintenance.

Planning this massive move was a gargantuan project: What was to go first—people (fighters, security, maintenance), weapons, ammunition, equipment, tents, food. There had to be people and equipment on each end to load and unload as well as to assemble and distribute the cargo in an orderly fashion. "President George Bush's national security advisor said... that the US deployment to the Persian Gulf was one of the smoothest military operations in memory..."[3]

One of the priorities was getting a sufficient number of latrines. Another was drinking water. When we saw service people on television, many times they were drinking water from plastic bottles while carrying a second bottle. And of equal importance were the mess tents that would serve hamburgers, pizza, and chicken, food that was familiar and that would be morale boosters.

Schwarzkopf, well-schooled and experienced in battle (Vietnam), is also one that cares about his troops. He likes being a part of them, sharing their rations, listening to their comments, their problems. At one time they were commenting that sand came through the ventilation holes in their boots and their feet couldn't breathe in the thick leather. As a result, he ordered new boots with a lighter covering.

Our troops were well equipped. A new bullet-resistant helmet gave more protection to the head and weighed less. "Over his desert camouflage outer garment, the trooper wore a Kevlar flak jacket and a load-bearing harness that carried ammo, a combat knife, first aid supplies, and a 9-mm Beretta pistol. His rucksack held two ponchos, a poncho liner, rations, underwear and personal hygiene items. Leg and hip pockets on his outer garment provided additional personal stowage space. An entrenching tool was strapped to the side of the rucksack and a pair of canteens hung from his combat belt. Strapped to the bottom of the pack was his bedroll, and he carried the standard issue M-16 A2 automatic rifle... (The Army and Marine troops were basically the same.)

Finally, there were two new items: a protective mask to filter out chemical and biological agents, and a protective suit (stowed in the rucksack)."[4] Within eight minutes they could be completely encased in the suit.

Paratroopers wore a "... T-10C main back parachute, a yellow static line that will open the chute, a reserve chest chute, a rectangular M1950 weapons case for a Colt M16A2 rifle and ... rucksack, below the waist."[5] They have a Kevlar ballistic helmet.

The armed forces involved in this war were all volunteers, average age of 27, six years older than the average in the Vietnam war, better trained, better educated, with most having a high-school diploma and many having at least some college. Most officers had some college and some, advanced degrees. Sixty-five percent were married and many had children.

Over thirty-two percent of the forces were black. "In the top NCO ranks, thirty percent of the Army's sergeant majors and 17.5 percent of Marine Corps' were black."[6]

Over ten percent were women. Three hundred two, out of three hundred fifty-one, occupational specialties were open to women; for example, they served as mechanics, nurses, physicians, heli-

Chemical gear. Courtesy Dept. of Defense and Robert F. Dorr.

copter pilots, and flight crew members. Women did their jobs well with very little complaining, even though they had practically no privacy except at latrines.

American troops in the Gulf had to adjust to a desert environment, extremely hot days (up to 130 degrees F.) and cold nights. Dehydration and heat stroke did not prove to be the problem it could have been, but diarrhea took its toll. Sand was constantly getting into clothing and equipment. There were false-horned vipers and seven-banded scorpions. "High-tech items of military equipment were melting, blowing up and springing leaks amid the harsh climate and blowing sand."[7]

The culture was radically different, not allowing alcohol, and women being treated much differently than in the States. Our women, if out of uniform and away from the job area, were to wear long, black dresses, covering arms and legs, be accompanied by a man and walk twelve paces behind him, the same as the native women. Islam was the only practiced religion, so other services for our troops were kept quiet, not publicized.

To make the troops feel as much at home as possible, 24-hour-a-day snack bars (commonly called roach coaches) were scattered around, offering sodas, chips, sandwiches, and sometimes even non-alcoholic beer.

While off duty, troopers washed their clothes in buckets, fought off the flies, swapped newspapers, played poker, volleyball, football, chess. And with the always-present Yankee humor and ingenuity, they joked and even came up with lizard races. Some of the workers produced their own newspaper for the troops.

During the buildup, the troops in place became bored and depressed just waiting for something to happen. They trained and trained some more, much of it at night. They rehearsed, moved, dug in, cleaned and oiled their guns and weapons. They "stretched condoms over the barrels of the rifles to keep out the gritty sand."[8] They sharpened their fighting knives, wrote letters home and sent souvenirs back. The hurry-up-and-wait period, even though they were doing busy work, gave room for a morale problem.

They ate their plastic-sealed rations, called MREs (Meals, Ready to Eat) when a chow hall wasn't close by. And again, with the usual humor, the term for MREs became "Meals Rejected by Ethiopia."[9]

The world, unlike in previous wars, kept eyes on the television for all the latest developments. On the day after the U.N. deadline for Iraq to withdraw from Kuwait, suddenly Bernard Shaw's voice interrupted a CNN program saying that the skies all over Baghdad were illuminated with bright flashes.

Along with Bernard Shaw were Peter Arnett and John Holliman, with the three giving, in their trembling voices, the first live, eyewitness, account of war as they crouched in their room, sometimes holding their microphones out the window to capture the sounds of war.

Relations between the military and the media were not particularly good. Understandably, the press wanted to give all the latest news to its readers or viewers. But, so that crucial information would not be given to the enemy unintentionally, the military decided what should be told and what should not be.

In fact, they were assuming that after Saddam's communication systems were knocked out, he was relying on CNN to get the news of the day-to-day happenings.

Each morning a briefing was given to the press and questions were accepted. The military would not speculate on what would be happening, but stuck to the facts.

Television was saturated with war coverage. In trying to find a new perspective, reporters began interviewing military people, asking what they would do or what they thought would be happening. General Schwarzkopf became very disgruntled with this approach because some of those military men could have easily given away his strategy.

On Thursday, January 17, 1991, 2:40 A.M. Israel time (Wednesday, January 16, 1991, 6:40 P.M. EST) nearly 700 aircraft of the coalition forces assembled in airspace beyond Iraqi radar range. "The USAF F-15 Eagles and F-16 Falcons, in concert with USN and USMC F/A-18 Hornets and coalition Hornets and Jaguars, would be given the mission of sweeping the skies of..."[10] Iraq's planes. The "... F-14 Tomcat fighter... as the Navy's fleet defense interceptor... was responsible for the protection of each carrier battle group..."[11]

"USAF tactical aircraft began flying combat air patrols within hours of arriving at airfields within Saudi... E-3 airborne surveillance aircraft (AWACs—Airborne Warning and Surveillance System) searched the skies for any enemy aircraft movement or hostile intent... Communications were monitored..."[12]

Also flying overhead were satellites which made it possible for ground troops to hold a receiving device in their hand and know their exact position. From satellites they could also get weather pictures and detect and track missile launches.

On January 17, with the first attack, the name Desert Shield changed to Desert Storm.

Ships made the first strikes with Tomahawk Land-Attack Missiles, flying at around 550 m.p.h., reaching heavily-defended targets several hundred miles away. Two-thousand pound shells from the 16-inch guns could be sent into the coastal area of Kuwait with extreme accuracy.

F-117 Stealth attack fighters sped in, followed by hundreds of coalition aircraft.

Eight AH-64 Apaches, flying low and without lights, cleared the way from intercepting aircraft by destroying two crucial radar stations.

Apache. Courtesy U.S. Coast Guard
(PA1 Chuck Kalnback) and Robert F. Dorr

AWACS (E)C-137D. Courtesy Air Force

Coalition aircraft flew 2,000 sorties during the first twenty-four hours (more than 1,000 by U.S. aircraft) with very little opposition from Saddam's fighters. This, in spite of the fact that Iraq had modern equipment and combat-experienced men, with its military ranking only after the Soviet Union, China, and the United States.

Once the command and control facilities, communications centers and supply lines were annihilated, coalition planes would give support to ground operations. Random bombing, that might cause civilians to be wounded or killed, was to be avoided.

Saddam had threatened to retaliate by striking Israel if he were attacked, and he did. But, the same night a Scud was fired at Saudi Arabia, it was shot down by American Patriot missiles, "... the first time one missile had destroyed another in midair."[13] TV audiences all over the world watched and cheered as these Patriot missiles continued to destroy Saddam's Scuds.

Stealth Fighter. Courtesy Dept. Defense and Robert F. Dorr.

Saddam's threats to retaliate by using chemical and biological weapons never materialized, but our troops had been prepared for such occasions.

Iraqi troops captured several of our fliers and, against the rules of the Geneva Convention which govern the treatment of prisoners, showed them on television, and, by so doing, created world-wide anger. He also announced that the POWs were to be housed at high-priority target areas.

Major Rhonda Cornum, an army officer and physician, one of three survivors from a helicopter crash while on a search-and-rescue mission, was taken prisoner and held for eighteen days. With two broken arms, among other injuries, she was almost helpless in many ways. Generally speaking, she was not mistreated. Blindfolded, she was moved from place to place. Since she couldn't use her arms, they fed her, what food there was, and gave her some medical treatment.

Army Specialist Melissa Rathbun had been the first female prisoner, having been captured when the truck broke down while taking supplies to the forward lines.

Oil wells and storage tanks were set ablaze by Saddam's men; huge oil slicks were created. Reports said that Saddam's men were continuing their rape, torture, murder, and looting, the victims numbering in the thousands.

After their-hurry-up-and-wait routine, finally the troops sensed that it would not be long before the ground war would start. They were allowed small fires to make their coffee but no open fires. A whisper sounded like a loud intrusion of the quiet. Music of the military-run FM radio stations could be listened to with earphones. They thought about home and how they would be treated. It seemed that people were supporting them because there was so much mail and many letters were addressed to Any Soldier. They prayed—not only for their own safety and that of their comrades but that they wouldn't let their comrades down. They prayed for bravery and strength in combat and then private things. The old saying that there are no atheists in foxholes seemed true.

"Coalition forces had as a distinct advantage over their enemy the ability to conduct at night almost the entire spectrum of military operations. Infrared and/or low-light sensors were installed in practically every armed combat vehicle, land and air. The M1A1

Abrams main battle tank had a superb night detection and aiming capability."[14] "But sand dunes lacked the texture of topographical features elsewhere and even when NVGs were working properly, a helicopter pilot could fly into a mound of sand simply because it produced no shadow."[15]

Marines used their Humm-Vee vehicles and some M60A1 tanks. The army mainly used M1 Abrams tanks with 105 mm guns. Some M551 Sheridan light tanks, that dated back to 1959 and could be airdropped, were used with their 152 mm guns.

Humm-Vee returned to National Guard Armory, Piqua, Ohio, after use in Desert Storm. Doris Eggleston

The air campaign took out the Iraqi Air Force, as well as supply lines, and communication systems. Only then, when Saddam had no way of checking on the allied forces, did the troops and supplies begin to move.

On Sunday, February 24, 1991, the ground offensive began. Coalition forces moved quickly, covering great distances, eating field rations during their very short breaks, never turning off the engines of their vehicles. Men and women in cargo trucks and helicopters struggled to have fuel, ammunition, food and water at the ready. "...an armored division could use more than a half-million gallons of fuel per day." [16] Med-evac helicopters were there to evacuate any wounded.

In this war there would be no body counts. Schwarzkopf had been through that routine in Vietnam, and was still outraged over the misleading conclusions to which it led.

Complete divisions of Iraqis could have been wiped out, but were instead given the opportunity to surrender. Leaflets were dropped from planes and in artillery shells telling the Iraqis that they would have good treatment if they surrendered; that we were not there to destroy Iraqi troops but to get the leaders to leave Kuwait.

After the first ten hours, Iraqi prisoners numbered over 5,500; hundreds more waited, wanting to give themselves up to anyone, even journalists.

The Iraqis held their hands high with "white pieces of cloth gripped in their fingers... They were all fatigued and hungry and many slogged through the sands on cloth-wrapped feet... The coalition forces felt little animosity toward... (them), knowing they were also just soldiers doing their job, and very poorly supported. The prevalent emotion of U.S. troops was pity. Most of the Iraqis, once they realized they were safe, smiled and enthusiastically nodded their gratitude. A few even embraced their captors."[17]

By Monday, February 25, it was estimated that 20,000 Iraqis had surrendered, so many that it was difficult to contain them.

Wednesday, February 27, the U.S. Embassy was being secured in Kuwait City. The Kuwaitis were ecstatic as they regained control of their capital city, and there were crowds of shouting and happy people in the streets. All were expressing their admiration and gratitude to the coalition forces.

Thursday, February 28, 1991, President Bush announced that he was ordering an end to hostilities, the order to take effect in three hours, at midnight Washington time.

"The war lasted 43 days. The Ground Assault, 100 hours. The United States deployed 540,000 troops. Our Allies, over 200,000... the pilots of Desert Storm dropped 142,000 tons of bombs on Iraq and Kuwait—about 5 percent of the total in the years of World War II... American casualties were 148 killed in action, of whom 35 were struck by friendly fire. Fifty-seven U.S. planes and helicopters were lost. Not one American tank was destroyed. Seldom, if ever, has a victory been so one-sided, or a defeat so massive."[18]

But with all the other devastation, Kuwait was left with over 600 burning oil wells, more than 5 million barrels of oil going up in smoke each day, filling their atmosphere with a blanket of black pollution.

DESERT STORM

THE HOMEFRONT

On August 2, 1990, Saddam Hussein aroused American and world hatred as his troops marched into Kuwait, killing, raping, torturing Kuwaiti people as they went. President George Bush said, "There are times in life when we confront values worth fighting for. This is one such time."[19] Americans rallied around him. Immediately Saddam was the bad guy in cartoons, on dartboards, and even in a song.

Tearful farewells were shown on television as troops were rapidly deployed to Saudi Arabia and the Persian Gulf. National Guard, Reserves, and even some retirees were called to serve. With 65 percent of servicemen being married and many having children, families were separated, children left with no understanding of why Daddy was going away. In some cases, since over 10 percent of the troops were women, mothers had to leave their children. And there were incidents where Mother and Daddy both were sent overseas; grandparents, other relatives, or friends took custody of the children. This was a different situation than in previous wars.

Support groups were quickly formed in most communities for those family members left behind. Besides being morale-boosters for one another and getting advice of all kinds, these groups made and distributed lists of things the service people (men and women) might like to have, or things that might make their lives a little easier. Some of the items mentioned were: Baby Wipes, fruit cups, Beanie Weenies, Jiffy Pop popcorn, instant cocoa mix, cup of soup, Pop Tarts, lip balm, insect repellent, goggles (dirt bike type), tape recorder and tapes...

The support groups had money-making events in order to send boxes to those in service. Businesses donated money to help. The groups had marches, carrying flags, banners, and posters. There were candlelight prayer vigils.

For the first time in history, television viewers could see the war as it happened—could see missiles hurtling overhead, could hear the bombs burst, could see the sky light up with the explosions, could share the fear. Occasionally, TV viewers could get a glimpse of loved ones.

Prime-time shows on television were ignored; people wanted to watch the stations carrying war news. The war seemed to be going so well that citizens believed it was going to end in a matter of days. General Schwarzkopf, Commander in Chief, and other leaders did not want that attitude to become prevalent for fear that the situation might change and morale and support would plummet. For this reason, when the media was briefed of a success story, it was also cautioned to not put too much significance on the story.

Enthusiastic displays of patriotism were all over America, the most since World War II. Yellow ribbons appeared in numerous places—on trees, mailboxes, yard lampposts, car antennas, car mirrors. Men and women wore them as lapel pins. Shopkeepers couldn't keep enough yellow ribbon in stock.

And the same with American flags. Homes and businesses that had never flown flags before were flying them high, many left up at night with lights shining on them. Desert Storm T-shirts and sweatshirts were the popular items to be wearing.

Making sure that our service people were receiving mail seemed to be a priority. School children of all ages practiced their letter-writing skills, many times developing on-going communication with a particular person. They sent Christmas cards and Valentines, crossword puzzles, word games, jokes, riddles. Upon their return to the States, many of these special friends visited the students in their classrooms.

Despite all the enthusiastic display of patriotism, there were those who did not feel we should be fighting another country's cause or fighting for oil. Protests and demonstrations erupted in the U. S., as well as in other countries, but nothing like during the Vietnam era.

An interesting occurrence was the marching by many Vietnam veterans all over the country to show their support of the troops in the Persian Gulf.

Church attendance in general rose and prayers for peace and for the safety of our servicemen in the Persian Gulf were almost always included.

Fuel prices did rise and there was talk of fuel shortages and conservation. Consumers griped and blamed the oil companies, thinking they were taking advantage of the situation.

During football season, NFL players had a small American flag on their helmets.There seemed to be a greater participation in the singing of the national anthem and with hands or hats placed over the heart.At the Superbowl people cheered and waved American flags during the singing of "The Star Spangled Banner." There had been discussion about canceling the game due to possible terrorist attacks; but because it is such an American tradition, it went on with extra security precautions.

Bob Hope took a Christmas show to the Persian Gulf, as he has done for American service members since WWII.The girls' costumes were not as skimpy and the jokes were selected a little more carefully, in respect for the Islamic customs. But the pretty girls were there, as was the Les Brown band, and someone sang the ever-popular White Christmas.As the program was replayed in the States, people at home watched for familiar faces.

As the troops came home, there were celebrations and parades similar to those after WW II.The service people did not need to worry about how they would be received.The country welcomed them with open arms.

HENRY M. CAMPBELL

SIDNEY, OHIO

Cook, Sergeant, Army National Guard, 1991, Desert Storm
Basic Training: Ft. Knox, KY
Duty in Saudi Arabia

On our flight to Saudi Arabia, it took about 24 hours from Volk Field in Wisconsin, on a commercial 747. The flight attendants had all volunteered to go over on that flight. One person refused to get on the plane. They were going to court martial her but found she had mental problems before; intended to charge her with failure to obey orders and failure to meet deadline.

Our mess sergeant had two sons also in the unit. There was another man and his son both there. Back in WW II there was something about not all the male members of a family being taken. Here I don't think they excused anybody. I had open heart surgery in 1983; had my gall bladder removed two months before being called up for this operation, and I didn't get excused. They still do have a 4F classification, but somehow or other, I was still able to stay in the Guard unit.

There was a two-hour fuel stop in Philadelphia, but we weren't allowed to get off the plane. They were afraid somebody might not get back on. Next stop was Brussels, Belgium—two hours, but we still couldn't get off.

We could see the shoreline of Italy from the plane, could actually see the shape of the boot. We took pictures of the oil fields in Saudi Arabia from the plane—look like big black spots in the pictures.

From Brussels we flew into King Faud airport in Saudi Arabia. As we disembarked, there was a sergeant major standing down at the bottom of the runway and he said, "Well, this is it, Sergeant!"

We loaded on buses and went to our barracks, what was called Scud Towers. This area was where a lot of the scud missiles came and were intercepted by the patriot missiles.

We had an underground garage that was converted into a mess hall. They told us we were fed the first couple of weeks by King Faud. Caterers brought the food in. With 500-1,000 people there, we had to wait in line for everything: 30-60 minutes for the mess hall; the telephone, 30-45 minutes. Calls had to be made from a phone center.

These buildings were nice, high-rise apartment buildings but had nothing in them besides running water, carpet, bathtub, commode, and shower. Each apartment was probably for two or three families. They told us these were built for the nomads, but they didn't want to live there—no place for their animals. They would rather be out on the desert. And another thing, they were built by Koreans and they brought the women of the night in; called it Sin City.

We finally got some cots. When we first arrived, we slept on the floor, which was concrete with a very thin carpet.

The place is messy and very dirty. They don't pick up anything that gets torn up, like a car. They walk away and leave it if they have a wreck. One time out on the desert we saw a bunch of black stuff laying out all over. When we got closer, it looked like a hundred or more sheep lying out there, dead. We went on down another hundred yards or so and there laid a dead camel decomposing. Their sheep are all black and look different from ours.

People from Saudi Arabia do not work. They are rich so they hire Palestinians, Koreans, and other foreigners to work for them.

We had bottled water; not allowed to drink the water in the building. We could shower with it, shave with it, brush our teeth, but we couldn't drink it. We got three or four 2-liter plastic bottles of water a day.

There's no grass anywhere. About the only thing they have looks like a thistle, and the camels and sheep eat it. Palm and date trees are about the only kind of trees they have. One day when it rained, there was a sea of mud in the center area of the apartment complex. There were some walkways, but no grass.

There was a fried chicken place—not Kentucky Fried or any of our franchises, but something similar.

If you want to go to a public restroom, there's about a 4-inch hole in the floor with a set of footprints on each side of it that you stand on. The women and the men seem to use the same ones. There was no toilet paper.

In the apartment buildings there was a regular stool. Right beside the stool was a hose about three feet long with a spray on the end and a trigger to operate it. You washed yourself off with this and then used a towelette, which was there (rather than toilet paper). This flushed; I'm not sure about the public ones.

We moved out of these apartments to CCPS (Convoy Control Point South). Out there our bus driver was a Palestinian. One day he pulled off the side of the road, got out of the bus, walked back beside the bus, squatted down, pulled his robes up, and did his business, picked up some gravel with his left hand. Their left hand is for sanitary purposes. That's the reason they never shake hands with their left hand. It's considered an insult to offer your left hand to shake. When he got to where he could, he washed his hands.

After we got out in the desert, everything was burned, garbage and whatever was in our latrine. The latrines were box-like. No chemicals. One of these was marked Urinal Only—Male; another, Solids only—Male. Then there was one of each for females. Every day, cause there were about one hundred sixty in our company, we had what we called Shit-burning detail. I didn't have to be on this detail since I was a cook. They took a 55 gallon drum and cut it in half. There was a seat with 4 holes. The back end lifted up and they pulled out the drum with handles that were on it. They pulled it away from the building, poured kerosene and gasoline on it together, and set it on fire—burned the waste. They stirred it to make sure it all burned up.

We went through an ancient city; we didn't know how old it was, but the houses were all adobe with flat roofs, like the ones in Jesus' time. They had decorated, patterned doors, mostly in blue. The streets were very narrow.

One day an Arab brought a camel around to let people sit on and have their picture taken; didn't ask any money for it. There were a lot of camels out on the desert. One man stuck his hand in the camel's mouth and told us that camels can't bite. Then he showed us that they have no lower teeth.

I got sick and had to come home—had a headache and diarrhea; they thought my heart trouble was coming back. I finally went to a field hospital and they kept me two or three days. Then they Med-Evac'd me by helicopter to King Faud airport. I flew out of there on a C141 transport to a hospital in Germany. A lot of people got diarrhea.

I've been checked out by the VA. They have what they call the Saudi Arabia, Persian Gulf Register. I have something and can't get straightened out. I'm depressed all the time, can't sleep good at night. We ended up with some people that had never had sugar diabetes or anything; they got so bad they were taken to Germany, where they took me, and given insulin.

I was in that hospital in Germany for a week or so. While there, they brought me a bologna sandwich—nothing ever tasted so good!

Back to the desert—after I left, they got A-rations, which is food like in the U.S. But until I left, we were eating what they called Top Shelf and Dinner Buckets. We had regular field mess equipment, two burner units. We'd take our big stock pot, heat water in it, and then drop the lunch buckets, or soup, in it. Whenever units moved up, we'd go out and get the stuff they left behind.

For our noon meal, (this was out in the field) we'd have MREs (Meals Ready to Eat), something like K-rations. We also had T-rations. We'd heat water and drop the Ts in; one would be enough to feed twelve people. There might be hotdogs. For breakfast there would be sausage links, scrambled eggs with cheese and sausage, fruitcake or some kind of cake, and usually some fruit. And then there was coffee. Each of these things came in a separate package, each one having enough for twelve.

Then our evening meal would consist of maybe meatloaf or chili con carne over rice. We dropped it in the water for 30-45 minutes, and then it was ready to serve. We did get milk, but it was what was called shelf-life. It was in paper cartons, but it was dated and good for a year, without being refrigerated. We didn't have much refrigeration. Whatever we drank was the temperature of whatever it was that day. We had some fruit occasionally. We'd get enough for one piece per person per day.

They didn't get any desert camouflage fatigues until after I left, around February 15. My unit stayed over there until September, 1991. They just wore regular fatigues. We were issued jungle boots—outside was leather on the bottom but canvas around the ankle and foot. The inside was completely lined with canvas.

Even though I was a cook, I carried a rifle at all times; also a gas mask, First Aid pouch, a mopp suit (chemical suit). When the war started, we had to put suits on because the scud missiles were coming in, and we didn't know for certain whether there were chemicals or not. After that, we ordinarily wore part of the outfit; then it wouldn't take long to get the rest on, if we needed it. Once the suit is exposed to chemicals, it has to be thrown away. So far as I know, we were never exposed to chemicals.The only way you can detect chemicals is through what I think you call a radon meter. It's always carried by the CBN person (Chemical, Biological, and Nuclear Warfare). The only thing, I think, we could have been exposed to was germ warfare in the scud missiles.

As far as vehicles, the jeep has been replaced by the Humm-Vee, an all-purpose car. They did use a Blazer for a while, but now it has been discontinued. The Humm-Vee can be used as an ambulance, a command car, a staff car, or a truck. It's a four-passenger vehicle, automatic shift, and runs on Diesel. Everything before that was standard shift and ran on gasoline. We got our gasoline over there from Saudi Arabia.

DAVID PATRICK DEAL

SIDNEY, OHIO

Line Haul Tractor and Trailer, E-5 Sgt., Ohio Army National Guard,
1971-92, Desert Storm
Basic Training: San Antonio Air Force Base, San Antonio, TX
Duty in Northern Saudi Arabia

I originally joined the Air Force Reserves my junior year of college. The understanding was that we would be called in time of war. Once I had my family started, I opted to serve in a little less, though essential, capacity. I joined the Ohio National Army Guard with ignorance of the fact we might serve in conflict. Thus our call to arms was a shock to myself, as well as others. This bit of history may give you an idea of the slant with which I viewed the events in Saudi. Homesick, angry, and frightened, I endured and welcomed the return home.

Vivid impressions of the war: Rows and rows of armored vehicles in Port Dammam. Unbelievable traffic on Dodge Road. Dodge ran parallel to Kuwait and Iraq. Many parts of the road came within five miles of the border. I came to know this road well. Our transportation company was included in the west push of men and supplies to flank the Iraqi forces. If you think of the traffic on I-75 or State Route 25A on a Friday night of a big holiday weekend, it would be very similar. The traffic was so thick you traveled at certain times. All spots were reserved. Add to that a domestic group of Saudi drivers who, in all honesty, were the Evel Knievels of the road. I believe more people died on Dodge road than the whole of U.S. battle casualties.

The grace of God was with us, though. I did not witness any of the battlefield casualties. I'm sure I would have had nightmares if I had.

My most memorable time took place shortly after we moved north from Port Dammam. Before we had any tents set up, we slept on the back of our trailers. I awoke in the middle of the night to the red streaking and shrill whistling Scuds flying over us, headed south into Saudi toward our previous positions.

We were treated to a heroes' welcome upon our return home. The American people were proud and showed it. Nobody felt heroic; we were just people put in a situation and made the best of it.

LYDIA FREEMAN

JACKSON CENTER, OHIO

Chapel Management Specialist, Airman First Class, Desert Storm
Duty in United Arab Emirates; Saudi Arabia

Like thousands of other female military personnel, Airman First Class Lydia Freeman performed her duties under the watchful eyes of Arabs who firmly believe a woman's place is at home.

"It was an eye-opening experience," she admits with a glint of determination and pride flashing in her dark brown eyes. "We did the jobs we were trained to do, and we did them well. The Arabs, particularly those in the military, came to realize that.

"I'm glad to be back in the United States where men and women are considered equal and freedom is something most of us take for granted. Sometimes a person has to go away for awhile to appreciate home and all that it offers."

The 20-year-old airman... was deployed to the United Arab Emirates, a tiny country located near Saudi Arabia on the Persian Gulf, in late August...

As members of an advance party, everyone was expected to pitch in and prepare the air base in the Emirates for the long haul. Thousands of sand bags were needed to fortify bunkers and existing buildings. Saddam Hussein had a well-trained air force in Iraq and no one knew precisely where he would send his planes and bombs.

"Every unit had a daily quota of sand bags to fill," she says. "It didn't matter what your area of specialization involved. Everybody, including officers, filled their 50 bags of sand day in and day out. We never ran out of bags and there was no chance whatsoever of depleting our supply of sand. There was nothing but sand as far as the eye could see, more than enough for millions and millions of bags.

"I heard quite a few people—men as well as women—comment that they never plan to visit the beach again. After living and working in the sand, the thought of spending another day in the sand is not very appealing."

Blazing heat made working outdoors unpleasant at best. Daytime temperatures of 120 to 130 were not uncommon during September, October and early November, and humidity levels ranged from 80 to 90 percent. Miss Freeman describes the weather "as being as hot as Arizona and as humid as Florida on the most unbearable summer day."

Men in the U.S. Air Force were permitted to strip off their camouflage shirts and work in military issue T-shirts because of the heat. Women remained in complete uniform out of deference to religious beliefs in the Middle Eastern countries that the female body should be covered from head to toe.

"I was incredibly hot but my heart went out to the women mechanics on the flight line," she says. "They had to deal with the blazing heat not to mention the heat from those big jet engines. Camouflage uniforms are heavier than standard issue because they have an extra layer or flap of fabric that absorbs perspiration."

All military personnel, regardless of their sex, seldom went anywhere without bottled water. They were to drink a designated amount to make up for body fluid lost through perspiration or run the risk of dehydration. Many servicemen, like Miss Freeman, remember being thirsty all the time. Nothing seemed to satisfy the craving for cold drinks and tepid water did little more than wash the dust from their throats.

As a chapel management specialist who worked with chaplains from all faiths and handled reams of paperwork, she did not encounter the cool reception Arabs accorded other female personnel.

"Although the Arabs never came out and said anything in the beginning, you could tell they didn't believe women should be flying planes or working on anything as sophisticated and vital as a jet engine.

"In the U.S. Air Force, we are viewed as equals. Men and women train for jobs in specialized areas. If you can't make the grade, you are out. It's as pure and simple as that. Women don't get any special consideration and we certainly don't expect any. We want to do the same jobs as men do and do them just as well."

The women gradually earned some begrudging respect from members of the Emirates' air force. Along with respect for performing their duties well came an easing of restrictions and a new-found sense of camaraderie.The friendly atmosphere never quite reached the stage of acknowledged equality but Miss Freeman admits with a chuckle that "it came pretty darn close."

The Americans also developed a deep respect for their hosts. No one volunteers for military service in the Emirates.The selection is made by a sheik after reviewing test scores, background checks and indepth interviews. Those successfully meeting the stringent qualifications are inducted and carefully trained. Officers are highly paid... Parking lots are filled with late model Mercedes Benz cars equipped with all the amenities such as air conditioning and telephones.

Many of the women in Miss Freeman's unit stayed in spartan barracks formerly occupied by enlisted men and low-ranking officers. (They were open-bay dormitories with twenty-forty girls in each bay.) Although the bunk beds were not especially comfortable and privacy was sorely lacking... they were glad to have a roof overhead and something other than sand at their feet.

"The room didn't matter all that much because most of us were only there long enough to sleep or change clothes," she says. "Dorm rats—those people who enjoy hanging around the dorm—were not too happy but anything is better than a tent."

During her stay in the Emirates, Miss Freeman had an opportunity to accompany a Roman Catholic priest on a trip to the USS Wisconsin, a battleship anchored in the Persian Gulf some 15 miles from shore. In addition to helping prepare the chapel for Mass, she received a tour of the huge ship and posed for pictures by its 16-inch guns. Those guns were fired in later months, spewing forth shells weighing as much as a Volkswagen in preparation for a ground assault.

"I definitely felt outnumbered aboard ship," she says. "It serves as home to 1,500 men and I was the only woman... talk about being in the minority."

Miss Freeman admits that female military personnel constituted the minority in all aspects of the Persian Gulf War. Her own unit consisted of 1,300 men and 50 women. While no official count has been made regarding the number of servicewomen stationed in the Mideast, military officials have said women represented about 8 percent of all 500,000 U.S. troops deployed in response to Hussein's invasion of Kuwait.

Lydia Freeman

"We may have been in the minority but every one of us successfully completed our duties," she says proudly. "We toted guns and gas masks just like the men and we knew how to use them. This was one war where women handled more than nursing or secretarial assignments. Women were on the front line in support positions and they were on the flight line. Some of the helicopters that played vital roles were piloted by women."

Miss Freeman is the first to admit that duty in the Emirates was far from being considered a hardship. She and her companions had an opportunity to leave base and go to nearby cities where the effect of westernization was clearly evident. Instead of field rations, they ate pizza at Pizza Hut and ordered dinners at Kentucky Fried Chicken. They dressed modestly but were not required to wear heavy, black veils when traveling to and from discotheques and clubs.

"No one forgot that war was brewing and the air of uncertainty grew as the Jan. 15 deadline for the Iraqi withdrawal loomed closer," she says. "It was like waiting for the other shoe to drop. We knew war was coming but we didn't know exactly when. It was like a big, black cloud looming on the horizon."

"Everyone held their breath when the air sorties began. We tried to count all the planes leaving the base and all those returning from bombing missions up north. We prayed all the crews would make it back home but sometimes our quick counts didn't coincide. Then everybody was sad, almost as if a friend or relative had died."

Although Miss Freeman never feared for her safety in the Emirates, she admits to being scared after being transferred to the Saudi Arabian city of Jiddah. The El Kalegh Hotel where she and other Americans stayed was rumored to be a prime objective for terrorists.

"There were times in the Emirates when security was tightened," she says. "Everything was different in Jiddah even though it was 650 kilometers from Riyadh. I only went into the city once and there were armed guards everywhere. After terrorists opened fire on a bus about a block from the hotel, I didn't venture out again unless it was to perform my duties. Three American servicemen and a Saudi guard were injured in the shooting. I never felt safe again until I stepped on American soil."

In late February, she was told to pack her belongings and be ready to leave Saudi Arabia in a matter of hours. The passengers were informed upon landing in Spain that a ceasefire agreement had been reached. The announcement was greeted with cheers and tears.

"I am glad to be home and I am proud to be an American," she says. "People ask me whether I think the war was justified. A war is something nobody likes but in this case it was inevitaable. I saw Kuwaitis who had fled to the Emirates and Saudi Arabia. Iraqis came in and stripped their country, murdered their friends and relatives and tortured their women. One power-hungry ruler came in and ravaged their homeland.

"For seven months I served my country and I am proud of the role I played. Yes, I lived with prejudice during those seven months but I like to think that the Saudis who would not look me or my friends in the eye will remember that women also played an important role in bringing this war to a swift and successful completion."

Reprinted with permission of *The Sidney* (Ohio) *Daily News* and Margie Wuebker.

DAWN LOZIS
DIXON, MISSOURI

Brigade Adjutant, Captain, Medical Service Corps, Desert Storm Duty in Saudi Arabia

I arrived in the Kingdom of Saudi Arabia on October 3. (We flew through Germany and I was there the day the wall came down.) Originally, I was assigned to the 32nd Medsom, which is a medical supply, optometry, and B10-Medical equipment repair unit. My unit supplied all the medical supplies to every unit in Saudi Arabia (including all army, air force, marine, and navy units, as well as the mercy and comfort hospital ships).

We worked 18-hour days, 7 days a week, and held the idea that our war was now. This was during the buildup phase of Operation Desert Shield, and if we could not get the units stocked with medical supplies before the casualties rolled in, then we lost the war. This was a tremendous task as supplies had to be transported long distances and under severe climatic conditions (Certain supplies and meds have to be refrigerated, particularly units of blood, not to mention they must be protected from dust!).

In addition, there was no infra-structure in place. We operated out of a warehouse, shared with the Saudis, though only 3rd country nationals worked there (Lebanese, Pakistanis, etc.) and they were wonderful to work with. They shared their ethnic food and had lots of questions about American life.

We used a newly-developed computer system to track all the supplies and orders (material request orders). I could not tell you how many we processed in one day or the number of lines we stocked, but it was tremendous and we were continually busy 24 hours a day.

During this time the unit lived in Dammam (outside the air base Dhahran) in a tent city called Cement City (as it was a cement factory). The conditions were absolutely appalling, white cement dust blew everywhere, the latrines and showers were outdoor ones made of wood, and were used by too many people. Many units were living here so no one took responsibility for these facilities; therefore, there was often feces on the toilet seats (nobody wanted to sit down so they squatted) and occasionally in the shower. Flies were everywhere and traveled from the latrines to the mess hall area. The food was the pre-packaged tin-rations or the pre-packaged Meals Ready to Eat. I caught gastroenteritis, as did many others, and was hospitalized for a week.

In November I was selected to be the brigade adjutant and moved up to the brigade headquarters. Life dramatically improved as the brigade headquarters was located in 3rd country national work housing. We had indoor plumbing and an indoor mess hall. Eight people shared a hooch. We celebrated Thanksgiving, Christmas, and New Year's on this compound (and eventually, Easter).

As the adjutant I had duties as the protocol officer, the secretary of the general staff, and served as the aide de camp for the commander. We had 67 subordinate units under the 44th Medical Brigade, ranging from 400-bed evacuation hospitals to med-evac helicopter units, preventive medicine units, dental units, medsoms (now there were two), mash hospitals, veterinary detachments, combat stress detachments, etc.

It was interesting being the adjutant as I got to attend many top level briefings. I knew in December that the air war was going to start around January 15. This was a heavy burden to bear. In addition, we had many dignitaries visit, such as Gen. Colin Powell, Dick Cheney, and the Army and Navy Surgeon General.

On January 15 the brigade and brigade headquarters again moved north, this time right on the Iraqi border and about 60 KM east of Rafha, Saudi Arabia. Again we lived in tents (co-ed), built bunkers, did all our laundry by hand, and used outdoor showers and latrines (this time much cleaner as it was just our unit). We stayed on this site for three months. It was very cold and we occasionally had snow or frost and it rained a lot.

Most of the patients that the brigade treated were Iraqis, both civilians and soldiers. All were awed by our facilities and seemed generally pleased to be with us and under our care; they were not hateful or resentful towards the U.S., but rather towards Sadaam Hussein. Many Iraqi POWs were a little scared as they were told that we would kill them. The Iraqi children we treated were delightful though very sick or injured. Much of the hospital staff gave the children teddy bears that had been sent to them or candy or cookies from care packages from home. Children are children all over the world, whether they're American, Honduran, or Iraqi.

In late March, the brigade redeployed back to Dammam, Saudi Arabia, to prepare for our trip home. We lived in the same

3rd country national work housing, but after 3 months in the desert, it looked like the Hilton to us.

After the ground war, most of the Arab people, particularly Saudis, were waving American flags and cheering us everywhere. Many would stop us and want to take a picture of us with them. I will always remember the friendships and comradeship developed during Operation Desert Shield and Desert Storm. I miss being with these people to this day. War does really bond people together.

On our trip back from Saudi we flew through Athens, Greece, Shannon, Ireland, and finally into Bangor, Maine. It was a 26-hour flight. As we were landing, the crew of the plane played the video "I'm Proud to be an American," by Lee Greenwood; it was very moving.

We landed at 6 o'clock A.M. in Bangor, and the town had amassed about 500 people that stood in a long line and cheered us as we got off the plane. They even had a band there. There was not a dry eye in the airport from either the 250 plus passengers or the townspeople, and we were not even their first flight! Finally, at about 9 o'clock A.M., we landed back at Fort Bragg, North Carolina. After almost seven months, it was great to be home!

MELISSA KAY WIFORD

SIDNEY, OHIO

Finance Specialist, Army Aiborne Air Assault Div., Desert Storm Duty in Saudi Arabia

"Have money will travel" could very well be the motto of Army Spec. Melissa Kay Wiford and her fellow finance-specialists...

Carrying locked metal boxes or olive drab-shoulder bags, they doled out $15 million over a period of eight months to thousands of troops deployed in the Mideast with Operation Desert Storm. Instead of setting up shop in a nicely appointed bank, they completed transactions from the rear of military vehicles, the interior of helicopter cockpits, the recesses of an underground sewer treatment plant or the shade of hastily erected tents.

Frequently the finance specialists did business at counters that were nothing more than planks of wood thrown over empty buckets or concrete blocks.

Their customers—men and women serving with the Division's Screaming Eagles and other military support units—showed up in camouflage uniforms with gas masks strapped to their belts and loaded M-16 rifles slung over their shoulders. Many laid their weapons on the counter as they leaned over to complete the necessary paperwork.

"In the beginning we were authorized to pay our people $50 in cash each month," she says. "Later the amount was upped to $100.The rest of their pay was deposited directly into their savings or checking accounts. It takes a real long time to pay out $15 million when you're doing it at $50 or $100 a pop.

"Some people are overwhelmed to hear about that much money. It doesn't affect me that way. When you work with money day in and day out, you disassociate yourself from its value. All those dollars become nothing more than pieces of paper bearing numbers and pictures of men who lived a long time ago."

Since there were no convenient federal exchange banks in the middle of the Saudi Arabian desert, all the money had to be brought in by members of the 101st Finance Support Unit at various times throughout the deployment. When Miss

Wiford... left Fort Campbell, KY August 19, she carried more than personal belongings to the waiting military plane.

"I was toting a big old green bag just like the other guys in my unit," she says. "The strap was over my shoulder and the handle was in my hand. It was kind of heavy so I might have been leaning a little bit."

Some servicemen preparing to board the same plane offered to help but she politely declined. They quickly backed away after catching sight of the M-16 rifles and .45-caliber sidearms the petite, dark-haired woman and her companions carried.

"They thought we were medics carrying drugs," she says trying to suppress a giggle. "I didn't have drugs in my bag. It was filled with lots of money, all in small bills.

"When you're assigned to carry $150,000 to $200,000 in cash, you don't let anybody help and you certainly don't let the bag out of your sight for one second. That bag literally became a part of me all during the long flight to the Mideast."

The military flight touched down some 23 hours later at the Saudi Arabian International Airport located about 45 miles north of Dhahran. Stepping onto the tarmack, Miss Wiford... was startled by the desolate location of the modern facility.

"The Saudis have been building the airport for 10 years and it will be another five years before everything is completed. It sits out in the middle of the desert surrounded by nothing but sand. Saudi planes have yet to use the new runways... American planes were the first to touch down."

Initially, the 101st Division was headquartered at the airport. It didn't take long for the Americans to receive their orders to move to other sites with code names like Camp Eagle II, Fort Camel and Log Base Cobra. When the division began to move, Miss Wiford and other finance personnel went along.

"When they moved, we moved," she says matter of factly. "Everybody knew something was brewing and we had to move closer to the expected action. It didn't matter if you were a man or a woman. You had duties to perform and you went where those duties took you."

Tent cities quickly sprang up in the Saudi Arabian desert and everybody pitched in to get the work done. As members of the advance party, servicemen and women set about digging in for what they hoped would not be a long haul. Day in and day out, there was always the same order—fill sandbags and fortify the compound.

"Sometimes I think we filled at least four million bags," she says with a sigh. "And we never came close to running out of sand. The heat was incredible, frequently rising as high as 137 degrees."

There was a growing sense of apprehension as the deadlines imposed by President George Bush neared and Iraqi leader Saddam Hussein showed no interest in pulling his troops from the oil-rich country of Kuwait. Security heightened in the days leading up to the start of the air campaign and the wail of an air raid siren frequently shattered the late night stillness.

"We were all busy practicing emergency procedures because no one knew what that guy over in Iraq was planning," she says. "He made a real big mistake by failing to capitalize on his advantage. There were only 150,000 American troops deployed initially. He had a whole lot more men and he could have done a lot of damage big time. I don't think Saddam Hussein ever believed Bush would send in the planes and the Infantry. He played the wrong hunch and that made all the difference."

As troops advanced further to the front and massed along the borders of Iraq and Kuwait, Miss Wiford and other finance specialists took to the air in military helicopters.

"When the soldiers can't come to us, we go to them," she says proudly. "They need their pay whether a war is brewing or not. As the helicopter approached you could see a line of guys waiting for us to land. They had their identification cards and papers ready. With their pay in hand, they went out to relieve their buddies in the bunkers.

"The guys came whether they needed the money or not. We joked around with them and they laughed. A lot of guys just wanted to talk and forget all about what might happen tomorrow or the day after that.

"I always enjoyed the helicopter rides and the opportunity to see the country. There was nothing but desert where we went... sand for as far as the eye could see. Sometimes out in the middle of nowhere there would be a band of nomads. The strangest thing I ever saw was a guy in a white Toyota pickup truck herding a whole bunch of camels. It reminded me of a cowboy rounding up cattle but this guy was using a different form of horsepower."

Unlike a lot of women in support units, Miss Wiford had an opportunity to be where the action was and feel the desert floor shake as a Scud missile landed with a bang.

"The sirens signaling an incoming Scud wailed so often," she says. "And within minutes the all-clear would sound. There were so many false alarms and then one night the real thing came."

Many military personnel were asleep or preparing for bed when the siren sounded. Some groaned and grumbled about the interruption. Miss Wiford remembers automatically reaching for her gas mask and getting up. Then came the explosion, less than a mile from the camp. Frightened servicemen and women bolted for the designated shelter.

"Three hours later the sirens went off again and this time nobody fooled around. I think we set a record getting into our gas masks and running for the shelter.

"Another night we watched as a Scud passed overhead with a Patriot missile in close pursuit. It was quite a sight when our Patriot intercepted Saddam Hussein's Scud. What an incredible display of fireworks! It was bigger and better than any Fourth of July fireworks display."

American military personnel cheered when they received news of Iraqi troops surrendering. Many members of the elite and highly touted Republican Guard left their heavily fortified bunkers after firing only one or two shots.

"They were not the emaciated prisoners the news media described," she says. "These guys were well-fed, well-armed soldiers. Had they stood their ground and fought as they had been trained, this would have been a very bloody battle. There never was any doubt who would win in the end, but the Republican Guard could have taken out thousands of our guys. They simply did not want to fight Saddam Hussein's battle, and that was to our advantage."

Two weeks before receiving her orders to return to the States, Miss Wiford boarded a helicopter and flew over to the Euphrates River Valley in Iraq to pay servicemen who had moved to that position. On the return trip the aircraft experienced problems and crashed just short of the Saudi Arabian border.

"One of the two hydraulic pumps in the tail section went out and we started spinning around helplessly," she says quietly. "I thought it was all over, but the pilot did an outstanding job regaining some control. We all walked away from the crash. If it wasn't for him and just enough hydraulic fluid in the other motor, we would have come down grinding into the earth and somebody would have had to pick up the pieces."

On April 3, Miss Wiford and 456 members of the 101st Airborne Air Assault Division climbed on board a chartered commercial aircraft in Saudi Arabia. After eight months and a maze of orders that always seemed to change at the last minute, the plane roared down the runway heading home to Fort Campbell and a long-awaited leave with friends and family in Sidney. "When the plane lifted off the runway, we all went wild," she says.

"Ever since I got home, people have been coming up to me and saying 'Thanks for all you did.' It surprises me because I didn't do anything special or heroic. I only did the job I was trained to do and I did it for my country."

BOOTS & COOTS

HOUSTON, TEXAS

Oil Well Fire Fighters and Blowout Specialists
Contract duty in Kuwait, 1991

In July, 1990, 100,000 Iraqi troops amassed at the border with Kuwait. By invading and annexing the prize oil fields of Kuwait, Iraq would become the leading oil power. Half a century earlier, drillers found that the Kuwait desert floated on an ocean of oil, more than 95 billion barrels. About twice the total U.S. reserves lay under an area that would easily fit into Rhode Island. These fields are dotted with more than a thousand oil wells that produced 150 million dollars each day.

Saddam Hussein invaded Kuwait August 2, 1990. Iraq practiced ecological terrorism on a scale unknown in modern times. Iraq sabotaged oil storage facilities and more than 138 million gallons of oil fouled the waters of the gulf around Kuwait.

Within four or five days of the invasion, Iraqi soldiers and engineers fanned out over the oilfields and packed most of the 1,080 working wellheads with explosives.

In December, Iraq detonated six wells. When Operation Desert Storm began on January 16, Iraq blew up sixty wells. Days before the allied ground offensive, destruction began in earnest. On February 12, 1991, at least 150 oil wells were set afire. The torching of the wells continued as tons of bombs, missiles, and artillery shells poured on to Saddam Hussein's position. In the aftermath of Saddam Hussein, 732 wells were critically damaged and set on fire. Many other wells which were not burning were flowing into the atmosphere, polluting our earth along with smoke from the burning wells.

Streaks of black smoke blanketed a quarter of the nation. Flames shot 150 feet high. Half a million tons of pollutants spewed into the atmosphere each day. Some scientists predicted devastation would create the equivalent of nuclear winter. Oil gushed and burned at the rate of five million barrels a day. Extinguishing fires would cost at least a million dollars a day and perhaps a great deal more. Predictions of how long it would take to extinguish the fires ran from two to five years.

Three companies from Houston and one from Calgary, Alberta, were called in. Each company would have two or three fire-fighting teams. Each team would have three or four fire fighters, supplemented by roughnecks supplied by Kuwait. These workers were in the field 28 days and off 28 days. Many other companies furnished equipment, men, and assistance. There were fire fighters, mud engineers, machinists, welders, heavy machine and crane operators, all the best in their fields and with years of experience in the most adverse conditions imaginable.

In addition to the sheer number of fires and brutal desert conditions, fire fighters encountered many unique dangers. Many of the wells were surrounded by unexploded bombs and artillery shells. Some were laced with land mines. Production lines that carried oil to the loading docks were severed and fire-fighting tools and equipment stored near the well sites had been looted.

The fire fighters were astonished when they arrived in Kuwait. The city was demolished. If Iraqi troops didn't find what they wanted, they carried all the contents of a building outside and smashed them. Cars were laying around everywhere. Iraqis couldn't take whole cars back to their country so they would disassemble them and take back the pieces, even the doorknobs. There was nothing left.

We spent two weeks on preparation, putting equipment together, and planning. Inadequate water supply caused the greatest delay. Iraqis had blown up water treatment plants. Millions of gallons were needed to fight the fires but only a trickle was available. We got big tanks, five hundred barrels each.

Kuwait wanted to cap wells around the airport first. Because of smoke, planes were having difficulty landing and getting our equipment in.

The wells burned at 3,000 degrees Fahrenheit at their center, hot enough to melt steel. We could pull the monitor in and be one hundred feet from the well and the temperature would run up to 450 degrees at the back of the monitor stand. We had to stand with a water bottle in our hand. We had paramedics whose main job was to keep us with water and potassium tablets.

Work was hampered by 40 mph winds and frequent sandstorms. When we first got there, at 10:30 in the morning it was pitch black, smoke everywhere. We could look 360 degrees and see fire all the way around. It sounded like one hundred jets taking off all day long.

We didn't use any artificial breathing apparatus, too cumbersome and bulky. There were methodical precautions, especially with the threat of gas. Some wells had traces of H2S but the wind blew it away. Safety technicians were responsible for checking for H2S.

Initial progress was slow. With the Kuwaiti government in disarray, fire-fighting efforts were swamped in red tape. Iraq had ransacked Kuwait oil companies, stealing trucks, bulldozers, and frontend loaders. It took about three months before we had everything we needed. They were moving it as fast as they could, but it was so heavy and there was so much that it was just a slow process. We built a lot of our own stuff, specialized tools and equipment.

Pipes that carried the oil to the ports were rigged to work in reverse, sucking water from the Persian Gulf and carrying it ten miles inland. To hold the water, pits, with a capacity of a million gallons, were dug in the desert. Four thousand gallons of water a minute were pumped. We got the water system going first.

Once the wellhead was whittled down to a single jet of flame, fire fighters relied on several techniques to extinguish the blazes. Depending on how big the fire was, they might be able to put it out with water, if there was enough water and pumps. If not, they shot it out with explosives. Extinguishing the fires would appear to pose the greatest difficulty, but the most dangerous work comes after the fire is out. Once the well is cooled, the crews must wade into the gushing crude and cap the well. The fire fighters are drenched in oil and gas. Static electricity and flames from a nearby well could easily re-ignite the well. Once the well was capped and killed, we turned it over to the Kuwaitis and moved on to the next one.

We were used to handling wells and blowouts. What we weren't accustomed to were the munitions and explosives laying around, the possibility of landmines and booby traps. We had to work in pools of oil laying around knee deep; we were concerned with what was under the oil. We didn't shuffle our feet. The U.S. army guys were in clearing the fields in front of us.

I don't think any fire fighters got hurt by ordnance, but there were other contract people hurt.

In July the first regular shipment of long-awaited caterpillar bulldozers began to arrive in C5A military transports. The Kuwait oil company drilling yard on the edge of the oil fields was a beehive of activity. It was used as the staging ground.

One reason our work went so fast was that there were no drilling rigs; they were all production wells. Seventy-five or eighty percent were shot off above, not below, the casing hanger. If they had been shot off below, instead of being a one, two, or three-day job, it would have been a fifteen, sixteen, or even a twenty-day job.

At six o'clock every evening representatives of the fire-fighter teams and the Kuwaiti government met to discuss the day's progress and coordinate future efforts and decide what materials would be needed the next day. We all tried not to interfere with each other. If one guy had something the other guy could use, we would lend it. We would trade. We all worked together.

The first fire was extinguished April 7. By August, an average of eight wells were capped each day. More than half the wells had been capped by then. Kuwait estimated they were losing five million dollars every hour they continued to burn.

Anxious to speed the rate at which the fires were extinguished, Kuwait formed their own fire-fighting team. They invited teams from China, Iran, Britain, France, Romania, Hungary, and the Soviet Union. Companies began arriving in September. Many had never extinguished an oil well fire before. We shared a lot of our fire-fighting secrets. It was a big job and there was enough room for everybody. We were just concerned with getting the job done.

Many individuals and organizations were anxious to get into the action. The office of Boots & Coots and other companies was beseiged with job applications and advice. We must have had ten or twelve boxes of suggestions on how to put the fires out.

One suggestion was getting an army tank to shoot away the coke mounds that build up around the wellheads and pose a problem in capping the well. At the behest of the military, we tried this one novel suggestion. The military brought in a tank and put it three or four hundred yards from the well and aimed it at the well. An explosion went off about a half mile away. We wondered, rather disgustedly, if that was the closest they could get with that thing. But by looking at a movie of it, we saw that the shot had hit the top of the coke mound and ricocheted. The next three shots hit the target but didn't blow the coke up. That amazed these army people. They said, "I can't believe this! This would demolish a tank!" Even though it didn't blow the coke away, it had fractured it so it could be swept away. They did this to four or five wells, but then the army stopped, because they had to have a well off by itself; most of them were too close together.

By August, 1991, Kuwait was producing 75,000 barrels of oil per day, just a fraction of the 1.6 million barrels a day it was pumping a year earlier. But it was enough to meet their requirements for electricity. The cost to restore their oil industry would be almost 20 billion dollars.

We had signed the contract on February 27, 1991. October 31, 1991, was the last job we did. We had guys stay to get equipment cleaned up and sent back. Our crew did 128 wells. The last well was extinguished November 6, 1991, with the Emir of Kuwait in attendance. The estimated time had been two to five years. The project was completed in eight months. When everyone joins in together to do a job, they can do it.

Boots & Coots had no serious injuries. All our methods had been used before; we know they work. People have been killed using new methods and taking shortcuts.

The blazing oil fields have altered the landscape of Kuwait forever. The predictions, however, of a nuclear winter and global environmental disaster have failed to come true.

Taken from the video, *Boots & Coots: Danger Zone, Kuwait 1991. Headed for the Future,* with permission of Boots & Coots, Houston, TX.

JOHN ADAMS

SIDNEY, OHIO

Naval Special Warfare, E-5, Navy, 1983-87
Basic Training: San Diego, CA

While John was not a Navy SEAL at the time of Desert Storm, his experiences in training give us some insight as to how the SEALs, along with other special forces, slipped into Iraq, undetected, to learn of Hussein's defenses.

I was an Intelligence Specialist in the BUDS (Basic Underwater Demolition Seals), a six-month program of arduous training. The first six months, they run you, swim you, mess with your mind. I was not an exceptional runner or swimmer; about all I had was heart. Basically, I was scared. I made everything, just barely.

First, they had to get us in shape, into trained fighting machines. We ran in boots, in sand, we rope climbed. There was a great big jungle gym on which we had to meet time requirements. We would train with telephone poles, had to do extended arm push-ups with them, raising them up over our heads. At the end of the first phase, we were lean and excellent specimens physically.

If we didn't act as a team, we failed. Then instructors really picked on you. In war, you have to act as a team, as a unit. In our job, you have to endure the weather, or whatever. The mission must be completed!

Team work was the key to Seals. They didn't want individuality. All students were broken up into 7-man squads called Boat Crews, 6 enlisted men and one officer. Everywhere we went and everything we did was with a squad. We had to paddle IBSs out into the surf zones and those waves were huge, 8-12 ft! Stars disappeared. For two weeks we didn't get through the surf zone. We were in a rubber boat and it was practically vertical, just crested a wave, but we made it! A couple of times we got turned over. We wore a Kapok, big old life preserver, and when it got wet, it weighed a ton.

The fourth week was Hell Week. We did everything we did the previous four weeks, but we got no sleep for five days. By

Wednesday we were seeing things. We ate four times a day; fell asleep in the chow hall, and they would pour ice water down our backs; went to the bathroom out in the water. We'd sit in the surf zone hours and hours and the surf would beat us to death.

We had probably 40-50 people quit during Hell Week. It was a voluntary program. If you wanted to quit, all you had to do was ring a bell three times and you were back in the fleet. Early in the first phase, you didn't want to go to a ship, you wanted to be a Seal. That was the great thing!

I made it through Hell Week. Early on in the week I cut my leg; later these sores became infected. We were on our feet all week. If we took our boots off, we couldn't get them back on because all our body fluids would go to our feet. We had medical checks every day. The navy took care of us. They didn't want anyone hurt. I was pulled out Friday morning. I collapsed, and they carried me to bed. But I had accomplished it!

The greatest pain was in the weeks after Hell Week, during the healing process. Our flesh was rubbed raw from sands and pants, unbelievable soreness everywhere. I was on antibiotics three or four weeks after that; didn't do anything for two weeks, just bedrest.

The instructors treated us differently then. I started out in a class with 105-110 students. We graduated 17, 75 percent attrition rate. We finished out with bookwork, letting our bodies heal for two weeks. This was Phase 1; each phase is 2 months.

Phase 2 was the diving phase, tower training, learning scuba, doing mock ship attacks, that is, putting limpid mines on rudders of ships; very basic at that stage. In each stage, your time decreases to pass it. They still run and swim you to death.

Phase 3 meant going to San Clemente Island, learning explosives, land navigation—very enjoyable. Learned all weapons.

Then to Ft. Benning, Georgia, to learn to sky dive. I was assigned to Seal Team 3, a brand new team. The military had deteriorated to an unprecedented state prior to President Reagan. Bases had deteriorated; gear was deteriorated; morale had deteriorated. You wouldn't believe what new gear and remodeling of a base does to morale. Reagan made the service tougher to get into. He made it a place where people wanted to go, people at all academic levels. They were quality people.

We had new gear, the latest. Ours was the first team ever to go to Subic, the entire team, six platoons, for overseas training. There were sixteen men in our platoon, two officers, two 8-man squads. We trained and had requirements to fulfill before being a fit platoon to go overseas. Some of the ops were diving, insertion, different modes of insertions. Combat Rubber Raiding Craft was one. We prepared through the week to do an op and did it in one night. It was fun. With one of the ops, the mode of insertion was a CRRC dropped out of a C130 at 800 ft. We pushed the platform out that had the boat on it, the motor, and all our gear for an 8-man squad. As that boat went out, eight men followed, parachuted in 800 ft. above the water. What a thrill! Scary, too! Hit the water, get rid of your chutes, which were picked up (always had support crews on the surface of the water), collect our chutes, get boat ready, cut it loose from the platform, and we were on our way.

Delmar was a marina on Camp Pendleton. One training op was, when the weather was bad, to drop an entire squad in at one time. We dropped three men in at a time. It was so windy. As soon as we hit the water we were gone. The chute was dragging me through the water, had to reach up and cut one side loose. Once everybody was in the water, we had to do a diving op on some boats that were stationed at Delmar Marina. The waves were so bad that everybody was sick. I ended up not doing the op. There was only one diving team that made it in.

We learned to dive with a closed circuit breathing apparatus, let off no bubbles. That was neat, thrilling, a test of our skills to swim, not leaving any trace of bubbles, into enemy territory, and put a bomb on a rudder of a ship and swim back out. Swimming into an enemy harbor is very difficult. Many harbors string up nets all around with tin cans tied to the top of it. If we hit that, they know we're there. All they need to do is throw a grenade into the water and we're dead.

We went to an island and trained to do desert ops. We had to parachute in darkness on to a desert and learn to survive, as well as navigate in the desert. Environment was always a key element to survival—desert, jungles, whatever—we had to train in every element and learn how to complete a successful mission in those elements. We always felt like we were Jack of all trades and master of none. Our missions were so broad.

Back to the breathing apparatus without bubbles. We were put on a line under water and had to swim on it, get a pace down. We had to swim a certain distance in one minute. We practiced and practiced, maybe three weeks. That pace was maybe three hundred yards in one minute. Once we developed this certain pace, then we could plot going into an enemy harbor, that is, basically navigating underwater. We used a compass. The pace was a set pace in a minute and we used tide tables. As a concept, instead of flying in the air, we are flying under the water. We would navigate under water with a compass board with a timer and a depth gage.

When we swam into enemy harbors we did legs. These legs were certain distances, and we would swim a leg for a certain amount of time, reset our chronometer, turn a different direction on our compass, swim across currents, either with the tide coming in or going out. We had to vector in, considering the tides. These things were done at night; it was dark, spooky, and noises were amplified.

One guy was the navigator and the other was a safety man. We always swam at twelve meters deep. I didn't like swimming any deeper. We always heard the story about something happening and a guy getting sucked up. One time we swam for three hours and twenty-seven minutes when we did a simulated mission on a submarine base. There are people who can stay in water longer than that. The French are supposed to be very good divers.

Other ops in training: We flew our entire team over to Subic, Philippines, six months. From there we went to other countries, Thailand, Malaysia, Korea, Australia, and trained with their elite, our counter-parts. We were on call.

For my first deployment, we were called at 8 o'clock at night. Our two officers walked in looking like they had seen a ghost. Some ship was mining the Gulf, the Red Sea, the transport of oil through the Gulf. Somebody was rolling mines off a ship. Our job was to get trained to board that vessel. We were all scared. We knew somebody was going to die. But as time went on, we gained confidence. There was a certain time frame. We boarded a C141 for Guam. One platoon, 18 guys, had the plane all to ourselves, a big jet. For two or three weeks all we did was train for this boarding of the ship. We set up plywood in the form of a bridge, a long corridor and the bridge of a ship. All we did was shoot and shoot, 12 hours a day for two weeks. There is an allotment of bullets for each deployment that goes to Subic. We used the entire allotment of 9 mm ammunition in that training. But we never went. Stormed the bridge with our AK machine guns. Tried it with night vision goggles—tunnelvision. It didn't work, so off with the night vision. We taped our flashlights to our weapons. You can buy this stuff now. You can buy gear that attaches to your weapons. But we used our plain old flashlights. Storming the bridge, clearing the bridge, basically killing the bad guys. Identifying the hostages vs the terrorists, just like in the Seal Team movie, "Close Quarter Battle." We wanted to do it.

Even the pilots who flew the CH46s did not want to fly the op. They were vectored in by a C2, mini small version of the Awax. It's what the navy launches off aircraft carriers. They had vectored in that helicopter. It would fly just above the surface of the water on night vision goggles. That is, pilots had to wear night vision, flare up just above the surface of the water, come up over the top of the ship, our guys would fast rope on to the deck of the ship. When we first did that, it was hilarious. We could put the eight guys on in seconds. As soon as you hit the ground, you want to be out of there. When you have eight guys storming down that rope, you either get out of the way or get crushed.

When we first started this training, the helicopter pilots were frightened. Dangerous stuff! We wore flak jackets, we improvised everything to make this op work. The second CH46 would come up alongside the ship with a machine gun mounted with a night vision scope. We put Infra Red chem lights on ourselves so that the gunner on the second helicopter would not be shooting us. Spot the enemy, take him out before we were taken out. We never got to use that, but the development of those techniques are still there. Extremely interesting!

Camaraderie in the platoon is very close. Gays in the military, just for that reason, just won't work.

Cold weather training, 13,000 ft., for a week—camped out; pulled sleds behind us, rigged up harnesses; pulled our gear. Pulled our sleds. Wore snowshoes. Good times! Lock in, lock out procedure, simulates locking in and locking out of a submarine.

When we did our next deployment, we had finished every op. When you are going through your training, you are graded. We were not the best platoon. We were not consistent. But our second time around, we had the best platoon out of Seal Team 3. We completed every exercise, op, overseas and in the Philippines, no matter what the weather or the situation was. Four weeks in a row we had an over-the-horizon insertion. Take your boat out, parachute in, over the horizon and bring those boats into your target area, CRRC (Combat Rubber Raiding Craft). Four weeks in a row we got beat up coming in. The weather was lousy, we were drenched, we were sopped, but that was what we went through Hell Week for. One boat went completely flat, had a hole in it somewhere. We tied it up, put it in tow, and the entire platoon was all in one boat. That was the mentality—we are going to finish everything we start, no matter what the conditions are.

We got overseas special pay for jumping, for diving— tacked on to regular pay. Good pay! I was in the navy five years, four years on the team. Fortunately, I was between conflicts.

I loved being a Navy Seal. I'd do it again, except now I wouldn't want to leave my family.

John Adams, Navy SEAL

EPILOGUE

War is all-encompassing, involving not only the military, who takes the brunt, but civilians as well, worldwide. Those on the battlefields would be in even more dire circumstances without the support of their country's citizens.

Since the ending of WW II fifty years ago (V-E and V-J Day), there have been three additional wars plus other skirmishes. Of those who did the fighting of these wars, most did it because it was an obligation; they tried to make the best of the situation. Many have never talked of their experiences, preferring to leave them behind.

Through the stories in this book we have had an inside glance, not just at battles, but at how men and women have coped, how they have endured under horrifying circumstances, how they have used humor to lighten the burden, to keep their sanity.

We must remember what men and women, civilians as well as military, have done for their country! Children must be taught this important history! Is it not true that that forgotten is oft repeated?

Rockport, Texas, Doris Eggleston

Lessons from war are harsh. Sacrifices are too great.
Mothers' tears cannot be ignored.
We Can't Forget!

WORLD WAR II
FOOTNOTE REFERENCES

1 Charles E. Glover, "Churchill Pledges to Fight Japanese," *The Dayton Daily News,* May 23, 1993, p.15A.

2 William Manchester, *Goodbye, Darkness.* (Boston: Little, Brown and Company, 1979, 1980), p. 78.

3 *Ibid.,* p. 61.

4 *Ibid.,* p. 95.

5 *Ibid.,* p. 161.

6 *Ibid.,* p. 162.

7 *Ibid.,* p. 257.

8 *Ibid,* p. 262.

9 *Ibid.,* p. 391.

10 Dave Hirschman (Scripps-Howard News Service), *The Dayton Daily News,* May 16, 1993, p. 13A.

11 Paul D. Casdorph, *Let the Good Times Roll, Life at Home in America During World War II.* (New York: Paragon House, 1989), p. 127.

12 William Manchester, *The Glory and the Dream, a Narrative History of America,* 1932-1972, Vol. 1. (Boston: Little, Brown and Company, 1974), p. 487.

13 *Information on Living Conditions and Recreational Facilities in Washington* (United States Civil Service Commission), enclosed with letter dated May 9, 1944.

14 Manchester, *op. cit., (The Glory and the Dream),* p. 362.

15 *Ibid.,* p. 289.

KOREA
FOOTNOTE REFERENCES

1 Eric M. Hammel, *Chosin. Heroic Ordeal of the Korean War.* (New York: The Vanguard Press, 1981), p. 4.

2 Brig. Gen. S.L.A. Marshall, USAR (Ret.), *The Military History of the Korean War.* (New York: Franklin Watts, Inc., 1963), book cover.

3 Max Hastings, *The Korean War.* (New York: Simon and Schuster, 1987), p. 145.

4 Hastings, *Ibid.,* p. 272.

5 Hastings, *Ibid.,* p. 166.

6 Hammel, *Op.cit.,* p. 265.
7 Hammel, *Op.cit.,* p. 264.
8 Hammel, *Op.cit.,* p. 286.
9 Hastings, *Op.cit.,* p. 152.
10 Hastings, *Op.cit.,* p. 152.
11 Marshall, *Op.cit.,* p. 5.
12 Hastings, *Op.cit.,* p. 88.
13 James L. Stokesbury, *A Short History of the Korean War.* (New York: William Morrow and Company, Inc., 1988), p.173.
14 *Ibid.,* p. 212.
15 Marshall, *Op.cit.,* p. 66.
16 Marshall, *Op.cit.,* p. 75.
17 Hastings, *Op.cit.,* p. 261.
18 Hastings, *Op.cit.,* p. 184.
19 Stokesbury, *Op.cit.,* p. 143.
20 Hastings, *Op.cit.,* p. 324.
21 Marshall, *Op.cit.,* p. 82.
22 Stokesbury, *Op.cit.,* p. 250.
23 Hastings, *Op.cit.,* p. 326.
24 Hastings, *Op.cit.,* p. 327.
25 Hastings, *Op.cit.,* p. 328.
26 Marshall, *Op.cit.,* p. 86.
27 Stokesbury, *Op.cit.,* p. 253.
28 Clark Dougan, et al., *The Vietnam Experience: A Nation Divided.* (Boston: Boston Publishing Company, 1984, p. 21.
29 Dougan, et al., *Ibid.,* p. 16.
30 Jeffrey Merritt, *Day by Day: The Fifties.* (New York: Facts on File, Inc., 1979), p. xvii.
31 Dougan, et al., *A Nation Divided, Op.cit.,* p. 28.
32 Dougan, et al., *A Nation Divided, Op.cit.,* p. 34.

VIETNAM

FOOTNOTE REFERENCES

1 William Broyles, Jr., *Brothers in Arms, A Journey from War to Peace.* (New York: Alfred A. Knopf, 1986), p. 99.

2 Clark Dougan, et al., The Vietnam Experience: A Nation Divided. (Boston: Boston Publishing Company, 1984), p. 6.

3 Don Lawson, *An Album of the Vietnam War.* (New York: Franklin Watts, 1986), p. 24.

4 Patience H. C. Mason, *Recovering from the War.* (New York: Penguin Books, 1990), p. 34.

5 *Ibid.,* p. 2.

6 *Ibid.,* p. 124.

7 *Ibid.,* p. 130.

8 *Ibid.,* p. 129-30.

9 *Ibid.,* p. 40.

10 Clark Dougan, et al., *The Vietnam Experience: Combat Photographer.* (Boston: Boston Publishing Company, 1983), p. 15.

11 *Ibid.,* p. 25.

12 Mason, *Op.cit.,* p. 208.

13 Mason, *Op.cit.,* p. 52.

14 Broyles, *Op.cit.,* p. 5.

15 Broyles, *Op.cit.,* p. 5.

16 Peter Goldman and Tony Fuller, *Charlie Company. What Vietnam Did to Us.* (New York: William Morrow and Company, Inc., 1983), p. 75.

17 Clark Dougan, et al., *The Vietnam Experience: A Contagion of War.* (Boston: Boston Publishing Company, 1983), p. 110.

18 Nhu Tang Truong, David Chanoff, and Doan Van Toai, *Vietcong Memoir, An Inside Account of the Vietnam War and Its Aftermath.* (New York: Harcourt Brace Jovanovich, 1985), p.167.

19 Stuart A. Herrington, *Peace With Honor.* (Novato, CA: Presidio Press, 1983), p. 83-5.

20 Dougan, et al., *The Vietnam Experience: The North.* (Boston: Boston Publishing Company, 1986), p. 150.

21 *Ibid.,* p. 150.

22 Lawson, *Op.cit.,* p. 71.

23 Dougan, et al., *The North,* Op.cit., p. 154.

24 Herrington, *Op.cit.,* p. 100.

25 Dougan, et al., *Combat Photographer, Op.cit.,* p. 160.

26 Herrington, *Op.cit.,* p. 153.

27 Broyles, *Op.cit.,* p. 236.

28 Dougan, et al., *The North, Op,cit.,* p. 160.

29 Broyles, *Op.cit.,* p. 267.

30 Broyles, *Op.cit.,* p. 46.

31 Broyles, *Op.cit.,* p. 93.

32 Everett Alvarez, Jr., and Anthony S. Pitch, *Chained Eagle.* (New York: Donald I. Fine, Inc., 1989), p. 2.

33 Broyles, *Op.cit.,* p. 269-70.

34 Goldman and Fuller, *Op.cit.,* p. 171-2.

35 Goldman and Fuller, *Op.cit.,* p. 162-3.

36 Dougan, et al., A Nation Divided, *Op.cit.,* p. 113.

37 Mason, *Op.cit.,* p. 190

38 Goldman and Fuller, *Op.cit.,* p. 130.

39 Dougan, et al., *A Nation Divided, Op.cit.,* p. 46.

40 Dougan, et al., *A Nation Divided, Op.cit.,* p. 167.

41 Dougan, et al., *A Nation Divided, Op.cit.,* p. 148.

42 Lawson, *Op.cit.,* 64.

43 Dougan, et al., *A Nation Divided, Op.cit.,* p. 151.

44 Dougan, et al., *A Nation Divided, Op.cit.,* p. 151.

45 Herrington, Op.cit., p. 234.

46 Al Santoli, "MIA Families Won't Give Up," *Parade Magazine* (May 30, 1993), p. 4.

47 Dougan, et al., *A Nation Divided,* Op.cit., p. 178.

48 Dougan, et al., *A Nation Divided,* Op.cit., p. 178.

49 Dougan, et al., *A Nation Divided,* Op.cit., p. 178-9.

50 Dougan, et al., *A Nation Divided,* Op.cit., p. 183.

51 Lawson, *Op.cit.,* p. 85.

52 Lawson, *Op.cit.,* p. 85.

53 Lawson, *Op.cit.,* p. 85.

DESERT STORM

FOOTNOTE REFERENCES

1 Robert F. Dorr, *Desert Shield. The Build-Up: The Complete Story.* (Osceola, WI: Motorbooks International Publishers and Wholesalers, 1991), p. 23.

2 *Ibid.,* p. 22.

3 *Ibid.,* p. 120.

4 Captain M. E. Morris, U.S.N. (Ret.), *H. Norman Schwarzkopf, Road to Triumph.* (New York: St. Martin's Press, 1991), p. 71-2.

5 Dorr, *Op.cit.,* p. 8.

6 Dorr, *Op.cit.,* p, 83.

7 Dorr, *Op.cit.,* p. 98.

8 Morris, *Op.cit.,* p. 111.

9 Dorr, *Op.cit.,* p. 50.

10 Morris, *Op.cit.,* p. 97.

11 Dorr, *Op.cit.,* p. 56.

12 Morris, *Op.cit.,* p. 56-7.

13 Morris, *Op.cit.,* p. 124.

14 Morris, *Op.cit.,* p. 184.

15 Dorr, *Op.cit.,* p. 109.

16 Morris, *Op.cit.,* p. 192.

17 Morris, *Op.cit.,* p. 193-4.

18 Jean Edward Smith, *George Bush's War.* (New York: Henry Holt and Company, 1992), p. 9.

19 Morris, *Op.cit.,* p. 107.

ADDITIONAL BIBLIOGRPAHY

Allen, Thomas B., F. Clifton Berry, Norman Polmar. *CNN: War in the Gulf.* Atlanta: Turner Publishing, Inc., 1991.

Berry, Darcie. "Former Fighting Men Enjoy Packed Calendar," *Outlook Parade/Community,* Alexander City, AL, February 29-March 1, 1992.

"Boots & Coots, Oil Well Fire Fighters and Blowout Specialists." Houston, Texas.

Brady, James. *The Coldest War.* New York: Orion Books, 1990.

Collier, Basil. *The Second World War: A Military History.* New York: William Morrow & Co., Inc., 1967.

Collier's Encyclopedia, Vol. 16, 1991.

Collier's Encyclopedia, Vol. 14, 23, 1988.

Cornum, Rhonda, as told to Peter Copeland. *She Went to War: The Rhonda Cornum Story.* Novato, CA: Presidio Press, 1992.

Encyclopedia Americana, Vol. 16, 1991.

Fehrenbach, T.R. *Crossroads in Korea.* New York: The MacMillan Co., 1966.

Glover, Charles E., "'Pappy' Leads Black Sheep in Pacific Raid," *Dayton Daily News,* Sunday, January 9, 1994.

Greene, Bob. *Homecoming—When the Soldiers Returned from Vietnam.* New York: G. P. Putnam's Sons, 1989.

Haley, Alex. "Why I Remember," *Parade, Houston Chronicle,* Sunday, December 1, 1991.

Hoyt, Edwin P. *The Day the Chinese Attacked Korea, 1950.* New York: McGraw-Hill Pub. Co., 1990.

The New Encyclopedia Britannica, Vol. 6, 15th Ed., 1992.

Phillips, Robert F. *To Save Bastogne.* New York: Stein and Day, Scarborough House, 1983.

Pitt, Barrie, Editor, and the late Sir Basil Liddell Hart, Editor-in-Chief. *History of the Second World War,* Parts 1-96. New York: Marshall Cavendish USA Ltd., 1973, 1974. (BPC Publishing Ltd., 1966,1972).

Rosenblatt, George L. "Pearl Harbor," *Houston Chronicle.* Sunday, December 1, 1991.

Rosholt, Malcolm. *Days of the Ching Pao, A Photographic Record of the Flying Tigers—14th Air Force in China in WW II.* Appleton, WI: Rosholt House II, Graphic Communications Pub. Div., 1986.

Rosholt, Malcolm. *Flight in the China Air Space, 1910-1950.* Rosholt, WI: Rosholt House, 1984.

The Sidney Daily News, Hometown Proud, Special Edition, December 11, 1990.

"War Still Taking Its Toll on Gulf Economies" *The Dayton Daily News,* Sunday, April 25, 1993.

Thompson, James. *True Colors, 1004 Days as a Prisoner of War.* Pt. Washington, New York: Ashley Books, Inc., 1989.

The World Book Encyclopedia, Vol. 5, 13, 19, 20, 1968.

ACKNOWLEDGMENTS

Acknowledgment is made to the publishers of the following copyrighted material to be reprinted in *We Can't Forget!*

"Churchill pledges to fight Japanese" by Charles E. Glover, *The Dayton Daily News.* By permission of Charles E. Glover.

Goodbye, Darkness by William Manchester. ©1979, 1980, by William Manchester. By permission of Little, Brown and Co.

"Memphis Belle gunner doesn't understand fuss" by Dave Hirschman. By permission of Dave Hirschman.

Let the Good Times Roll, Life at Home in America During World War II, by Paul D. Casdorph. Paragon House, 1989. By permission of Paul D. Casdorph.

The Glory and the Dream, by William Manchester. ©1974. By permission of Little, Brown and Company.

Chosin, Heroic Ordeal of the Korean War, by Eric M. Hammel. Vanguard Press, 1981. Permission by Presidio Press.

The Military History of the Korean War, by Brig. Gen. S.L.A. Marshall. ©1963. By permission of Franklin Watts, Inc.

The Korean War, by Max Hastings. ©1987 by Romadata Ltd. Reprinted by permission of Simon & Schuster, Inc.

24 line excerpt, *A Short History of the Korean War,* by James L. Stokesbury. Text: ©1988 by James L. Stokesbury. Ill: Copyright ©. By permission of William Morrow & Company, Inc.

The Vietnam Experience, series by Clark Dougan, et. al., Boston Publishing Co., 1984. By permission of Boston Publishing Co.

Day by Day: The Fifties, by Jeffrey Merritt. ©1979 by Jeffrey Merritt. Reprinted by permission of Facts on File, Inc.

Brothers in Arms, by William Broyles Jr. ©1986 by William Broyles Jr. Reprinted by permission of Alfred A. Knopf Inc.

An Album of the Vietnam War, by Don Lawson. ©1986. By permission of Franklin Watts, Inc.

Recovering from the War, by Patience Mason. ©1990 by Patie1

nce H. C. Mason. Used by permission of Viking Penguin, a division of Penguin Books USA Inc.

15 line excerpt, *Charlie Company: What Vietnam Did to Us,* by Peter Goldman and Tony Fuller. Text: ©1983 by Newsweek, Inc. Ill: Copyright ©. By permission of William Morrow & Company, Inc.

Excerpt from *A Vietcong Memoir,* ©1985, by Truong Nhu Tang, David Chanoff, and Doan Van Toai, reprinted by permission of Harcourt Brace & Company.

Peace with Honor, by Stuart A. Herrington. Presidio Press, 1983. By permission of Stuart A. Herrington.

Chained Eagle, by Everett Alvarez, Jr., and Anthony S. Pitch. ©1989. By permission of Donald I. Fine, Inc.

"MIA Families Won't Give Up" by Al Santoli.
Reprinted with permission of Parade, ©1993.

Desert Shield. The Build-up: The Complete Story, by Robert F. Dorr. Motorbooks International Publishers and Wholesalers, 1991. By permission of Motorbooks International Publishers and Wholesalers and Robert F. Dorr.

H. Norman Schwarzkopf: A Road to Triumph, by Captain M. E. Morris. ©1991 by Captain M. E. Morris. By permission of St. Martin's Press, Inc. New York, NY.

George Bush's War by Jean Edward Smith. ©1992.
By permission of Henry Holt and Company, Inc.